POST MEMES

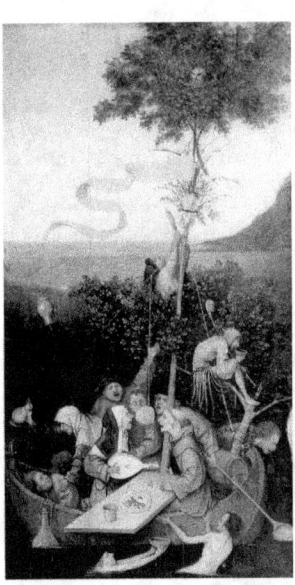

Fig. 1. Hieronymus Bosch, *Ship of Fools* (1490–1500)

First published in 2019 by punctum books, Earth, Milky Way.
https://punctumbooks.com

ISBN-13: 978-1-950192-43-4 (print)
ISBN-13: 978-1-950192-44-1 (ePDF)

DOI: 10.21983/P3.0255.1.00

LCCN: 2019947997
Library of Congress Cataloging Data is available from the Library of Congress

Book Design: Vincent W.J. van Gerven Oei

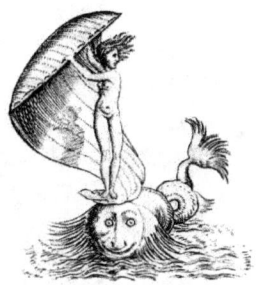

HIC SVNT MONSTRA

Post Memes

Seizing the Memes of Production

Edited by
Alfie Bown
& Dan Bristow

Contents

Memes, misperceived by us, subjects, as means of our communication, effectively run the show (they use us to reproduce and multiply themselves) [...]. The true aim of the process, its end-in-itself, is the development of the productive forces, and the satisfaction of our needs and desires (i.e., what appears to us as the goal) is effectively just the means for the development of the productive forces.

— Slavoj Žižek, *Organs Without Bodies*

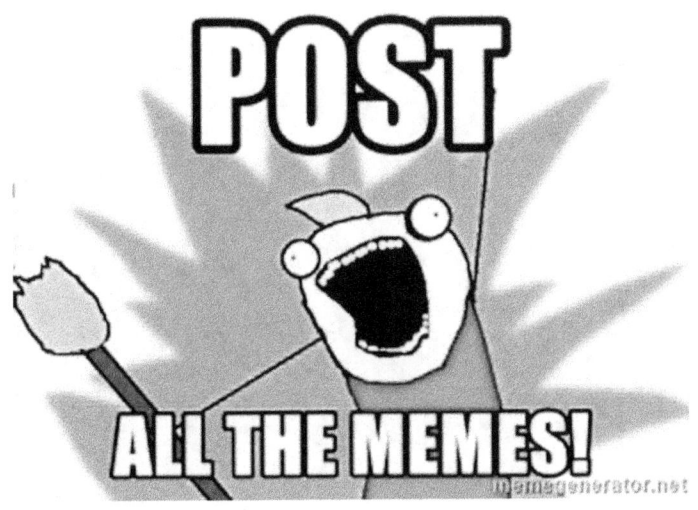

Introproduction

Dan Bristow

What's in a meme? The Internet proffers almost an infinity of answers, mostly by way of examples, which go on to teasingly court and taskingly contort definition in myriad ways, leaving meming an enigmatic signifier — and memes sublime objects — to say the least.[1] Prior to the Internet, the meme had another life, one which is reflected on briefly at the beginning of this collection (and nodded to throughout). Conceptually born into this world as an eminently adaptable element, it has to be remembered that this entails not only being adaptable *to* new conditions, but adaptable *by* them: the Internet

---

1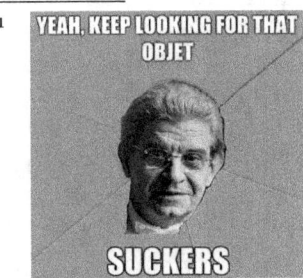

This "theory meme" depicts the psychoanalyst Jacques Lacan, who theorized the *objet petit a,* a little "object" that we desire, without knowing precisely why, or what it is, or truly realizing its unattainability.

DOI: 10.21983/P3.0255.1.02   17

(with its *ads* and *apps*) has, transformationally and irrevocably, adapted the meme.

In earlier, halcyon days of Internet theory, there was great hope — a sense of utopianism — in certain circles for what its near-infinite network could bring; it is often suggested now that this hope was a rose-tinted and premature misfiring (along the lines of the trope of the Internet being the greatest resource pool of, and tool for, knowledge, but getting used primarily for porn and funny pictures of cats…). But hope should not too readily be conflated with naïveté. Whilst a text like Gregory L. Ulmer's *Internet Invention* (2003) is full of strange, businessy applications and a slightly archaic, '60s-ish sense of cool, it launches from a precise understanding of new technologies — even something of a founding insight — particularly applicable to memes: "the Internet as a medium […] puts us in a new relation to writing."[2] From this statement — steeped in the grammatology of the philosopher of deconstruction, Jacques Derrida — comes the expansion: "the technology supports graphic imaging along with text: one writes with the whole page, so to speak—text, picture, layout. Moreover, there is an exact correspondence between the cut-and-paste tools and the collage and juxtapositional rhetoric of twentieth-century vanguard poetics."[3]

From rebuses (coded picture-puzzles, or pictograms, which Sigmund Freud drew on as dream analogues) to readymades (the re-presentations of everyday items as defamiliarized works of art; most famously perhaps, Marcel Duchamp's *Fountain* (1917), a urinal signed with the name "R. Mutt"), memes have had an array of precursors throughout the history of inscription — art, graphics, and writing (particularly in folk art and the avant-garde, for example, which Internet art seemingly draws on in equal measure aesthetically). Images are excerpted, recycled, copy-and-pasted; memes often utilize stock photography, or "poor images," fuzzier and less sharpened, unairbrushed, not photoshopped; paused frames, often of accidental facial expres-

---

2   Gregory L. Ulmer, *Internet Invention* (New York: Longman, 2003), 1.
3   Ibid., 2.

sions overflowing with a particular emotion, or archly wry, or saturated in gormlessness; celebrities and Joe Bloggses alike.[4]

This collection of essays seeks to look at these images and elements known as memes, and at their means of production, and to think them through — their practices and politics — and to think through them, too. We aim to look at the work memes do — and what structures that work — and the uses to which they are put, culturally and politically; how they enter into the service of politics, how they *politicize,* what they *produce,* and what that production is for, or gets used for; and at the dialectic between online phenomena and IRL ("in real life") phenomena, how political entities, statist and governmental, interact with online culture, how they fail to, what of their ideologies seeps through into it, how these ideologies are modified by it, where hegemony lies in these regards; how to seize memes as future-building blocks, what to head towards.

In Akala's *Natives,* he states:

[W]hile the overtly racist regimes have fallen, one only has to spend a little time on the Internet, looking at comments on videos or following social media threads about migrants, police brutality, terrorism or any other potentially racialised issue to see that the idea of race and racial hierarchy is perhaps as strong as it ever was for many millions of people today.[5]

In this, this highlighted side of the Internet has begun to do the work of those racist regimes for them. This is so often, sadly, where that hope referred to earlier has ended up (in parallel, in

---

4   The ex-Everton goalkeeper Neville Southall's Twitter account — a wonderfully "woke" platform that he regularly gives over for use to LGBTQ+ activists, sex workers, international crises organizations, etc. — utilizes something of both the meme image (a football sticker-esque photograph of him goalkeeping with a large "1" on it is the profile picture) and its humor/seriousness ("I realise I am just a big cock really/People s [sic] voices must be heard/that's my goal") to get its progressive messages across.

5   Akala, *Natives: Race and Class in the Ruins of Empire* (London: Two Roads, 2018), 168.

terms of memic presentation, we might trace the famous image of Barack Obama over the word "hope" ending up in Donald Trump and Pepe the Frog in the US).

The essays in this collection analyze this state of affairs and envisage how to re-*envisage* things, reimagine them, reimage them. Bookended by two manifestos, the loose trajectory to the contributions' presentation herein takes us from memic origins, through memic possibilities — imaginaries, utopias, action plans — to online culture wars, and beyond (punctuated with occasional interludes and oddities). Dominic Pettman's "Memtic Desire: Twenty Theses on Posthumanism, Political Affect, and Proliferation" sets the scene for memes, outlining the technological, virtual, human, and posthuman contexts of memic production and political affectivity. This is followed by Roy Christopher's deliberation, in part a historicity that tracks memes from their conceptual origins in the work of Richard Dawkins to their prevalence on the Internet, which offers an introductory overview to the work to follow. Bogna M. Konior's "Apocalypse Memes for the Anthropocene God: Mediating Crisis and the Memetic Body Politic" is an astounding odyssey of a tabulation of trends in meme production that reflect on a truly cosmological scale, in which memes are like monads of a gargantuan conceptology, encompassing everything from the Anthropocene to the apocalypse.

Lightening the load, Jay Owens's enlightening "Post-Authenticity and the Ironic Truths of Meme Culture" delivers an astute assessment of how authenticity is revaluated in meming, how irony is marshalled, and gone beyond, and how new generations interact with the Internet: the teens of memes. My own contribution looks at political and intersectional themes in memes through their reliance on form, content, and structure. Eric Wilson's article specifically focuses on the theory of anthropological philosopher René Girard in relation to memes, relevance, and desire down through the Ages to the aegis of the Internet, and takes the form of something like an elegy-as-emoji.

Roisin Kiberd's "Chaotic, Good" takes alignment charts, from the game *Dungeons and Dragons,* and their memed forms, and relays them against the online categorization of people (ourselves as Internet users included). The next article, by Tom Whyman, keys his passion for *The Simpsons* into Internet culture, and extrapolates from it fascinating analyses of equally fascinating *Simpsons'* practices (Simpsonswave music and seas of shitposting), exploring memic nostalgias for lost futures and the creations of alternative spaces. After this, we delve into the meme-making world itself with an insider interview with the admins of the Non-Existent Existentialist Memes (NEEM) group conducted by Angus Reoch, "fashioning a cap from a page of Camus," as Joanna Newsom once put it...

Then, we hop into a corporate world quite distinct from that belonging to proletarian and lumpenproletarian memes producers. Yvette Granata's survey of memes takes into account their labor-power and that used to create them, and revolves around the American fast food restaurant chain Wendy's' weird foray into the realm of memes, looking to use meme magic in their advertising, but really rather forcing Pepe the racist frog to become their number one burger flipper.

Patricia Reed's "Meso-Memetics, Service Fetishism, and Deep Mediation" is a deep meditation on meme production, and its types of labor, relayed against Marxist and post-Marxist theoretic frameworks; in so many ways it thoroughly interrogates both elements of this book's title. Scott and McKenzie Wark's essay continues in a similar vein and carries over similar themes. Like Marx's own second volume of *Capital,* its main preoccupation is circulation, and it uses this as a grid, on which it decodes meme magic and its fetishizations. Out of these groundwork essays come futural calls to oneiric possibilities of memic automation and the autonomization of means, and the memic rise of AI, in C_YS's sci-fi-y "In the Future, the Means of Production Will Own Themselves," and of machinic loving grace in Tom Hobson and Kaajal Modi's imaginative work on Fully Automated Luxury Communism and Fully Automated Luxury Gay Space Communism, written specifically in relation to UK left politics and its online manifestations and momentum.

With the future firmly in view, it falls to the remainder of the collection to focus on the political present — the conjuncture that gives us the alt-right, Donald Trump, Brexit, Jordan B. Peterson, and so on and so on — and to track it from the West out globally.[6] Ian Parker's ruminations on Donald Trump, and his mediatization, interrogate the very theory it relies on in an autocritique that holds up psychoanalysis, as a blanket applicatory force, to scrutiny along the intersecting lines of politics and class prejudice, etc., especially in relation to the "four discourses" — and the fifth — of psychoanalytic theorist Jacques Lacan (his very own memes of a sort, known as mathemes).

Using the work of philosopher Søren Kierkegaard, on irony, Giacomo Bianchino launches his piece by looking into intentionality in relation to the creation of Pepe the Frog and spreads out into assessing comicality and irony, and its limits, (mis)interpretations, pitfalls, and productions. Beginning similarly, Gabriele de Seta's penultimate essay trajectorily shifts to show appropriations and reinterpretations of Pepe in China. Practices of reclamation and meaning/meming-shifting are at work in the phenomena being arrayed in the essay, which leads swiftly into the manifesto that brings this collection to a close before the concluding statements of the Afterword by Alfie Bown and Francis Russell, Seong-Young Her's "Post-Pepe Manifesto." Putting the height of Pepeism at its center, it calls for the abolition of private memic property, at a time now all the more pressing; for example, with reports emerging of copyright controls threatening memes as we know 'em, Jim.[7] The Afterword then takes us out, post_meme, post-meme.

---

6   While Peterson is currently the "intellectual" darling of this conjuncture, for an interesting summary of its recent ideologue antecedents, see Mike Wendling, *Alt-Right: From 4chan to the White House* (London: Pluto Press, 2018), 17–39.

7   See, for example, "Memes 'Will be Banned' under New EU Copyright Law, Warn Campaigners," *Sky News*, June 9, 2018, https://news.sky.com/story/memes-will-be-banned-under-new-eu-copyright-law-warn-campaigners-11398577. [Article brought to the attention of the author by Kaajal Modi.]

Editorially, we have aimed to strike a balance between preservation of individual writing styles and introducing certain forms of standardization. We hope that the text reads fluidly and fluently as a result.

Bibliography

Akala. *Natives: Race and Class in the Ruins of Empire.* London: Two Roads, 2018.

"Memes 'Will be Banned' under New EU Copyright Law, Warn Campaigners." *Sky News,* June 9, 2018. https://news.sky.com/story/memes-will-be-banned-under-new-eu-copyright-law-warn-campaigners-11398577.

Ulmer, Gregory L. *Internet Invention.* New York: Longman, 2003.

Wendling, Mike. *Alt-Right: From 4chan to the White House.* London: Pluto Press, 2018.

2

Memetic Desire: Twenty Theses on Posthumanism, Political Affect, and Proliferation

Dominic Pettman

1. The human is always already posthuman.

   The human is the animal that relies on technology in order to realize its humanity.
   The "post-human" is thus an ontological category, more than a historical one. The very first humans were, from this perspective, as posthuman as we are today. We are ever using tools and prostheses to get ahead of ourselves.
   This perspective is known as "originary technicity" (see Bernard Stiegler, David Wills, and others).

2. Politics is built into the bones of (post)human culture.

   See, for example, the bone which one chimp uses to beat the other at the beginning of Kubrick's *2001: A Space Odyssey*; or the bones used by our early human ancestors as tools for painting, adornment, or charms.

3. Technology and art stem from the same root in *technē*.

DOI: 10.21983/P3.0255.1.03

Technē being the ancient Greek word incorporating "art, artifice, making, fashioning, bringing-forth, revealing."

4. Technology and politics stem from the same root in *cybernetics*.

   Cybernetics comes from the ancient Greek word *kybernētikē*, meaning "governance," especially through the metaphorical act of steering or navigation (*kybernēsis*).

5. Art and politics are thus connected and mediated by *technics*.

   Technics being the wider or deeper logic (social, economic, mechanical) nestled within technology itself.

6. Different technological artifacts enlist humans in their campaign to come into existence.

   Just as different human groups favor specific media and technologies in order to realize their aspirations and express their affections.

7. We call "media" the manifold tools and assemblages that not only comprise the interface for our attempts at communication, but that — perhaps more importantly — also engineer new "structures of feeling" (Raymond Williams).

8. Each new technological object or arrangement allows and encourages a new aesthetic orientation out of the detritus of former aesthetic materials, which in turn foster new affects. This happens by way of new vectors of proliferation.

9. We call the volunteer maintenance staff of these new vectors of proliferation "artists."

10. Proliferation in the posthuman context is largely an instance of contagion and enthusiasm, obliging us to focus on what Hayden White calls "the content of the form" (that is, the ways in which the medium shapes and pre-determines the message). Such contagion occurs in different degrees of technical mediation, and the medium of enthusiasm can often be its own message.

11. Analogue proliferation is at once amplified, accelerated, and complicated by digital proliferation.

    Think, for instance, of an irresistible rumor. Last century this would have been transmitted by word-of-mouth, and then perhaps picked up by radio or television. Today such rumors take on new textures, temporalities, scales, and impacts by virtue of being distributed through the Internet.

12. Some forms of proliferation depend on visibility within the attention economy (trending topics, hashtags, viral videos, political movements, etc.).

13. Other forms of proliferation depend on *the lack* of personal, public, or political attention (computer viruses, Bitcoin, pollution, arms, etc.).

14. Some forms of proliferation depend on a complex combination of both visibility and invisibility; contagion and excommunication (terrorism, extremism, state violence, etc.).

15. The Internet — especially so-called "social media" — can be viewed as a planetary proliferation chamber, or global meme machine, communicating micro- and macro-enthusiasms on a scale and speed never seen before (and cancelling earlier enthusiasms in the process).

    Memes are an idea, behavior, or style that spreads from person to person within or across cultures.

A meme is a "cultural unit" for carrying ideas, symbols, or practices that can be transmitted from one mind to another through media.

Richard Dawkins considers memes to be something akin to cultural genes.

More specifically, however, memes have begun to describe those deliberately clunky images, with accompanying text, designed to make us laugh, feel, and/or think, and that circulate primarily through social media, spreading like a virus.

An especially effective or popular meme is described as "dank."

16. For example, the ideological identity-position known as being "pro-life" uses deliberate modes of image "pro-liferation" in an attempt to influence others into feeling indignant righteousness: an affect that Spinoza classed as one of "the sad passions." This in turn encourages an overdetermined biopolitical relationship to women's bodies, personal freedoms, medical technologies, etc.

17. A propos, predatory professionalized proponents of the pro-life position misappropriate the proprietary proliferation of yet more proponents of pro-life propaganda, lead-

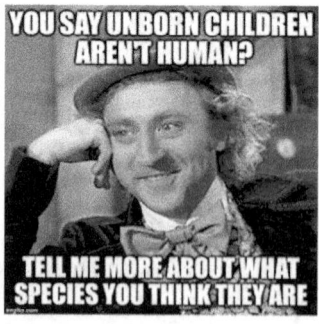

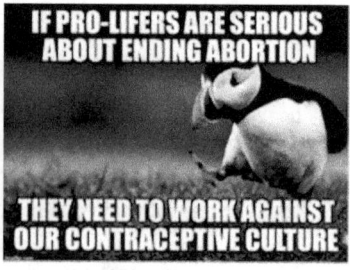

ing — appropriately perhaps — to prolific ideological pria-
pisms beyond all propriety.

18. We may go so far as to consider memes as a new folk-art,
     often given powerful signal boosts by corporate, political,
     and ideological interests.

19. We thus live in the Golden Age of Memetic Desire.

     "Memetic desire" is related to, but also distinct from, "mi-
     metic desire," made famous by theorist René Girard. (The
     latter identifies the origin of all desires as *external* to the
     desiring subject, whereby the rival or role model inspires
     desire, more so than the object upon which such desire
     eventually rests.)
        Memetic desire also derives from elsewhere, but is not
     born in imitation, but rather infection or contagion. It re-
     tains traces of the original and essential triangular structure
     (desirer–mediator–desired), but fractalizes this throughout
     the network — to the degree that a specific mediator can
     no longer be confidently ascribed. The subject is therefore
     less an ape of established ideological patterns, and more the
     reflex, medium, or host, through which memetic currents
     flow or grow. The human is revealed to be less an impres-
     sionable marionette than an extension of the string. (Or bet-
     ter yet, the tension which guides the connecting threads.)
        So to say, where the posthumans of the pre-Internet age
     desired what *other* people already found desirable (e.g., Don
     Quixote, Emma Bovary), the posthumans of today desire
     to be told what to desire — and indeed *how* to desire — by
     trending algorithms and recommendation engines (e.g.,
     anyone of us in conversation with Siri, Echo, and others).
     Indeed, we ourselves now function as semi-organic nodes
     of the memetic network.

20. The Golden Age of Memetic Desire is thus the dawning of
     an era in which our structures of feeling are liquified into

reflecting pools upon which bloom and float these sad and passionate "cultural units" of compressed affect; the blue-green algae of the general intellect.

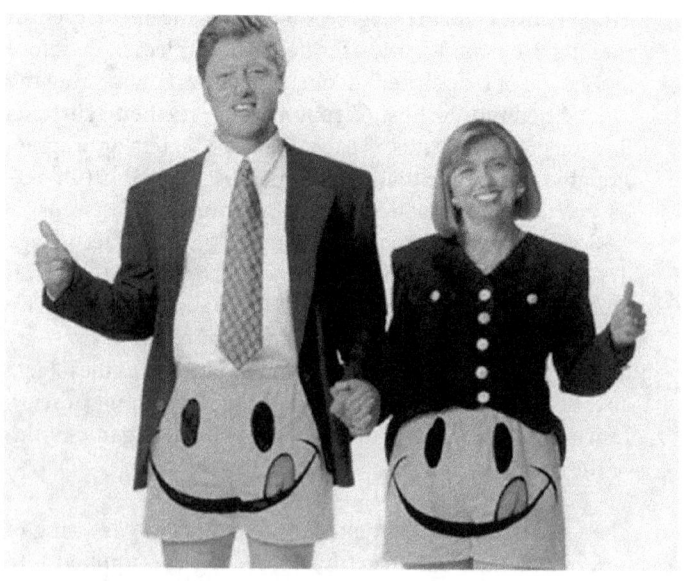

3

The Meme is Dead, Long Live the Meme

Roy Christopher

> "This proud picture of human grandeur is
> unfortunately an illusion and is counterbalanced
> by a reality that is very different."
> — C.G. Jung[1]

We're all home for the holidays. Looking around the living room today at the family assembled there, most were clicking around on laptops, two were also wearing headphones, one was fingering a smartphone. The television was on, but no one was watching it. Each of us engrossed in his or her own digital experience, be it a game, a TV show, or some social meta-medium.

My friend Mark Wieman noted recently that the Long Tail has gotten so long and so thick that there's not much left in the Big Head. As the Internet-enabled market supports a wider and wider variety of cultural artifacts with less and less depth of interest, the big, blockbuster hits have had ever-smaller audiences. This wasn't the case just a decade ago, and it certainly wasn't two

---

1   C.G. Jung, *The Undiscovered Self* (Princeton: Princeton University Press, 1990), 24.

DOI: 10.21983/P3.0255.1.04

or even three decades ago. The audiences seem to decrease in proportion to the size of the screens. I have found this splintering more and more in the classroom as I try to pick somewhat universal media artifacts to use as examples. Even the biggest shows and movies I brought up this semester left most of my students out, and if I ever got into the stuff I actually like, I was greeted with little more than cricket sounds. The postmodern promise of individual viewpoints and infinite fragmentation is upon us.

Attempts to unify this splintering are nothing new. In the 1990s, events like the X-Games and Gravity Games and websites like Hardcloud.com and Pie.com tried to gather long-tail markets that were too small by themselves into viable mass markets. It happened with the recording artists of the time like Sheryl Crow, Alanis Morissette, Dave Matthews Band, and Counting Crows. What was the label "alternative" if not a feeble attempt at garnering enough support for separate markets under one tenuous banner? If you can get both the kids and their parents, you might have a real hit. As Mark Lewman writes, "this is teen cool *and* mom cool."[2] Then in the 2000s, sub-brands like Nike 6.0 (in which the "6.0" referred to six domains of extreme activities: BMX, skateboarding, snowboarding, wakeboarding, surfing, and motocross) tried again. Whatever the practitioners of such sports might share in attitudes or footwear, they do not normally share in an affinity for each other. We remain in our silos, refusing to cross-pollinate in any way.

If marketing can't bring us together, mass tragedy will. In his 2009 novel, *Neuropath,* R. Scott Bakker describes the unifying effect of news of a mass or serial murderer, in this case, "The Chiropractor" (so named because he removes his victims' spines):

In these days of broadband it was rare for anything nonpolitical to rise above the disjointed din of millions pursuing millions of different interests. The niche had become all-pow-

---

2   Mark Lewman, "The Coolhunter," 2009. [URL defunct]

erful. The Chiropractor story was a throwback in a sense, a flashback to the day when sitcoms or murders could provide people a common frame of reference, or at least something to talk about when polite questions gave out.[3]

Regarding recent actual events of a mass and violent nature, Mark Follman at *Mother Jones* writes:

> When I asked threat assessment experts what might explain the recent rise in gun rampages, I heard the same two words over and over: social media. Although there is no definitive research yet, widespread anecdotal evidence suggests that the speed at which social media bombards us with memes and images exacerbates the copycat effect. As Meloy and his colleagues noted earlier this year in the journal *Behavioral Sciences and the Law,* "Cultural scripts are now spread globally… within seconds.[4]

Cliff Goddard and Anna Wierzbicka describe cultural scripts as "common sayings and proverbs, frequent collocations, conversational routines and varieties of formulaic or semi-formulaic speech, discourse particles and interjections, and terms of address and reference—all highly 'interactional' aspects of language."[5] Cultural scripts are the way our fragmented networks coalesce into unified interests and concerns.

The mainstream might not be much of a stream anymore. It seems now like culture is sliced and split among various niches, but in trial or tragedy that mist can condense into a wave as quickly as it needs to. The question is *how?*

---

3   R. Scott Bakker, *Neuropath* (New York: Tor Books, 2009), 71.
4   Mark Follman, "Inside the Race to Stop the Next Mass Shooter," *Mother Jones,* Nov./Dec. 2015, https://www.motherjones.com/politics/2015/10/mass-shootings-threat-assessment-shooter-fbi-columbine/.
5   Cliff Goddard and Anna Wierzbicka, "Cultural Scripts: What Are They and What Are They Good For?" *Intercultural Pragmatics* 1, no. 2 (2004): 153–66, at 154.

Meme Weavers

As you know if you're reading this book, as originally conceived by Richard Dawkins, a meme is a unit of humanity, "a unit of cultural transmission, or a unit of imitation."[6] It is the smallest spreadable bit or iteration of an idea. Where some try to reconcile his original conception with the Internet version, I think we can call a moratorium on Dawkins's original idea.[7] This is an elegy for the meme.

Memes are based on genes, Dawkins's original analogy contends. He writes:

> Examples of memes are tunes, ideas, catch-phrases, clothes fashions, ways of making pots or of building arches. Just as genes propagate themselves in the gene pool by leaping from body to body via sperms or eggs, so memes propagate themselves in the meme pool by leaping from brain to brain via a process which, in the broad sense, can be called imitation.[8]

Others have taken the idea, the "meme" meme, further. Kate Distin has perhaps taken up the idea most earnestly with two books, *The Selfish Meme* (2005) and *Cultural Evolution* (2011), the latter of which moved away from memes and looked closer at languages, written, spoken, and musical.[9] In her book *The Meme Machine* (1999), Susan Blackmore distinguishes between memes that copy a product and memes that copy instructions.[10] Similarly, in *The Electric Meme* (2002), Robert Aunger extends the meme metaphor by adding phenotypes and conflating them

---

6   Richard Dawkins, *The Selfish Gene* (Oxford: Oxford University Press, 2006), 192.

7   Limor Shifman, *Memes in Digital Culture* (Cambridge: MIT Press, 2013), for example.

8   Dawkins, *The Selfish Gene,* 192.

9   Kate Distin, *The Selfish Meme* (New York: Cambridge University Press, 2005); Kate Distin, *Cultural Evolution* (New York: Cambridge University Press, 2011).

10 See Susan Blackmore, *The Meme Machine* (New York: Oxford University Press, 1999).

with artifacts.[11] With *Memes in Digital Culture* (2013), Limor Shifman does a noble job attempting to reconcile Dawkinsian memes with internet memes.[12]

Distinguishing imitation or replication as a process of communication, as well as integrating Everett M. Rogers's closely related diffusion of innovations theory, Brian H. Spitzberg proposes an operational model of meme diffusion. He writes, "communication messages such as tweets, e-mails, and digital images are by definition memes, because they are replicable transmitters of cultural meanings."[13]

In his book of the same name, J.M. Balkin imagines memes as bits in a "cultural software" that makes up ideologies.[14] In *Genes, Memes, Culture, and Mental Illness* (2010), Hoyle Leigh writes that "a meme is a memory that is transferred or has the potential to be transferred."[15] There's even *The Complete Idiot's Guide to Memes,* which only discusses Internet memes in one chapter of its 23, and as an afterthought (Appendix E).[16]

Both biological and cultural evolution require competition and collaboration, and no one knows at what level the selection, transfers, and changes happen: Genes? Individuals? Groups?[17] Where memetic theories are concerned, another major problem is one of scale. What size is a meme? Where are its borders? What do memes add up to? Like genes, germs, and viruses, Dawkins gave memes "fitness," which means that a very "healthy" meme that grows big and strong can still be very negative and quite

---

11 See Robert Aunger, *The Electric Meme: A New Theory of How We Think* (New York: Free Press, 2002).

12 See Shifman, *Memes in Digital Culture.*

13 Brian S. Spitzberg, "Toward A Model of Meme Diffusion (M3D)," *Communication Theory* 24 (2014): 311–39, at 313.

14 J.M. Balkin, *Cultural Software: A Theory of Ideology* (New Haven: Yale University Press, 2003).

15 Hoyle Leigh, *Genes, Memes, Culture, and Mental Illness: Toward an Integrative Model* (New York: Springer, 2010), 91.

16 See John Gunders and Damon Brown, *The Complete Idiot's Guide to Memes* (New York: Alpha, 2010).

17 See Spitzberg, "Toward A Model of Meme Diffusion (M3D)."

dangerous.[18] As Brodie told me, "memetic theory tells us that repetition of a meme, regardless of whether you think you are 'for' it or 'against' it, helps it spread. It's like the old saying 'there's no such thing as bad publicity.'"[19] This is an overlooked aspect of memetics that also applies to Internet memes.[20] Retweets might not equal endorsements, but they do strengthen the memes.

Another problem you may have noticed in the "meme" meme via the brief and selective literature review above, is that the genetic analogy is not universal. Some theorists prefer an analogy with viruses. As many aspects as they might share as useful metaphors, genes and viruses are not the same thing. Douglas Rushkoff's *Media Virus!* (1994), Richard Brodie's *Virus of the Mind* (1995), and Aaron Lynch's *Thought Contagion* (1996) all take up the virus analogy over the gene one.[21] Maybe it's a better model, as when something is "viral," it spreads. When something is "genetic," it doesn't necessarily. Sure, genes are passed on, but viruses are inherently difficult to stop. Spreading is what they do. This epidemiological view of culture has been most thoroughly explored by anthropologist Dan Sperber. His 1996 book, *Explaining Culture,* goes a long way to doing just that, using a naturalistic view of its spread.[22] Some prefer to skip the memes altogether. Malcolm Gladwell, whose 2000 bestseller, *The Tipping Point,* also takes an epidemiological view

---

18 See Carol Cadwalladr, "Interview with Daniel Dennett: 'I Begrudge Every Hour I Have to Spend Worrying about Politics,'" *The Guardian,* February 12, 2017, https://www.theguardian.com/science/2017/feb/12/daniel-dennett-politics-bacteria-bach-back-dawkins-trump-interview.

19 Interview with the author, June 2, 1999.

20 Think here of Internet users reposting memes with which they do not agree and commenting to say so. Regardless of the context, the meme still spreads. That is, even if it is presented in a negative light, the meme is fitter, healthier, and stronger as long as it spreads.

21 See Douglas Rushkoff, *Media Virus! Hidden Agendas in Popular Culture* (New York: Ballantine, 1994); Richard Brodie, *Virus of the Mind: The New Science of the Meme* (Seattle: Integral Press, 1995); Aaron Lynch, *Thought Contagion: How Belief Spreads Through Society* (New York: Basic Books, 1996).

22 See Dan Sperber, *Explaining Culture: A Naturalistic Approach* (New York: Blackwell, 1996).

of culture and marketing but without ever mentioning memes, told me in 2002:

> As for memetics, I hate that theory. I find it very unsatisfying. That idea says that ideas are like genes — that they seek to replicate themselves. But that is a dry and narrow way of looking at the spread of ideas. I prefer my idea because it captures the full social dimension of how something spreads. Epidemiologists are, after all, only partially interested in the agent being spread: they are more interested in how the agent is being spread, and who's doing the spreading. They are fundamentally interested in the social dimension of contagion, and that social dimension — which I think is so critical — is exactly what memetics lacks.[23]

If memes are indeed analogous to genes, then the real power of memes is that they add up to something. I'm no biologist, but genes are bits of code that become chromosomes, and chromosomes make up DNA, which then becomes organisms. Plants, animals, viruses, and all life that we know about is built from them.[24] "The meme has done its work by assembling massive social systems, the new rulers of this earth," writes Howard Bloom. "Together, the meme and the human superorganism have become the universe's latest device for creating fresh forms of order."[25]

Perhaps that was true two decades ago, when Bloom wrote that, or three decades ago when Dawkins wrote *The Selfish Gene,* but the biases and affordances of memes' attendant infrastructure has changed dramatically since. After all, memes have to replicate, and in order to replicate, they have to move from one mind to another via some conduit. This could be the oral culture of yore, but it's more and more likely to be technologically ena-

---

23 Interview with the author, November 12, 2002.
24 See Elizabeth Parthenia Shea, *How the Gene Got Its Groove: Figurative Language, Science, and the Rhetoric of the Real* (Albany: SUNY Press, 2008).
25 Howard Bloom, *The Lucifer Principle: A Scientific Expedition into the Forces of History* (New York: Atlantic Monthly Press, 1995), 101.

bled. Broadcast media supports one kind of memetic propagation. The internet, however, supports quite another.

Units vs. Unity

Since the meme came on the scene, the mainstream has become less of a stream and more of a mist. Narrowcasting and narrowcatching, as each of us burrows further into our own interests, we have less of them in common as a whole.

Cultural divisions as such used to be framed as high versus low culture. *New Yorker* writer John Seabrook argues that we have evolved past such hierarchies into what he calls "nobrow culture."[26] Definitely erring on the high side, Seabrook doesn't know Stormtroopers from Sand People. Depending on which side of the high/low fence you stand, he and his ilk have "condescended and/or pandered" to you for far too long.[27] The monobrow mixing of high culture's concerns with low culture's lack thereof only makes sense if there's a market in the middle.

It's never made much sense to describe something aesthetically in terms of the mainstream, and now it makes less than ever. Working the ends against the middle trying to get the best of both worlds, so-called "nobrow culture" ends up with the bad of both without any of the good. Watered-down, diluted, widely disseminated, what's left of the mainstream is the cultural equivalent of the muddy, middle heartland viewed from an airplane window: flyover culture.

In our switch from television screens to computer screens and on to mobile screens, we fundamentally changed the infrastructure by which memes spread. We gather together around the former big screens to watch passively, while we individually

---

26 See John Seabrook, *Nobrow: The Marketing of Culture and the Culture of Marketing* (New York: Knopf, 2000).

27 Hal Foster, "Slumming with Rappers at the Roxy," *London Review of Books* 22, no. 18 (2000): 16–18.

engage with the latter smaller screens also to watch passively but also to connect actively with each other.[28]

What Means These Memes

How are we to understand culture through a metaphor that's based on another metaphor? Genes are figurative as well, a rhetorical tactic deployed simply to give a name to something.[29] Meta-metaphors are known as pataphors, and they are so useless as to be called a fake science by their originator Alfred Jarry. Pataphysics is to metaphysics what metaphysics is to physics. It's one level up. "Pataphysics [...] is the science of that which is superinduced upon metaphysics," wrote Jarry, "whether within or beyond the latter's limitations, extending as far beyond metaphysics as the latter extends beyond physics." He added, "Pataphysics is the science of imaginary solutions, which symbolically attributes the properties of objects, described by their virtuality, to their lineaments."[30] If ever there were a scientific concept that proved pataphysical, it is sure to have been the meme. Virtual. An imaginary solution.

In her book, *How the Gene Got Its Groove,* Elizabeth Parthenia Shea writes:

> As a rhetorical figure, the 'gene' moves from context to context, adapting to a broad range of rhetorical exigencies (from the highly technical to the intensely political to the ephemeral and the absurd), carrying with it a capacity for rhetorical work and rhetorical consequences. As the examples in this book show [...] the rhetorical consequences of the figure of the gene often include the assertion of boundaries, with

---

28 See S. Craig Watkins, *The Young and The Digital: What the Migration to Social Network Sites, Games, and Anytime, Anywhere Media Means for Our Future* (New York: Beacon, 2009), passim.

29 See Shea, *How the Gene Got Its Groove.*

30 Alfred Jarry, *Exploits & Opinions of Dr. Faustroll, Pataphysician* (Cambridge: Exact Change, 1965), 21–22.

authoritative knowledge on one side and playful language, stylistic devices, and rhetoric on the other.[31]

Sound familiar? Memes only work if they move. If they are units of culture then in order to build and maintain that culture, they have to move.[32]

Memes are what supposedly make us different from all other species in that we can deny our biological genes because of our cultural memes.[33] As we've seen, memes have been touted as units of thoughts, belief, ideology, memory, learning, influence, and, of course, culture. As media theorist Douglas Rushkoff told me in 1999:

> I've been into memes off-and-on since *Media Virus!* (1994), and I still think they're an interesting way to understand culture. But meme conversations spend much more time explaining memes than they accomplish. In other words, the metaphor itself seems more complex than the ideas it is meant to convey. So, I've abandoned the notion of memes pretty much altogether.[34]

Even in the 1990s, the web's salad days, the concept was so beleaguered by explanation that one of its major champions dropped the idea. Rushkoff continues:

> I remember I was doing an interview about *Media Virus!* for some magazine, and it was taking place at Timothy Leary's house. And he overheard me mention memes, and the journalist asking me to explain to him what 'memes' are. Afterwards, Timothy teased me. 'Two years you've been carrying

---

31 Shea, *How the Gene Got Its Groove*, 3.
32 See Greg Urban, *Metaculture: How Culture Moves Through the World* (Minneapolis: University of Minnesota Press, 2001); E.M. Rogers, *Diffusion of Innovations*, 5th edn. (New York: Free Press, 2003)
33 See Daniel Dennett, *Darwin's Dangerous Idea: Evolution and the Meanings of Life* (New York: Simon and Schuster, 1995).
34 Interview with the author, June 2, 1999.

on about memes,' he said. 'If you still have to explain what they are every time you mention them, it means they just haven't caught on. Drop 'em.'[35]

Now everyone knows what a meme is. One is far less likely to have to explain what memes are as you are what they aren't. Forget it. An Internet meme is a meme now. Dawkins's idea has been hi-jacked by the jacked-in.

Ludwig Wittgenstein once said there was no such thing as a private language.[36] The presumption being that language, the prime mover of ideas if ever there were such a thing, only works if it is shared. The same can be said of culture. It only works if it is shared. If memes never add up to anything larger than memes, the concept is dead, and so is its culture.

---

35 Ibid.
36 See Ludwig Wittgenstein, *Philosophical Investigations*, trans. G.E.M. Anscombe (Hoboken: Blackwell Publishing, 1953). Conflating the idea further, Daniel Dennett says that "words are memes that can be pronounced" (Daniel Dennet, "Daniel C. Dennett: Religion's Just a Survival Meme," 2006, https://ase.tufts.edu/cogstud/dennett/papers/ScienceTheologyNews.pdf).

Bibliography

Aunger, Robert. *The Electric Meme: A New Theory of How We Think*. New York: Free Press, 2002.

Bakker, R. Scott. *Neuropath*. New York: Tor Books, 2009.

Balkin, J.M. *Cultural Software: A Theory of Ideology*. New Haven: Yale University Press, 2003.

Blackmore, Susan. *The Meme Machine*. New York: Oxford University Press, 1999.

Bloom, Howard. *The Lucifer Principle: A Scientific Expedition into the Forces of History*. New York: Atlantic Monthly Press, 1995.

Brodie, Richard. *Virus of the Mind: The New Science of the Meme*. Seattle: Integral Press, 1995.

Cadwalladr, Carol. "Interview with Daniel Dennett: 'I Begrudge Every Hour I Have to Spend Worrying about Politics.'" *The Guardian,* February 12, 2017, https://www.theguardian.com/science/2017/feb/12/daniel-dennett-politics-bacteria-bach-back-dawkins-trump-interview.

Dawkins, Richard. *The Selfish Gene*. Oxford: Oxford University Press, 2006.

Dennett, Daniel. "Daniel C. Dennett: Religion's Just a Survival Meme." *Tufts University,* 2006. https://ase.tufts.edu/cogstud/dennett/papers/ScienceTheologyNews.pdf.

———. *Darwin's Dangerous Idea: Evolution and the Meanings of Life*. New York: Simon and Schuster, 1995.

Distin, Kate. *Cultural Evolution*. New York: Cambridge University Press, 2011.

———. *The Selfish Meme*. New York: Cambridge University Press, 2005.

Follman, Mark. "Inside the Race to Stop the Next Mass Shooter." *Mother Jones,* Nov./Dec. 2015, https://www.motherjones.com/politics/2015/10/mass-shootings-threat-assessment-shooter-fbi-columbine/.

Foster, Hal. "Slumming with Rappers at the Roxy." *London Review of Books* 22, no. 18 (2000): 16–18.

Goddard, Cliff, and Anna Wierzbicka. "Cultural Scripts: What Are They and What Are They Good For?" *Intercultural Pragmatics* 1, no. 2 (2004): 153–66. DOI: 10.1515/iprg.2004.1.2.153.

Gunders, John, and Damon Brown. *The Complete Idiot's Guide to Memes.* New York: Alpha, 2010.

Jarry, Alfred. *Exploits & Opinions of Dr. Faustroll, Pataphysician.* Translated by Simon Watson Taylor. Cambridge: Exact Change, 1965.

Jung, C.G. *The Undiscovered Self.* Princeton: Princeton University Press, 1990.

Leigh, Hoyle. *Genes, Memes, Culture, and Mental Illness: Toward an Integrative Model.* New York: Springer, 2010.

Lynch, Aaron. *Thought Contagion: How Belief Spreads Through Society.* New York: Basic Books, 1996.

Rogers, E.M. *Diffusion of Innovations.* 5th Edition. New York: Free Press, 2003.

Rushkoff, Douglas. *Media Virus! Hidden Agendas in Popular Culture.* New York: Ballantine, 1994.

Seabrook, John. *Nobrow: The Marketing of Culture and the Culture of Marketing.* New York: Knopf, 2000.

Shea, Elizabeth Parthenia. *How the Gene Got Its Groove: Figurative Language, Science, and the Rhetoric of the Real.* Albany: SUNY Press, 2008.

Shifman, Limor. *Memes in Digital Culture.* Cambridge: MIT Press, 2013.

Sperber, Dan. *Explaining Culture: A Naturalistic Approach.* New York: Blackwell, 1996.

Spitzberg, Brian S. "Toward A Model of Meme Diffusion (M3D)." *Communication Theory* 24 (2014): 311–39.

Urban, Greg. *Metaculture: How Culture Moves Through the World.* Minneapolis: University of Minnesota Press, 2001.

Watkins, S. Craig. *The Young and The Digital: What the Migration to Social Network Sites, Games, and Anytime, Anywhere Media Means for Our Future.* New York: Beacon, 2009.

Wittgenstein, Ludwig. *Philosophical Investigations*. Translated by G.E.M. Anscombe. Hoboken: Blackwell Publishing, 1953.

4

Apocalypse Memes for the Anthropocene God: Mediating Crisis and the Memetic Body Politic

Bogna M. Konior

The End Times

> *When the ax came into the forest, the trees said:*
> *'The handle is one of us.'*
> — Alice Walker, *Possessing the Secret of Joy*[1]

Human thought, whether in word or meme, has long been molded by the fact that the *Homo sapiens* are a species of ape, living on a rock surrounded by a deafening void, circling around a slowly dying star. Philosophy trades in re-articulating this matter, from Nietzsche's poetic vision of humans as "clever animals," whose knowledge cannot save them from the universe's relentless entropy, to Ray Brassier's recent attempt at unbinding philosophy from the paralysis of unthought so-

---

1   Alice Walker, *Possessing the Secret of Joy* (New York: Simon and Schuster, 1997), 15.

DOI: 10.21983/P3.0255.1.05

lar extinction.[2] "A refounder of future ruins, if you like," writes François Laruelle, "that's the best definition of philosophy."[3] This ostensibly cosmological problem casts its shadow over human affairs. It is historically ubiquitous to believe that things are not only worse now than they had been before but that, despite our cosmic insignificance, our times are the most significant of all: the end times. Who would not want to witness the end of the world, to feel that one dies without regret, leaving nothing behind? In 1995, Jean Baudrillard wrote:

> Imagine the amazing good fortune of the generation that gets to see the end of the world. This is as marvellous as being there at the beginning [...]. Let us therefore apply ourselves to seeing things — values, concepts, institutions — perish, seeing them disappear. This is the only issue worth fighting for.[4]

The desire for destruction, apocalypse, and disintegration takes different forms, from eschatological to bloodthirsty. "There are no breaks on this train!" proclaims a popular meme series that pictures the President of the United States as the alt-right mascot Pepe the Frog, helming what can be identified as "the rape-train," which in this memeplex functions as a symbol of joyful, unstoppable victory through destruction. *The Pursuit of the Millennium: Revolutionary Millenarians and Mystical Anarchists of the Middle Ages* outlines how medieval Christendom abounded in apocalyptic movements, where the book of *Revelations* was

---

2   Friedrich Nietzsche, "Truth and Lie in the Extra-Moral Sense," *The Portable Nietzsche,* trans. and ed. Walter Kaufmann (New York: Penguin Books, 1997), 42–46; Ray Brassier, *Nihil Unbound: Enlightenment and Extinction* (New York: Palgrave Macmillan, 2007).

3   François Laruelle, quoted in "Laruelle: Concept-Collider," *fragilekeys* (blog), December 10, 2017, https://fragilekeys.com/2017/12/10/laruelle-concept-collider/.

4   Jean Baudrillard, *Fragments: Cool Memories III, 1990–1995,* trans. Emily Agar (London and New York: Verso, 2006), 33–34.

considered indispensable to political comprehension.[5] *The ISIS Apocalypse: The History, Strategy, and Doomsday Vision of the Islamic State* shows how the cataclysmic vision of Abu Bakr al-Baghdadi echoes violent Christian millenarian movements in the 16th century; and in *Divine Destruction,* journalist Stephanie Hendricks studies contemporary Christian Dominionists, who believe that climate change should not be stalled but accelerated in order to bring about the Second Coming of Jesus and the beginning of God's Kingdom on Earth.[6] No breaks on the planetary train! Physicist Stephen Hawking and engineer Elon Musk present us with an atheist version of the Final Judgment, warning that accelerated technological progress will bring about an artificial intelligence singularity and a *de facto* end of the human species once the AI realizes how immoral or inefficient humans are.[7] In the Greco-Christian narrative, ever since Apollo spat in the mouth of the oracle Cassandra, history has been filled with prophets of doom to the extent that, as Justin Clemens perceptively writes, "a certain apocalypticism is perhaps a condition for [...] thinking as such."[8]

If, as we can read in a quoted passage in Richard Dawkins's *The Selfish Gene,* "memes should be regarded as living structures [...] when you plant a fertile meme in my mind you literally parasitize my brain," then a prominent subspecies of these

5   Norman Cohn, *The Pursuit of the Millennium: Revolutionary Millenarians and Mystical Anarchists of the Middle Ages* (Oxford: Oxford University Press, 1992).

6   Will McCants, *The ISIS Apocalypse: The History, Strategy, and Doomsday Vision of the Islamic State* (New York: St. Martin's Press, 2015); Stephanie Hendricks, *Divine Destruction* (New York: Melville House Publishing, 2005).

7   See, for example, Rory Cellan-Jones, "Stephen Hawking Warns That Artificial Intelligence Could End Mankind," *BBC,* December 2, 2014, http://www.bbc.com/news/technology-30290540; Melia Robinson, "Elon Musk Thinks Artificial Intelligence is Ultimately More Dangerous than Nuclear Weapons," *Business Insider,* March 12, 2018, http://www.businessinsider.com/elon-musk-ai-more-dangerous-than-nuclear-weapons-sxsw-2018-3.

8   Justin Clemens, "After After Finitude: An Afterword," in *Aesthetics after Finitude,* eds. Baylee Brits, Prudence Gibson, and Amy Ireland (Victoria: re.press, 2016), 229.

brain parasites that we call "memes" — units of digital culture with substantial cultural and now also political capital gained through circulation — feeds on various strains of apocalypticism.[9] While eschatology remains indispensable to diverse cultures, these days it is especially visible in English-language memes, also for the fact that they are the most visible on the Western Internet, whose social media interfaces are provided largely by American corporations. An early sign was the first wave of disaster memes that rose just after the dust of the World Trade Center fell. Analyzing 398 of these "collage jokes," as she labels them, Giselinde Kuipers suggested that they were a coping mechanism for dealing with an exceedingly "unreal and fiction-like" world by deploying humor.[10] These images were, for example, of King Kong fending off terrorist planes on top of the World Trade Center, with a caption: "Where was King Kong when we needed him?" or of Osama Bin Laden in an advertisement for "Taliban Airlines: Exploring New Destinations!" Similarly, one of the first viral videos was about the end of the world, uploaded to YouTube shortly after the website's launch, the light-hearted "End of Ze World" (2003) by Fluid, which generated millions of views and has since warranted a sequel, "End of Ze World... Probably For Real This Time" (2018), which laments neo-Nazism, Donald Trump, the refugee crisis, terrorism, nuclear danger, climate change, and Twitter as possible signs of doom. While the original is hardly political, dealing rather in harmless humor based in national stereotypes, the sequel addresses global news headlines through the lens of crisis clothed in campy digital aesthetics.

Nowadays, in the meme-heaven that is Reddit, users chart "end-of-world scenarios that frighten you the most," which include solar flares, sex comets from Neptune, overpopulation, nanotechnology, famine, nuclear war, super viruses, infertility

---

9   N.K. Humphrey, quoted in Richard Dawkins, *The Selfish Gene* (Oxford: Oxford University Press, 2006), 192.

10   Giselinde Kuipers, "Media Culture and Internet Disaster Jokes: Bin Laden and the Attack on the World Trade Center," *European Journal of Cultural Studies* 5, no. 4 (2002): 450–70, at 468.

and, of course, "that we run out of memes."[11] The anxiety-ridden, left-leaning in its focus on ecological overshoot subreddit r/collapse, with around 60,000 members, includes a monthly meta-thread in which users note down the signs of downfall around them, from crumbling infrastructure to rising unemployment. On some days, they discuss Ted Kaczynski's neo-Luddite books, on others, they pick at major headlines, such as "Doomsday Prep for the Super Rich" (*New Yorker*) or "Silicon Valley Billionaires are Preparing for the Apocalypse with Motorcycles, Guns, and Private Hideaways" (*Business Insider*).[12] A corresponding r/LateStageCapitalism channel, with 260,000 members, is devoted to "zesty memes [...] that critique [and mock] the decay of western capitalist culture" as it is "digging its own grave."[13] The subreddit also links to dozens of other channels, from apocalyptic fiction to survival guides. Lagging well behind is a young channel r/Cowwapse, which describes itself as "an antidote to the fear-mongering and doom-porn of these subreddits" and focuses mainly on climate change denial ("Snow in Sahara Desert for third time in 40 years") as well as on celebrating free markets and "the unprecedented equality of the 21st century."[14] The infamous r/The_Donald has in excess of half a million members, and labels itself a "national suicide prevention lifeline," celebrating how Donald Trump's election stalled the disaster toward which his supporters believed America had been heading.[15] The alt-right alike relies on a reactionary civilizational decline narrative, as Angela Nagle writes, a testament to a long line of collapse thought that ties decadence to doom.[16]

As Matt Goerzen writes in "Notes Towards the Memes of Production," for years "memes were perceived as a negligible

---

11 See Reddit, s.v. "collapse," https://www.reddit.com/r/collapse/.
12 Ibid.
13 See Reddit, s.v. "LateStageCapitalism," https://www.reddit.com/r/LateStageCapitalism/.
14 See Reddit, s.v. "Cowwapse," https://www.reddit.com/r/Cowwapse/.
15 See Reddit, s.v. "The_Donald," https://www.reddit.com/r/The_Donald/.
16 Angela Nagle, *Kill All Normies: The Online Culture Wars from Tumblr and 4chan to the Alt-right and Trump* (Hants: Zero Books, 2017), 63–64.

artefact until meme magic elected Trump."[17] Memes are now the focal point of an increasingly visible debate about the state of contemporary political divisions and the online cultural identity war. Circulated mainly within the sphere of American politics that is simultaneously a forum of global digital pop culture, they are associated with the alt-right's strategy of trolling while "bypassing the dying mainstream media and creating an Internet-culture and alternative media of their own."[18] Yet, while Nagle writes that the alt-right successfully built its "transgressive" aesthetics by arguing that "we are not 'five minutes to midnight' as the anti-immigration right had long claimed but well past midnight," the desire to grapple with or inhabit apocalypticism is present across the political spectrum.[19] From Afro-pessimism to queer negativity, there is a rising conviction that, as an anonymous graffiti in France proclaimed to the world a few years ago, "another end of the world is possible."[20] One meme, for example, contrasts neo-reactionary philosopher Nick Land with Afro-pessimist philosopher Frank Wilderson III, denouncing the first as a "techno-commercialist" who advocates a "thirst for annihilation but [is] scared of Islam [and] not at all ready for meltdown," while praising the latter's work as a "total apocalyptic epistemic World negation [...] unflinching paradigmatic dissatisfaction with humanity," calling him a "doomsday scion who brings about Afrofuturist singularity."[21] Marxist scholar and science-fiction writer China Miéville alike advocates that progressives should embrace "a strategy for ruination [...] a state

---

17 Matt Goerzen, "Notes Towards the Memes of Production," *Texte zur Kunst* 106 (2017): 86–107, https://www.textezurkunst.de/106/uber-die-meme-der-produktion/

18 Nagle, *Kill All Normies*, 41.

19 Ibid., 102.

20 A photo can be found here: Le Comptoir, "Une autre fin du monde est-elle possible?" *Le Comptoir*, May 29, 2017, https://comptoir.org/2017/05/29/une-autre-fin-du-monde-est-elle-possible/.

21 The post uses a "virgin versus chad" meme format in which an unsuccessful male introvert is compared with an attractive but crude one. See, for example, @viralpraxis's Facebook post, September 3, 2017, https://www.facebook.com/viralpraxis/posts/1487585427945169.

of an undefeated despair because *it's done,* this is a dystopia, a worsening one, and dreams of interceding don't just miss the point but are actively unhelpful."[22]

Next to this apocalyptic cultural capital on both sides of the political spectrum are memes that do not connect easily with the existing political options. An interest in annihilation, at least on the surface, might be the attractor between diffuse political factions, which often share very little apart from their collapse drive. This interrogation happens alongside the debates around posthumanism, transhumanism, automation, extinction, and climate nihilism that have been drawing increased academic, political, cultural, and scientific attention over the last two decades. Pondering abstraction, dehumanization, and disintegration, they play out against the recent Euro-American history of "a not merely 'non-political' but a 'post-political' generation grappling with its own politicisation under the aegis of austerity, neoliberalism, and financial-managerial political corruption," and — we should add — the growing realization of geological peril on top of that.[23] Questions about humanity, agency, and the very scale at which "politics" must be thought emerge as the main problem of this apocalyptic inquiry. Twitter's meme culture, for example, is created by humans and bots alike and thus circulating memes on Twitter is a different form of meme commentary than if we were doing so on predominately "human" social media like Snapchat. A recent joint study at the Center for Complex Networks and Systems Research at the University of Indiana and the Information Sciences Institute at the University of Southern California estimates that up to 15% (around 50 million) of Twitter accounts are not human.[24] Outsourcing human agency to machines and experimenting with a nonhu-

---

22 "A Strategy for Ruination: An Interview with China Miéville," *Boston Review,* January 8, 2018, http://bostonreview.net/literature-culture-china-mieville-strategy-ruination.

23 See Metahaven, *Can Jokes Bring Down Governments? Memes, Design and Politics* (Moscow: Strelka Press, 2014), 44.

24 Onur Varol et al., "Online Human-Bot Interactions: Detection, Estimation, and Characterization," *arXiv,* 2017, https://arxiv.org/abs/1703.03107.

man vision of politics informs this variant of apocalyptic meme culture. Anonymous account @dogsdoingthings, for example, generates dismissive commentaries of human affairs: "Dogs exiting political discourse, preferring instead to lie prone forever in puddle of ooze,"[25] or "Dogs asserting there is no such thing as history and citing the preceding eons of nothingness as evidence."[26] Add to that the general reputation of Twitter as a grim, soul-crushing place. Musician Mikel Jollett described it as such: "Instagram: My life is a party. Snapchat: My life is a quirky tv show. Facebook: My life turned out great! Twitter: We're all going to die."[27] Aside from Twitter, many loosely distributed memes cultivate an appetite for void and a desire to relinquish human agency. Take two of the most popular memes featuring r/surrealmemes's emblematic "Meme Man," a bad 3D model of a human face. The first one introduces him as an open source figure for an unknown transformation: "meme man is a conduit through which tortured souls may channel their rage and misery into something more [...] an entity which resides in the unspace between this world and the next."[28] Another portrays him opening a gift, inside which is an all-encompassing obliteration that splits his face into pieces. "Thank you," he responds.[29]

How can we understand this proliferation of apocalypticism in contemporary meme cultures? Slavoj Žižek writes that we indeed live in the end times, marked by the ecological crisis, the biogenetic revolution, accelerating social inequality, and struggles over resources.[30] All of this is happening against the background of sweeping technological changes, which, as Alvin

---

25 See @dogsdoingthings, *Twitter,* February 23, 2018, 5:20pm, https://twitter.com/dogsdoingthings/status/967071664356937728.

26 See @dogsdoingthings, *Twitter,* August 22, 2017, 9:35pm, https://twitter.com/dogsdoingthings/status/900078876398931968.

27 See @Mikel_Jollet, *Twitter,* January 8, 2017, 9:35am, https://twitter.com/Mikel_Jollett/status/818149100717621248.

28 See Know Your Meme, s.v. "Meme Man," http://knowyourmeme.com/photos/1090174-meme-man.

29 Ibid.

30 Slavoj Žižek, *Living in the End Times* (London: Verso, 2010).

Toffler wrote, provoke a cultural "future shock [...] the dizzying disorientation brought on by the premature arrival of the future [...] a product of the greatly accelerated rate of change in society."[31] While apocalyptic memes can be explained by the medium's inherent — often ironic — humor, they are also the evidence of grappling with the insufficiency of politics at this moment of perceived crisis. Some express panic about civilizational decline, some joke about doom becoming our *status quo.* Others still wrestle with abstraction and, perhaps unwillingly informed by the possibility of actual extinction in the era that has been called the Anthropocene, challenge the idea of sufficient human agency. Dehumanization, anonymity, and doom are symptomatic not only of what the current (Western) political sphere on the Internet styles itself to be, but also of a larger shift in experiencing the inefficiency of human politics. Various theories of film and media already predicted this moment; tending toward posthumanism, they informed proto-meme theories of technologically mediated forms of anonymous or virtual political subjectivity. This legacy could explain online collapse cultures, and account for the rise of a specific strand of dehumanized apocalypticism, which can only be understood alongside a larger reconsideration of human agency in the age of socio-geological crisis that is the Anthropocene.

The Medium Is the Apocalypse

> *"There is no other world, but it can't be this one."*
> — @mckenziewark, January, 17, 2018[32]

Barry Vacker, director of the Center for Media and Destiny affiliated with Temple University, writes that "media technologies can be divided into *cosmic media* and *social media,* while the

---

31 Alvin Toffler, *Future Shock* (New York: Random House, 1970), 13.

32 See @mckenziewark, *Twitter,* January 17, 2018, 9:44am, https://twitter.com/mckenziewark/status/953684423790252032.

media content itself can be understood in terms of memes."[33] For him, *all* media within this duplet, from telescopes to television screens, can loop apocalyptic messages because they contribute to revising prevalent forms of human subjectivity, placing it either within the context of the cosmos or the perpetually expanding and contracting network society. The Internet features prominently in his argument, as it represents both the destruction of stable meaning due to its multiple information flows, and a foreshadowing of the biological end of the human species, where the predictions about the singularity to come true. The link between the beginning of the "dehumanizing" industrial revolution and the ascent of moving image technologies, which prefigured digital images, is evident in cinema studies through the linkage of the train and the film projector.[34] Both symbolize not only the onset of the age of technological innovation and environmental pollution, but a change in perception itself: to be able to perceive the world in movement while ourselves remaining stable and still, whether from the window of a moving train or on the cinema screen, changed the very speed at which people viewed reality. No longer, as it was in Renaissance painting, was the human eye the holy perceiver and meaning-maker for which the whole universe arranged itself geometrically and purposefully. Early cinema theorists, such as Jean Epstein and Dziga Vertov, wrote that alongside the telescope and the microscope lens, the inhuman cinema lenses participated in decentralizing the human ego, displacing it from its position at the center of the universe.[35] As Jacques Aumont writes, these tech-

---

33 Barry Vacker, *The End of the World — Again: Why the Apocalypse Meme Replicates in Media, Science, and Culture* (Philadelphia: Center for Media Destiny, 2012), 5.

34 See Jacques Aumont, "The Variable Eye, or Mobilization of the Gaze," in *Image in Dispute: Art and Cinema in the Age of Photography,* ed. Dudley Andrew (Austin: University of Texas Press, 1997), 31–259.

35 Dziga Vertov, *Kino-Eye: The Writings of Dziga Vertov,* ed. Annette Michelson, trans. Kevin O'Brien (Berkeley and Los Angeles: University of California Press, 1984); I wrote about Epstein's nonhuman cinema theory in Bogna Konior, "Towards Nonhuman Personhood: Reading Jean Epstein's Cinema Essays," in *Filmmakers' Theory: Contributions to Cinema*

nological changes were not only reconfiguring how people experienced spatio-temporality but morality itself, producing new desires such as "the desire for acceleration or the wish to sever roots."[36] It is within this genealogy that we understand media as a crucial component in posthumanist debates. If, following Marshall McLuhan, we agree that the medium is the message and that every medium destroys some form of subjectivity to introduce another, we can also repeat after Vacker: "the medium is the apocalypse."[37]

While this linear story bypasses alternate options both within and outside of the "West," it could partially account for why apocalyptic memes express both a sense of aggrandizement and a desire to relinquish control at the same time. It would be a way for humans to deal with what Vacker describes as the paradoxical effect of the media: a sense of insignificance that they produce by exposing the negligibility of humans within the world, as the telescope and the microscope did, and a sense of importance within a networked system that we experience as centering on us, as social media are purported to do. The train, the symbol of this accelerating, schizophrenic industrial modernity appears in one popular meme. Already mentioned, the "Rape Train" is a reference to a tactic used in *Call of Duty*, when the player creates a string of zombies following him and eventually stacking up to be easily defeated. When it became apparent that Donald Trump had a legitimate chance of winning the election, it mutated into a "Trump Train," which celebrated the supposed accelerating destruction of "the elites," often represented by the Democratic Party, or the "fake news" media. This genre is decisively about asserting control rather than relinquishing the centrality of human agency, yet its interest in destruction and its unintended connection to accelerated media modernity, where humans exist as mere carriers of an unstoppable force, make it

---

Theory, eds. Manuela Penafria et al. (Covilhã: Labcom Books, 2016), 117–38.

36 Aumont, "The Variable Eye," 235.

37 Marshall McLuhan, *The Medium is the Message: An Inventory of Effects* (London: Penguin Books, 1967); Vacker, *The End of the World,* 7.

a part of a larger apocalyptic tendency in memes, or, as some would argue, in the Internet at large.

Digging into the decentralized, leaky archive of viral digital culture, we might uncover a pervasive sense of crisis and anxiety around new forms of political subjectivity that informs early investigations into the politics of the Internet. In 2002, the Institute for New Culture Technologies in Austria, led by Konrad Becker, hosted a tactical workshop, "Dark Markets: Infopolitics, Electronic Media and Democracy in Times of Crisis", with guiding questions like "has the Internet still its digital potential to foster a 'network democracy from below'" or "can the Internet be reclaimed as a digital commons"?[38] The conference marked a rapid decline of trust in the ideals of global democracy once ecstatically arisen with the fall of the Berlin Wall in 1989, and then quickly put to rest as the project of the free market guided by the EU, NATO, and the IMF was already turning into a "disaster," signaled by, among others, "the rise of Europe's populist and 'culturalist' right," "global warming and the Kyoto treaty drama" and "the astonishing roller coaster ride from dotcom mania to plummeting stock markets." The conference already questioned whether anything like an "electronic democracy" can exist but, nevertheless, in a then-popular spirit of Deleuze and Guattari's philosophy, advocated for a "rhizomatic" decentralization of digital networks and "a rigorous involvement and implementation of social movements into technology." The becoming-networked of the human species was only about to begin, and while many watched with uneasiness the decentralization of markets, the idea of a decentralized, subversive, anarchic digital politics held sway in the early 2000s. Crisis in consequence of technological advancement could model forms of political subjectivity that were considered productive precisely because of their de-individualizing form.

This decentralized political subjectivity is connected to the ideals of anonymity and cyber-utopian virtual realities that were

---

38 These, and the further quotations, are taken from the digital archive. See http://darkmarkets.to.or.at/concept.htm

prominent in early Internet scholarship. Throughout the 1990s, the promise of these ostensibly non-hierarchical spaces was their ability to erase any physical manifestation of identity and central control — where, under strings of avatars, we would be able to escape the scanning gaze of repressive social structures, which befall us because our bodies appear to others in terms of ethnicity or sex. In "The Sex Appeal of the Inorganic," Thomas Foster outlines how the idea of posthuman or machine body appears in tandem with a machinic desire: desire for machines or desire to be like one.[39] Anonymity, mutability, and invisibility that online spaces afforded were the revolutionary horizon for feminist critiques, such as in the novels of Melissa Scott, which saw emancipatory potential in the diffused world of alternative and virtual realities, where utopias could be constructed anew, and identity would no longer be defined by what we cannot control: the racialized and sexed ideologies projected onto our bodies.[40] As Donna Haraway noted, "social subjects who are already [used] to thinking about their bodies as constructed, usually by others, and therefore available to reconstruction" would be most incited by the freedom from bodily determinism that living in the meatspace forces on us.[41] It was the left-leaning, posthumanist space of socially transgressive and technologically inclined science fiction that advocated for a maximum subtraction of physical markers of identity by engaging the medium of the Internet.

In the early 2010s, it was still argued that politics could be projected into an endlessly mutable digital space, where basic social and political terms would have to be remodeled. Heather Brooke's *The Revolution Will be Digitised: Dispatches from the Information War* argues that technology will break down social

---

39 Thomas Foster, "'The Sex Appeal of the Inorganic': Posthuman Narratives and the Construction of Desire," in *Centuries' Ends, Narrative Means,* ed. Robert Newman (Stanford: Stanford University Press, 1996), 276.

40 For example, Melissa Scott, *Burning Bright* (New York: Tor Books, 1994).

41 In Foster, "'The Sex Appeal of the Inorganic,'" 281.

divisions by creating an even playing field.[42] Yet, as Nagle noticed, this kind of anti-establishment, DIY online culture "that cyberutopian true believers have evangelized for many years" has taken a specific political form in the meme magic of the alt-right, who embrace "the freewheeling world of anonymity and tech" but reinforce a reactionary order of things, rather than creating a mutable space for a new social order.[43] In their Kickstarted book, *Neoreaction: A Basilisk,* Elizabeth Sandifer also notices that the "neoreactionary" (by their own designation), racist-libertarian movements connected to the alt-right aped the cultural techniques of the left to portray themselves as rebels, while evoking the aesthetics of "Basilisks, Cthulhu, and shuddering voids of inescapable reality."[44]

Memes, as is common knowledge by now, became a tool of choice in this new cultural war. Despite the resulting claims that "the left can't meme," discussed also in this collection, the political potential of memes themselves was first celebrated by left-leaning scholars, and not so long ago. Considering contemporary digital culture in times of austerity and in a post-financial crisis Europe, which they describe as "the Pandora's box of disastrous consequences," in *Can Jokes Bring Down Governments?,* the Metahaven collective believe that jokes, including memes, can operate outside of state power because they disrupt what counts as political reality management, that is, what counts as reasonable within public political discourse.[45] Discussing Anonymous, the Arab Spring, the Cute Cat Theory of Digital

---

42 Heather Brooke, *The Revolution Will be Digitised: Dispatches from the Information War* (Portsmouth: William Heinemann, 2011).

43 Nagle, *Kill All Normies,* 18. In Alexander Galloway and Eugene Thacker, *The Exploit: A Theory of Networks* (Minneapolis: University of Minnesota Press, 2007), the authors also describe how the utopian idea of a decentralised network society turned out to be perversely hostile to the kind of utopias that scholars once ascribed to it; instead, it turned into a new model of control, with governments and corporations alike adapting to this mode of distributing power.

44 Elizabeth Sandifer (with Jack Hartman), *Neoreaction a Basilisk: Essays On and around the Alt-Right* (Eruditorum Press, 2016), 54.

45 Metahaven, *Can Jokes Bring Down Governments?,* 9.

Activism, and 4chan's trolling of the Church of Scientology in 2008, they go as far as to suggest that memes can be an alternative to representative democracy: an idea previously advocated by scholars who saw the Internet as a permissive space where those who could not access real political representation could nevertheless claim it.[46] In this vision, memes could have been the realization of Jürgen Habermas's ideal of the public sphere, a non-legislative space of communication for the people, which Habermas dates back to the eighteenth century and the ideals of the Enlightenment in Europe.[47]

Before the alt-right became the most visible dealer of memes, there were at least three noticeable traditions of proto-meme-politics on the left: one in the 1990s, which celebrated the anonymous, mutable spaces of the Internet as a way of erasing oppressive identities; the other two in the early 2000s, when the Internet was portrayed both as a disruptive space of nonsensical humor, and an accessible public sphere. And yet, Goerzen writes that it was the neo-Luddite thinking on the left, which forgot its own roots in political techno-experimentations, that led to the right reappropriating the techniques of the avant-garde, such as provocation, anonymity, and irony to advocate for a return to a paleo-libertarian value system. This is true enough — equally visible in Internet scholarship are works that lament its ascent as the end-all of politics. Hubert Dreyfus's *On the Internet* builds on Søren Kierkegaard's impressive hatred of the daily press — "Europe will come to a standstill at the Press and remain at a standstill as a reminder that the human race has invented something which will eventually overpower it"[48] — to argue that a disembodied experience characteristic of the online

---

46 Limor Shifman, *Memes in Digital Culture* (Cambridge: MIT Press, 2014), 119–51.

47 Jürgen Habermas, *The Structural Transformation of the Public Sphere,* trans Thomas Burger and Frederick Lawrence (Cambridge: MIT Press, 1989).

48 Søren Kierkegaard, *Journals and Papers,* Vol. 2: F–K, ed. and trans. Howard V. Hong and Edna H. Hong (Bloomington: Indiana University Press, 1970), 480.

sphere is in itself a political catastrophe.[49] For Dreyfus, anonymity and information overload turn everyone into a dilettante and a nihilist. Kierkegaard despised the principle of equivalence that the daily press introduced into information flows. He found the idea that God was "equally concerned with the salvation of humanity and the fall of one sparrow" the expression of utmost nihilism, an annihilation of political relevance and concern.[50] We can only imagine his outrage at Mark Zuckerberg's famous claim that "a squirrel dying in your front yard may be more relevant to your interests right now than people dying in Africa," a comment that prefigured the trouble he was about to get in after Trump's victory, when Facebook had to withstand a lot of criticism pertaining to its information bubbles.[51] Dreyfus alike tells us that because of the Internet, there is nothing worth dying for — everything matters equally, invading your attention span with equal force. Stands are to be taken no more! Flow of information postpones action indefinitely, memes drown us in their self-replicating digital flood, rabbit holes down subreddits tear you away from practice and insert you into an information-producing machine, until you are nothing but an ever-sharpening set of refined "views on issues." You have become an epistemological halo, trapped in the apparatus of the Internet, which produces knowledge but stalls action. This process, as Dreyfus tells us, rests in the fact of the Internet's "deindividualized" and "abstract" nature, detached from local practices.[52] Kierkegaard predicted that this abstract, mediated public sphere will proliferate apocalyptic prophecies, proposing that humans, overwhelmed by the nihilism brought on by the media, will refuse ethical thought entirely, prioritizing instead involvements in the aesthetic sphere, where the goal is to "make enjoyment of all possibilities the center of their lives."[53] He would probably say that

---

49 Hubert Dreyfus, *On the Internet,* 2nd edn. (London: Routledge, 2008), 73.
50 Ibid. 79.
51 Eli Pariser, "When the Internet Thinks It Knows You," *New York Times,* May 23, 2011, http://www.nytimes.com/2011/05/23/opinion/23pariser.html.
52 Dreyfus, *On the Internet,* 76.
53 Ibid., 79–80.

it is not the content that makes memes apocalyptic but rather that *all* aesthetic production that the media sphere necessitates is hopelessly rooted in the annihilation of ethical concern. The medium is the apocalypse.

These traditions — one pro-Internet, the other anti — disagree primarily on the points of abstraction and dehumanization. Starting from the same point — the Internet is abstracting and disrupting politics — they arrive either at a utopian vision, in which digital spaces become materials out of which a new politics can be borne, or generate a dystopian disengagement with politics as humanity is increasingly trapped in aesthetics. Habermas was immediately critical of how the public sphere worked, complaining that it deteriorated into mediocrity and conformism, but he still believed in rescuing it. Kierkegaard, however, predicted that for media nihilism to occur, "a phantom must first be provided, its spirit, a monstrous abstraction, an all-encompassing something that is a nothing, a mirage — this phantom is the *public*."[54] Of course, for him, this was an entirely deplorable fact, a monstrous, occult uprising of unethical and perversely aesthetic nihilism. Any type of harm can be waged in the name of "the people" as they are but a phantom, delighted by aesthetic speculation and detached from localized practices. A faceless online army, we could say, spewing apocalyptic prophecies, entertaining themselves with unethical, aesthetic nihilism, is precisely what Kierkegaard feared that the media would produce.

Given the failed utopianism of techno-anarchism on the one side, and the dystopian relativism of the memetic public sphere on the other, could a different opening still be created within this phantom politics? Rather than demonizing the phantom nature of meme politics, Tiziana Terranova suggests that "meme theory" is an appropriate way of understanding all technological mediation, precisely because "what Dawkins' theory allows is the replacement of the individual by the unit" and if we should stick with the biological undertones of the original term, it is

---

54 Ibid., 73.

because of its "immense productivity of the multitude, its absolute capacity to [...] mutate."[55] Putting forth the possibility of collapse as productive, she believes that such technologies enable "an acceleration of history and an annihilation of distance within an information milieu, it is a creative destruction" which allows for social reconstruction.[56] Perhaps the desire to erase oneself, to anonymize the Internet, to thrust ourselves — as a phantom public — into destruction is not an entirely aesthetic project but, as any legitimately nihilist drive, speaks to a deeper impulse toward a *revaluation* of what counts as political in the first place. Could this phantom subjectivity that the media called into existence be also a specter of reformation?

Memes of the Anthropocene

> "the question that once seemed to be: are
> you happy? has been replaced with: can you
> breathe? neither can be answered"
> — @atlajala, August 2, 2017[57]

Konrad Becker notices that "disorganization creates crisis cults or projective systems resulting from culture strains."[58] The Global Financial Crisis in 2008, which was, in fact, a doom event with disastrous consequences, surprisingly did not provoke a surge in meme production.[59] In the same year, however, there were dozens of apocalyptic memes related to the Large Hadron Collider particle accelerator and the possibility of creating a black hole that could swallow our universe. A status-indicator single site, active until today, titled "Has The Large Hadron Col-

---

55   Tiziana Terranova, *Network Culture Politics for the Information Age* (London and Ann Arbor: Pluto Press, 2004), 124, 118.

56   Ibid., 2–3.

57   See @atlajala, *Twitter*, August 2, 2017, 5:54pm, https://twitter.com/atlajala/ status/892911463009992705.

58   Konrad Becker, *Tactical Reality Dictionary: Cultural Intelligence and Social Control* (Vienna: Edition Selene, 2010), 44.

59   To the best of my knowledge.

lider Destroyed The World Yet?" was launched. In 2012, there was a flood of catastrophic memes, this time devoted to the Mayan calendar, including images depicting the Nibiru Cataclysm, a theory of planetary collision first proposed in 1995 by Nancy Lieder who claimed to have received the prophecy from aliens. The theory was so popular that it compelled NASA to inform the Internet that Nibiru actually did not exist. Like the memes commenting on a doomsday scenario from just a year before fabricated by Christian preacher Harold Camping (The May 21, 2011 Rapture), the overall tone was mockery — *as if* we were going to die! Grumpy Cat, the Internet's favourite cynical retort at the height of the mid-2010s obsession with animal reaction memes, provided a subtle celebratory tone: "The world is ending in December? Good." In 2016, when Donald Trump ran for President, the "This is Fine" meme brought another brand of ironic defeatism to the table. Sourced from K.C. Green's Gunshow comics, this continually popular meme portrays a dog sitting at a table amidst burning flames, assuring himself that everything is fine — "this is fine, I'm okay with the events that are unfolding currently" — as the fire engulfs his house and eventually melts his face off. *Elite Daily* collected several end of the world memes to honor the end of 2017, which joke about Hurricane Ophelia in London and the possibility of a nuclear war.[60] Donald Trump's inauguration inspired many memes which equated it with no less than the coming of the beast.[61] The unintentionally ominous picture of Trump, Saudi king Salman, and Egyptian president Abdel Fattah el-Sisi touching a mysterious glowing orb, originally posted by @SaudiEmbassyUSA, was widely circulated and drew comparisons to *Lord of the Rings* and Marvel universe villains. The Church of Satan retweeted the photo, clarifying that

---

60 Thea Glassman, "5 End of the World Memes to Honor Going into 2018," *Elite Daily,* December 19, 2017, https://www.elitedaily.com/p/5-end-of-the-world-memes-to-honor-going-into-2018-7523572.

61 Jay Hathaway, "'Here's the Livestream of Trump's Inauguration' Meme Prepares for the Apocalypse," *The Daily Dot,* January 20, 2017, https://www.dailydot.com/unclick/livestream-trump-inauguration-apocalypse-meme/.

it was not a Satanic ritual.[62] John Hodgman tagged conspiracy theorist Alex Jones in his retweet, asking him to "pay attention" as — it was implied — the orb was clearly about to jumpstart a communist-reptilian reckoning.[63] It is not only the alt-right that trades in the aesthetics of civilizational decline.

In 1922, shortly after the October revolution, Russian historian Yevgeny Tarle wrote that "revolution is foremost a death, then a life; we risk forgetting that not far under the elegant carpet of our cabin there is a dark and fathomless abyss."[64] Based in his conviction that crisis was temporary, his strategy was to advocate for a calm resistance to the sway of the unknown, for asserting, rather than overthrowing the persuasions of the olden days. Or, the Internet would say, keep calm and carry on. Yet, what if crisis is not a transitory stage but the rhythm to which society marches without break? What if crisis is perpetually but unequally distributed? Mark Fisher uses the term "capitalist realism" to describe how capitalism manages to ostensibly unhinge itself from economy, where Karl Marx defined it chiefly through the production of surplus value, to encompass the past and the future, as if it was the only thing that ever existed and the only one that ever will.[65] To sustain this tautology, capitalism trades in producing and maintaining crisis as its main cultural currency, thus naturalizing itself as the only alternative. Achille Mbembe describes a similar mechanism underlying necro-political states, which must maintain a sense of danger — you have no idea of the threat that is underway! — to justify large-scale physical violence toward (typically racialized) populations.[66] Necro-political nation-states must then maintain both the sense

---

62 See @ChurchofSatan, *Twitter,* May 22, 2017, 2:41am, https://twitter.com/ChurchofSatan/status/866453928535236608.

63 See @hodgman, *Twitter,* May 21, 2017, 11:56am, https://twitter.com/hodgman/status/866367178248945664.

64 Yevgeny Tarle, quoted in Paul Dukes, *Minutes to Midnight: History and the Anthropocene Era from 1763* (London: Anthem Press, 2011), 70.

65 Mark Fisher, *Capitalist Realism: Is There No Alternative?* (London: Zero Books, 2009).

66 Achille Mbembe, "Necropolitics," trans. Libby Meintjes, *Public Culture* 15, no. 1 (2003): 11–40.

of crisis and the fantasy of protection at their hands to stay in power. The difference now is that instead of analyzing how capitalism manages culture and crisis within the nation state, we should be charting a far more encompassing, planetary necropolitics parallel to what is called the Anthropocene. The power fantasy that it produces is not security but inevitability.

First coined by the Dutch chemist Paul J. Crutzen in 2000, the term "Anthropocene" gained currency in 2007, when paleobiologist and stratigrapher Jan Zalasiewicz requested that the Geological Society of London's Stratigraphy Commission review the case for a new geological epoch to replace the currently prevailing Holocene. While climate change and the Anthropocene are often conflated, in 2009 *Nature* published an article in which a team of scientists led by Johan Rockström of the Stockholm Resilience Centre list several different factors that, if accelerated by humans, would lead to the 6th global extinction.[67] Climate change is only one of them, alongside ocean acidification, stratospheric ozone depletion, global freshwater depletion, biodiversity loss, changes in nitrogen and phosphorus cycles, industrial agriculture, chemical pollution, and atmospheric aerosol loading.[68] Although these phenomena are environmental, the Anthropocene denotes their civilizational origin: industrial capitalism and fossil fuel extraction, the global slave trade, the Great Acceleration, and the bombing of Hiroshima and Nagasaki have all been suggested as the starting points of this geosociological, or socio-geological era.[69] This prophecy of doom,

---

67 Biologist Scott Gilbert compares it to a K-T event such as the Cretaceous-Tertiary boundary and the extinction of non-avian dinosaurs 66 million years ago, or the Permian-Triassic extinction that wiped out more than 90% of all species 252 million years ago, in Donna Haraway et al., "Anthropologists Are Talking — About the Anthropocene," *Ethnos* 81, no. 3 (2016): 535–64.

68 See Johan Rockström et al., "A Safe Operating Space for Humanity," *Nature* 461 (2009): 472–75.

69 See Heather Davis and Etienne Turpin, "Art and Death: Lives Between the Fifth Assessment & the Sixth Extinction," in *Art in the Anthropocene: Encounters Among Aesthetics, Politics, and Epistemologies,* eds. Heather Davis and Etienne Turpin (London: Open Humanities Press, 2015), 5;

however, grounded as it is in the scientific consensus, does not inspire apocalypticism in memes in the same way that everyday political headlines do. Climate change memes are popular but are rather didactic tools for educating the masses about the prescience of the subject, or deceiving them into climate change denialism.[70]

If the Anthropocene informs apocalyptic memes, it does so in a less direct way. Precisely because the points of contestation discussed here are abstraction, phantom politics, and posthumanism, the Anthropocene as an organizing principle must tell us something about the vectors of dehumanization and doom that we currently inhabit. This extends beyond portraying current events as apocalyptic into a symptomatic denouncing of the importance of humanity as such. As a counterpart to Reddit's collapse channels mentioned in the introduction, r/antinatalism and r/vhemt are devoted to antinatalism and voluntary human extinction movements, where human hubris is harshly criticized.[71] Discussions there are resentful, defeatist, and often angry. Annihilation, some users argue, is what humans deserve, exhibiting a sentiment similar to the many millenarian movements throughout history. However, they advocate rather for a definite death of the whole human species as a moral duty — the Earth is already overpopulated and full of suffering — rather than a political purge of unworthy groups. In an indirect parallel to these are r/surrealmemes memes, where humans are often portrayed as a funnily insignificant element of a much more interesting and alien universe.[72] A popular meme titled "Compared to him, they are nothing" portrays humans devoured by a

---

Simon Lewis and Mark Maslin, "Defining the Anthropocene," *Nature* 519 (2015): 171–80.

70 See, for example, Madhuri Sathish, "11 Hilarious Climate Change Memes to Quiet The Naysayers Who Keep Denying It's Real," *Bustle,* August 19, 2015, https://www.bustle.com/articles/105138-11-hilarious-climate-change-memes-to-quiet-the-naysayers-who-keep-denying-its-real.

71 See Reddit, s.v. "antinatalism," https://www.reddit.com/r/antinatalism/; Reddit, s.v. "vhemt," https://www.reddit.com/r/vhemt/.

72 Reddit, s.v. "surrealmemes," https://www.reddit.com/r/surrealmemes/.

presumably alien octagon, with a caption "They run, for he consumes their entire existence." Another, "Sentient beings be like," pictures a gigantic humanoid face in a meditative-hallucinatory state, with a caption "Yes, we observe the memes, but do we even fucking exist?" An "exploding brain" meme, in which each panel describes a more mind-blowing revelation than the last, begins with "confused screaming," moves through "revolution and reform are two sides of the same utopian coin" and "awaiting 'the collapse' as if it were a singular event [...] is merely a crude inversion of utopia" to end again at "confused screaming." Neither of these memes are didactic about geo-social problems. Yet, the Anthropocene is "a social imaginary that has exceeded its intended categorization and whose parameters delimit ways of thinking about the world well beyond the confines of geo-scientific debate."[73] On the level of politics and culture, this catastrophic narrative marks the moment when we are collectively redefining our idea of the "human" and the types of social agency that this figure might have in the times when our species seems both powerful enough to bring about our own destruction through technological expansion, and at the same time *not* powerful enough to save itself, or to even at a minimum provide a model of industrial society that would not be based in rapidly accelerating social inequality and political polarization.

Alexander Galloway writes that the Anthropocene narrative is a contemporary form of *amor fati* to which the allegedly rational moderns have surprisingly succumbed.[74] Karl Marx wrote about the strange "ghost dance" of capitalism, where material conditions are reduced to an abstraction, while the intangible is made into something concrete — subjects become objects and objects become subjects, commodities seem more alive than the workers whose labor creates them.[75] Marx described how the

73 Davis and Turpin, "Art and Death," 7.

74 Alexander Galloway, "Warm Pride," October 29, 2014, http://cultureandcommunication.org/galloway/warm-pride

75 See Jacques Derrida, *Specters of Marx: The State of the Debt, the Work of Mourning, and the New International*, trans. Peggy Kamuf (London: Routledge, 1994), 153.

ruling classes mask the actual ways in which they organize labor, thus giving the impression of the market itself as a sentient being, separate from human agency. Galloway's concept of the "warm pride" can be understood as an extension of this condition in the context of the Anthropocene and the climate, where humanity's global geological agency is masked by a theoretical and aesthetic scaling down of humans to just one being among many others:

> Like the "landfill" trashcan, the concept of the Anthropocene teeters with postmodern vertigo. It indicts mankind for its fiduciary failings, only to promulgate a new historical narrative with mankind at the center. Tell me I failed, then put me in the spotlight. Remove agency, then assign it again. Which is it? Are we special or aren't we? Are we special enough to go toe to toe with the planet? Or are we merely another desiring machine, no different from the lowly mouse, or the deoxyribonucleic acid? [...] [Contemporary theory would often tell us that] we're impactful in matters of existence, but peripheral in matters of ontology, [it says,] I may display hubris toward the natural world, provided I subscribe to annihilation at the level of being; [it is the] pride of place in geological history within a declension narrative that only ends one way [— in collapse].[76]

This thought spells out a paradox, an asymmetry in line with Vacker's diagnosis that it is the combination of both decentralising and narcissistic effects of cosmic and social media that makes all media forms prone to apocalypticism. In this context, it is hardly surprising that apocalyptic memes are plentiful on the Western Internet — through colonialism, Western European culture was "the first memetic global pandemic."[77] The Anglo-Saxon colonial empire at the center of the Industrial Revolution that led us to the Anthropocene is now generating apocalyptic

---

76 Galloway, "Warm Pride."
77 Sandifer, *Neoreaction a Basilisk,* 174.

signifiers, because it is — perhaps — witnessing its own end. If everyday events in the West provoke apocalyptic panic, it is because the empire cannot picture itself as peripheral to history and so it embraces apocalypticism to turn inevitability into a comforting thought, removing unknowns by predicting the end. This could account for many of the doom-memes that relate quite visibly to current political events. However, if the Anthropocene maps both a recognition of the power of colonial industrial societies and an embarrassment at any suggestions that this power could be used to erase its own ill effects, political *agency* in itself becomes one of the most important questions. The ways in which less obviously political memes inhabit the aesthetics of collapse could signal a shift in how (post)human agency is experienced against the background of a looming extinction event, which — despite its specific historical origins — interpellates humanity at large as the subject.

Such warm pride turns the Western Internet into an apocalyptic space of *dank dystopia,* where anonymously sharing doom memes becomes a commodified version of cyberpunk utopia and its failed promise of equalising facelessness. If for Deborah Danowski and Eduardo Viveiros de Castro the Anthropocene announces that for the first time in known history that a dominant geological form — humans — is self-aware, the proliferation of apocalyptic memes signifies the desire of that force for its own dissolution achieved by memetic automation and dehumanization of political subjectivity.[78] Within this submissive fantasy, the scale of current and coming geo-social damage is experienced as far too great to comprehend, much less to act on. Humans are insignificant and anonymous in the face of planetary collapse. Abandoning themselves to anonymous, ever-replicating networks of doom memes provides the solace of discarding the idea of a sufficient human agency, alongside any values that this species-being may confer, including what is coded as political or ethical. Humans, newly clothed in a self-

---

78   Deborah Danowski and Eduardo Viveiros de Castro, *The Ends of the World* (New Jersey: John Wiley and Sons, 2016), 33.

chastizing impulse and perceiving themselves as just one element of the ever-expanding planetary cyberspace, are but survival bunkers for memes, who spread their power both across the biological space of the human organism, planting and replicating ideas, and the digital space of the Internet, where they travel as image. Becker already diagnosed this desire to renounce human agency by filtering it through media networks, writing that memes "[live] off humans, eating brain when they do not battle themselves in memetic cannibalism, preying on each other like flip-flop cellular automatons."[79] In his dystopian novel *World War Z*, only one of hundreds of literary and visual dystopias that have flooded popular culture over the last two decades, Max Brooks describes how, in order to survive a zombie apocalypse, some humans started impersonating zombies, convincing themselves that if they could become like those who want to eat them, they will not be eaten.[80] (They all died.) Relinquishing the idea of a sufficient individual, human presence within the global crisis narrative could function in a similar way — withdrawing humanity into these surreal, fatalistic, apocalyptic memes corresponds to the general experience of human politics as either heading toward grotesque failure or being insufficient as a rule.

Yet, this does not necessarily mean that apocalyptic memes translate into passivity or that they want no part in constructing the future. They map — at times with pleasure and curiosity rather than fear — both the decline of the Western empire and the global reckoning with the crisis of the Anthropocene. Crisis cults function as a way of identification with a set of values, even if this value is the mutual agreement on the impossibility of the present and coming world. In this world that is "increasingly unthinkable," to use Eugene Thacker's term, either on the level of perceived political catastrophe and civilizational decline or on the planetary scale of the Anthropocene, the way that these memes grapple with the insufficiency of human politics is val-

---

79 Becker, *Tactical Reality Dictionary*, 30.
80 Max Brooks, *World War Z: An Oral History of the Zombie War* (Danvers: Crown Publishing Group, 2006).

id.[81] How is it at all possible to think about politics unless they are scaled up to a planetary level, where the dehumanizing abstractions of capitalism, the laments about civilization decline, and the extractions of what used to be called "natural" converge? Apocalyptic memes do not provide an answer but they do express a crisis in the conventional experience of human agency in an orderly world, and as such a willingness to pose the question.

---

81 Eugene Thacker, *In the Dust of this Planet: Horror of Philosophy, Vol. 1* (Hants: Zero Books, 2011).

Bibliography

"A Strategy for Ruination: An Interview with China Miéville." *Boston Review,* January 8, 2018. http://bostonreview.net/ literature-culture-china-mieville-strategy-ruination.

@atlajala. *Twitter,* August 2, 2017, 5:54pm. https://twitter.com/ atlajala/status/892911463009992705.

Aumont, Jacques. "The Variable Eye, or Mobilization of the Gaze." In *Image in Dispute: Art and Cinema in the Age of Photography,* edited by Dudley Andrew, 31–259. Austin: University of Texas Press, 1997.

Baudrillard, Jean. *Fragments: Cool Memories III, 1990–1995.* Translated by Emily Agar. London and New York: Verso, 2006.

Becker, Konrad. *Tactical Reality Dictionary: Cultural Intelligence and Social Control.* Vienna: Edition Selene, 2010.

Brassier, Ray. *Nihil Unbound: Enlightenment and Extinction.* New York: Palgrave Macmillan, 2007.

Brooke, Heather. *The Revolution Will be Digitised: Dispatches from the Information War.* Portsmouth: William Heinemann, 2011.

Brooks, Max. *World War Z: An Oral History of the Zombie War.* Danvers: Crown Publishing Group, 2006.

Cellan-Jones, Rory. "Stephen Hawking Warns That Artificial Intelligence Could End Mankind." *BBC,* December, 2, 2014. http://www.bbc.com/news/technology-30290540.

@ChurchofSatan. *Twitter,* May 22, 2017, 2:41am. https://twitter. com/ChurchofSatan/status/866453928535236608.

Clemens, Justin. "After After Finitude: An Afterword." In *Aesthetics after Finitude,* edited by Baylee Brits, Prudence Gibson, and Amy Ireland, 229–35. Victoria: re.press, 2016.

Cohn, Norman. *The Pursuit of the Millennium: Revolutionary Millenarians and Mystical Anarchists of the Middle Ages.* Oxford: Oxford University Press, 1992.

Danowski, Deborah, and Eduardo Viveiros de Castro. *The Ends of the World.* New Jersey: John Wiley and Sons, 2016.

Davis, Heather, and Etienne Turpin. "Art and Death: Lives Between the Fifth Assessment & the Sixth Extinction." In *Art in the Anthropocene: Encounters Among Aesthetics, Politics, and Epistemologies,* edited by Heather Davis and Etienne Turpin, 3–31. London: Open Humanities Press, 2015.

Dawkins, Richard. *The Selfish Gene.* Oxford: Oxford University Press, 2006.

Derrida, Jacques. *Specters of Marx: The State of the Debt, the Work of Mourning, and the New International.* Translated by Peggy Kamuf. London: Routledge, 1994.

@dogsdoingthings. *Twitter,* August 22, 2017. 9:35pm, https://twitter.com/dogsdoingthings/status/900078876398931968.

———. *Twitter,* February 23, 2018. 5:20pm, https://twitter.com/dogsdoingthings/status/967071664356937728.

Dreyfus, Hubert. *On the Internet.* 2nd Edition. London: Routledge, 2008.

Dukes, Paul. *Minutes to Midnight: History and the Anthropocene Era from 1763.* London: Anthem Press, 2011.

Fisher, Mark. *Capitalist Realism: Is There No Alternative?* Hants: Zero Books, 2009.

Foster, Thomas. "'The Sex Appeal of the Inorganic': Posthuman Narratives and the Construction of Desire." In *Centuries' Ends, Narrative Means,* edited by Robert Newman, 276–301. Stanford: Stanford University Press, 1996.

Galloway, Alexander. "Warm Pride." October 29, 2014. http://cultureandcommunication.org/galloway/warm-pride.

——— and Eugene Thacker. *The Exploit: A Theory of Networks.* Minneapolis: University of Minnesota Press, 2007.

Glassman, Thea. "5 End of the World Memes to Honor Going into 2018." *Elite Daily,* December 19, 2017. https://www.elitedaily.com/p/5-end-of-the-world-memes-to-honor-going-into-2018–7523572.

Goerzen, Matt. "Notes Towards the Memes of Production." *Texte zur Kunst* 106 (2017): 86–107. https://www.textezurkunst.de/106/uber-die-meme-der-produktion/.

Habermas, Jürgen. *The Structural Transformation of the Public Sphere.* Translated by Thomas Burger and Frederick Lawrence. Cambridge: MIT Press, 1989.

Haraway, Donna, et al. "Anthropologists Are Talking — About the Anthropocene." *Ethnos* 81, no. 3 (2016): 535–64. DOI: 10.1080/00141844.2015.1105838.

Hathaway, Jay. "'Here's the Livestream of Trump's Inauguration' Meme Prepares for the Apocalypse." *The Daily Dot,* January 20, 2017. https://www.dailydot.com/unclick/livestream-trump-inauguration-apocalypse-meme/.

Hendricks, Stephanie. *Divine Destruction.* New York: Melville House Publishing, 2005.

@hodgman. *Twitter,* May 21, 2017, 11:56am. https://twitter.com/hodgman/status/866367178248945664.

Kierkegaard, Søren. *Journals and Papers,* Vol. 2: F–K. Edited and translated by Howard V. Hong and Edna H. Hong. Bloomington: Indiana University Press, 1970.

Konior, Bogna. "Towards Nonhuman Personhood: Reading Jean Epstein's Cinema Essays." In *Filmmakers' Theory: Contributions to Cinema Theory,* edited by Manuela Penafria et al., 117–38. Covilhã: Labcom Books, 2016.

Kuipers, Giselinde. "Media Culture and Internet Disaster Jokes: Bin Laden and the Attack on the World Trade Center." *European Journal of Cultural Studies* 5, no. 4 (2002): 450–70. DOI: 10.1177/1364942002005004296.

"Laruelle: Concept-Collider." *fragilekeys* (blog), 10 December 2017. https://fragilekeys.com/2017/12/10/laruelle-concept-collider/.

Le Comptoir. "Une autre fin du monde est-elle possible?" *Le Comptoir,* May 29, 2017. https://comptoir.org/2017/05/29/une-autre-fin-du-monde-est-elle-possible/.

Lewis, Simon, and Mark Maslin. "Defining the Anthropocene." *Nature* 519 (2015): 171–80. DOI: 10.1038/nature14258.

Mbembe, Achille. "Necropolitics." Translated by Libby Meintjes. *Public Culture* 15, no. 1 (2003): 11–40. https://muse.jhu.edu/article/39984.

McCants, Will. *The ISIS Apocalypse: The History, Strategy, and Doomsday Vision of the Islamic State.* New York: St. Martin's Press, 2015.

@mckenziewark. *Twitter,* January 17, 2018, 9:44am. https://twitter.com/mckenziewark/status/953684423790252032.

McLuhan, Marshall. *The Medium is the Message: An Inventory of Effects.* London: Penguin Books, 1967.

Metahaven. *Can Jokes Bring Down Governments? Memes, Design and Politics.* Moscow: Strelka Press, 2014.

@Mikel_Jollet. *Twitter,* January 8, 2017, 9:35am. https://twitter.com/Mikel_Jollett/status/818149100717621248.

Nagle, Angela. *Kill All Normies: The Online Culture Wars from Tumblr and 4chan to the Alt-right and Trump.* Hants: Zero Books, 2017.

Nietzsche, Friedrich. "Truth and Lie in the Extra-Moral Sense." In *The Portable Nietzsche,* translated and edited by Walter Kaufmann, 42–46. New York: Penguin Books, 1997.

Pariser, Eli. "When the Internet Thinks It Knows You." *New York Times,* May 23, 2011. http://www.nytimes.com/2011/05/23/opinion/23pariser.html.

Robinson, Melia. "Elon Musk Thinks Artificial Intelligence is Ultimately More Dangerous than Nuclear Weapons." *Business Insider,* March 12, 2018. http://www.businessinsider.com/elon-musk-ai-more-dangerous-than-nuclear-weapons-sxsw-2018-3.

Rockström, Johan, et al. "A Safe Operating Space for Humanity." *Nature* 461 (2009): 472–75. DOI: 10.1038/461472a.

Sandifer, Elizabeth (with Jack Graham). *Neoreaction a Basilisk. Essays On and around the Alt-Right.* Eruditorum Press, 2016.

Sathish, Madhuri. "11 Hilarious Climate Change Memes to Quiet The Naysayers Who Keep Denying It's Real." *Bustle,* August 19, 2015. https://www.bustle.com/articles/105138-11-hilarious-climate-change-memes-to-quiet-the-naysayers-who-keep-denying-its-real.

Scott, Melissa. *Burning Bright.* New York: Tor Books, 1994.

Shifman, Limor. *Memes in Digital Culture.* Cambridge: MIT Press, 2014.

Terranova, Tiziana. *Network Culture Politics for the Information Age*. London and Ann Arbor: Pluto Press, 2004.

Thacker, Eugene. I*n the Dust of this Planet: Horror of Philosophy, Vol. 1*. Hants: Zero Books, 2011.

Toffler, Alvin. *Future Shock*. New York: Random House, 1970.

Vacker, Barry. *The End of the World — Again: Why the Apocalypse Meme Replicates in Media, Science, and Cultur*e. Philadelphia: Center for Media Destiny, 2012.

Varol, Onur, et al. "Online Human-Bot Interactions: Detection, Estimation, and Characterization." *arXiv,* 2017. https://arxiv.org/abs/1703.03107

Vertov, Dziga. *Kino-Eye: The Writings of Dziga Vertov*. Edited by Annette Michelson. Translated by Kevin O'Brien. Berkeley and Los Angeles: University of California Press, 1984.

@viralpraxis, *Facebook,* September 3, 2017, https://www.facebook.com/viralpraxis/posts/1487585427945169.

Walker, Alice. *Possessing the Secret of Joy*. New York: Simon and Schuster, 1997.

Žižek, Slavoj. *Living in the End Times*. London: Verso, 2010.

5

Post-Authenticity and the Ironic Truths of Meme Culture

Jay Owens

Media Isn't Really Real

I n the last couple of years, fakery seems to have accelerated. The term "fake news" appeared out of next-to-nowhere in November 2016 (fig. 1).

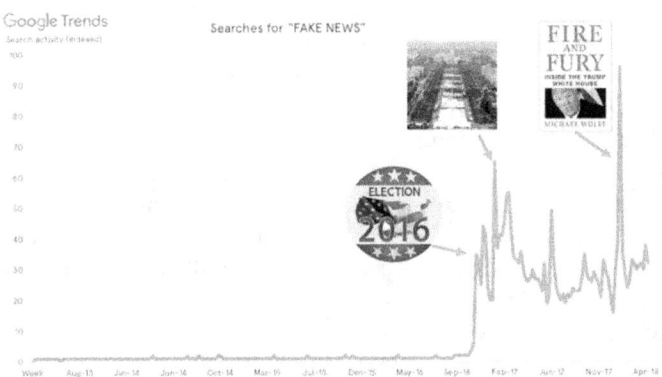

Fig. 1. Source: Google Trends. See https://trends.google.com/trends/explore?date=today%205-y&geo=US&q=fake%20news.

DOI: 10.21983/P3.0255.1.06

The press has published myths, falsehoods, and exaggerations for about as long as there has been a press—and even the term "fake news" dates back to the 1890s, the *Merriam-Webster* dictionary reports.[1] Lying is, surely, as old as humanity.

But the term has twisted. "Fake news," as used in the last 18 months, doesn't really mean "fake" in the conventional sense of the word — as in unreal, or incorrect, or false news. As used by the US President, the most mainstream and fact-checked news media is "fake" if he disagrees with it. The term means something more like "troublesome news," or "news I vehemently disagree with, and wish to discredit."

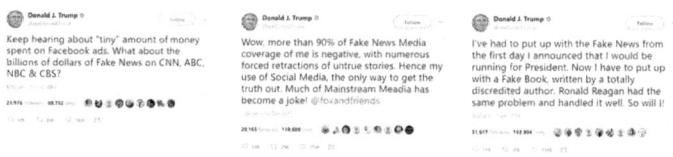

Fig. 2. Tweets by us President Donald J. Trump, @realDonaldTrump.

The US President helped spur 29 million tweets about "fake news" in the last year, keeping the topic always present in public discourse (figs. 2 and 3).

Meanwhile, in the UK, "fake news" becomes a political point-scoring exercise in headlines such as: "Theresa May's 'Fake News Unit' Announcement Has Itself Been Branded 'Fake News.'"[2] Your boy Kafka is proud.

The work of making real news: the fact-checking and triangulating processes by which news organizations ensure their coverage is accurate, and professional principles of integrity; journalists talk about this continually on Twitter. Yet is the message getting through?

---

1   See "The Real Story of 'Fake News,'" *Merriam-Webster,* https://www.merriam-webster.com/words-at-play/the-real-story-of-fake-news.

2   See Mikey Smith, "Theresa May's 'Fake News Unit' Announcement Has Itself Been Branded 'Fake News,'" *Mirror,* January 30, 2018, https://www.mirror.co.uk/news/politics/theresa-mays-fake-news-unit-11940423.

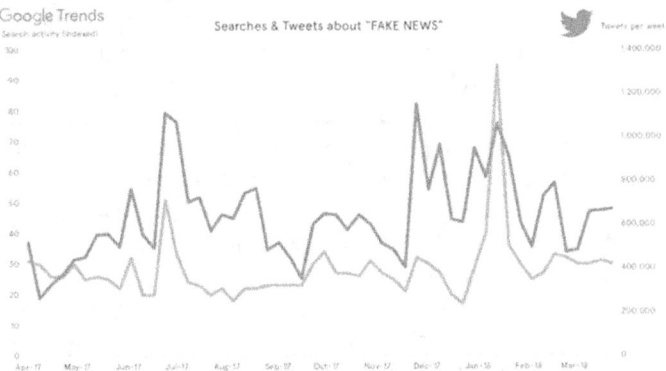

Fig. 3. Source: Google Trends and Pulsar Trends. See https://trends.google.com/trends/explore?date=2017-04-01%20 2018-04-01&geo=US&q=fake%20news.

Public trust both is and isn't holding up.

Kantar's 2017 Trust In News survey finds that people still believe in the principle of "real news": Across the USA, UK, France, and Brazil, 73% of people agreed that quality journalism is key to a healthy democracy.[3] The reputational impact of the "fake news" issue has been predominantly borne by digital and social media channels: 58% now trust social media coverage of politics and elections less and 41% trust online-only news sources less. Traditional TV and print media channels have held up comparatively well.

However, the stat to remember is that only slightly more than half (56%) believe what they read overall is true "most of the time." The principle of a shared factual reality among the general public has become tenuous, and cannot be taken for granted.

Last month, an anonymous academic posted to Reddit saying: "I'm a college philosophy professor. Jordan Peterson is mak-

---

3   See Kirsty Cooke, "'Fake News' Reinforces Trust in Mainstream News Brands," *Kantar,* October 31, 2017, https://uk.kantar.com/business/brands/2017/trust-in-news/.

ing my job impossible."[4] They report how a minority of students who have been reading and watching "internet outrage merchants" come into class no longer merely disagreeing with some of the ideas taught "that I'm used to dealing with; it's the bread and butter of philosophy") — but newly angry, deeply hostile, and believing in complete fabrications about what feminist or postmodernist or Marxist philosophy entails. "To even get to a real discussion of actual texts it takes half the [class] time to just deprogram some of them."

As danah boyd pointed out at SXSW EDU this year, attempts to increase media literacy in schools can often backfire. Examining the credibility of a Fox News article in class risks being perceived by working class or evangelical youth as an "elite" attack on their values. Teaching young people to make sense of the information landscape without exacerbating distrust is, boyd fears, very difficult: "when youth are encouraged to be critical of the news media, they come away thinking that the media is lying."[5]

In 2004, a previous Republican presidency gave us the concept of the "reality-based community," a term meant as pejorative: why be so short-sighted as to limit your vision to the way things were, rather than what the Administration's actions made possible?[6]

"We're an empire now, and when we act, we create our own reality," the unnamed official (generally understood to be Karl Rove) said.

---

4   See annoyed_professor, "I'm a College Philosophy Professor. Jordan Peterson Is Making My Job Impossible," *Reddit*, March 24, 2018, 16:20 GMT+1, https://www.reddit.com/r/enoughpetersonspam/comments/86tnz7/im_a_college_philosophy_professor_jordan_peterson/.

5   See danah boyd, "You Think You Want Media Literacy…Do You?" *Points*, March 9, 2018, https://points.datasociety.net/you-think-you-want-media-literacy-do-you-7cad6af18ec2.

6   See *Wikipedia*, s.v. "reality-based comunity," https://en.wikipedia.org/wiki/Reality-based_community/.

So this present state of things isn't really new. Kurt Andersen dates the rise of this present "truthiness" back to the 1960s, and the rise of an "it's all relative" mode of thinking.[7] And yet.

Technology Is Warping Reality in New Ways

The post-authenticity of fake news isn't solely a technological or media problem, but a social one, symptomatic of declining trust in a shared civic project. Nonetheless, new media technologies really aren't helping.

In the last year or two,

- Technologies have become available to fake people's voices, so that you can appear to make them say anything you want. In 2016, Adobe released a tool, VoCo, which needed 20 minutes of audio to train on.[8] In May 2017, Lyrebird, a Montreal-based AI startup, claimed to be able to synthetically mimic any person's voice based on just 60 seconds of speech.[9]
- Faking video has also become accessible. In March 2016, researchers from the University of Erlangen-Nuremberg, the Max Planck Institute for Informatics, and Stanford University presented a novel approach for creating fake videos — e.g., making Putin smile, or George W. Bush appear to lipsync to ridiculous material. Through capturing the facial expressions of a source actor on a webcam, and using facial mapping, they demonstrate they're able to manipulate and re-render a YouTube video photorealistically.

7   Kurt Andersen, "How America Lost Its Mind," *The Atlantic,* September 2017, https://www.theatlantic.com/magazine/archive/2017/09/how-america-lost-its-mind/534231/.

8   See Matthew Gault, "After 20 Minutes of Listening, New Adobe Tool Can Make You Say Anything," *Motherboard,* November 5, 2016, https://motherboard.vice.com/en_us/article/jpgkxp/after-20-minutes-of-listening-new-adobe-tool-can-make-you-say-anything.

9   Bahar Gholipour, "New AI Tech Can Mimic Any Voice," *Scientific American,* May 2, 2017, https://www.scientificamerican.com/article/new-ai-tech-can-mimic-any-voice/.

The Face2Face team note that "computer-generated videos have been part of feature-film movies for over 30 years. [...] These results are hard to distinguish from reality and it often goes unnoticed that the content is not real." What's new is the way the technology is newly mass-accessible: now, "we can edit pre-recorded videos in real-time on a commodity PC."[10]

- Where video goes, porn is first to take advantage. In December 2017, Samantha Cole of *Motherboard* reported that "AI-Assisted Fake Porn Is Here and We're All Fucked."[11] She reports how a Redditor by the name of deepfakes worked out how to combine celebrity facial images from Google image search, stock photos, and YouTube videos, with porn videos, using open-source neural-network "deep learning" library Keras and TensorFlow.

  A month later deepfakes turned the process into an app — and *Vice* reported that "We Are All Truly Fucked," as the faceswap porn trend swept Reddit.[12] It then got banned, but you know, that horse had already bolted.

- Various smaller events, too. The ongoing march of fake social media followers and fake "likes," as reported most recently in the *New York Times*'s snazzy longread investigation "The Follower Factory," a somewhat late-to-the-party but nonetheless welcome dig into the entirely fictional world of celebrity and

---

10 See, for a demonstration, Matthias Niessner, "Face2Face: Real-time Face Capture and Reenactment of RGB Videos (CVPR 2016 Oral)," YouTube, March 18, 2016, https://www.youtube.com/watch?v=ohmajJTcpNk.

11 See Samantha Cole, "AI-Assisted Fake Porn Is Here and We're All Fucked," *Motherboard,* December 11, 2017, https://motherboard.vice.com/en_us/article/gydydm/gal-gadot-fake-ai-porn.

12 See Samantha Cole, "We Are Truly Fucked: Everyone Is Making AI-Generated Fake Porn Now," *Motherboard,* January 24, 2018, https://motherboard.vice.com/en_us/article/bjye8a/reddit-fake-porn-app-daisy-ridley.

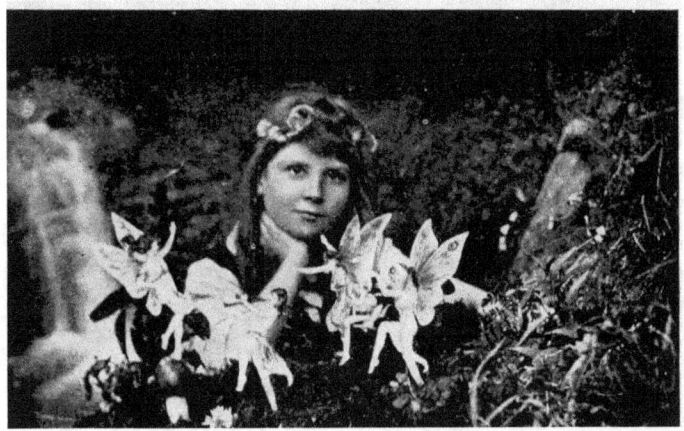

Fig. 4. Fake fairies. Image credit: Kristian Nordestgaard via flickr/CC BY 2.0.

influencer social media metrics.[13] More fake metrics over on Trip Advisor, too, as Oobah Butler of *Vice* made his garden shed the #1 rated restaurant in London.[14]

Again, none of this is new exactly — in 1917, two young girls went down to a stream at the bottom of a garden in Cottingley, England, and took some photographs of fairies which traveled the world (fig. 4).[15] Doubtless some wily courtier seeing some opportunity for gain painstakingly inscribed fake news on a Sumerian stone tablet.

---

13 See Nicholas Confessore et al., "The Follower Factory," *New York Times*, January 27, 2018, https://www.nytimes.com/interactive/2018/01/27/technology/social-media-bots.html.

14 Oobah Butler, "I Made My Shed the Top Rated Restaurant on Trip-Advisor," *Vice,* December 6, 2017, https://www.vice.com/en_uk/article/434gqw/i-made-my-shed-the-top-rated-restaurant-on-tripadvisor.

15 See Rosa Lyster, "The Cottingley Fairy Hoax of 1917 Is a Case Study in How Smart People Lose Control of the Truth," *Quartz,* February 17, 2017, https://qz.com/911990/the-cottingley-fairy-hoax-of-1917-is-a-case-study-in-how-smart-people-lose-control-of-the-truth/.

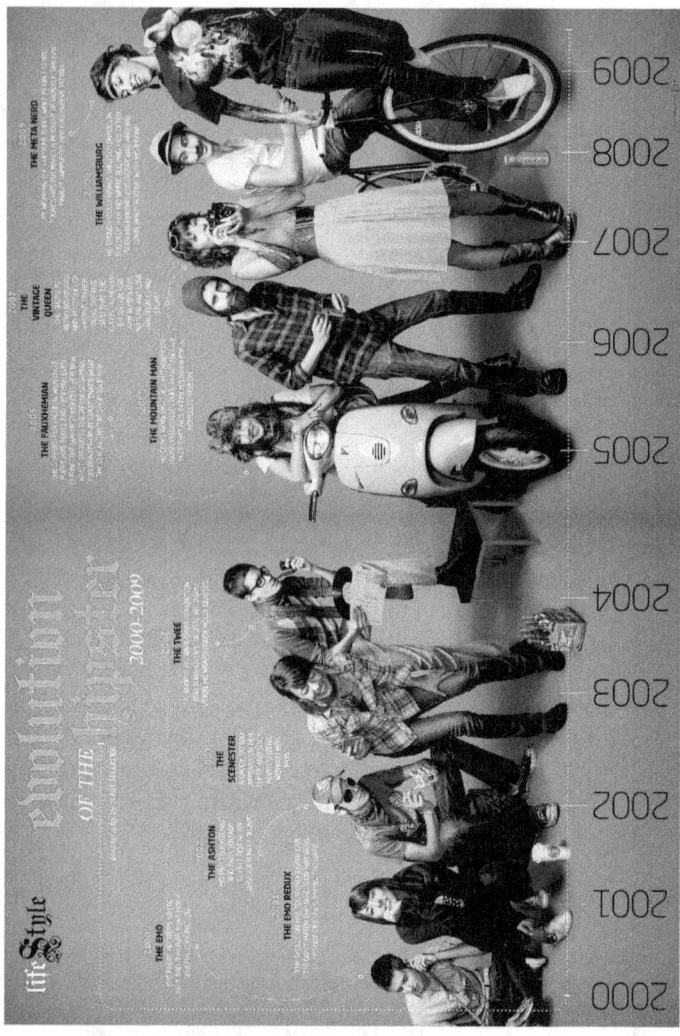

Fig. 5. Which ones did you date? Source: *Paste Magazine*. See Kate Kiefer, "The Evolution of the Hipster 2000–2009," *Paste*, December 3, 2009, https://www.pastemagazine.com/articles/2009/12/the-evolution-of-the-hipster-2000-2009.html.

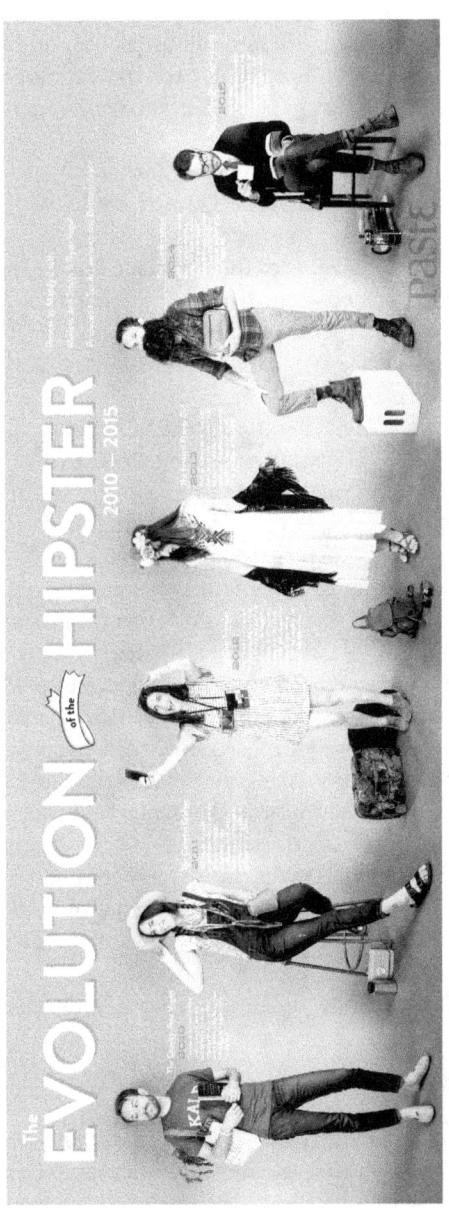

Fig. 6. Gotta catch them all. Source: *Paste Magazine.* See Brittany Joyce and Sarah Lawrence, "The Evolution of the Hipster 2010–2015," *Paste,* June 18, 2015, https://www.pastemagazine.com/articles/2015/06/the-evolution-of-the-hipster-2010-2015.html.

Yet, something is up — something in culture has moved, quite recently, and now the world is different: the pace and extent of fakery has accelerated. It's not just happened in media, it's happened in pop culture too.

In Fashion, Authenticity Imploded Some Time around 2015

"Authenticity" was the defining value of the late-stage hipster.

How the hipster transformed from trucker-cap-clad 2000s nu-rave machine to bearded artisanal flannel shirt connoisseur is recorded in various lifestyle magazine features — best and most visually in *Paste Magazine* (figs. 5, 6)

Though, seeing as this is my generation we're talking about, I might also comment that we just grew up and slowed down a bit (the UK government also made mephedrone — the "white powder that smells faintly of cat piss [which] defined the UK's party scene from 2008 to 2010" — illegal.[16])

Rewind eight years, to 2010. In this period, as smartphones and digital media took over our lives, the dominant aesthetic of middle-class consumption — fashion, interior decor and lifestyle — went the other way: rough-hewn, wholesome. Authentic. God, do you remember the beards? And the flannel, and the workwear, and the artisan everything: coffee, bread, burgers. Ostentatious unpretentiousness: cocktails in mason jars, wine in tumblers, and ridged, deeply textured wooden tables and walls. Flower crowns and neo-boho festival fashion.

Driving this trend was a small magazine — print, of course, published on heavyweight matte paper stock — run out of Portland, Oregon, called *Kinfolk*. The visual language it defined spread far and wide (fig. 7).

Summer Allen noticed just how much of a template this look was:

---

16 See JS Rafaeli, "The Story of Mephedrone, the Party Drug That Boomed and Went Bust," *Vice,* January 17, 2017, https://www.vice.com/en_uk/article/9aa53a/the-story-of-mephedrone-the-party-drug-that-boomed-and-went-bust.

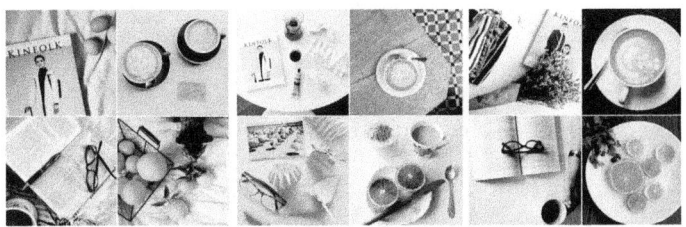

Fig. 7. From left to right: Instagram users @MaryHoagland, @UpTheWoodenHills, and @NuanceAndBubbles Photo coordination credit: SummerAllen.

I started the The Kinspiracy tumblr after I noticed a pattern emerging from dozens of Instagram users — my own personal Beautiful Mind moment. It was suddenly so clear: Every account cultivating that Kinfolk look seemed to follow a specific formula. Every account had a photo (or several) of the following: A latte with a foam leaf design, a fresh piece or two of citrus, a glimpse of a pair of small feet — often in a well-worn pair of boots — an ice cream cone, weather permitting, some glasses here and there, twine, the occasional fixed-gear bike. And always, in every damn account, *Kinfolk*.[17]

The "authentic" look wasn't just shaping people's Instagram feeds, but real-world spaces and places too in a feedback loop between social media and IRL that journalist Kyle Chayka called AirSpace:

It's marked by an easily recognisable mix of symbols — like reclaimed wood, Edison bulbs, and refurbished industrial lighting — that's meant to provide familiar, comforting surroundings for a wealthy, mobile elite, who want to feel like they're visiting somewhere "authentic" while they travel, but who actually just crave more of the same: more rustic interi-

---

17 Summer Allen, "Wood, Citrus, Lattes, Feet, Twine, Repeat: The Kinfolk Kinspiracy Code," *Gawker,* March 31, 2015, http://gawker.com/wood-citrus-lattes-feet-twine-repeat-the-kinfolk-1693115156.

ors and sans-serif logos and splashes of cliché accent colours on rugs and walls.[18]

Later, Chayka was blunter about his frustrations — tweeting in October 2017 that "'authenticity' is the plague of the 21st century," in a thread about the cynical falseness of so many of its iterations.

The contradictory appeal of AirSpace was best summed up by artist and designer Lauren Schwulst: "it's funny how you want these really generic things but also want authenticity, too."[19]

The authentic aesthetic is too clearly a facsimile, too obviously a template rolled out by the operations directors of VC-funded Millennial Pink-branded startups and Airbnb megahosts putting the same framed inspirational quotes in every identikit, resident-displacing condo. Airbnb rebranded in 2014 with a campaign about how you can "belong anywhere," a profoundly inauthentic claim that strips belonging of all meaning.

Around 2015 there was a wave of articles about how "the hipster" was, finally, dead as a cultural archetype ("Why London decided to move on from beards, beanies and fixie bikes" was the title of a Richard Godwin article in the *Evening Standard*[20]) — and "authenticity" as a cultural value expired along with it:

The typology has become a caricature and the terms once associated with it — craft, artisan, making — have also become cartoonish. When McDonald's boasts about artisanal chicken

---

18 Kyle Chayka, "Same Old, Same Old: How the Hipster Aesthetic is Taking Over the World," *The Guardian*, August 6, 2016, https://www.theguardian.com/commentisfree/2016/aug/06/hipster-aesthetic-taking-over-world.

19 Lauren Schwulst, quoted in Kyle Chayka, "Welcome to Airspace: How Silicon Valley Helps Spread the Same Sterile Aesthetic Across the World," *The Verge*, August 3, 2016, https://www.theverge.com/2016/8/3/12325104/airbnb-aesthetic-global-minimalism-startup-gentrification.

20 Richard Godwin, "Death of the Hipster: Why London Decided to Move on from Beards, Beanies and Fixie Bikes," *Evening Standard*, April 16, 2015, https://www.standard.co.uk/lifestyle/death-of-the-hipster-why-london-decided-to-move-on-from-beards-beanies-and-fixie-bikes-10178615.html.

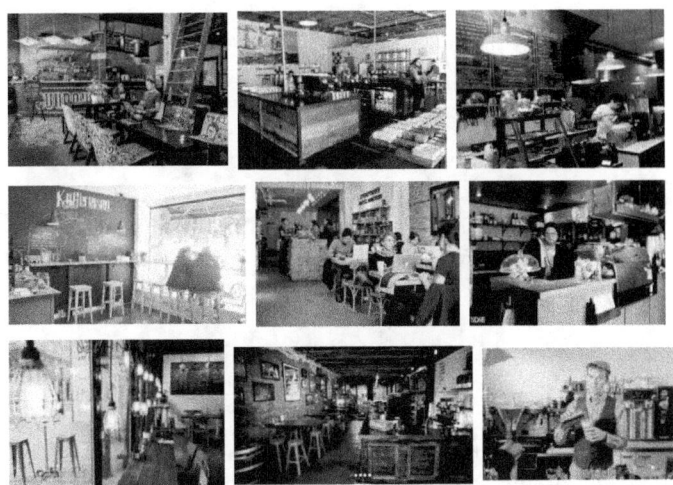

Fig. 8. All hipster coffee shops have the same stools. Source: Google Image search.

(complete with "artisan chicken" and "artisan roll") you know the message has gone awry.[21]

What came next? "Minimalist brands" was one answer from marketers — but that mood didn't last.[22] In Spring 2016, Demna Gvasalia shocked the fashion press with bootleg anti-fashion at Vetements — selling meta-referential hoodies, DHL-branded T-shirts, and reworked secondhand jeans for hundreds and thousands of Euros.[23] Meanwhile, in the hipper echelons of design we're back to postmodernism, with 1980s Memphis Group

21 Daniela Walker, "The Hipster is Dead, Let's Start an Anti-authenticity Movement," *Campaign,* September 29, 2015, https://www.campaignlive.co.uk/article/hipster-dead-lets-start-anti-authenticity-movement/1366143.

22 See Ed Silk, "Authenticity as We Know It Is Dead as Brands Go Minimalist to Express Their Craft and Quality," *The Drum,* February 12, 2016, http://www.thedrum.com/opinion/2016/02/12/authenticity-we-know-it-dead-brands-go-minimalist-express-their-craft-and-quality.

23 See Jake Woolf, "There's an $800 Hoodie That's Selling Out Everywhere," GQ, February 22, 2016, https://www.gq.com/story/vetements-hoodie-buy-sold-out-price.

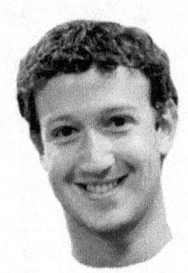

"Having two identities for yourself is an example of a lack of integrity"

-- Mark Zuckerberg, 2010

Fig. 9. Quote from Facebook founder Mark Zuckerberg.

aesthetics and terrazzo replacing Insta'd-out white marble (if the pages of *Elle Decoration* and the graphic design of Chayka's Studyhall journalist co-op is anything to go by).[24] "Authenticity" and the desire to focus on the perceived, more-real "essence of things" is no longer in vogue: surface and clever references are all.

Something similarly playful is happening, I argue, in how the post-Millennial "Generation Z" present themselves online.

Generation Z Are Pioneering Post-authentic Social Media

Back in 2010, Mark Zuckerberg made the case for the single, real-name Facebook account as the "authentic" way to do social media, and sought to impose this model of self-presentation on hundreds of millions of users, with Facebook's controversial (and partially rolled-back) "real names policy" (fig. 9).[25]

But authenticity became a performance, as we started to speak to audiences of hundreds and thousands beyond our "real" pools of friends and family, and "likes" and follower counts trained us to create the kinds of content that would be

---

24 See http://studyhall.xyz/.
25 See Dave Lee, "Facebook Amends 'Real Name' Policy after Protests," BBC, December 15, 2015, http://www.bbc.co.uk/news/technology-35109045.

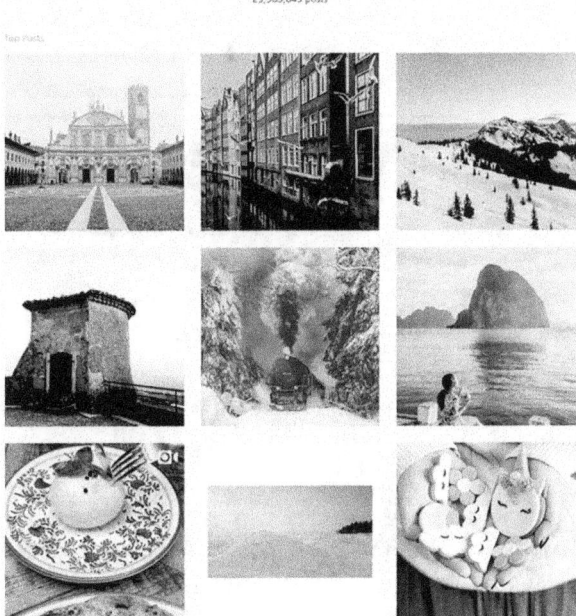

Fig. 10. Instagram #liveauthentic stream.

the most popular, over the realistic depictions of our day-to-day. Our Instagram feeds professionalized: the quality of photography got better, the captions wittier. The relationship to our real lives became more complicated

The ur-point of this, for me, is the #liveauthentic hashtag on Instagram (fig. 10): a compendium of the most *Kinfolk*-perfect depictions of an enviable foodie, travel lifestyle, Rise-filter tinted for that "golden hour" glow.

Meanwhile, young people were reporting that looking right in social media was stressing them the hell out.

A survey from the Girl Guides Association in the US last year found that teenage girls weren't just seeing social media risks like their parents did, as a place where they might be threatened

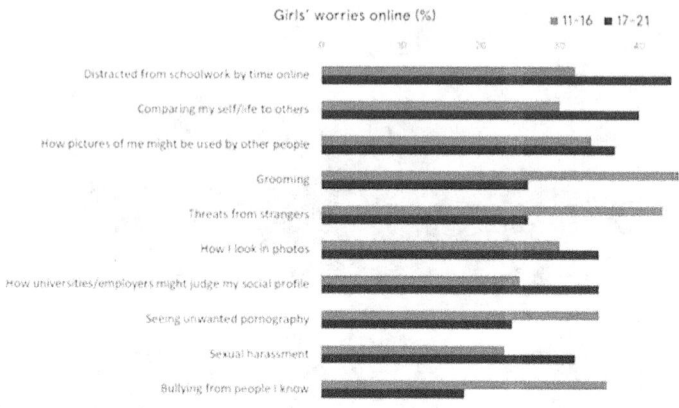

Fig. 11. Girls' worries online (%). Source: Girl Guides, Girls Attitude Survey 2017.

by bullying and "stranger danger." Instead, their second biggest worry online was the pressure of "comparing my self/life to others." Their sixth biggest concern, "how I look in photos" (fig. 11).[26]

Social media has, after all, dramatically changed the field of social comparison, from operating mostly at the transient, real-world social scale of a few hundred people around you at your school and in your neighborhood, to one that's media-scale, global, and permanent. Eric Herber, then a 17-year-old in high school, wrote in 2015:

When I post a photo on Instagram I know that just about every person I am connected to in the real life will see my photo, decide whether or not to like it, and then judge me subconsciously.

---

26 See Girlguiding, "Girls' Attitudes Survey 2017," 2017, https://www. girlguiding.org.uk/globalassets/docs-and-resources/research-and-campaigns/girls-attitudes-survey-2017.pdf.

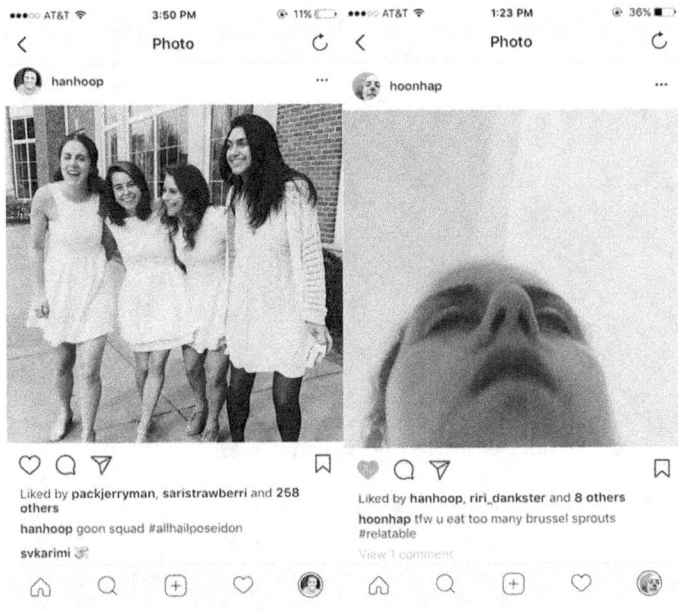

Fig. 12. Instagram accounts @hahoop and @hoonhap, via Mic.com.

Because of this, Instagram is seen as a huge stressor for many teenagers.

Your Instagram defines who you are.[27]

Teenagers, being young and adaptable, have modified their social media behaviors to fit this new landscape accordingly.

An 18-year-old American high school student, interviewed by journalist Justine Harman, details the heavily strategized social media management playbook she and her peers use:

---

27 Eric Herber, "Finstagram: The Instagram Revolution," *Medium,* February 10, 2015, https://medium.com/bits-pixels/finstagram-the-instagram-revolution-737999d40014.

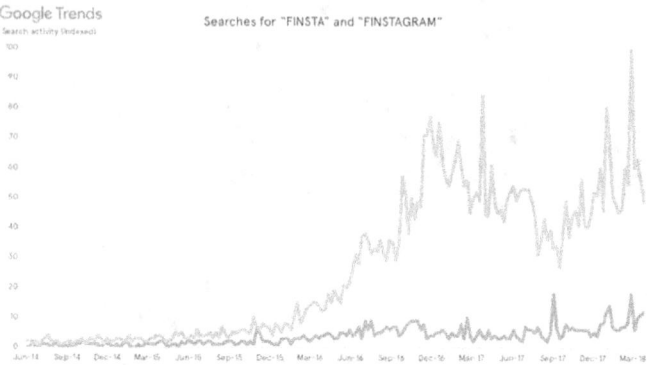

Fig. 13. Source: Google Trends. See https://trends.google.com/trends/explore?date=today%205-y&q=finstagram,finsta.

I would never post twice in one day because if I am expecting to get 200 likes on a picture, I have to post sparingly.

First you have to edit the picture, make sure no one in your friend group is already posting it, send it to your friends for approval, think of a clever caption, and then post it at a time of day that will hopefully afford you the most amount of likes.

Yes, it's insane. But this is what girls do.[28]

As a result, Finstagram.

What? Fake Instagram, for trash pics and the outtakes reel of your main, hyper-curated Instagram account (fig. 12).[29]

Finstagram has been a thing since, ah yes, January 2016: coincidentally or not, just after hipster "authenticity" died.

---

28 Justine Harman, "The Crazy Way Teens are Hiding Their Imperfections Online: Finstagram," *Elle,* July 9, 2015, https://www.elle.com/culture/tech/a29243/finstagram/.

29 See Taylor Lorenz, "The Secret Instagram Accounts Teens Use to Share Their Realest, Most Intimate Moments," *Mic,* March 3, 2017, https://mic.com/articles/175936/the-secret-instagram-accounts-teens-use-to-share-their-realest-most-intimate-moments.

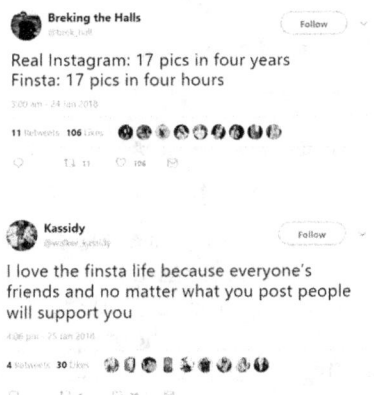

Fig. 14. Finsta tweets.

Freed from having to maintain a singular, authentic, official identity, it turns out young people feel they can be a lot more real on their fake accounts.

Snapchat offers the same promise too: ephemeral social media. It's digital "safe space" in the real sense of that word: setting boundaries and expectations in order to make difficult things — here, your imperfect, unfiltered self — possible to speak about.

The Meme Generation

"Generations" are a bullshit marketing concept, right? Except all of us looking at the remarkable teenagers of Parkland High School and their astonishing media campaigning ways are also aware that damn, something's different about kids today.

For the last two or three years I've been doing a bit of work for a tech company client on understanding first Millennials and then Generation Z: what are they doing, how are they different, and what makes them tick. For Generation Z — born in 2000 onward — there are two interesting, seemingly opposite cultural tendencies in play.

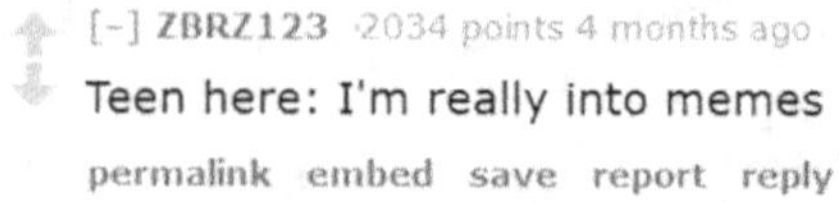

[-] **ZBRZ123** 2034 points 4 months ago

Teen here: I'm really into memes

permalink   embed   save   report   reply

Fig. 15. Comment on Reddit post "Teens of Reddit, what is considered cool right now?"

On the one hand, they're the Sensible Generation. Every measure of risk-taking behavior is down, across the US and Europe: drinking, smoking, drug use, early sexual activity, and teenage pregnancy.[30] Spurred on by the prospect of massive educational debt, they try harder in school and have heart-breakingly modest and, well, sensible aspirations for their future lives.

On the other hand…

Let me introduce you to a cultural goldmine. In September last year, an AskReddit thread enquired, "Teens of Reddit, what is considered cool right now?"[31]

The answers are brilliant:

17 here. The word "lit", trap music, being "THICC", Vans, Converse, Gucci flip flops, chokers, crop tops, ripped jeans, bomber jackets, Kendrick Lamar, acrylic nails, going to the gym, athletic clothing, taking aesthetic pics of your dog or yourself or both together, being "relationship goals", grinding at school dances, prom, being confident, being smart, being artistic, ooh and MEMES!!!!!

idk what else but those are the basics lol.[32]

---

30 See Sarah Kliff, Soo Oh, and Sarah Frostenson, "Today's Teens Use Hallucinogens/Watch Television/Fight/Drink/Use Heroin/Have Babies/Use Meth/Binge Drink/Carry Weapons to School Less than You Did," *Vox,* June 9, 2016, https://www.vox.com/a/teens.

31 rasras4, "Teens of Reddit, What Is Considered Cool Right Now?" *Reddit,* September 9, 2017, 16:55 GMT+2, https://www.reddit.com/r/AskReddit/comments/6z23rj/teens_of_reddit_what_is_considered_cool_right_now/.

32 Majestichuman, Comment on rasras4, "Teens of Reddit, What Is Considered Cool Right Now?" *Reddit,* September 9, 2017, 20:20 GMT+2, https://www.reddit.com/r/AskReddit/comments/6z23rj/teens_of_reddit_what_is_considered_cool_right_now/dms4g57

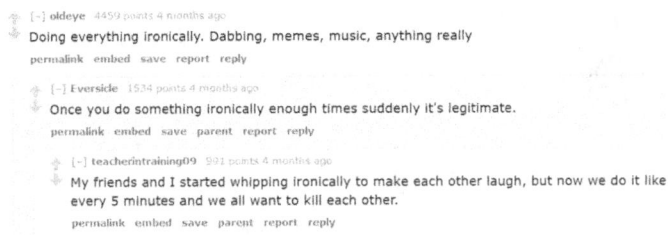

[-] oldeye 4459 points 4 months ago
Doing everything ironically. Dabbing, memes, music, anything really
permalink embed save report reply

[-] Everside 1534 points 4 months ago
Once you do something ironically enough times suddenly it's legitimate.
permalink embed save parent report reply

[-] teacherintraining09 991 points 4 months ago
My friends and I started whipping ironically to make each other laugh, but now we do it like
every 5 minutes and we all want to kill each other.
permalink embed save parent report reply

Fig. 16. Comment on Reddit post "Teens of Reddit, what is considered cool right now?"

The most up-voted answers stressed irony as a fundamental orientation (fig. 16).

Youth culture today, in two words: Sensibleness, and Memes. Seriousness, and taking nothing seriously.

Teenagers may be shifting away from posting Facebook status updates — partly because Facebook is where your mum and your aunties are hanging out — but one part of Facebook is thriving: Groups. Zuckerberg emphasized Groups in his "Building Global Community" strategy last year, with a putatively civic-minded goal to "strengthen people's online and offline connections."[33] But he probably wasn't thinking of groups like these (fig. 17).

Frequented mostly by an audience under 25, many of these groups are just sharing funny, ironic, meme-y content. Roots lie in what was called Weird Facebook — as documented by Jordan Pedersen in 2014, the group Shit Memes then had 30,000 followers, and was one of the bigger groups around.[34] Prior to that, Internet meme culture in the period 2008–2012 was being heav-

---

33 Mark Zuckerberg, "Building Global Community," *Facebook,* February 16, 2017, https://www.facebook.com/notes/mark-zuckerberg/building-global-community/10154544292806634/.
34 Jordan Pedersen, "Inside the Inscrutable World of Weird Facebook," *Daily Dot,* August 5, 2014, https://www.dailydot.com/unclick/weird-facebook/.

Post Memes

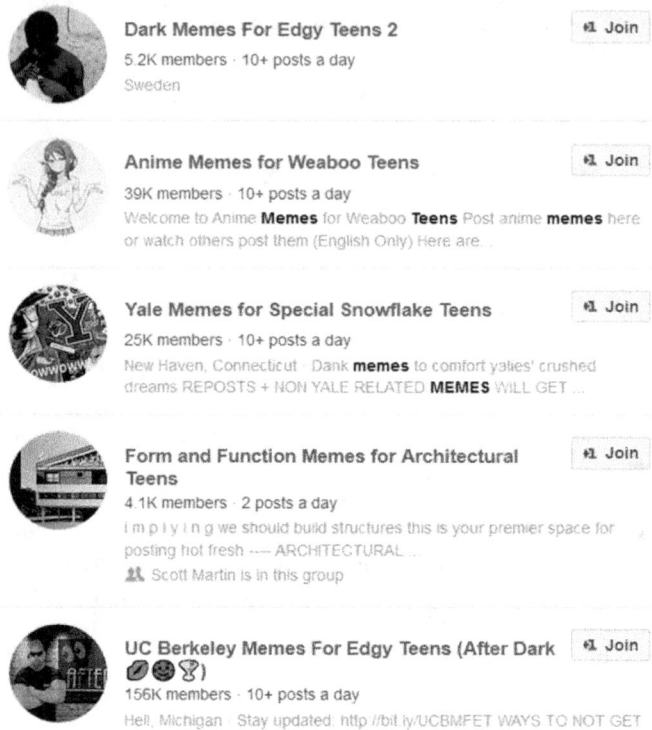

Dark Memes For Edgy Teens 2
   +1 Join
5.2K members · 10+ posts a day
Sweden

Anime Memes for Weaboo Teens
   +1 Join
39K members · 10+ posts a day
Welcome to Anime **Memes** for Weaboo **Teens** Post anime **memes** here or watch others post them (English Only) Here are...

Yale Memes for Special Snowflake Teens
   +1 Join
25K members · 10+ posts a day
New Haven, Connecticut · Dank **memes** to comfort yalies' crushed dreams REPOSTS + NON YALE RELATED **MEMES** WILL GET ...

Form and Function Memes for Architectural Teens
   +1 Join
4.1K members · 2 posts a day
i m p l y i n g we should build structures this is your premier space for posting hot fresh ---- ARCHITECTURAL ...
Scott Martin is in this group

UC Berkeley Memes For Edgy Teens (After Dark ⊘☺🏆)
   +1 Join
156K members · 10+ posts a day
Hell, Michigan · Stay updated: http //bit ly/UCBMFET WAYS TO NOT GET B&: 1) Don't resubmit the same meme over ...

Haram Memes For Jahannam Minded Teens
   +1 Join
57K members · 10+ posts a day

Fig. 17. Meme groups on Facebook

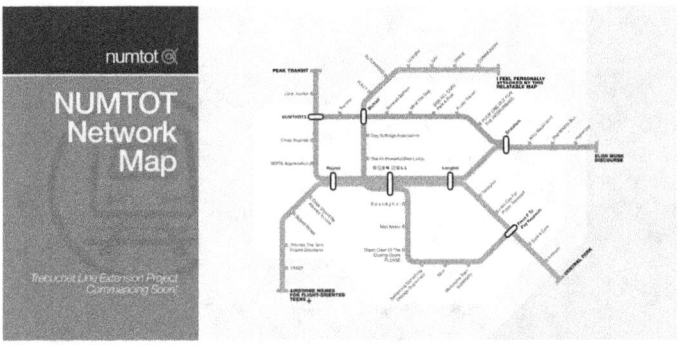

Fig. 18. NUMTOTS's mapping of their intersecting obsessions, from peak transit to Elon Musk. Design: Mitchell Sheldrick.

ily driven by 4chan /b/ board, as Whitney Philips notes in *This Is Why We Can't Have Nice Things*.[35]

But in the last couple of years, the Facebook meme group really took off. Articles started being written like "The Rise of Weird Facebook: How the World's Biggest Social Network Became Cool Again (and Why It Matters)" and "The Future of College is Facebook Meme Groups."[36]

College and university meme groups are particularly interesting spaces, because here the seriousness and the memeyness of the present generation of youth culture intersect, to often startling degree.

Sometimes it's simply very educational, such as in groups like NUMTOTS: New Urbanist Memes for Transit-Oriented Teens, with 70K+ members.[37] This group mixes an irrepressible

---

35 Whitney Philips, *This Is Why We Can't Have Nice Things* (Cambridge: MIT Press, 2015), xx.

36 See Hudson Hongo, "The Rise of Weird Facebook: How the World's Biggest Social Network Became Cool Again (and Why It Matters)," *New York Magazine,* February 25, 2016, http://nymag.com/selectall/2016/02/weird-facebook-became-cool-again.html; Paris Martineau, "The Future of College Is Facebook Meme Groups," *New York Magazine,* July 10, 2017, http://nymag.com/selectall/2017/07/martin-shkreli-teens-and-college-facebook-meme-groups.html.

37 See https://www.facebook.com/groups/whatwouldjanejacobsdo/.

adult: What are your plans after LSE ?
me:

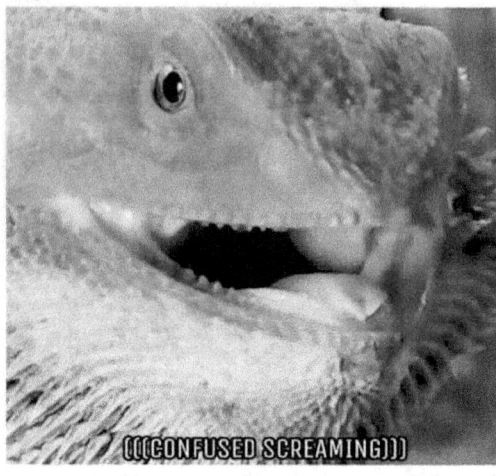

((((CONFUSED SCREAMING))))

Fig. 19. Source: Facebook Group Robust Memes for LSE Teens, https://www. facebook. com/memes. LSE.Robust/.

repurposing of other internet meme forms, from dog meme vocabulary where every thing is a "boi" — "sad reaccs only for this r e p l a c e m e n t b o i" replacement bus service — with contemporary meme formats such as the recent *American Chopper* meme made into a debate about Shinkansen vs. Maglev trains, alongside serious discussion about the reforms needed to the transportation systems and urban planning of American cities.[38]

One testimonial notes: "I joined this group expecting memes and all I got was the equivalent of a bachelor's in urban planning."

But teenagers are using humor and irony — through the form of memes — to find ways to face up to and discuss deeper stresses and anxieties, too.

---

38 See Martin Belam, "Meme Explained: Why Do I Keep Seeing the Same Two Angry Men on Social Media?," *The Guardian,* April 6, 2018, https://www.theguardian.com/media/2018/apr/06/meme-explained-why-do-i-keep-seeing-the-same-two-angry-men-on-social-media; "New Urbanist Memes for Transit-Oriented Teens," Facebook Group, https://www.facebook.com/groups/whatwouldjanejacobsdo/permalink/946290535530568/.

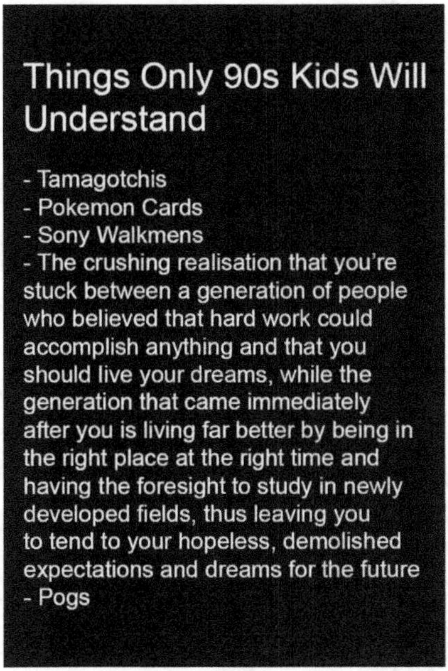

Things Only 90s Kids Will Understand

- Tamagotchis
- Pokemon Cards
- Sony Walkmens
- The crushing realisation that you're stuck between a generation of people who believed that hard work could accomplish anything and that you should live your dreams, while the generation that came immediately after you is living far better by being in the right place at the right time and having the foresight to study in newly developed fields, thus leaving you to tend to your hopeless, demolished expectations and dreams for the future
- Pogs

Fig. 20. Source: Facebook Group Nihilist Memes, https://www.facebook.com/nihilistmemes/.

My alma mater, the career-obsessed cultural desert that is the London School of Economics, has a good line in memes which are almost entirely about the pressures students face in their studying and to get a good job (read: a banking or consultancy job) after graduation (fig. 19).

The LSE Memes admin gives barbed benedictions to its anonymous contributors: "may they become one of our top banking lizard overlords," "may their hourly consultancy rate collapse a small country's economy," and "may she get an unconditional offer from Rothschild so none of this matters." The irony here is complex, capturing the students' ambitions and their doubts and their critics, all at once.

Meanwhile, groups like Nihilistic Memes (1.9M followers) and Dank Memes (890K followers) are some of the biggest in

Facebook, trafficking in — again — a kind of doomy empathy (fig. 20).[39]

What's going on? Paris Martineau interviewed some of the founders of college meme groups for *New York Magazine* last year.[40] The admins emphasize the empathetic function of the communities they have created: "my friends and I always say that memes come from a place of stress and anxiety," notes Ephraim Sutherland, co-founder of Yale Memes for Special Snowflake Teens.

And "before the page, I had never seen anyone get together and talk about these issues," Tril of UC Berkeley Memes for Edgy Teens recalled. "now, I feel like people aren't afraid to talk about them out in the open."

So through humor, and exaggeration, and irony — a kind of truth emerges about how people are feeling. A truth that they may not have felt able to express straight. And there's more community here as in many of the more traditionally civic-oriented Groups Zuckerberg's strategy may have had in mind.

But why memes?

The formal properties of the meme make it a particularly effective format for delivering an indirect payload of empathy.

A major vector in meme content in the past couple of years has been "relatability" — from the "Common White Girl" @girlposts Twitter account (fig. 21) celebrating the small failings of the everyday basic bitch (now suspended for stealing tweets), to reaction GIFs turning particularly expressive gestures into reusable, quotable forms (and particularly appropriating the emotional labor of black women, as Lauren Michele Jackson noted last year[41]). In consuming these memes — in liking and

---

39 See https://www.facebook.com/nihilistmemes/, and https://www.facebook.com/PlaceForMemes/.

40 See Martineau, "The Future of College is Facebook Meme Groups."

41 *Know Your Meme,* s.v. "Common White Girl," http://knowyourmeme.com/memes/common-white-girl; Julia Reinstein, "Twitter Just Suspended a Ton of Accounts Known for Stealing Tweets," *Buzzfeed,* March 10, 2018, https://www.buzzfeed.com/juliareinstein/twitter-dory-girlposts-suspended-accounts-tweetdecking; and Lauren Michele Jackson, "We Need to Talk

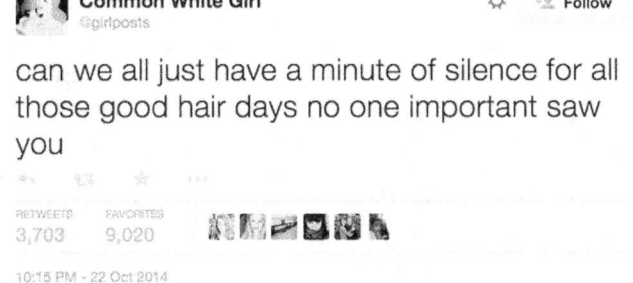

Common White Girl
@girlposts

⚙   + Follow

can we all just have a minute of silence for all those good hair days no one important saw you

RETWEETS   FAVORITES
3,703   9,020

10:15 PM - 22 Oct 2014

Fig. 21. Tweet by Twitter account @girlposts.

sharing — the social media user is participating in a moment of commonality. They're saying, "I am like this too." These memes are predicated on a recognition of common human similarities.

Meme formats — from the recent *American Chopper* dialectic model to the "Exploding Brain," "Distracted Boyfriend," and "Tag Yourself" templates — are by their very nature iterative and quotable. That is how the meme functions, through reference to the original context and the memes that have gone before, coupled with creative remixing to speak to a particular audience or topic or moment. Each new instance of a meme is thereby automatically familiar and recognizable. The format carries a meta-message to the audience: "this is familiar, not weird." And the audience is pre-prepared to know how to react to this: you like, you "haha" emoji, and you tag your friends in the comments.

The format acts as a kind of Trojan Horse, then, for sharing difficult feelings — because the format pre-primes the audience to respond in a hospitable mode. There isn't that moment of feeling stuck about how to respond to your friend's big emotional disclosure, because she hasn't made the big statement quite directly, but through irony and cultural quotation — distanced

---

about Digital Blackface in Reaction GIFs," *Teen Vogue,* August 2, 2017, https://www.teenvogue.com/story/digital-blackface-reaction-gifs.

through memes typically using stock photography (as Leigh Alexander notes) rather than anything as gauche as a picture of oneself.[42] This enables you the viewer to sidestep the full intensity of it in your response, should you choose (but still, crucially, to respond). And also to DM your friend and ask, "hey, are you alright?" and cut to the realtalk should you so choose, too.

So a space is created, to talk about being stressed and overwhelmed and unsure of the meaning of anything we do — space which is, I believe, more open than it has been in the past. As the mod of UC Berkeley Memes for Edgy Teens says, this "gets the conversation going, as I don't think it would have even started without it."[43]

And this is how memes help people speak truths.

What Does "Authenticity" Mean, Anyway?

> *"Thrown, in spite of myself, into the great world, without possessing its manners, and unable to acquire or conform to them, I took it into my head to adopt manners of my own, which might enable me to dispense with them."*
> — Jean-Jacques Rousseau, *Confessions*[44]

The concept of personal authenticity arises as part of Enlightenment rationality and a new, distinctively modern conception of the self. Rousseau argued that authenticity is diminished by the need for the esteem of others; one's guide to conduct in life should come not from social pressures or external rules (e.g., the Church), but rather a source within — the sovereign, rational individual.

---

42 Leigh Alexander, "The Many Faces of 'Distracted Boyfriend': On Stock Photography Memes and the Illusion of Reality," *Medium,* September 29, 2017, https://medium.com/s/i-o/the-many-faces-of-distracted-boyfriend-299836ba4c89.

43 See Martineau, "The Future of College is Facebook Meme Groups."

44 Jean-Jacques Rousseau, *The Confessions* [1781] (Ware: Wordsworth, 1996), 357.

Twentieth-century philosophers — Sartre, Heidegger — recognized that this was perhaps a little more difficult than Rousseau claimed: the external world and its influences is inescapable and not straightforward to slough off, and nature and society shape us as much as our own choices. And so authenticity must always be negotiated in complex interdependency with its opposite — that is, you were never really authentic in the first place.

That tension is what meme culture is negotiating: these unexpected, witty truths emerging through the most inauthentic, borrowed, or stolen stock photograph content possible.

Because people still want to tell the truth about their lives, and the world: absolutely nothing has changed there.

What is changing, I argue, are the cultural formats people are using for discussion — the carrier waves for this signal. This is where "authenticity" isn't a useful claim any more, having been wholly co-opted and commodified into its opposite. Culture and the way we communicate — shaped by media affordances — have got more complex and ironic and multi-layered than that.

It turns out, even people who share fake news stories are trying to tell a kind of truth too.

At SXSW EDU this year, technology researcher danah boyd argued that we've been rather uncharitable in our analyses of why people share fake news. The assumption is that people really believe the claims they share — that is, they're ill-informed; that is, they're stupid. It turns out not to be quite so simple:

> Yet, if you talk with someone who has posted clear, unquestionable misinformation, more often than not, they know it's bullshit. Or they don't care whether or not it's true. Why do they post it then? Because they're making a statement. The people who posted this meme [fig. 22] didn't bother to fact check this claim. They didn't care. What they wanted to signal loud and clear is that they hated Hillary Clinton. And that message was indeed heard loud and clear. As a re-

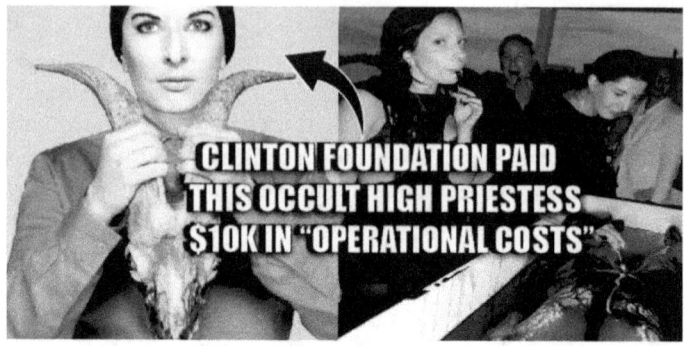

Fig. 22. Source: *Truthfeed*. See Amy Moreno, "Breaking: Clinton Foundation Paid Occult 'Spirit Cooking' Priestess 10K For 'Operational Support'," *Truthfeed*, November 5, 2016, http://truthfeed. com/breaking-clinton-foundation-paid-occult-spirit-cooking-priestess-10k-for-operational-support/34116/.

sult, they are very offended if you tell them that they've been duped by Russians into spreading propaganda. They don't believe you for one second.[45]

The people sharing this story are seeking to tell a kind of moral truth through metaphor and cultural quotation (the person shown in the picture is in fact performance artist Marina Abramovic). Not entirely unlike our meme-ing teens on Facebook.

What I've sought to argue in this essay, then, is that we are indeed living in an a strange, surface-centric moment in popular, digital culture right now — where the original "essence of things" has indeed become somewhat unfashionable (or just less entertaining). Social and media technologies, optimised for the diffusion of highly emotive, reaction-generating content, encourage a rapid trade in attention-grabbing ideas, over slower-burning systematic, contextualized thinking.

Yet, even as "authenticity" as a claim and as an aesthetic feels outdated, deeper forms of "realness" in our communica-

---

45 See boyd, "You Think You Want Media Literacy…Do You?"

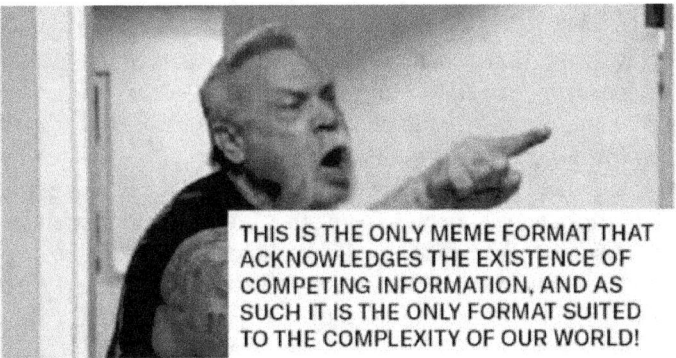

THIS IS THE ONLY MEME FORMAT THAT ACKNOWLEDGES THE EXISTENCE OF COMPETING INFORMATION, AND AS SUCH IT IS THE ONLY FORMAT SUITED TO THE COMPLEXITY OF OUR WORLD!

Fig. 23. Source: *Meme*. See https://me.me/i/american-chopper-memes-are-compelling-rhetorical-devices-that-could-be-f9f92fe24d2f4296af0bb20b1a63322e/.

tions still persist. People are still seeking to communicate their deepest personal truths: their values, hopes, and fears with each other. Through sharing media, we're still creating community.

Nonetheless, the kind of truth in play is changing form: emotional and moral truths are in ascendance over straightforwardly factual claims. Truth becomes plural, and thereby highly contested: global warming, 9/11, or Obama's birthplace are all treated as matters of cultural allegiance over "fact" as traditionally understood. "By my reckoning, the solidly reality-based are a minority, maybe a third of us but almost certainly fewer than half," Kurt Andersen posits.[46] Electorates in the US and Europe are polarizing along value-driven lines — order and authority vs. openness and change.[47] Building the coalitions of support needed to tackle the grand challenges we face this century will require a profound upgrade to our political and cultural leaders' empathic and reconciliation skills.

---

46 See Andersen, "How America Lost Its Mind."

47 See Eric Kaufmann, "It's NOT the Economy, Stupid: Brexit as a Story of Personal Values," *LSE* (blog), July 7, 2016, http://blogs.lse.ac.uk/politicsandpolicy/personal-values-brexit-vote/.

So perhaps to say that this post-authentic moment is one of evolving, increasingly nuanced collective communication norms, able to operate with multi-layered recursive meanings and ironies in disposable pop culture content…is kind of cold comfort.

Nonetheless, author Robin Sloan described the genius of the *American Chopper* meme as being that "THIS IS THE ONLY MEME FORMAT THAT ACKNOWLEDGES THE EXISTENCE OF COMPETING INFORMATION, AND AS SUCH IT IS THE ONLY FORMAT SUITED TO THE COMPLEXITY OF OUR WORLD!"[48]

May it yet save us.

---

48 https://twitter.com/robinsloan/status/982303299264069632. [URL defunct]

Bibliography

Allen, Summer. "Wood, Citrus, Lattes, Feet, Twine, Repeat: The Kinfolk Kinspiracy Code." *Gawker*, March 31, 2015. http://gawker.com/wood-citrus-lattes-feet-twine-repeat-the-kinfolk-1693115156.

Alexander, Leigh. "The Many Faces of 'Distracted Boyfriend': On Stock Photography Memes and the Illusion of Reality." *Medium*, September 29, 2017. https://medium.com/s/i-o/the-many-faces-of-distracted-boyfriend-299836ba4c89.

Andersen, Kurt. "How America Lost Its Mind." *The Atlantic*, September 2017. https://www.theatlantic.com/magazine/archive/2017/09/how-america-lost-its-mind/534231/.

annoyed_professor. "I'm a College Philosophy Professor. Jordan Peterson Is Making My Job Impossible." *Reddit*, March 24, 2018, 16:20 GMT+1. https://www.reddit.com/r/enoughpetersonspam/comments/86tnz7/im_a_college_philosophy_professor_jordan_peterson/.

Belam, Martin. "Meme Explained: Why do I Keep Seeing the Same Two Angry Men on Social Media?" *The Guardian*, April 6, 2018. https://www.theguardian.com/media/2018/apr/06/meme-explained-why-do-i-keep-seeing-the-same-two-angry-men-on-social-media.

boyd, danah. "You Think You Want Media Literacy…Do You?" *Points*, March 9, 2018. https://points.datasociety.net/you-think-you-want-media-literacy-do-you-7cad6af18ec2.

Butler, Oobah. "I Made My Shed the Top Rated Restaurant On TripAdvisor." *Vice*, December 6, 2017. https://www.vice.com/en_uk/article/434gqw/i-made-my-shed-the-top-rated-restaurant-on-tripadvisor.

Chayka, Kyle. "Same Old, Same Old: How the Hipster Aesthetic Is Taking Over the World." *The Guardian*, August 6, 2016. https://www.theguardian.com/commentisfree/2016/aug/06/hipster-aesthetic-taking-over-world.

Cole, Samantha. "AI-Assisted Fake Porn Is Here and We're All Fucked." *Motherboard*, December 11, 2017. https://

motherboard.vice.com/en_us/article/gydydm/gal-gadot-fake-ai-porn.

————. "We Are Truly Fucked: Everyone Is Making AI-Generated Fake Porn Now." *Motherboard,* January 24, 2018, https://motherboard.vice.com/en_us/article/bjye8a/reddit-fake-porn-app-daisy-ridley.

Confessore, Nicholas, et al. "The Follower Factory." *New York Times,* January 27, 2018. https://www.nytimes.com/interactive/2018/01/27/technology/social-media-bots.html.

Cooke, Kirsty. "'Fake News' Reinforces Trust in Mainstream News Brands." *Kantar,* October 31, 2017. https://uk.kantar.com/business/brands/2017/trust-in-news/.

Gault, Matthew. "After 20 Minutes of Listening, New Adobe Tool Can Make You Say Anything." *Motherboard,* November 5, 2016. https://motherboard.vice.com/en_us/article/jpgkxp/after-20-minutes-of-listening-new-adobe-tool-can-make-you-say-anything.

Gholipour, Bahar. "New AI Tech Can Mimic Any Voice." *Scientific American,* May 2, 2017. https://www.scientificamerican.com/article/new-ai-tech-can-mimic-any-voice/.

Girlguiding, "Girls' Attitudes Survey 2017," 2017. https://www.girlguiding.org.uk/globalassets/docs-and-resources/research-and-campaigns/girls-attitudes-survey-2017.pdf.

Godwin, Richard. "Death of the Hipster: Why London Decided to Move on from Beards, Beanies and Fixie Bikes." *Evening Standard,* April 16, 2015. https://www.standard.co.uk/lifestyle/death-of-the-hipster-why-london-decided-to-move-on-from-beards-beanies-and-fixie-bikes-10178615.html.

Harman, Justine. "The Crazy Way Teens are Hiding Their Imperfections Online: Finstagram." *Elle,* July 9 2015. https://www.elle.com/culture/tech/a29243/finstagram/.

Herber, Eric. "Finstagram: The Instagram Revolution." *Medium,* February 10, 2015. https://medium.com/bits-pixels/finstagram-the-instagram-revolution-737999d40014.

Hongo, Hudson. "The Rise of Weird Facebook: How the World's Biggest Social Network Became Cool Again (and Why It Matters)." *New York Magazine,* February 25, 2016. http://nymag.com/selectall/2016/02/weird-facebook-became-cool-again.html.

Jackson, Lauren Michele. "We Need to Talk About Digital Blackface in Reaction GIFs." *Teen Vogue,* August 2, 2017. https://www.teenvogue.com/story/digital-blackface-reaction-gifs.

Joyce, Brittany, and Sarah Lawrence. "The Evolution of the Hipster 2010–2015." *Paste,* June 18, 2015. https://www.pastemagazine.com/articles/2015/06/the-evolution-of-the-hipster-2010–2015.html.

Kaufmann, Eric. "It's NOT the Economy, Stupid: Brexit as a Story of Personal Values." *LSE* (blog), July 7, 2016. http://blogs.lse.ac.uk/politicsandpolicy/personal-values-brexit-vote/.

Kiefer, Kate. "The Evolution of the Hipster 2000–2009." *Paste,* December 3, 2009. https://www.pastemagazine.com/articles/2009/12/the-evolution-of-the-hipster-2000–2009.html.

Kliff, Sarah, Soo Oh, and Sarah Frostenson. "Today's Teens Use Hallucinogens/Watch Television/Fight/Drink/Use Heroin/Have Babies/Use Meth/Binge Drink/Carry Weapons to School Less than You Did." *Vox,* June 9, 2016. https://www.vox.com/a/teens.

Lee, Dave. "Facebook Amends 'Real Name' Policy After Protests." *BBC,* December 15, 2015. http://www.bbc.co.uk/news/technology-35109045.

Lorenz, Taylor. "The Secret Instagram Accounts Teens Use to Share Their Realest, Most Intimate Moments." *Mic,* March 3, 2017. https://mic.com/articles/175936/the-secret-instagram-accounts-teens-use-to-share-their-realest-most-intimate-moments.

Lyster, Rosa. "The Cottingley Fairy Hoax of 1917 is a Case Study in How Smart People Lose Control of the Truth."

Quartz, February 17, 2017. https://qz.com/911990/the-cottingley-fairy-hoax-of-1917-is-a-case-study-in-how-smart-people-lose-control-of-the-truth/.

Majestichuman. Comment on rasras4, "Teens of Reddit, What Is Considered Cool Right Now?" *Reddit,* September 9, 2017, 20:20 GMT+2. https://www.reddit.com/r/AskReddit/comments/6z23rj/teens_of_reddit_what_is_considered_cool_right_now/dms4g57.

Martineau, Paris. "The Future of College Is Facebook Meme Groups." *New York Magazine,* July 10, 2017. http://nymag.com/selectall/2017/07/martin-shkreli-teens-and-college-facebook-meme-groups.html.

Moreno, Amy. "Breaking: Clinton Foundation Paid Occult 'Spirit Cooking' Priestess 10K For 'Operational Support.'" *Truthfeed,* November 5, 2016. http://truthfeed.com/breaking-clinton-foundation-paid-occult-spirit-cooking-priestess-10k-for-operational-support/34116/.

Niessner, Matthias. "Face2Face: Real-time Face Capture and Reenactment of RGB Videos (CVPR 2016 Oral)." *YouTube,* March 18, 2016. https://www.youtube.com/watch?v=ohmajJTcpNk.

Pedersen, Jordan. "Inside the Inscrutable World of Weird Facebook." *Daily Dot,* Augusts 5, 2014. https://www.dailydot.com/unclick/weird-facebook/.

Philips, Whitney. *This Is Why We Can't Have Nice Things.* Cambridge: MIT Press, 2015.

Rafaeli, JS. "The Story of Mephedrone, the Party Drug That Boomed and Went Bust." *Vice,* January 17, 2017. https://www.vice.com/en_uk/article/9aa53a/the-story-of-mephedrone-the-party-drug-that-boomed-and-went-bust.

rasras4, "Teens of Reddit, What Is Considered Cool Right Now?" *Reddit,* September 9, 2017, 16:55 GMT+2. https://www.reddit.com/r/AskReddit/comments/6z23rj/teens_of_reddit_what_is_considered_cool_right_now/.

Reinstein, Julia. "Twitter Just Suspended a Ton of Accounts Known for Stealing Tweets." *Buzzfeed,* March 10, 2018.

https://www.buzzfeed.com/juliareinstein/twitter-dory-girlposts-suspended-accounts-tweetdecking.

Rousseau, Jean-Jacques. *The Confessions* [1781]. Ware: Wordsworth, 1996.

Schwulst, Lauren. Quoted in Kyle Chayka, "Welcome to Airspace: How Silicon Valley Helps Spread the Same Sterile Aesthetic Across the World." *The Verge,* August 3, 2016. https://www.theverge.com/2016/8/3/12325104/airbnb-aesthetic-global-minimalism-startup-gentrification.

Silk, Ed. "Authenticity as We Know It Is Dead as Brands Go Minimalist to Express Their Craft and Quality." *The Drum,* February 12, 2016. http://www.thedrum.com/opinion/2016/02/12/authenticity-we-know-it-dead-brands-go-minimalist-express-their-craft-and-quality.

Smith, Mikey. "Theresa May's 'Fake News Unit' Announcement Has Itself Been Branded 'Fake News.'" *Mirror,* January 30, 2018. https://www.mirror.co.uk/news/politics/theresa-mays-fake-news-unit-11940423.

"The Real Story of 'Fake News.'" *Merriam-Webster.* https://www.merriam-webster.com/words-at-play/the-real-story-of-fake-news.

Walker, Daniela. "The Hipster is Dead, Let's Start an Anti-authenticity Movement." *Campaign,* September 29, 2015. https://www.campaignlive.co.uk/article/hipster-dead-lets-start-anti-authenticity-movement/1366143.

Woolf, Jake. "There's an $800 Hoodie That's Selling Out Everywhere." *GQ,* February 22, 2016. https://www.gq.com/story/vetements-hoodie-buy-sold-out-price

Zuckerberg, Mark. "Building Global Community." *Facebook,* February 16, 2017. https://www.facebook.com/notes/mark-zuckerberg/building-global-community/10154544292806634/.

The Work of Art(iculation) in the Age of Memic Rhythmicality: Memes between Form, Content, and Structure

Dan Bristow

In the preface to the first edition of his *Critique of Pure Reason,* Immanuel Kant states:

> If we measured the size of a book, not by the number of its pages, but by the time we require for mastering it, then it could be said of many a book *that it would be much shorter if it were not so short.* On the other hand, if we ask how a wide-ranging whole of speculative knowledge that yet coheres in one principle can best be rendered intelligible, we might be equally justified in saying that *many a book would have been clearer if it had not tried to be so very clear.* The reader does not arrive quickly enough at an overview of the whole, and the bright colours of illustrations hide and distort the articulation and organization of the system, which, after all, matter most if we want to judge of its unity and solidity.[1]

---

1   Immanuel Kant, "Preface to the First Edition," in *Critique of Pure Reason,* trans. and ed. Marcus Weigelt (London: Penguin Classics, 2007), 11. My

Similar criteria could be applied in a critique of pure memage: in any meme-building exercise, brevity and clarity are requisite, but can also naturally come at the cost of a fuller appreciation of a situation's complexity, which mightn't be open to so reductive a rendering; a well-crafted meme will jostle but should ultimately balance correlatively with its wider contextualization, which it will also offset in some catchy, critical, or farcical way, although it is of course this that might misconstrue further problematics inherent in that upon which it is a commentary (none of which it might be too bothered by), in its quest for virality; if misjudged, a meme will fail in its intended purpose, remaining pat and static — although, of course, a meme can easily run off from authorial grasp, as Pepe has proven — and endlessly be de- and reterritorialized.[2] Thus, a meme in part is a play between reduction, *reductiveness,* and also often irreducibility; that is, a meme *can* encompass that kernel, or *bit,* that sticks, that resonates, that may illuminate — however fleetingly, or only introductorily — the principle in which its subject matter coheres (however temporary this phenomenon of coherence itself might prove be upon the dank waves of discursivity).[3] The

---

emphasis.

2   Even in terms of the articulation of the spread of memes, and of memic popularity, something of a dichotomy can be seen between the terms most commonly used to describe this: the disease-laced, parasitic "virality," and the equality-couched (re)distributive "shareability."

3   I have in previous work relayed this against *"sinthomic"* processes in Lacanian psychoanalytic theory, conceptualising the sinthome as a sort of *empty signified,* or *memic blank,* in which a "little bit of real" can get stuck and effloresce *enjoyable* meaning, or myriad meanings (*"enjoymeants"*). An early instance that chimes with this current work can be found in EDA Collective, "The *Sinthomic* Blank in Future Bass and Dubstep," in *Twerking to Turking: Everyday Analysis, Volume 2* (Alresford: Zero Books, 2015), 158–59. In this vein, much in the way of memes and the analysis of their modes of operation can be run through a musicological lens, from the (formal) units into which musical measurement is divided, to practices like that employed by the band The Books, of selecting instances of "found sound" (as the content) to construct their songs around (which can perhaps be likened to practices involved in shitposting); see their collected works: The Books, *A Dot in Time* (New York: Temporary Residence

ur-meme is rhythmical — like a beat, or measure, or, better still, like a *riddim,* as utilized in reggae and dancehall music — over which the memic message may dance (to put this in Nietzschean terms: the Apollonian opens out onto the Dionysian), but the argument to be made here will posit that this is not simply a matter of form, or forms, being filled with content, but something more dialectical, structural.

The object of the brief analysis ahead will thus be to look at memes, alongside other instances of internet activity — comments, for example, into which memes are often posted — through the spectral lens of three interconnected categories: form, content, and structure. Its aim will be to postulate some of the ways in which the subject matter of these activities gets spectralized through such means (that may in fact amount to — however consciously or unconsciously — *methods*) of representation. For example, let's take a "meme" (approximating more the Dawkinsian sense here; as something that has been reduced into a transferrable *bit,* or kernel) to begin at; that of sexism: what might sprout out of just this decontextualized, memically presented phenomenon — that is, excerpted here as only something like a trigger word — might be instances of fragile male egoic fears over just what behaviors men are "any longer permitted," and the attendant victim blaming and berating that comes with these attitudes; essentialist universalizations based on psycho-social and medico-nominative promulgations of sex and gender, and the misapprehension of the ideologies underlying these; structuralist accounts of how sexism is inscribed in the very contours of systematicities that format and formulate how sex and gender are experienced by modern and historical subjects. From the structuralist position that this essay launches from, form and content will come to be conceived as something like *sides,* both unified to, and separated from, each other by structure, or structures, understandings, or apprehensions, of which may be able to rein back in from other sides biases or

Limited, 2012). For more on memic-musical crossings, see Tom Whyman's chapter on the online art of *The Simpsons* in this collection.

prejudices rigid adherence to them can give rise to. This is not say that structuralism is something like "neutrality," or a claim to some inherent truth, but that it can be utilized as a principle for apprehending and contemplating division, contradiction, and antagonism, and that it is in the thus dialectically materialist place of these that it takes up its very position. For each category we will take up discussion of a topic that makes it regularly into meme posting and online activity in the political realm: for form, feminism; for content, racism; and for structure, capitalism.

Form

> "*The Queen being the Queen isn't an emancipatory feminist fact.*"
> — Dawn Foster, *Lean Out*

In her extremely insightful short tract *Lean Out* (2015), Dawn Foster exposes a great deal of what we might term "formalist feminism" (including corporate feminism, choice feminism, lifestyle feminism, etc.), encompassed for Foster in the project and projected image of Sheryl Sandberg, and her book — the title of which Foster of course flips — *Lean In* (2013). Its subtitle, *Women, Work, and the Will to Lead,* sums up its stance: if women *will* it, it will come; success *is* achievable in the workplace, top positions are available to women, if the requisite effort is put in. Just look at this case in point: Sandberg made it to Chief Operating Officer (COO) of Facebook. But because one woman has, doesn't mean all women *can*, which is what the argument seems to boil down to.[4]

---

4   Although they're brilliant for young readers, and a very welcome publishing event, this is something that Elena Favilli and Francesca Cavello's *Goodnight Stories for Rebel Girls* books, for example — and probably necessitously, given the complexity to be communicated to a younger audience who are less likely to have had, or to have been parentally more protected from, directly oppressive experiences — structurally elide. Such subsequent publications as *The*

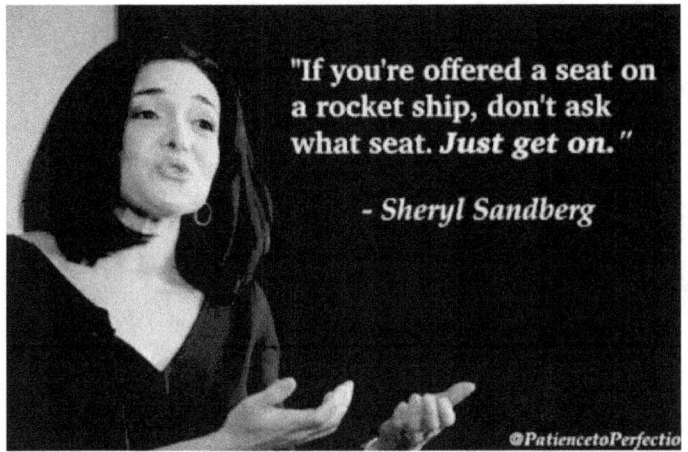

Thanks Sheryl. (r/getmotivated)

Fig. 1. Source: Sizzle. See https://onsizzle.com/i/if-youre-offered-a-seat-on-a-rocket-ship-dont-15875341.

An inspirational message tacked on to a professional corporate photograph mightn't tend to be what we first think of in terms of dank meme stashes, but such of Sandberg exist (quoting her "if you're offered a seat on a rocket ship, don't ask what seat. *Just get on*" soundbite, for example), and are no doubt shared, most likely on "professional networking" social media sites like LinkedIn, where they'll be posted with the intention of chivvying along the aspiration-shy into becoming better ladder climbers, while they really partake of a form of policing dissent — from those who might bemoan the fact that however far they've leant in, it hasn't worked out for them — and any potential break-ins of emotional, or political (not business-minded politics, that is), subjectivity, through a sort of accidental, or un-

Good Guys: 50 Heroes Who Changed the World with Kindness, which focuses on compassionate men only, not only ride the bandwagon, and miss the point, but can only seem a tad reactionary.

conscious, user-generated, and mob/mod-moderated, panopti-cal surveillance (fig. 1).

The form that this takes in corporate feminism is that if *she* could, *you* can; in corporate egalitarianism (in other words, the sovereign rule of individualism, in emulation of the "free" market economy), if they could, you can (and if you don't, that's down to you): nothing else should be considered (e.g., the con-ditions into which one was born, opportunities, nepotism, etc.). The ideological maneuver of the formalism at work here has repackaged and re-presented — even *sold* (such professional networking sites often offer a paid premium service boasting of boosting success rates) — a universalized individual as an *individualized universal*; that is, they make out such successful figures to merely be individuals who have achieved the *univer-sally achievable,* and then attach this to a social cause as an add-on: advancements made in feminism, "social mobility," "self-makeable success," etc. This (self-help 101) formula is simple: "because *a* woman, so *all* women"; because *a* worker got a pro-motion — perhaps even jumped a class boundary — *all* workers can, because *a* success was self-made, *all* successes can be.

What is occurring is the transposition of an individual con-tent into a universal form. Foster explains this in the confused conflation of feminism with anything that pertains to women, or even a particular woman, in the phenomenon of "choice fem-inism [that] states that any choice is feminist purely by virtue of having been made by a woman: that she is in a position to, and has, made a choice is thereby feminist. There's little analysis paid to what this means for women in society as a whole."[5] A part — which in this instance happens to be of the correctly cor-responding gender — is mistaken for, or wilfully construed as, the whole. This is what feeds into how feminism becomes appre-hended by its antagonists. Most often male (though also anti-feminist female) resentment becomes stoked up by the idea — a tautological extension of its original — that *because* a woman *is* a woman, they *can* do this and that, and may even be un-

---

5   Dawn Foster, *Lean Out* (London: Repeater Books, 2016), 61–62.

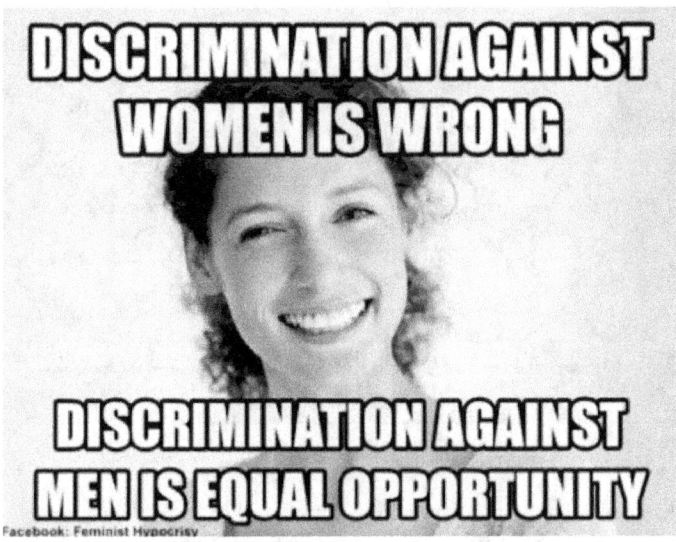

Fig. 2. Source: Meme. See https://me.me/i/discrimination-against-women-is-wrong-discrimination-against-men-isequalopportunity-facebook-5565821.

fairly *favored* to. (This finds voice, for example, in a supposedly meritocracy-advocating railing against "equal opportunities" in employment law: memes along these lines contain such messages as, "Discrimination against women is wrong/Discrimination against men is equal opportunity," or Morpheus from *The Matrix* saying, "What if I told you/the term 'equal opportunity' has become a euphemism for: 'straight white males need not apply'" (figs. 2, 3). There then may also arise the paranoid male fear that women have become untouchable, *a priori,* by any criticism or reprobation — not to mention, in its creepiest manifestation, sexually; misrecognition of what consent, and conversation, is being paramount to this — *because* of their status *as* women (which completely misrecognizes the culturally promulgated and then unquestioningly *assumed* possessive right to — or something like unpaid debt from — women; women's bodies, and minds). And yet this can also extend into paranoiacally checking oneself for hallmarks of anti-feminism (and this is the

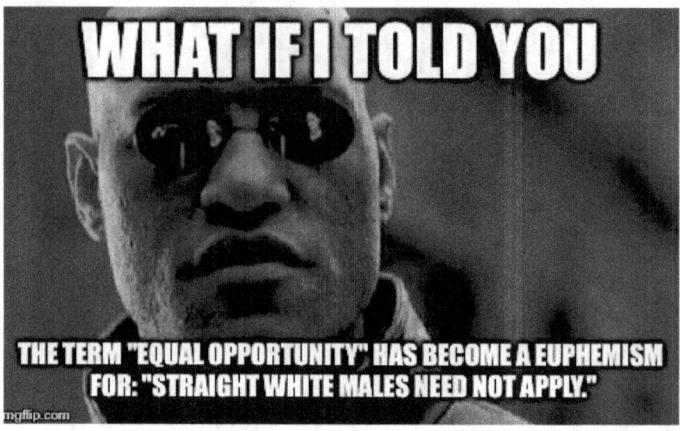

Fig. 3. Source: Imgflip. See https://imgflip.com/i/18ri2u.

kind of formalism that can get mobilized by liberals; for example, against the straw man of universalized "brocialism"[6]). In her

---

6   While there are of course actual 'Bernie Bros," the construal of all
    Sanders supporters being such is preposterous. On this, Angela Nagle
    is illuminating: "while the alt-right regard the Guardian [*sic*], BBC and
    CNN as the media of 'the left,' espousing 'Cultural Marxism,' it became
    obvious when the possibility of any kind of economically 'left' political
    force emerged that liberal media sources were often the most vicious
    and oppositional. Liberal feminist journalist Joan Walsh called Bernie
    Sanders's supporters 'Berniebot keyboard warriors,' while Salon [*sic*] was
    one of the main propagators of the Berniebro meme with headlines like,
    'Bernie Bros out of control: Explosion of misogynist rage...' and, 'Just like
    a Bernie Bro, Sanders bullies Clinton...' Meanwhile *Vice*, a magazine that
    made its brand on the most degenerate combination of vacuous hipster
    aesthetics and pornified transgression, published things like 'How to spot
    a brocialist." Before the elections *The Guardian* [*sic*] newspaper ran a piece
    with the comically cultish wording: 'Time to hail Hilary Clinton — and
    face down the testosterone left.' Despite overwhelming evidence of Bernie's
    popularity among young women, the myth was relentlessly peddled until
    it passed into the realm of Internet truth. The old liberal establishment
    then weighed in; for example, when feminist Gloria Steinem claimed
    that these numerous female Bernie fans were merely trying to impress
    their male peers. In the UK, an almost identical phenomenon occurred
    when the British liberal media establishment, in particular *The Guardian*
    [*sic*], joined forces with their more youthful online offspring in smearing

book, Foster effortlessly puts paid to these notions with these statements: "criticism of any woman isn't anti-feminist purely because she is a woman: women occupy all sections of society now. The Queen being the Queen isn't an emancipatory feminist fact. Margaret Thatcher harmed more than helped women by becoming Prime Minister."[7]

A reduction to, and reliance on, form in these instances is a cruel and dominative, often unconscious, circular logic that yet will regularly misrecognize itself — if not more insidiously motivated — as a clear, logical response to progressive social change. Feminism in these instances is mistaken for, and distilled into, formalism. This distillation is handy for those who want to criticize feminism, as through characterizing it as formalist makes it appear illogical. Cunningly and connivingly, form is relied upon in this maneuver, while it is railed against, and anything beyond it (that might surface in terms of content — particular women's experiences, which are formally subsumed into grand and overarching narratives about those types of experience — or structure, which might hint at other, outside forces at work) is constrained to silence and the shadows.

Content

> *"It's clear that equality doesn't quite cut it. Asking for a sliver of disproportional power is too polite a request. I don't want to be included. Instead, I want to question who created the standard in the first place. After a lifetime of embodying difference, I have no desire to be equal. I want to deconstruct the structural power of a system that marked me out as different. I don't wish to be assimilated into the status quo. I want to be liberated from all negative*

Corbyn and his supporters as being motivated primarily by this nefarious tide of brocialism, despite his squeaky-clean track record on women's issues in the UK." See Angela Nagle, *Kill All Normies: Online Culture Wars from 4chan and Tumblr to Trump and the Alt-Right* (Alresford: Zero Books, 2017), 43–44.

7   Foster, *Lean Out*, 79.

> *assumptions that my characteristics bring. The onus is*
> *not on me to change. Instead, it's the world around me."*
> — Reni Eddo-Lodge, *Why I'm No Longer Talking to White*
> *People about Race*[8]

Racism, like sexism (most overtly, yet not exclusively), operates along formalist lines: it reduces anything and everything that is subjectively individual to an "ineluctable modality" (to use James Joyce's famous words), to the color of one's skin (or another racial marker). It is of course, and it can only be, those on the receiving end of it that will know this best.[9] While presenting in form is obvious, racism does a better job at hiding behind content (whether its hosts in such circumstances wittingly know

---

8   Reni Eddo-Lodge, *Why I'm No Longer Talking to White People about Race* (London: Bloomsbury, 2018), 184.

9   In the introduction to Mike and Trevor Phillips's *Windrush* — published on the fiftieth anniversary of the *Empire Windrush*'s arrival on British shores in 1948 — they discuss the fact that "few black British people can be in any doubt that the majority of their fellow citizens take the colour of their skins to be a characteristic which defines what they are and what they can do," and how this has affected citizenship status: "if we were engaged in a struggle, it wasn't about our 'acceptance' as individuals. Instead, it was about our status as citizens, and it seemed obvious that if our citizenship was to mean more than the paper on which it was written, it would be necessary for the whole country to reassess not only its own identity, and history, but also what it meant to be British." See Mike Phillips and Trevor Phillips, *Windrush: The Irresistible Rise of Multi-Racial Britain* (London: HarperCollins, 1998), 5. The Windrush scandal, that broke over the course of 2018 (another significant anniversary), clearly indicates the retardation that this reassessment has met with, with governmental policy still operating along fundamentally formalist racist lines in its intentional creation of a "hostile environment" that would lead to deportations to meet target figures. (One resultant meme — utilizing a homophonic play on words — shows a back-and-forth between former Home Secretary, and architect of these scandalous policies, Prime Minister Theresa May and then-Home Secretary (who resigned in light of the scandal, and fell on May's Sword) Amber Rudd: "One of my constituents is going to the Caribbean"/"Jamaica?"/"Yes." It is featured in Paul Sorene, 'Windrush Children Only Became Visible When They Became Criminals," *Anorak*, April 17, 2018, http://www.anorak.co.uk/449047/politicians/windrush-children-only-became-visible-when-they-became-criminals.html.

it — or rather, *understand* it — or not). Content is what often gets mobilized and deployed against anti-racism, and is, in the deepest sense, reactionary. Race itself might remain untouched — issues pertaining to race unacknowledged — in conversations ostensibly on the topic, due to this maneuver; for example, if in flagging up elements of the structural racism of white people and institutions, it gets met with a "but" (the famous "but" that always implies a little more than meets the eye in matters of racism; i.e., in the commonplace "I'm not racist, but..."), we can often provide the translation: "*but I'm* not racist, so that notion's invalid." What is probably often missed, even by the (supposed) defendants, in this defense, is the fact that it defends *beyond itself*. In this unnecessary retort, the individual is (perhaps unwittingly) *universalizing*, deflecting not only from oneself, but, due to recourse to this method of defense, from the structure(s) under critique. In relation to clashes stoked by racism in the city of Nottingham in the UK in 1958, Reni Eddo-Lodge talks of "white resentment towards the city's black residents [being] rife, and black resentment at white resentment [...] simmering."[10] What's occurring, *absurdly*, in these abovementioned content-fueled reactions, are thus manifestations of white resentment at black resentment at white resentment.

As she delineates time and again in her extraordinary book *Why I'm No Longer Talking to White People about Race*, when conversations go this way, the original topic is quickly gotten away from; the focus most often becomes the injured ego of the other party; racism and race dissolve away, and "reverse racism" — a perennially memed concept — rears its head. In the added chapter to the paperback edition, "Aftermath," Eddo-Lodge discusses the book's publication, and the waves it ended up making. Even before its release, she discusses how the title (taken from the name she gave to the 2014 blog post that in many ways launched the project) and the cover were received: "when I posted the cover to social media, roughly a year before publication, the shares were out of control, and the anticipation

---

10 Eddo-Lodge, *Why I'm No Longer Talking to White People about Race*, 23.

was palpable. Much of this response was thanks to that cardinal sin — judging a book by its cover."[11] The cover portrays the title in black against a white background, except for the words "to white people," which are debossed into the white of the cover (and appear in white on white on the spine) (it is hoped that handholding through metaphorical decoding here should be unnecessary).[12]

> Like a red rag to a bull, the attention came in droves. It enthralled some, and sent others into a rage. In amongst the praise were early signs of ire from white people; some lectured me about segregation, or told me Martin Luther King Junior would never approve of my work. Others admonished me for my prejudice.
>
> [...] This was the scenario an east London bookseller relayed to me after I visited her shop to sign books. An elderly white man had entered the shop, saw the book in the window, and, shaking with rage, proceeded to make a scene at the counter, angry because 'it wouldn't be allowed the other way round'. 'He was so angry, I couldn't speak to him', she told me. Then there was the young black man who, on reading the book in public, had to endure the displeasure of a white woman approaching him to let him know that the book he was reading 'really didn't help the conversation'. White middle class people can be particularly calculated with their discomfort.[13]

---

11 Ibid., 231.

12 In an earlier, and probably quite inadequate, essay, I briefly explored similar ways in which Audre Lorde has shown up the social *hiddenness* of whiteness and racism in her work (the word "white," for example, being always lowercase in contrast to the always capitalized signifier "Black"). See Daniel Bristow, "New Spellings: Auto-orthographies in *Zami* and *Vanity of Duluoz*," *Life Writing* 11, no. 3 (2014): 275–92.

13 Eddo-Lodge, *Why I'm No Longer Talking to White People about Race*, 231–32.

In a meme, Dr Evil from the *Austin Powers* film franchise looks quizzically to camera with this statement superimposed: "I noticed that you hate racism and openly protest against it/But you are being racist by accusing anyone who's white of being racist."[14] (Whether the substitution of "anyone" for "everyone" was deliberate or unconscious, it nonetheless highlights the racism out of which the meme originates.) The (very *personal*) instances of offense taken in the quotation above accord to these "reverse racism" lines: the first seems unabashedly racist in identifying something as racist and then bemoaning that "it wouldn't be allowed the other way round"; the second in denial, specifically of *structural* racism, in suggesting that it is not "helping the conversation," but not asking by whom this "conversation" has been set; if it's even really taking place; or why it should be a "conversation" at all, as if whether racism is valid or not is, and *should be,* up for debate.

As Eddo-Lodge simply and unequivocally puts it: "racism does not go both ways. There are unique forms of discrimination that are backed up by entitlement, assertion and, most importantly, supported by a structural power strong enough to scare you into complying with the demands of the status quo. We have to recognise this."[15] The elision of the structural in not *thinking* privilege — hallmarked in "entitlement," "assertion," and "power" — can only make the *content claim* show its disingenuousness. We arrive back at the *assumed* meritocracy (as if it is the unchallengeably societally inherent order of things), and the kind of sentiment that underwrites the memes that champion it (a meme supposedly in sympathy with Rachel Dolezal — the former president of the National Association for the Advancement

---

14 This meme and the one (of Rachel Dolezal) mentioned below are featured and discussed in Tabi, "Memes as Racialized Discourse," *Medium,* December 28, 2017, https://medium.com/digital-sociology-at-vcu/memes-as-racialized-discourse-ef73e23798d5. For another analysis of a racist meme that utilizes the idea of "reverse racism," see my "Refugees and the Racism Crisis," in EDA Collective, *Politactics: Political Conversations from Everyday Analysis* (Alresford: Zero Books, 2016), 88–92.

15 Eddo-Lodge, *Why I'm No Longer Talking to White People about Race,* 98.

of Colored People who lied about being black, and identifies as "transracial" — puts over a picture of her the words: "When you have to lie about being black/Just to get a job"). Eddo-Lodge deftly puts paid to these notions:

> The underlying assumption to all opposition to positive discrimination is that it just isn't fair play.
>
> The insistence is on merit, insinuating that any current majority white leadership in any industry has got there through hard work and no outside help, as if whiteness isn't it its own leg-up, as if it doesn't imply a familiarity that warms an interviewer to a candidate. When each of the sectors I mentioned earlier have such dire racial representations, you'd have to be fooling yourself if you really think that the homogeneous glut of middle-aged white men currently clogging the upper echelons of most professions got there purely through talent alone. We don't live in a meritocracy, and to pretend that simple hard work will elevate all to success is an exercise in wilful ignorance.[16]

What can be discerned in these supposedly meritocracy-advocating responses is the fact that content mobilizes itself to militate against its perceived accusers (non-structurally-informed content feels persecuted), which it singles out in any suggestion that form (structurally co-opted form, that is) may have had a part to play in one's success, privilege, power, attainment of private property, etc. — down to whatever last vestige can be hierarchically held onto *against* another. Its range of memic tropes — from "I'm alright, Jack" to "wan't me, guv" — want to be seen to be de-logicizing, and thereby delegitimizing, discussions that touch on race and (structural manifestations of) racism (by appearing to quarantine racism off as a purely formal prejudice that others may have, and which one's own *content* thus entirely resists ("nothing to do with me"), thus mistaking the opposite of racism as (passive) non-racism, as opposed to

---

16 Ibid., 78–79.

(active) anti-racism). But these *contented* tropes — in both the senses of relying on content and resting on laurels — are really rather purposefully evading any dialectical engagement with the issues at hand.

Structure

> *"At this point, it may be useful to try to identify some of the important characteristics and implications of a structural approach to symbolic systems and cultural forms. First, meaning does not arise in the world, it is not there waiting to be discovered. Meaning is not something which is out there in the world apart from language which language, acting simply like a mirror, reflects. The world is what it is, and societies use the instrumentality of symbolism to make certain relations in the world intelligible to them. They have to impose a system of meaning on the world. [...] Meaning and intelligibility are articulated onto the world. It is not given or already present in the world and then simply expressed or reproduced through language."*
> — Stuart Hall, *Cultural Studies 1983*[17]

Memes present an indeterminate face; their messages, if in earnest, often verge so much on the absurd that it is difficult to tell if they're irony or iron-fistedness. Indeed, with many memes, satire is in the irony of the beholder.[18] The range of responses in typical comments sections (encompassing earnestness, gullibility, failure to "get" the joke, trolling) is indicative here. Memes become, and are infinitely open to becoming, *overdetermined.* As cultural creations, in their origination they are steeped in meaning (or even attempts at anti-meaning, amongst certain

---

17 Stuart Hall, *Cultural Studies 1983: A Theoretical History* (Durham: Duke University Press, 2016), 66.

18 See Jay Owens's article above and Giacomo Bianco's below for more on how irony is marshalled, and is inherent, in relation to memes.

avant-gardists), but — to use Stuart Hall's words above — meaning and intelligibility are also articulated *onto* memes.

Hall outlines in a series of lectures newly collected as *Cultural Studies 1983* some vital lessons about capitalism, hegemony, and (prefiguring to some extent Kimberlé Crenshaw's intersectionality) the crossovers between different struggles: gender, race, class. Fundamentally, culture is presented by Hall as operating on the plane of *articulation*:

> The relationship between social forces and ideology is absolutely dialectical[.] It is the articulation, the nonnecessary link between a social force which is making itself and the ideology or conceptions of the world which make intelligible the process they are going through, which begins to bring onto the historical stage a new social position and political position, a new set of social and political subjects.[19]

In the Internet age, the memic field is one on which the process of articulation plays out. Capitalism is a complex structural and structuring system that, like the meme itself, thrives on its indeterminacy, as it does on its crises.[20] That is to say, the less it can be made sense of, the more mystically essential and necessitous it can seem. Plenty of pro-capitalist or anti-socialist reaction memes will sarcastically juxtapose pictures of unidentified Western suburban streets with those of (equally unidentified) rundown "foreign" slums, presented in a sort of "no-brainer-between-these-alternatives" manner, without any questioning of, e.g., population demographics; whether comparable streets and areas exist vice versa, and in what proximity to each other; where — if that's the case — has greater inequality or larger di-

---

19 Hall, *Cultural Studies 1983*, 145–46.

20 The structure of capitalism is a *sublime* force, incalculable (it demands so many different sets of sums, so variegated an array of economic *approaches* to the very idea of doing the maths, in its current metastases) in its massiveness. Often it is whimsicality that is the only thing that can look in the face of the sublime, hence…Cats Against Capitalism (and similar Facebook groups, Twitter feeds, memes, etc.).

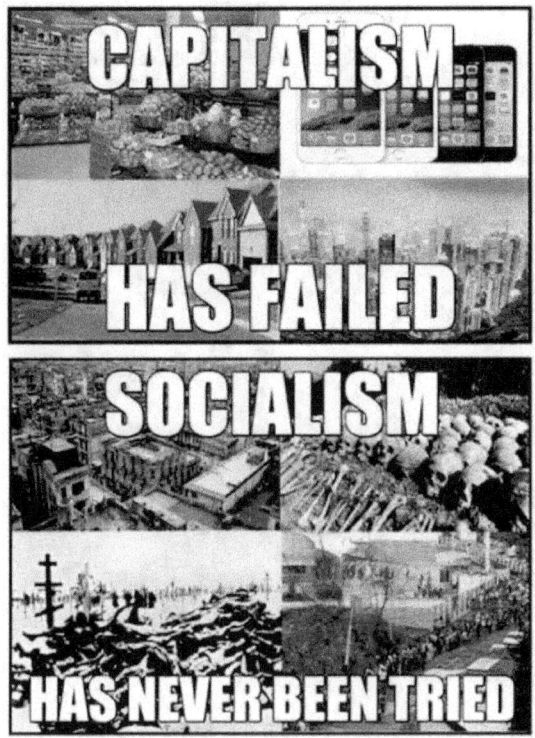

Fig. 4. Source: Sizzle. See https://onsizzle.com/i/capitalism-do-has-failed-socialism-hasnever-been-tried-~spaulding-1060226.

vides between rich and poor, and what sections of society might be affected by these divides (racially, in terms of gender, etc.); whether what we see on the "non-capitalist" side is in fact an effect of global(ized) capitalism; whether there's an amount of glee taken in the implicit conclusion that the pro-capitalist memer (and their intended audience) belongs to the suburban and not the slum scene, and if this is indicative of class prejudice, etc. (figs. 4, 5). As both Foster and Eddo-Lodge delineate in their books, while there are important differences in respective intersectional struggles that must be respected, capitalism is a structuring force that more often than not doesn't respect these, and

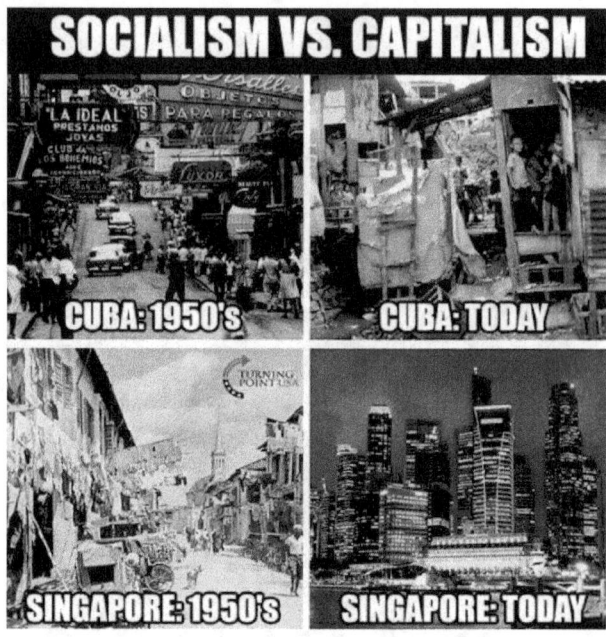

Fig. 5. Source: Ballmemes. See https://ballmemes.com/i/socialism-vs-capitalism-la-ideal-s-para-regalos-prestamos-joyas-20705320.

which can separate society along not only class lines, but within these, further along gender and race lines (Foster: "women have been disproportionately affected by austerity, with single mothers and pensioners particularly affected"; Eddo-Lodge: "in the wake of the 2015 summer budget, analysis from race equality think tank the Runnymede Trust found that 4 million black and minority ethnic people would be worse off as a result of it, that BME people were over-represented in areas hit by the budget, and that race inequality will worsen over time because of it").[21]

---

21 See Foster, *Lean Out,* 20 (her data is taken from Tracy McVeigh, "Spending Cuts Hit Women Worse, Says Report," *The Guardian,* September 21, 2013, https://www.theguardian.com/society/2013/sep/21/spending-cuts-women-report, and the Women's Budget Group report), and Eddo-Lodge, *Why I'm No Longer Talking to White People about Race,* 192.

Hall identifies "an interdiscursive field generated by at least three different contradictions (class, race, gender), each of which has a different history; a different mode of operation; each divides and classifies the world in different ways."[22] In memes we see concretised ways in which the world gets cut up into elements of its ideological representation; snapshots of thought within the conjunctural articulation; "ways in which class, race, and gender are articulated with one another to establish particular condensed social positions[, which are] by definition overdetermined."[23] It is on the plane of articulation that their overdetermination is hegemonically fought over. As Hall states: "the domain of culture and ideology is where those new positions are opened and where the new articulations have to be made. And in that domain, people can change and struggle."[24]

Memes are bits lodged in the cultural, and are part of the stuff that makes it up. Seizing the memes of production means that

> we need to see resistance as the continual practices of working on the cultural domain and opening up cultural possibilities. [...] The conditions within which people are able to construct subjective possibilities and new political subjectivities for themselves are not simply given in the dominant system. They are won in the practices of articulation which produce them.[25]

What Hall articulates most pertinently is a properly structural analysis that favors neither form nor content in highlighting the

---

22 Hall, *Cultural Studies 1983*, 150.

23 Ibid.

24 Ibid, 190.

25 Ibid., 206. One example of the memic jostling for socially just articulation can be seen in Spike Lee's *Do the Right Thing* (1989), in Buggin Out's (Giancarlo Esposito) campaign to have black heroes featured on Sal's (Danny Aiello) Wall of Fame in his Famous Pizzeria, and in Smiley's (Roger Guenveur Smith) symbolic seizure of the wall, redistributing its representation with Martin Luther King Jr. and Malcolm X, after the uproarious events brought on by the brutal police murder of Radio Raheem (Bill Nunn).

irreducibility of difference (which sustains intersectional unity), and the politics that can arise out of such an analytic:

> It is necessary […] to acknowledge the irreducibility of one contradiction to another. Different contradictions have different effects in the social field, and it is the tendency to reduce one to the other that is the theoretical problem. For this reason, the suspension of the capitalist mode of production in a particular society will not guarantee the liberation of blacks, women, or subordinate classes.
>
> […] The only alternative is a Marxist politics which recognises the necessary differentiation of different struggles and the importance of these struggles on different fronts, that is to say, a Marxist politics which understands the nature of a hegemonic politics, in which different struggles take the leading position on a range of different fronts. Such […] rejects reductionism in favor of an understanding of complexity in unity or unity through complexity.[26]

What memes can and do teach us is that the very dialectic between form and content is structural, and in its effects is material. Thus, while — as Hall puts it, apropos of the above — "the mode of production does not command every contradiction," the mode of articulation can come to positively alter the contradictions if seized successfully.[27] In terms of the work of art(iculation) in the age of memic rhythmicality, then, we are such stuff as memes are made on, and it is in memes that one source of such articulable potential resides.

∴, *carpe meme.*

---

26 Hall, *Cultural Studies 1983*, 84–185.
27 Ibid., 185.

Bibliography

The Books. *A Dot in Time*. New York: Temporary Residence Limited, 2012.

Bristow, Daniel. "New Spellings: Auto-orthographies in *Zami* and *Vanity of Duluoz*." *Life Writing* 11, no. 3 (2014): 275–92.

EDA Collective. *Politactics: Political Conversations from Everyday Analysis*. Alresford: Zero Books, 2016.

———. "The Sinthomic Blank in Future Bass and Dubstep." In *Twerking to Turking: Everyday Analysis, Volume 2*. Alresford: Zero Books, 2015.

Eddo-Lodge, Reni. *Why I'm No Longer Talking to White People about Race*. London: Bloomsbury, 2018.

Favilli, Elena, and Francesca Cavello. *Goodnight Stories for Rebel Girls: 100 Tales of Extraordinary Women*. Venice: Timbuktu Labs, 2016.

———. *Goodnight Stories for Rebel Girls 2*. Venice: Timbuktu Labs, 2017.

Foster, Dawn. *Lean Out*. London: Repeater Books, 2016.

Hall, Stuart. *Cultural Studies 1983: A Theoretical History*. Durham and London: Duke University Press, 2016.

Kant, Immanuel. "Preface to the First Edition." In *Critique of Pure Reason,* translated and edited by Marcus Weigelt, based on the translation by Max Müller. London: Penguin Classics, 2007.

Kemp, Rob, and Paul Blow. *The Good Guys: 50 Heroes who Changed the World with Kindness*. London: Wren & Rook, 2018.

McVeigh, Tracy. "Spending Cuts Hit Women Worse, Says Report." *The Guardian,* September 21, 2013. https://www.theguardian.com/society/2013/sep/21/spending-cuts-women-report.

Nagle, Angela. *Kill All Normies: Online Culture Wars from 4chan and Tumblr to Trump and the Alt-Right*. Alresford: Zero Books, 2017.

Phillips, Mike, and Trevor Phillips. *Windrush: The Irresistible Rise of Multi-Racial Britain*. London: HarperCollins, 1998.

Sorene, Paul. "Windrush Children Only Became Visible When They Became Criminals." *Anorak,* April 17, 2018. http://www.anorak.co.uk/449047/politicians/windrush-children-only-became-visible-when-they-became-criminals.html.

Tabi. "Memes as Racialized Discourse." *Medium,* September 28, 2017. https://medium.com/digital-sociology-at-vcu/memes-as-racialized-discourse-ef73e23798d5.

7

An Emoji for René Girard: Memes, Memesis, and the Apocalypse of the Eternally Irrelevant

Eric Wilson

"Of all the sorrows which afflict mankind, the bitterest is this, that one should have consciousness of much, but control over nothing."
— Herodotus

"Men think themselves free simply because they are conscious of their actions and ignorant of the causes by which they are determined."
— Benedict de Spinoza

"I have given a name to my pain."
— Friedrich Nietzsche

"All desire is a desire for being."
— René Girard

DOI: 10.21983/P3.0255.1.08

> *"'This is my first chance to do some work*
> *that actually means something.'*
> *'Means "something" to who? You had a career, Dad, before*
> *the third comic book movie. When people began to forget*
> *who was inside that Bird costume. You're doing a play*
> *based on a book written sixty years ago for a thousand*
> *rich old white people whose only concern is where they're*
> *going to go for their cake and coffee when it's over. Nobody*
> *gives a shit but you. And...let's...face it...Dad...you*
> *are not doing this for the sake of Art, you are doing this*
> *because you want to feel relevant again. Well, guess what?*
> *There is an entire world out there where people fight to be*
> *relevant every single day and you act like it doesn't exist!*
> *Things are happening in a place that you ignore, a place*
> *that—by the way—has already forgotten about you. I*
> *mean, who the fuck are you? You hate bloggers, you mock*
> *Twitter, you don't even have a Facebook page. You're the*
> *one who doesn't exist! You're doing this because you're*
> *scared to death, like the rest of us, that you don't matter.*
> *And you know what? You're right. You don't. It's not*
> *important—okay? You're not important—get used to it...*
> *...Dad?"'*

— Michael Keaton and Emma Stone discussing the problem
of being relevant in Alejandro Gonzalez Iñárritu, dir., *Bird-
man, or (The Unexpected Virtue of Ignorance)* (2014)

❝ *Il existe à la base de la vie humaine, un principe d'insuffisance,"*
as Georges Bataille would say. Living under the aegis of social media, the central question of *Existenz* has become:
what does it mean to be "relevant"? The answer is: being relevant means Being-Model-for-Other. The underlying problem
for us is that "the disappearance of the subject [is], more or less,
the mirror image of the disappearance of the real."[1] If the real
question, as Jean Baudrillard darkly hints, has never been the

---

1   Jean Baudrillard, *Why Hasn't Everything Disappeared?*, trans. Chris Turner
     (London: Seagull Books, 2009), 26.

nature of reality but the *value* of reality, then our entire historical predicament can justifiably be denoted as the *post-human*:
the irreversible disappearance of the traditional ontological referent (the Self) into the annihilating domain of pure virtuality.
We should have seen this coming.

It is not as though we hadn't been warned. The first sign
(excluding for now those prophesized by Jacques Ellul) came
with the publication of Guy Debord's *The Society of the Spectacle* in 1967. Within the soulless heart of Debordean society
lies the detritus of the wholesale collapse of politics into mass
media, yielding us the hegemony of "spectacular power" which
is subsumed within the onto-politics of the *integrated spectacle,*
the cultural reification of media as the sole arbiter of "truth":
"the whole life of those societies in which modern conditions of
production prevail presents itself as an immense accumulation
of spectacles. All that once was directly lived has become mere
representation."[2] We call these "modern conditions of production" late capitalism, under which there has been a parallel collapse within the political economy of use value into exchange
value. For Baudrillard, Debord's very approximate successor,
the integrated spectacle has been superseded by *integral reality,* the collapse of the integrated spectacle into social media;
if the Society of the Spectacle was the sign of what we call the
post-modern, then integral reality is the sign of the successor
state of the post-human which brings in its wake its own form
of political economy, what I call post-human capitalism: the
collapse of post-use exchange value into simulation, or what
Baudrillard refers to as "The Code." "Everything within production and the economy becomes commutable, reversible and
exchangeable according to the same indeterminate specularity
as we find in politics, fashion or the media"[3] — which, although
perfectly "real" is, paradoxically, utterly "impossible" (or un-

---

2   Guy Debord, *The Society of the Spectacle,* trans. Donald Nicholson-Smith
    (New York: Zone Books, 1995), 12.
3   Jean Baudrillard, *Symbolic Exchange and Death,* trans. Ian Grant (London:
    Sage Publications, 1993), 16.

bearable), for, as Baudrillard assures us, a "world of total, instantaneous, perpetual communication is unthinkable and, in any case, intolerable."[4] Which nonetheless happens to be exactly where we now find ourselves. Unknowingly, we, as the denizens of integral reality, are fundamentalists of a sort, the devotees of the "only true fundamentalism," which, "giving rise to the only true terror, is the fundamentalism of a fluid, mobile technocracy, the technocracy of flows and networks, of an inexorable dissemination and mental diaspora: *a fundamentalism without foundations*."[5] We are fanatical in our commitment to the evacuation of the grounds of our being and by our fruits (signs?) the world shall know us:

— The despair of having everything
— The despair of being nothing
— The despair of being everybody
— The despair of being nobody[6]

The orthodox left, both political and cultural, hates, and therefore fears, simulation[7] — "the precession of models and images,[8] the stratagem that erases the boundaries between the true and the false" — precisely because it constitutes a particularly decadent form of inauthenticity, a "flight" from the (allegedly) natural, but in fact unbearably integral world."[9] The continuing fascination with the neo-Foucauldian model of the panoptical surveillance state (the-one-who-sees-everything) is nothing more than nostalgia, reflecting the longing for an enemy that can be identi-

---

4   Jean Baudrillard, *The Agony of Power,* trans. Ames Hodges (Los Angeles: Semiotext(e), 2010), 45.

5   Jean Baudrillard, *Carnival and Cannibal,* trans. Chris Turner (London: Seagull Books, 2010), 48. Emphasis in the original.

6   Baudrillard, *The Agony of Power,* 87.

7   See Jean Baudrillard, *The Divine Left: A Chronicle of the Years 1977–1984,* trans. David L. Sweet (Los Angeles: Semiotext(e), 2014), generally.

8   For René Girard, the two are identical. See Jean-Michel Oughourlian, *The Mimetic Brain,* trans. Trevor Cribben Merrill (East Lansing: Michigan State University Press, 2016), 68, and below.

9   Baudrillard, *Carnival and Cannibal,* 87–88.

fied and fought against — the restoration of "authentic" reality (and the reality principle) in the face of an alien domination (it also goes without saying that the One who sees everything can also be *blamed* for everything — a universal scapegoat. More on that below.) The hegemony of "The Code" however — the sum total of that absence of autonomy that *is* our "every-thing" — reduces this lingering leftist pseudo-theological piety to post-metaphysical hash: "the real itself is still what it is, but there is no longer any sense in thinking it, or in reflecting on it, as such."[10] The political catastrophe here is that domination (control) has been replaced by hegemony ("The Code") rendering all forms of social critique obsolete through the voiding of the master referent of authenticity: "contemporary hegemony [...] relies on a symbolic liquidation of every possible value. The terms 'simulacrum,' 'simulation' and 'virtual' summarize this liquidation, in which every signification is eliminated in its own sign, and the profusion of signs parodies a by now unobtainable reality."[11] We are left, in "truth," with nothing other than the continuous and high-speed circulation of models and images — which prove to be horrifyingly reversible. Even worse — the universal and immediate circulation of the model is the only means left to us of validating the reality of the self; that is, of being "relevant."

But in truth none of this is new. We have all been here before. We have simply chosen to forget that the post-human is directly pre-figured within the *pre-human*.

When I teach my introductory course on Law, Literature, and Cinema, I offer my students the extra bonus, at no additional cost, of learning from me the secret(s) of literature.[12] Working

---

10 Baudrillard, *The Divine Left*, 42.
11 Baudrillard, *The Agony of Power*, 35.
12 The most brilliant exposition of this that I know of is Tom McCarthy's appropriately titled *Tintin and the Secret of Literature* (London: Counterpoint, 2008). This section is a re-working of my earlier discussions in Eric Wilson, "Warring Sovereigns and Mimetic Rivals: On Scapegoats and Political Crisis in William Golding's *Lord of the Flies*," *Law and Humanities* 8, no. 2 (2014): 147–73; Eric Wilson, "The Ballad of Ed and Lewis: Conflictual Mimesis and the Revocation of the Social Contract in James Dickey's *Deliverance*," *Law and Humanities* 10, no. 1 (2016): 115–60.

on the defensible premise that literature is any written work that instils a specifically aesthetic, or literary, response within the reader, I identify at least three of literature's secrets (although I am certain that there are more than just three). Somewhat to my surprise, I came to understand that all of the three secrets were central to the literary scholarship of René Girard (1923–2015). The first secret is that literature is subversive; to paraphrase Jim Thompson, the first rule of writing is that nothing is what it seems. In Girardian terms, subversiveness is not a question of mis-perception; at issue is the nature of "commonsense" re-ality as a *myth* which is (etymologically) a "lie" that causes to remain hidden a truth that is unspeakable but capable of ex-plaining everything — literature-as-subversion, -as-revelation. The second secret is that subversiveness of literature lies with the centrality of doubles to the narrative drama. The double may signify either the external (exoteric) relationship between the protagonist ("the self") and one or more of the other characters (e.g., Joseph Conrad, *Heart of Darkness*; *The Secret Sharer*) or the internal (esoteric) relationship among the contending parts of the sub-divided, or "split" personality of the protagonist (e.g., Fyodor Dostoevsky, *Notes from the Underground*; *The Brothers Karamazov*). Here, literature is reflecting the social conscious-ness of early hominids:

> Our hypothesis makes it logical to imagine that the rigor-ous symmetry between the mimetic partners[,] the living obstacle[13] of the model that is automatically transformed into a rival[,] must bring about two things among man's ances-

---

13 Girard uses the word "obstacle" in two different senses: (i) as shorthand for the *external mediator,* the person or thing that acts as a circuit-breaker of escalating mimetic rivalry; and (ii) the pathologized version (a "mimetic paroxysm") of an "ordinary" mimetic rivalry contaminated by *metaphysical desire,* in which mimetic rivalry "increases to the point that the subject is no longer interested in anything but the rivalry itself" — which is psychosis. See Jean-Michel Oughourlian, *The Genesis of Desire,* trans. Eugene Webb (East Lansing: Michigan State University Press, 2010), 12, and below. Both senses will be used in this essay.

tors, little by little: the ability to look at the other person, the mimetic *double,* as an *alter ego* and the matching capacity to establish a *double* inside oneself, through processes like reflection and consciousness.[14]

The third secret is that the plot, or drama, of the novel is driven by an escalating rivalry over mimetic desire that eventually explodes into full-scale mimetic conflict. For Girard, the archetypal plot of all literature is that the self (protagonist) will model its relationship to the other (double) on the basis of imitation (mimetic rivalry) that will narratively culminate in the self attempting to either replace and/or destroy the double (mimetic conflict):

> Rivalry does not arise because of the fortuitous convergence of two desires on a single object; rather, *the subject desires the object because the rival desires it.* In desiring an object the rival alerts the subject to the desirability of the object. The rival, then, serves as the model for the subject, not only in regard to such secondary matters as style and opinions but also, and more essentially, in regard to desires.[15]

The rivalry that mimetic desire unleashes will, in the end, assume the most extreme and grotesque form of the violent, or "monstrous" doubles who are the signifiers of the crisis of undifferentiation: as the rivals intensify their mimetic struggle they effectively become identical, triggering a pathological crisis of identity which can only be resolved through an act of extreme violence, whether physical, emotional, or symbolic.[16] Utilizing

---

14 René Girard, *Things Hidden Since the Foundation of the World,* research undertaken in collaboration with Jean-Michel Oughourlian and Guy Lefort, trans. Stephen Bann and Michael Metteer (New York: Continuum, 1978), 284, 285. Emphases in the original.

15 René Girard, *Violence and the Sacred,* trans. Patrick Gregory (Baltimore: Johns Hopkins University Press, 1977), 145.

16 See ibid., 143–68. "Violence is the process itself when two or more partners try to prevent one another from appropriating the object they all desire

a series of anthropological assumptions, Girard speculates that the logic of social formation is exchangeable with the logic of literary narrative.[17] As mimetic rivalries are to be proscribed because of their ultimately violent consequences, the mimetic rivals must displace, or discharge, their common violence against a convenient surrogate victim that serves as the transference object of the violence — the scapegoat.[18] Girard explains the "magical" efficacy of the scapegoat by identifying two variants of mimetic desire: divisive acquisitive mimesis, which leads two or more individuals to desire the exact same object at the same moment in time, and unifying conflictual mimesis, which induces all of the parties to the conflict to settle upon a common rivalry, or enemy, whom they all wish to "strike down."[19] Historically, the ritualistic enshrinement of the scapegoat, or sacrificial, mechanism was the domain of religion, which is anthropologically grounded upon the intermediary of the surrogate victim — the one who must die so that the community may live by being spared the apocalypse of the unlimited conflict of the monstrous doubles:[20]

To understand human culture it is necessary to concede that only the damming of mimetic forces by means of the prohibition and the diversion of those forces in the direction of

---

through physical or other means." René Girard, cited in Vittorio Gallese, "The Two Sides of Mimesis: Mimetic Theory, Embodied Simulation, and Social Identification," in *Mimesis and Science: Empirical Research on Imitation and the Mimetic Theory of Culture and Religion,* ed. Scott R. Garrels (East Lansing: Michigan State University Press, 2011), 88.

17 See Oughourlian, *The Mimetic Brain,* 3–31; Oughourlian, *The Genesis of Desire,* 81–106.

18 See Girard, *Things Hidden Since the Foundation of the World,* 93. The preferred term of evolutionary psychologists is "emissary victim." The concept is identical. See Zoey Reeve, "Mechanisms of Internal Cohesion: Scapegoating and Parochial Altruism," in *How We Became Human: Mimetic Theory and the Science of Evolutionary Origins,* eds. Pierpaolo Antonello and Paul Gifford (East Lansing: Michigan State University Press, 2015), 161–86.

19 See Girard, *Things Hidden Since the Foundation of the World,* 26.

20 See ibid., 48.

ritual are capable of spreading and perpetuating the recon-
ciliatory effect of the surrogate victim. Religion is nothing
other than this immense effort to keep the peace. *The sacred
is violence,* but if religious man worships violence it is only
insofar as the worship of violence is supposed to bring peace;
religion is entirely concerned with peace, but the means it
has of bringing it about are never free of sacrificial violence.[21]

In other words, hominization is the by-product of the scapegoat
mechanism.[22] Against Freud, we did not invent civilization in
order to prevent murder — rather, we invented civilization in
order to create the pre-conditions for a *certain kind* of murder:
the sacrificial killing that postpones the apocalypse of unlimited mimetic rivalry, the ritualistic slaying that guarantees the
victory of conflictual mimesis over acquisitive mimesis. Girard's
thesis is not a theory of religion but a theory of the genesis of
civilization that is grounded upon ritualistic human sacrifice
(or, even more subversively, the ritualistic sacrifice of "the human"); as Jean-Michel Oughourlian has observed, Girard's
"theory of religion is simply a particularly noteworthy aspect of
a fundamental theory of mimetic relations,"[23] for it is in primitive societies that "the mimetic crisis culminates in a phase of
unbearable un-differentiation that is resolved by the violence of
the sacrifice,"[24] and it is religious thought that led early human-

---

21 Ibid., 32. For the integrative function of Religion, see Oliver Dietrich
    et al., "The Role of Cult and Feasting in the Emergence of Neolithic
    Communities: New Evidence from Gobekli Tepe, South-Eastern Turkey,"
    Antiquity 86 (2012): 674–95, passim.

22 "All systems that give structure to human society have been generated
    from [the scapegoat mechanism]: language, kinship systems, taboos,
    codes of etiquette, patterns of exchange, rites, and civil institutions. Thus
    a theory of sacrifice has produced a comprehensive account of human
    social formation, religion, and culture." See Burton Mack, "Introduction:
    Religion and Ritual," in *Violent Origins: Walter Burkert, René Girard, and
    Jonathan Z. Smith on Ritual Killing and Cultural Formation,* ed. Robert G.
    Hammerton-Kelly (Stanford: Stanford University Press, 1987), 7.

23 Jean-Michel Oughourlian, cited in Girard, *Things Hidden Since the
    Foundation of the World,* 44.

24 Michel Treguer, cited in ibid., 68.

kind to "make the victim the vehicle and transforming agent of something sacred—mimesis—which is never conflictual or undifferentiated except in so far as it is spread throughout the community; its concentration in a victim makes it a pacifying and regulating force, the positive mimesis found in ritual."[25] But this same process audaciously "doubles" as Girard's theory of literature: every literary depiction of human drama, which is always a form of social phenomena, is ultimately about envy.[26] As for both Georges Bataille and Jean-Paul Sartre, the essence of the human dilemma is the absence of an essential self—anthropological *non-being*. "The human subject does not really know what to desire, in the last resort"; thus, the human subject "desires *being*, something he himself lacks and which some other person [the 'model'] seems to possess. The subject thus looks to that other person to inform him of what he should desire in order to acquire that being."[27] The entirety of human desire, the libidinal dimension of man's social existence, is subsumed under mimesis — "desire itself is essentially mimetic, directed toward an object desired by the model," from which comes rivalry, "the mimetic nature of conflict, which is to say the ultimate absence of any object proper to it."[28] Rivalry, therefore, is the flipside of the crisis of un-differentiation, that potentially boundless state of existential anguish in which no one is anything in particular because all inhabit the universal space of absent identity, a hellish crisis of the collective of the loss of personal differences that triggers an avalanche of reciprocal and escalating violence; "sameness is the terrible war in which twins [or 'monstrous doubles'] are personally engaged, right up until the moment when one manages to kill the other [...] When it spreads it becomes

---

25 Ibid., 48.

26 See René Girard, *Desire, Deceit and the Novel: Self and Other in Literary Structure*, trans. Yvonne Freccero (Baltimore: The Johns Hopkins University Press, 1976).

27 Girard, *Things Hidden Since the Foundation of the World*, 343; Girard, *Violence and the Sacred*, 146.

28 Girard, *Things Hidden Since the Foundation of the World*, 31; Girard, *Violence and the Sacred*, 146.

the famous war of all against all of which Hobbes spoke."[29] The un-differentiated are devoid of relevance and the sameness of this un-differentiation reduces society to the zero condition of chaos — a "virtual" apocalypse.

Hence, Girard's radically anti-secularist proposition that religion is the true foundation of society.[30] Much of Girard's work constitutes a highly unorthodox form of legal anthropology, a hybridization of both Durkheim's functionalist sociology of religion and Freud's cultural criticism, primarily *Totem and Taboo*. The key marker demarcating the boundary between the modern and the pre-modern is a judicial one: the substitution (or not) of a reified and de-personalized rule of law that denies the catharsis of a direct and spontaneous communitarian will-to revenge:

> [I]f we compare societies that adhere to a judicial system with societies that practice sacrificial rites, the difference between the two is such that we can indeed consider the absence or presence of these [judicial] institutions as a basis for distinguishing primitive societies from "civilized" ones.[31]

The foundational, but thoroughly repressed, continuity between the archaic and the post-archaic is a classic trope of Freudian psychoanalysis. Yet, Girard largely eschews the Freudian theory of instinct, or drive (*Trieb*), finding greater utility in the application of psychoanalysis to the collective (impersonal) dynamics of cultural formation; in effect, the translation of Freud's late metapsychology into the referential terms of Durkheim's notion of function: "the purpose of the sacrifice is to restore harmony to the community, to reinforce the social fabric. Everything else derives from that."[32] For Girard, the "fundamental truth about violence" is that, "if left unappeased, violence will accumulate

29 René Girard, *The One by Whom Scandal Comes*, trans. M.B. DeBoise (East Lansing: Michigan State University Press, 2014), 104–5.
30 See Girard, *Violence and the Sacred*, generally. See also Michael Kirwan, *Discovering Girard* (Chicago: Cowley Publications, 2005), esp. 43–50.
31 Girard, *Violence and the Sacred*, 8–19.
32 Ibid., 8.

until it overflows its confines and floods the surrounding area. The role of sacrifice is to stem this rising tide of indiscriminate substitutions and redirect violence into 'proper' channels."[33] Key to the success of the sacrificial mechanism is its status as ritual, which is invariably a "re-enactment of a 'prior event.'"[34] Since every ritual is a re-enactment, its governing logic is mimesis, the ritual is both a representation of and a substitution for an earlier crisis of violence. But this governing logic is anti-representational: under the sign of substitution, all differences are abolished and any one thing can be traded for and replaced with any other thing.[35] In Girard's case the vital ritualistic dimension of the sacrificial mechanism is the mimetic evocation of an earlier act of killing that was successful in resolving social crisis:

> [T]he sacrificers [...] are striving to produce a replica, as faithful as possible in every detail, of a previous crisis that was resolved by means of a spontaneously unanimous victimization. All the dangers, real and imaginary, that threaten the community are subsumed in the most terrible danger that can confront a society: the sacrificial crisis. The rite is therefore a repetition of the original, spontaneous 'lynching' that restored order in the community by reestablishing, around the figure of the surrogate victim [the scapegoat], that sentiment of social accord that had been destroyed in the onslaught of reciprocal violence [...]. In the scapegoat theme we should recognize the very real metamorphosis of reciprocal violence into restraining through the agency of unanimity.[36]

---

33 Ibid., 10.

34 See Mack, "Introduction: Religion and Ritual," 8.

35 According to Girard, "it is not possible to resolve the problem of violence with the surrogate victim without at the same time elaborating a theory of the sign and signification." See Girard, *Things Hidden Since the Foundation of the World*, 99.

36 Girard, *Violence and the Sacred*, 94–95, 96.

Every ritual bears the traces of a double movement: the re-invo-
cation of the past event and the projection of that earlier event's
cathartic effect into future time. The "prior event" that all ritual
killings represent through mimetic substitution is a collective
murder, an act of mob violence. "'Sacrifice' then becomes a term
that can be used to refer to the complex phenomenon of the collective killing of a human victim, its mythic rationalization, and
its ritualization."[37] The necessary precondition for the historical survival of the community is the successful exorcism of the
unclean spirit of revenge. This is secured through the periodic
enactment of the rituals of the machinery of sacrifice, which is
itself the mimetic repetition of an earlier killing of a designated
victim (the scapegoat) which successfully broke the cycle of re-
tributive violence.

To summarize: the pre-human (the hominid) became the
human (in hominization) by re-directing the violence un-
leashed by mimetic conflict — a war of all against all over models — against a sacrificial victim who was the reified substitute of
an original that is now absent.

Sounds great — but is it "true"?

Oughourlian, a psychoanalyst and a self-proclaimed devo-
tee of Girard, has done the most to translate Girardian theory
into the terms of meta-psychology; the result is *interdividual
psychology*, a post-Freudian innovation that owes as much to
Marcel Proust as it does Girard. To summarize: mimetic rivalry
"is always rooted in one of the two following claims: the claim
of the self for the ownership of its own desire; and the claim of
desire for its anteriority, its seniority over the other's desire, the
other desire that has generated it, on which it is modelled."[38] The
failure of either claim reduces the self to no-one; in truth, we are

---

37 Mack, "Introduction: Religion and Ritual," 8.

38 Jean-Michel Oughourlian, "Desire Is Mimetic: A Clinical Approach,"
    Contagion: Journal of Violence, Mimesis, and Culture 3 (1996): 43–49, at
    43. "The desire that constitutes the self is itself modelled on, copied from,
    inspired by, and communicated by the other. It is the other's desire that
    causes the desire to appear that will engender the self." See Oughourlian,
    The Genesis of Desire, 98.

all "legion." Crucial is the temporal dimension of mimesis: mimetic rivalry, in both its latent and manifest form, is embedded within the structural parameters of psychological time, which is incommensurable with linear (non-reversible) physical time. In Oughourlian's notation, conflict follows a strict pattern of migration from two nodal points, N and N':

> The constitution of the self in physical time can be summed up by a linear vector going from the past toward the future. Desire D [the model] mimetically elicits the birth of desire d [the subject], which, in turn, brings self s [the 'habitual self'; *habitus*] into existence. Such is the real sequence of events that unfold in physical time going from the past to the future. But this sequence has no meaning on the psychological level, for it unfolds completely without the knowledge of all the protagonists.[39]

The signature feature of nodal point N is "the self's claim to the ownership of its desires" — which is, of course, an illusion:[40]

> The self, at point N, in the most banal and normal case, cannot survive unless it is persuaded that it is the owner of its desire. The simplest solution for the self consists in forgetting the otherness of the desire that constituted it and in considering that this desire truly belongs to it. In reality, it is not a matter of mere forgetting because if one forgets something, this implies that one once knew it. It is in fact a matter of active mis-recognition, though at this stage remaining peaceful and non-adversarial.[41]

---

39 Oughourlian, *The Mimetic Brain*, 39.

40 Ibid., 38. "Consciousness, like the self, is a function of the relation to otherness. The self as such is a mythic notion." See Jean-Michel Oughourlian, *The Puppet of Desire: The Psychology of Hysteria, Possession, and Hypnosis,* trans. Eugene Webb (Stanford: Stanford University Press, 1991), 198.

41 Oughourlian, *The Mimetic Brain*, 39.

Amnesia is our truth. "Forgetting preserves harmony in the self and keeps it in existence [...]. Forgetting presides over the constitution of the self at the moment of its creation"; the new self s is always "built on the overlooking of the otherness of desire."[42] In a perfect inversion of Sartre, it is not the case that man is condemned to be free — it is ten times worse than that. Man is condemned to eternally "forget" (mis-recognize) that he is a slave (unconditionally un-free) precisely because the phenomenological basis of his sense of Being — his Self — is the by-product of a set of processes, psychical and social, which are intrinsically mimetic in nature. [43] "This otherness with which we are saturated and that constitutes us is the human condition; but it is very difficult to accept. Its mis-recognition is initial and necessary to the maintenance of the self in its existence."[44] Paradoxically, to the extent that we are real (or relevant) we are false, not truly of ourselves — which takes us directly into the domain of Saint Augustine and the true meaning of "original sin"; that we are depraved not because we are positively evil but because we are unable to (self-)author the good. And, just to turn the screw one more time, the logic of mimetic relationships must *necessarily* lead to mimetic conflict — or violence, physical and/or symbolic. "What is the clinical expression of mimetic desire? *Rivalry.* What I see every day in my practice is not mimicking, nor copying, nor learning; it is rivalry."[45] Why? When viewed in

---

42 See Ibid., 74, 76.

43 For "mimesis to function in the constitution of the self in desire, it is essential that the desire gradually forget its mimetic origin, forget even as it comes from the other [Desire *D*] that it belongs to the other, in order, precisely, to feel itself autonomous, to exist as such, to constitute a self. Desire, as Hegel said, *negates* the desire of the other." Oughourlian, *The Puppet of Desire*, 232–33.

44 Oughourlian, *The Mimetic Brain*, 45. Oughourlian follows Girard in illustrating *N* with the Teacher/Pupil relation; I would replace this with the Celebrity/Nobody. "While the model becomes circumfused with divine light, his follower sees himself relegated to the shadows, a mediocrity, abandoned and non-existent" — that is, a Nobody. We might call this "The Day of the Locust" syndrome.

45 Oughourlian, "Desire Is Mimetic," 43.

meta-psychological terms, the relationship between model and subject is fraught with peril. Firstly, just as with language, desire is never private or personal, it is always public and collective: both language and desire partake, in equal degree, in "otherness."[46] The mis-named "self" is, in truth, the "collective self of a collective desire, which is to say of a purely mimetic, contagious, irresistibly attractive, violent, labile desire; plural somnambulism [...] [a] merging of desires, mimetic hypertrophying, dissolution of each person's self—such is the crowd."[47] (Here we are not far from a wholly phenomenological rendition of Marx's fetish of the commodity). Secondly, the model actively "wishes to be copied" for a model with no imitators fails to qualify as a "model" (just as the master "needs" slaves); for the hierarchically subordinate subject, "identifying with a model is consolation for not possessing all his or her belongings, since one [thereby] *becomes* that model."[48] But then so does everyone else — "imitative desire is always a desire to be Another" — which is both intolerable and unsustainable, rendering every social relation inherently unstable.[49] Compounding that toxic brew which is community is our own private "hermeneutic of suspicion": at all times we are dimly aware that the model, vampire-like, establishes her relevance through the semi-voluntary alienation of our own — "the imitator often [...] envies the model because the model is [...] seeing his [the model's] role as a possession to be jealously guarded."[50] In other words, the Girardian constant of inter-individual relations is an *a-symmetrical reciprocity* with the result that the subject "is torn between two opposite feelings toward his model — the most submissive reverence and the

---

46 See Oughourlian, *The Genesis of Desire,* 14. The other of this other-ness is nothing other than the archaic victim: "human consciousness takes shape as attention is fixed on the other and particularly that special Other who is the scape-goat victim, the fountainhead of all signifiers, the transcendental signifier." Oughourlian, *The Puppet of Desire,* 39.

47 Oughourlian, *The Mimetic Brain,* 75.

48 Ibid., 47.

49 Girard, *Desire, Deceit and the Novel,* 83.

50 Giuseppe Fornari, *A God Torn to Pieces: The Nietzsche Case,* trans. Keith Buck (East Lansing: Michigan State University Press, 2013), 38.

most intense malice. This is the passion we call *hatred* [...]. Only someone who prevents us from satisfying a desire that he himself has inspired in us is truly an object of hatred."[51]

The raw core of interdividual psychology is phenomenology[52] ("it is desire that gradually brings the self into existence by constituting it as a *self-of-desire*"[53]) and the critical factor is the subject's varying experiences of the incompatible modalities of Time: the irreparable dis-junction between the psychological time of forgetting and the physical time of "irrelevance," for it is within psychological time that "self *s* declares itself the bearer and owner of desire *d* at nodal point *N* and desire d is [only later] scandalized to discover a desire *D* identical to itself and bearing on the same object, whose belatedness it will assert at nodal point *N'*."[54] (Note how this temporal dis-junction replicates perfectly the quantum-like temporality of the Internet, which is global instantaneity.[55]) Conversely, nodal point *N'*, "representing the self's claim to anteriority over the other's desire, which was responsible for inspiring and generating it" is the spawning ground of both neurosis and psychosis, which for Oughourlian are quintessentially mimetic in nature.[56] "At nodal point *N'* [...] desire *d* will assert its anteriority [coming earlier in time] with respect to desire *D*. Such that self *s*, which

---

51 Girard, *Desire, Deceit and the Novel*, 10–11. Naturally, this mimetic a-symmetry of relevance reflects an ontological a-symmetry: the model (desire *D*) is more "real," more replete with Being, in a manner in which self *s* (desire *d*) never is.

52 See Oughourlian, *The Puppet of Desire*.

53 Oughourlian, *The Genesis of Desire*, 98. This might be re-phrased as: "I desire; therefore, I AM [THAT AM]." The vital nexus of mimesis with psychosis lies with metaphysical desire; see above, n. 13. "The focus [of metaphysical rivalry] becomes the business itself of the rivalry and antagonism between individuals vying for the unlimited good of more-potent-being or identity." Reeve, "Mechanisms of Internal Cohesion," 163.

54 Oughourlian, *The Mimetic Brain*, 39.

55 Somewhat unhelpfully, Oughourlian writes: "it seems to me that memory [...] obeys the laws of quantum physics." See ibid., 41. He would perhaps have been more convincing if he had said that memory obeys the laws of Proustian narrative.

56 Ibid., 38.

is in [physical] reality the self-of-desire *d,* will lay claim loud and clear to the possession of the object of the two desires *d* and *D*."[57] In the final analysis, our mimetic *"illness of desire"*[58] is not orientated towards "power" (*pace* Nietzsche) but towards Being ("psychological subjectivity"[59]) along with its necessary attribute, autonomy ("self-grounding"). The neurotic/psychotic root of mimetic crisis, the ultimate ground of mimetic rivalry and violence, is the subjective awareness of self s that it is phenomenologically "un-real," that it does not really exist.[60] Clinically, this uncannily resembles the classic definition of (what used to be known as) *hysteria* and which presents us with an unsolvable double-bind.[61] Without exception, self s is alienated within psychological time: "the whole psychological sequence will constitute a new time—psychological time, the time of memory, the only time that has any meaning for the subjectivity of human beings, the only one that appears true and in accord with

---

57 Ibid., 39–40. See also ibid., 107: "all normal, neurotic, and psychotic phenomena exist in a continuum due to the gradual exacerbation of the mimetic mechanism [...] Neurotic phenomena are essentially due to a claim at nodal point *N* and psychotic phenomena to a claim at nodal point *N'*, the two claims always being present."

58 Oughourlian, *The Genesis of Desire,* 104.

59 Ibid., 101.

60 "If one accepts the hypothesis of mimetic desire, it becomes clear that we must abandon the idea that the self is the source of desire. Rather, it is the movement of desire that gradually engenders in a subject a dynamic structure that is both changing and persisting and that can be designated as the 'self'." Ibid., 98. And, because of the intolerable nature of its phenomenological "prison" self *s* will have to rebel in order to establish the truthfulness of its sense of "being a being": "self-individuation is a process originating from the necessity of disentangling the Self from the [Otherness] dimension in which it is originally and constitutively embedded." Gallese, "The Two Sides of Mimesis," 102.

61 "When the classical [19th-century] studies of hysteria said that the hysteric 'suffers from memories,' it was only the plural that was incorrect: it is a single, unique memory, always the same one essentially—the memory that brings back to the subject an awareness of the otherness of 'his own' desire" — or lack of relevance. See Oughourlian, *The Genesis of Desire,* 108.

reality."[62] Psychological time, within the unstable dynamics of mimetic relationships, operates as a kind of mystification:

> The physical time has no psychological reality although it is accessible to intelligence and therefore cognitive reality, but only when the first step toward wisdom is taken, that first step being the questioning or the recognition or the beginning of the recognition of the precedence [in physical time] of the other's desire, its priority over my desire, and therefore the non-ownership of "my" desire.[63]

But to attain this wisdom the first thing that self s must do is to admit her total and complete irrelevance — which is tantamount to committing phenomenological "suicide."[64] A no-thing cannot become a some-thing by renouncing its nothingness which is its being. Or, as the saying goes: Everybody wants to go to Heaven, but nobody wants to die.[65] Hence:

> Rivalry is recurrent, it repeats itself. The repetition syndrome identified by psycho-analysis is mimetic for two reasons: 1) because it is always the clinical expression of a rivalry and that rivalry is always mimetic; 2) because it reproduces itself,

---

62 Oughourlian, *The Mimetic Brain,* 40.

63 Ibid. Again, note the family resemblance to hysteria: "hysteria is one particular mode of [the] misunderstanding of interindividual relation and of the mimetic nature of desire." Oughourlian, *The Genesis of Desire,* 109. For Oughourlian, hysteria is not an illness: rather "it is a particular form of misunderstanding of the interindividual relation, a certain type of reaction to mimetic conflict. It is a phenomenologically varied manifestation of a certain dialectic of desire, a multiform expression of desire's pretension to its own priority and anteriority." Oughourlian, *The Puppet of Desire,* 183.

64 Self-awareness of our mimetic condition "requires us to re-think in the most fundamental way the notions of the subject and of desire and, despite all our shared beliefs, to renounce the glorious but mythic autonomy with which we have adorned humanity—to renounce, too, the pleasure we experience through being the playthings of those hidden mechanisms." Ibid. 20.

65 "The vanishing of self *s,* the 'habitual self,' is equivalent to a 'ritual death.'" Oughourlian, *The Mimetic Brain,* 196.

duplicates itself, imitating the circumstances of the first rivalry and always looking for an impossible victory. That victory is impossible, since it stems from a situation which mimics the circumstances of defeat. But those circumstances are the only ones of interest, since the only battle worth winning is the one that has every chance to be lost.[66]

Sisyphus had it easy. We have it much worse, as there are no gods to impose the limit of the absolute upon us and to maintain the "natural" relationship between Self and model. The fatal logic of substitution condemns us to eternal frustration.

But it was not always so. Girard argues that, historically, there are two ways to mediate mimetic rivalry: external and internal. Historically, external mediation corresponds to class-based societies; as Wolfgang Palaver explains, "as long as social difference or any other form of differentiation is present to channel mimetic desire, its conflictual dimension remains contained."[67] When external mediation prevails, the model can operate as an effective *obstacle* to the proliferating mimetic desires of the subject by precluding the possibility of true rivalry — a serf can never be "like" a knight (that is, Don Quixote can imitate the model of Amadis of Gaul, but not Sancho Panza[68]). Internal mediation,

---

66 Oughourlian, "Desire Is Mimetic," 43.

67 Wolfgang Palaver, *René Girard's Mimetic Theory,* trans. Gabriel Borrud (East Lansing: Michigan State University Press, 2013), 59.

68 Similarly, Quixote can never enter into mimetic *rivalry* with Amadis (as opposed to mere imitation) because the latter's insurmountable status as the "ideal" enables "him" to act as an external mediator: Amadis is the supreme "real" although he is totally un-real. See Oughourlian, *The Genesis of Desire,* 20–21. Cervantes brilliantly demonstrates that the affective power of the mediator stands in an *inverted* relationship to his ontological status — the less real it is *as* the "Ideal" the more powerful he becomes. What Cervantes presents us with is a double-edged Girardian practical joke: in a manner that prefigures the *drama* of the enactment of his dis-order (the "quest"), Quixote's original error lies in his mis-taking (or, even better, *re-naming*) the false for the real: he "reads" (interprets) the chivalric romances of Amadis as historical accounts. Ergo, when he imitates ("actualizes") the un-real Ideal, he does not technically suffer a delusion. Rather, he substitutes the world-view of the un-real but

by contrast, is a sign of the egalitarian society (i.e. the abolition of obstacles) in which mimetic conflict is resolved through the direct competition between the model and the imitating/envious subject, spawning interminable violence, physical and symbolic.[69] Crucially, the efficacy of external mediation rests upon the absence of direct and immediate communication (both spatial and temporal) between social actors. The true catastrophe is when rigid social hierarchies begin to break down and give way to proliferating "democratic" choices: as "the metaphysical distance between desiring subject and model diminishes—the key component of internal mediation—the potential for rivalry and violence increases. The more negligible this distance becomes, the more probable it is that mimesis will end in rivalry and violence."[70] Commenting on Girard, Stefano Tomelleri writes that it is "where social differentiation has practically disappeared [that] the power of mimesis is most destructive." Hence:

> While the social distance between individuals gradually decreases, the mutual imitation of individual desires grows. In contemporary society, the transition from external mediation to internal mediation increases the person's illusion that

---

all-powerful mediator for the perceptual consensus of the everyday and then behaves accordingly ("they might be giants"), indicating that he has entered into the realm of *simulation*: "generalized imitation has the power to create worlds that are perfectly disconnected from reality; at once orderly, stable, and totally illusory." See Jean-Pierre Dupuy, "Naturalizing Mimetic Theory," in *Mimesis and Science,* 209. Quixote's problem is not cognitive but libidinal; with Quixote/Amadis, we are moving away from "ordinary" mimesis to a state more akin to *possession,* which Girard understands as "an extreme form of alienation in which the subject totally absorbs the desires of another." Girard, *Violence and the Sacred,* 165. What social media presents us with, in stark contrast, is the Girardian dilemma of hyper-potent electronic models whose mimetic affectivity is in *direct* relationship to their *lack* of "reality": the more un-real it is, the more mimetically powerful it becomes. The digitalized models of social media can never act as mediators precisely because they can never be mis-taken for the real. See below, n. 88.

69 Palaver, *René Girard's Mimetic Theory,* 25.

70 Ibid., 61.

> he or she has a unique, autonomous, and individual desire, whereas actually differences among people are progressively disappearing. Everyone feels legitimated to compare him- or herself to others and to desire what the other has, independently of any distinction in terms of social role, job or group of reference.[71]

The scapegoat mechanism is Girard's own onto-political "remedy" for the eternal failure of the community to restrain the paroxysms of mimetic crisis and the epistemological key to the scapegoat is the logic of substitution: a new victim can be sacrificed as one member of an un-broken series of replicants of the original. But this same process of substitution — that which re-introduces the "breaking effect" of objective difference into the community through the binary opposition between society and scapegoat — is the same mechanism of political economy that drives *ressentiment,* the onto-phenomenological foundation of "bourgeois morality" and, therefore, of the politics of modernity. The "secret" of consumerism is that we can all replace each other through the accumulation of the external accruements of the Other. Tragically for the fetishizing consumer, "ressentiment is a symptom of internal mediation. It arises from the illusion of infinite freedom within a mimetic context. It is an invasive emotion that does not just affect private life, but also dominates the public sphere."[72] Just as there is a dis-junction between physical (objective) and psychological (objective) time, so there is an equally powerful and parallel dis-junction between private and public desires: "society seems increasingly individualistic, but an analysis of mimetic *ressentiment* shows that an individualist mentality also arises from the logic that leads to *ressentiment.*"[73] It is a question of illusion again:

---

71 Stefano Tomelleri, *Ressentiment: Reflections on Mimetic Desire and Society* (East Lansing: Michigan State University Press, 2015), 92–93.

72 Ibid., 94.

73 Ibid., 93.

People [imagine] realizing an individualist and authentic desire when in reality everything needs a mediator in order to
find a new desire, a need that is increasingly exaggerated by
the paradoxical combination between growing competition
among equals and an equally arising social inequality. All are
thus condemned to a fundamental dissatisfaction that leads
to a desire that finds no rest.[74]

Receiving its classic contemporary expression in the eponymous
work published by Max Scheler in 1912, *ressentiment* is "a self-
poisoning of the mind," the result of the long-term repression of
otherwise normal emotional faculties whose denial lead to the
obsessive (mimetic?) indulgence of "certain kinds of value delusions and corresponding value judgments" which, like the Tenth
Commandment, include but are not limited to "revenge, hatred,
malice, envy, the impulse to detract, and spite."[75] Broadly following Nietzsche (and Moses), Scheler views *ressentiment* as seeking natural expression through the antithesis of public reason,
the "spirit of revenge," the thing "most suitable source for the
formation of *ressentiment.* The nuances of language are precise.
There is a progression of feeling which starts with revenge and
runs via rancor, envy, and impulse to detract all the way to spite,
coming close to *ressentiment.*"[76] In our era of Post-Human Capitalism and the abolition of all traditional (and presumably legitimate) forms of relationships of external mediation, the specific
form that revenge is most likely to assume will be envy; "while
each has the 'right' to compare himself with everyone else, he
cannot do so in fact. Quite independently of the character and

---

74 Ibid., 93–94.
75 Max Scheler, *Ressentiment,* trans. Lewis B. Coser and William W.
    Holdheim (Milwaukee: Marquette University Press, 2010), 25.
76 Ibid., 25. The Mosaic linking of envy with both resentment and violence
    runs like a vein through Girardian scholarship. Compare Gil Bailie on
    this point: "when I speak of [...] mimetic desire[,] the word 'desire' means
    the influence of others." [...] The mimetic passions include jealousy, envy,
    covetousness, resentment, rivalry, contempt, and hatred." Gil Bailie,
    Violence Unveiled: Humanity at the Crossroads (New York: The Crossroad
    Publishing Company, 1995), 112.

experiences of individuals, a potent charge of ressentiment is here accumulated by the very *structure of society*" — the "system of free competition," as Scheler calls it is but in fact a phenomenological version of Marx's notion of capitalism as the substitution of contractual relationships for natural ones.[77] Important to note here is that Scheler does not restrict envy to the frustrated coveting of "objects" (fetishized commodities) alone but extends it equally to the unbridled competition for social capital ("values") now wholly unregulated by external mediation, yielding the ultra-toxin of *existential envy*. Paradoxically, envy, owing to its existential rather than materialistic nature, operates to reduce the acquisitive impulse rather than to strengthen it. The outcome, however, is lethal: envy "leads to *ressentiment* when the coveted values are such as cannot be acquired and lie in the sphere in which we compare ourselves to others. The most powerless envy is also the most terrible. Therefore, *existential envy*, which is directed against the other person's very *nature*, is the strongest source of *ressentiment*."[78] Even worse, existential envy operates in a wholly mimetic fashion, a near-exact parallel of Girard's concept of violence-as-contagion.

Through its very origin, *ressentiment* is therefore chiefly confined to those who serve and are dominated at the moment, who fruitlessly resent the sting of authority. When it occurs elsewhere, it is either due to psychological contagion — and the spiritual venom of *ressentiment* is extremely contagious — or to the violent suppression of an impulse which subsequently revolts by "embittering" and "poisoning" the personality.[79]

---

77 Scheler, *Ressentiment,* 28. Emphases in the original.

78 Ibid., 29, 30.

79 Ibid., 27. This is wholly consistent with Girard's notion of Modernity as "the universalization of internal mediation"; we collectively lack social domains of existential privacy resulting in the construction of "beliefs and identities [that] cannot but have strong mimetic components." See René Girard, Pierpaolo Antonello, and Joao Cezar de Castro Rocha, *Evolution and Conversion: Dialogues on the Origins of Culture* (New York: Continuum, 2008), 240.

Which sounds like a "troll." Girard's relationship with Scheler is complex; although he critiques the latter for his failure to situate the elements of ressentiment into a social dynamic, he concedes that "everything becomes clear, everything fits into a coherent structure if, in order to explain envy, we abandon the object of rivalry as a starting point and choose instead the rival himself, i.e., the mediator, as both a point of departure for our analysis and its conclusion."[80]

Why, then, is the will-to-revenge so central to human affairs? The answer, according to Girard, is that the sheer ferocity of violence, both physical and symbolic, is structurally embedded within the form of its transmission, which is best understood as a form of contagion:

> Why does the spirit of revenge, wherever it breaks out, constitute such an intolerable menace? Perhaps because the only satisfactory revenge for spilt blood is spilling the blood of the killer; and in the blood feud there is no clear distinction between the act for which the killer is being punished and the punishment itself. Vengeance professes to be an act of reprisal, and every reprisal calls for another reprisal. The crime to which the act of vengeance addresses itself is almost never an unprecedented offense; in almost every case it has been committed in revenge for some prior crime.[81]

But what, precisely, is this "prior crime"? It is nothing other than mimesis itself; the very thing that creates us (or, through which we are created) is, in a cosmically paradoxical fashion, the very thing that prevents us from ever becoming real — or relevant. The loss of amnesia, the recovery of the memory of insufficiency, calls forth the demand for vengeance against the reality that condemns us to irrelevance. "The infinite or absolute outcome of desire is tragic: to recognize that one can never fill in the gap between oneself [the irrelevant] and the model-rival [the rele-

---

80 Girard, *Desire, Deceit and the Novel*, 13.
81 Girard, *Violence and the Sacred*, 14.

vant] is to realize that the model can never be reached; thus does it become an obstacle."[82] Historically, however, there has been a catch: a mimetic-rival is not the same as a mimetic-obstacle, for the latter is governed by external mediation:

> Faced with the obstacle, which is to say the rival who is always already there, who is so to speak insurmountable, the "normal" attitude consists in renouncing competition with the other and in re-directing one's desire in a more constructive [agonistic?] direction, in accepting one's own limits as well as those imposed by social structure (for example, by the law). Renunciation is at the foundation of all hierarchical societies. This is because renunciation shows desire its impossibility. The obstacle is there, absolute. The mediator [of desire] is always external, even if he is right in front of you.[83]

Fortunately for us, mass media has changed all of that. Under the shadow of consumption, freedom has been reduced to "choice." From a Girardian perspective, the illusory "trick" of consumerism (a.k.a. "advertising") is not to mimetically seduce us into all wanting the same thing; rather, it is to collectively hypnotize all of us into believing that we are radically individualistic, *while desiring exactly the same thing*.[84] It is by this means that post-human capitalism is able to indefinitely postpone a fatal crisis of un-differentiation within technological society: the mirage of freedom-through-consumption imposes a deadly veil of ignorance over the abject reality of our total lack of authenticity.[85] Unfortunately for us, there is a fatal flaw — as always.

---

82 Oughourlian, *The Mimetic Brain*, 84.

83 Ibid., 84–85.

84 See Girard, Antonello, and de Castro Rocha, *Evolution and Conversion*, 77–83.

85 Predictably it was the Pied Piper of Pop Art, Andy Warhol, who expressed it best: "What's great about this country is that America started the tradition where the richest consumers buy essentially the same thing as the poorest. You can be watching TV and see Coca-Cola, and you can know that the President drinks Coke, Liz Taylor drinks Coke, and just think, you can drink Coke too. A Coke is a Coke and no amount of money can get

The crucial weakness lies within the Derridean-style "pun" (via iterability) that links Baudrillard's integral reality with Girard's mimetic rivalry: the reversibility between "model" and "image," both of which are signified within social media by the *meme*. For Baudrillard, the master-sign of the transition from capitalism to late capitalism (and onward to post-human capitalism) is the replacement of the "serial" (the hall-mark of industrial production) with the "model" (the signifier of the hegemony of the "The Code"). For Girard, the "model" is the libidinal object of desire that is, weirdly, always absent because never original: our desires are fake because they are really someone else's. The meme encapsulates both meanings perfectly: as an electronic image that is endlessly circulated, it qualifies as a "model" (Baudrillard); as an image that is endlessly circulated, it establishes both itself and its author as a "model" (Girard). After Facebook, the only way to prove our being-relevant is not by claiming the anteriority of our desire (which is now not merely impossible but objectively inconceivable); rather, it is to use the seemingly "democratic" platform of social media as a template through which to self-author *ourselves* as models by circulating images — electronic pictographs. Even better (worse?) is that we are no longer confined to the limits of the traditional ("natural"?) community; thanks to the global absence of external mediation we are now directly integrated into a universal community that creates an unbridled domain of unstable mimetic relationships.[86] To the best of my knowledge, neither Girard or Oughoularian contemplate the mimetic dilemma that presents itself to

---

you a better Coke than the one the bum on the corner is drinking." Andy Warhol, cited in Girard, Antonello, and de Castro Rocha, *Evolution and Conversion,* 91n11. Integral reality places all of its bets on staving off a final mimetic reckoning through the deranged but brilliant gimmick of getting the Rich (desire d) to model their own desires on the Poor (desire D).

86 Oughoularian expresses this in Dostoevskyian terms: "if nothing is forbidden, everything is thus permitted and this leads to a transformation of the world: everyone can take anyone whatsoever for a model and thus immediately for a rival." Jean-Michel Oughoularian, *Psychopolitics: Conversations with Trevor Cribben Merrill,* trans. Trevor Cribben Merrill (East Lansing: Michigan State University Press, 2012), 54.

us: the need for the *model* (Desire *D*) rather than self *s* (desire d) to claim possession of the anteriority of his/her/its desire, to prove that he or she is the "real" model.[87] We post ourselves as the model to prove our relevance and in so doing de-personalize ourselves through the annihilating integration into the nameless community; as we know by now, the "claim to originality [...] prepares the way for resentment."[88] The more that the model is circulated through unmediated communication the more un-real the model/image becomes, precisely because the meme be-longs to no one — exclusivity of both possession and originality has been abolished in advance. The cosmic-level horror of social media is that it electronically imitates the primitive, which is the anteriority of the modern, and that the meme is the perfect simulation of the scapegoat mechanism as pure symbolic vio-lence. The Girardian will-to-revenge is the mimetic equivalent of Nietzsche's eternal return of the same: the "same" that returns eternally is nothing other than the imitation of an archaic "lost" time now re-enacted in the present through a purely digitalized scapegoat mechanism.[89]

---

87 The closest example that I can think of is Girard's nomination of anorexia as an outstanding example of how self *s,* via external mediation, enters into a direct competition with the model with the pre-meditated intent of replacing her. Once victory is attained, the starving imitator "becomes" the new model who must then continuously prove her model status through un-ending performances of self-mortification — until the true end is reached. See René Girard, *Anorexia and Mimetic Desire,* trans. Mark R. Anspach (East Lansing: Michigan State University Press, 2013).

88 Oughourlian,*The Mimetic Brain,* 81.

89 For Nietzsche as himself the ultimate victim of psychotic mimetic rivalry ("metaphysical desire") and, therefore, of *ressentiment,* see Fornari, *A God Torn to Pieces.* The artfully concealed truth of the grandiosely self-proclaimed Truth-Sayer was the metaphysical desire to-be (*zu sein*) the anti-Wagner. See above, n. 13. The "case of Nietzsche" revolves around Richard Wagner's embodiment of the *dual* nature of the obstacle: his elevated cultural status should have operated as a form of external mediation with the young Nietzsche (as Amadis the Gaul did with Don Quixote) but instead, the composer was reconstituted by the philosopher as an object of metaphysical desire, unconsciously revealing the psychotic nature of Dionysus-Zagreus re-born (it should not be forgotten that

The meme: the neo-primitive pictograph that overcomes all obstacles.

The killing joke of René Girard: *"Let's all come together in order to make a...**difference!**"*

The mimetic psychosis: an egalitarian community of models.
Diagnosis?
The apocalypse of the eternally irrelevant.
Prognosis?
Unlimited.

---

the "pet" name of Cosima Wagner, Richard's spouse, was Ariadne/Arianna — the bride of Dionysus).

Bibliography

Bailie, Gil. *Violence Unveiled: Humanity at the Crossroads.* New York: The Crossroad Publishing Company, 1995.

Baudrillard, Jean. *The Agony of Power.* Translated by Ames Hodges. Los Angeles: Semiotext(e), 2010.

———. *Carnival and Cannibal.* Translated by Chris Turner. London: Seagull Books, 2010.

———. *The Divine Left: A Chronicle of the Years 1977–1984.* Translated by David L. Sweet. Los Angeles: Semiotext(e), 2014.

———. *Symbolic Exchange and Death.* Translated by Ian Grant. London: Sage Publications, 1993.

———. *Why Hasn't Everything Disappeared?* Translated by Chris Turner. London: Seagull Books, 2009.

Debord, Guy. *The Society of the Spectacle.* Translated by Donald Nicholson-Smith. New York: Zone Books, 1995.

Dietrich, Oliver, Manfred Heun, Jens Notroff, Klaus Schmidt, and Manfred Zarnkow. "The Role of Cult and Feasting in the Emergence of Neolithic Communities: New Evidence from Gobekli Tepe, South-Eastern Turkey." *Antiquity* 86 (2012): 674–95.

Dupuy, Jean-Pierre. "Naturalizing Mimetic Theory." In *Mimesis and Science: Empirical Research on Imitation and the Mimetic Theory of Culture and Religion,* edited by Scott R. Garrels, 193–213. East Lansing: Michigan State University Press, 2011.

Fornari, Giuseppe. *A God Torn to Pieces: The Nietzsche Case.* Translated by Keith Buck. East Lansing: Michigan State University Press, 2013.

Gallese, Vittorio. "The Two Sides of Mimesis: Mimetic Theory, Embodied Simulation, and Social Identification." In *Mimesis and Science: Empirical Research on Imitation and the Mimetic Theory of Culture and Religion,* edited by Scott R. Garrels, 87–108. East Lansing: Michigan State University Press, 2011.

Girard, René. *Anorexia and Mimetic Desire.* Translated by Mark R. Anspach. East Lansing: Michigan State University Press, 2013.

―――. *Desire, Deceit and the Novel: Self and Other in Literary Structure.* Translated by Yvonne Freccero. Baltimore: Johns Hopkins University Press, 1976.

―――. *The One by Whom Scandal Comes.* Translated by M. B. DeBoise. East Lansing: Michigan State University Press, 2014.

―――. *Things Hidden Since the Foundation of the World.* Research undertaken in collaboration with Jean-Michel Oughourlian and Guy Lefort. Translated by Stephen Bann and Michael Metteer. New York: Continuum, 1978.

―――. *Violence and the Sacred.* Translated by Patrick Gregory. Baltimore: Johns Hopkins University Press, 1977.

Girard, René, Pierpaolo Antonello, and Joao Cezar de Castro Rocha. *Evolution and Conversion: Dialogues on the Origins of Culture.* New York: Continuum, 2008.

Kirwan, Michael. *Discovering Girard.* Chicago: Cowley Publications, 2005.

Mack, Burton. "Introduction: Religion and Ritual." In *Violent Origins: Walter Burkert, René Girard, and Jonathan Z. Smith on Ritual Killing and Cultural Formation,* edited by Robert G. Hammerton-Kelly, 1–47. Stanford: Stanford University Press, 1987.

McCarthy, Tom. *Tintin and the Secret of Literature.* London: Counterpoint, 2008.

Oughourlian, Jean-Michel. "Desire Is Mimetic: A Clinical Approach." *Contagion: Journal of Violence, Mimesis, and Culture* 3 (1996): 43–49. DOI: 10.1353/ctn.1996.0006.

―――. *The Genesis of Desire.* Translated by Eugene Webb. East Lansing: Michigan State University Press, 2010.

―――. *The Mimetic Brain.* Translated by Trevor Cribben Merrill. East Lansing: Michigan State University Press, 2016.

―――. *The Puppet of Desire: The Psychology of Hysteria, Possession, and Hypnosis.* Translated by Eugene Webb. Stanford: Stanford University Press, 1991.

————. *Psychopolitics: Conversations with Trevor Cribben Merrill.* Translated by Trevor Cribben Merrill. East Lansing: Michigan State University Press, 2012.

Palaver, Wolfgang. *René Girard's Mimetic Theory.* Translated by Gabriel Borrud. East Lansing: Michigan State University Press, 2013.

Reeve, Zoey. "Mechanisms of Internal Cohesion: Scapegoating and Parochial Altruism." In *How We Became Human: Mimetic Theory and the Science of Evolutionary Origins,* edited by Pierpaolo Antonello and Paul Gifford, 161–86. East Lansing: Michigan State University Press, 2015.

Scheler, Max. *Ressentiment.* Translated by Lewis B. Coser and William W. Holdheim. Milwaukee: Marquette University Press, 2010.

Tomelleri, Stefano. *Ressentiment: Reflections on Mimetic Desire and Society.* East Lansing: Michigan State University Press, 2015.

Wilson, Eric. "Warring Sovereigns and Mimetic Rivals: On Scapegoats and Political Crisis in William Golding's Lord of the Flies." *Law and Humanities* 8, no. 2 (2014): 147–73. DOI: 10.5235/17521483.8.2.147.

————. "The Ballad of Ed and Lewis: Conflictual Mimesis and the Revocation of the Social Contract in James Dickey's *Deliverance." Law and Humanities* 10, no. 1 (2016): 115–60. DOI: 10.1080/17521483.2016.1174417.

8

Chaotic, Good

Roisin Kiberd

Briefly, for a single day in 2018, it appeared to the world that hell had been canceled.

In March of this year an interview was published with Pope Francis, written by 93-year-old reporter and *La Repubblica* editor Eugenio Scalfari. Asked where "bad souls" go after death, the pope was quoted as replying: "a hell doesn't exist, the disappearance of sinning souls exists."

Almost immediately the Vatican scrambled to discredit Scalfari's interview. They denied the meeting had ever been authorized, and pointed out Scalfari's habit of conducting interviews with important public figures without taking notes or making recordings. They issued a statement ordering that "no quotation of the article should be considered as a faithful transcription of the words of the Holy Father."

In the months since, the Pope's denial of hell has been relegated to Internet rumor. The story appears as an entry on Snopes.com, where it has been given the rating "UNPROVEN."

What are we to believe, those of us zealous and fragile enough to worry about one day waking up in hell? Was the cancelation of hell fake news? And if not, how did the pope arrive at this decision?

If hell doesn't exist — and never did — perhaps we should go looking for hell in different places.

DOI: 10.21983/P3.0255.1.09

Let us make hell a place on earth. Hell is on the Internet. Hell is social media.

* * *

For as long as I can remember, morality has appeared to be deeply out of fashion. The Internet, especially, is meant to have broadened our horizons beyond morality; the dream of the cyber-hippies was a technological new age, a hivemind dwelling on an elevated plane, where users would coexist in harmony.

Yet the Internet is full of reductive moral judgment. It speaks in binaries, because it is built on binary code. We rush to define ourselves with hashtags and labels. We express ourselves in solidarity and hate. We swipe left or swipe right, and post hearts or snake emojis under Instagram posts made by famous people, because very few people are motivated to post online about things they feel ambivalent towards. Rather, people have "feelings" and "feels"; good things are "pure," while bad things, like hell, are "canceled" (if you're a drag queen, these things can also be "deceased"). Images can be "cursed" or they can be "blessed." Other things are "woke," though that term is rarely used seriously anymore. The opposite of "woke" is "problematic," a self-defeating term which by definition fails to identify the problem.

On social media, a block list or trigger warning provides a moral framework for those unsure which opinion to hold. Memes, too, offer guidance in the form of semi-satirical commentary. One such meme is the alignment chart.

The alignment chart comes from *Dungeons and Dragons,* the name of which will likely cause certain readers to roll their eyes. In its first 1974 edition, *Dungeons and Dragons* (*D&D*) allowed players to choose between three alignments: lawful, neutral, and chaotic. They are as they sound, intended as a prompt for creating characters as part of the game's collaborative fiction.

By 1977 a new alignment axis was introduced: that of good and evil. It wasn't until the fourth edition of the *D&D* handbook that the axes evolved into nine clearly delineated options:

Lawful Good, Neutral Good, Chaotic Good
Lawful Neutral, True Neutral, Chaotic Neutral
Lawful Evil, Neutral Evil, Chaotic Evil

Switching alignments during a game incurs penalties, although dungeon masters, who lead *D&D* gameplay, are looked down on if they enforce an alignment too harshly. Some plot twists can make a character's alignment spontaneously change, like finding a cursed item, or sudden demonic possession. Alignments don't always feature in other tabletop games, and by the game's fifth edition in 2014 they became optional. This corresponded, oddly enough, with the rise of the alignment chart as meme.

The TV Tropes page for "character alignments" features a warning:

> Due to the controversial nature of this trope, and not to mention, it's considered shoe-horning to categorize people with these kind of tropes, there will be no real life examples under these circumstances, since it invites an Edit War.[1]

* * *

Wherever images are shared on the Internet, you will find alignment charts. Wherever there is variety, diversity, nuance, you will find people who want to divide things into categories.

Let's begin with nations, which are categorized in one of the oldest alignment charts. On this chart Sweden is labelled as lawful good. The UK is lawful neutral. Israel is somehow true neutral, and Iran is lawful evil. The US, interestingly, is judged to be chaotic neutral.

Another very old alignment chart categorizes websites. Twitter is lawful good, Wikipedia is true neutral, 4chan is chaotic neutral, and the Pirate Bay, bearing the tagline "Information is

---

1 See TV Tropes, s.v. "Character Alignment aka: Grid Alignmen/," http://tvtropes.org/pmwiki/pmwiki.php/Main/CharacterAlignment?from=Main.GridAlignmen/.

free," is chaotic good (Facebook, intriguingly, is nowhere to be seen).

The bulk of alignment memes are about pop culture, including Nintendo games (*Smash Bros* is lawful evil, *Zelda* is chaotic neutral), paint software (MS Paint is neutral evil, Photoshop is true neutral, despite its monthly subscription fee) and characters from *The Room* (Lisa is chaotic evil, Tommy is apparently lawful good). From here we move into more arcane territory: a number of alignment charts examine Internet culture itself, including expressions of amusement ("kek" is apparently lawful evil, "lol" is true neutral, "lel" is chaotic neutral and "lmao" is chaotic good) and frog memes (Dat Boy is chaotic good, Pepe is chaotic evil, and "Tea Lizard" Kermit is neutral evil).

2016 saw a rush of US election alignment charts, which commonly classified Donald Trump as chaotic evil. Some, from 4chan and outlets like the subreddit /r/The_Donald, list him as chaotic good. Hillary Clinton is most often a neutral, either lawful neutral or neutral evil depending on who made the meme. There is one alignment chart I've found which features Ted Cruz as chaotic evil. Under his name, the artist has placed a line of Wingdings symbols instead of a quote. The picture of Cruz is in black and white, but his eyes glow with a fiery red.

* * *

As a meme, the alignment chart has never quite peaked in popularity. This has, very likely, guaranteed its longevity. Another factor is its versatility: it's a structure, a "meta-meme" rather than an end in itself, which collates and critiques other memes in turn. Like the "Starter Pack" meme, or the Political Compass, it is a way to make sense of internet culture from within.

The alignment chart endures because of its near-endless capacity for customization; it is literally an empty grid, waiting to be filled with pictures. Like a YouTube video thumbnail, or a picture in the *Daily Mail*'s sidebar of shame, it crams multiple images into a single frame. The nine characters who personify the alignments don't have to come from the same book,

TV show, or fandom. They don't even have to all be fictional, or all real. Sometimes they speak volumes about the taste of the person who made them — for instance, there's a surplus of Alignment Charts originating on 4chan which combine characters from *South Park, Family Guy, The Dark Knight,* and *Super Mario,* outlining the cultural diet of a 2012-era teenage boy.

Google Trends shows a spike in interest in the alignment chart around 2012. It fell again soon after that, but its popularity has climbed steadily upward again over the last six years. The reddit community /r/AlignmentCharts was formed in 2010, and in 2012 an empty alignment template was posted to Polyvore.

The alignment chart closely resembles demotivation pictures, another elderly meme, and is, in a sense, simply a "demotivation collage." Sometimes the images have a quote from the character below their assignation, explaining the creator's reasoning for categorising them this way. But increasingly they don't; they just post a picture and leave it at that.

The chart format was never official to *Dungeons and Dragons* — instead it originated online, becoming commonplace on DeviantArt and later Tumblr. KnowYourMeme.com cites the earliest known example as a 5×5 alignment chart, which appeared on DeviantArt in 2011.[2] It included two extra horizontal categories — "social" and "rebel," and two extra vertical ones ("moral" and "impure"), and featured an assembly of figures taken from TV (*Family Guy*'s Peter Griffin, Arnold, of *Hey Arnold* fame, and *The Simpsons'* Ned Flanders) and film (Rocky, Hannibal Lecter, Darth Sidius, and, likely the most commonly-named Chaotic Evil character of all time, Heath Ledger's Joker). It features, in my opinion, one of most accurate true neutrals of all: Wilson, the ball from *Cast Away.*

* * *

---

2   See *Know Your Meme,* s.v. "Alignment Charts," http://knowyourmeme.com/photos/1137323-alignment-charts.

There are almost as many alignment charts about food as there are about every other kind of alignment chart put together.

As children we're told about the food pyramid. As adults we're told about the keto diet, the paleo diet, about the benefits of veganism and the moral superiority of kale. It follows, then, that foods would be sorted by their "chaotic" spirit and inherent virtue. Intentional or not, food is the form of morality we practise daily.

One of the best-known food alignment charts brings to mind the habits of good housemates and bad ones; the chart is about different ways to store bread. Once opened, putting a loaf of bread in a bread bin is deemed lawful good. Tying up the bag with a rubber band is true neutral. Tying a knot, however, is lawful evil (this one I don't understand — my parents taught me and my younger brother to do this, and it seems to preserve the bread just as well as a rubber band).

Other charts concern themselves with condiments. Newman's Own salad dressing is lawful good, as the company gives its profits to charity, while canned tomato sauce is chaotic evil. There's also a biscuit alignment chart. Thin Mints are chaotic evil (this chart was clearly made by an American), and "Toffeetastics" are chaotic neutral. Even the vegetable aisle can be navigated with an alignment chart: carrots, apparently, are lawful good, while mushrooms are chaotic evil.

My personal favourite is a chart titled "I Can't Believe It's Not an Alignment Chart." It's about butter substitutes, and each box on the chart is filled with a creamy yellow tub held close to the camera. Most of the pictures are grainy and poorly lit; furtive, somehow, as though taken undercover in the fake dairy aisle of a Walmart, late at night. In the neutral good box is a tub marked "You'd Butter Believe It." Neutral evil is "Unbelievable: This is Not Butter." The chaotic evil box is filled by a tub scrawled with what could be Comic Sans. It says "What, not butter!" That the creator of this chart skipped over Memories of Butter, another highly meme-able oil-based butter substitute, strikes me as a tragedy.

Do food alignment charts reveal a neurosis with which we treat food, an impossibility of ethical consumption contrasted with the marketing of foods as distinctly "good" and "bad"? Would anyone even want to consume a "lawful" food? Is consuming "chaotic" produce somehow aspirational? (I, for one, view Monster Energy drink as chaotic, a shot of pure, caffeinated "dragon energy.")

These charts, all of them made by ordinary web users (I have yet to see an "official" food alignment chart put out by manufacturers as marketing), reflect how we have internalized the morality of food advertising — the "naughty" chocolate bar, the "clean" protein, and the "dirty" burger — even as it is critiqued with self-awareness and humor.

* * *

In the *D&D* handbook, players are advised to choose a good or lawful good alignment ("playing an evil or chaotic evil character disrupts an adventuring party and, frankly, makes all the other players angry at you," the fourth edition says). Similarly, in online commentary the neutral alignments are those which attract the most criticism. Neutral evil is sometimes called "the jerk alignment," and all five of the neutral alignments, which cross the board and occupy the most space, are regarded with a degree of distrust. A neutral good character can be a pacifist, but lacking in conviction or loyalty, while a lawful neutral character is an unimaginative bureaucrat. True neutral can imply that a character works to preserve balance, but it can also imply that they're apathetic and vacuous. A chaotic neutral character, meanwhile, is exciting but inconsistent and self-interested. Chaotic neutral is the favorite alignment of edgelords.

Perhaps it's too difficult to trust a centrist, however "lawful" or "chaotic" they might be. Even if a character succeeds at playing with "true" neutrality, to those on either side of them they're only working to maintain a vacuum.

In life, as in tabletop games, the glory goes those who are most vocal about holding strong opinions. This tendency has increased in the era of Twitter, Facebook, Reddit, and Instagram. To be bombarded daily with information and opinion, as most social media users are, requires discernment and a keen sense of self, a "personal brand." Millennials, a magpie generation, are offered the world but burdened with the task of sorting through it, like so many NSA agents reading other people's emails.

The alignment chart speaks to this dilemma. It boils online discourse down to its essence: pop culture, pictures, and uncomplicated judgment.

* * *

Pinterest attributes a certain quote to Dante, but I am unwilling to judge for certain if it's true. The quote reads: "the darkest places in hell are reserved for those who maintain their neutrality in times of moral crisis."

Certain parts of pop culture play a role in keeping the idea of hell alive. Horror films, of course, tend to dwell on the concept; there's *Drag Me to Hell,* the (criminally underrated) *As Above So Below, Insidious* (hell, here, is a place where they play Tiny Tim), and the *Hellraiser* franchise, for starters. Hell also appears frequently in *Futurama, Spawn, Hellboy,* and occasional episodes of *South Park.*

Hell also features prominently in video games. *Devil May Cry* is loosely based around the *Divine Comedy,* while in *Saint's Row 3: Gat Out Of Hell,* the hero flies around an open-world hell, equipped with weapons inspired by the seven deadly sins. Two well-regarded indie titles, *Limbo* and *Pinstripe,* send their protagonists through the darker locales of the afterlife, and there is even a PS3 game titled *Dante's Inferno.* Classics of the "hell game" genre include the *Doom* series and 1987 ZX Spectrum title *Soft and Cuddly,* which features an intricately drawn neon portrait of Alice Cooper as its closing image, with the caption "Go to Hell."

I cannot help but think, sometimes, that the reason hell endures as the muse of geek culture, even now after it has fallen out of fashion, and after even the Pope is rumored to have given up on it, is that hell corresponds with an enduring black-and-white morality, one which serves as the muse of pop culture. It's something we don't speak about out loud very often, perhaps because we can't, but which thrives in the silence between laptop user and screen. It drives people to segment pop culture and everyday life into "alignments," for the purpose of entertainment and instruction.

* * *

There are nine alignments. Conveniently, there are also nine circles of hell.

At the entrance to Dante's hell is the "Vestibule of the Futile," where the opportunists, the "uncommitted" and "pusillanimous" suffer. Those who were too cautious in life, too cowardly or *neutral* to take sides and make their opinions known, are cursed to chase after a moving banner which they will never grasp. While doing this, they are also tormented and stung constantly by wasps. Their tears and blood and pus drip onto the ground, and the bilious mixture is feasted upon by maggots. It's a vision beyond the imagining of even the most sadistic game designer, even *Soft and Cuddly*'s teenage punk progenitor John George Jones.

By placing this particular form of torture at the entrance to hell, Dante is playing a trick on the reader. He's daring you to make up your mind, and choose to believe in his narrative or not to. He's asking you to decide where you're aligned.

A similar tactic, more crudely executed, occurs with alignment chart memes: even the avowedly "neutral" risk finding themselves placed on the chart. According to Dante, you're implicated, and subject to judgment, simply by bearing witness. *You're damned,* and if you're reading this it's too late.

* * *

When you type the word "millennial" into Google, you'll quick-ly find the term "millennialism," or "chialism." In eschatology, millennialism is a belief popular with certain sects within Chris-tianity that there will be a golden age of righteousness, lasting for 1000 years, before the Final Judgment and the World to Come. Heaven will be a place on earth, for a time, but after that the world will end.

Millennialism finds its inspiration in the Book of Revela-tions, in a verse which describes an angel descending from the heavens, holding the key to a bottomless pit. He seizes the devil, throws him into the pit and locks the door. Then John, the nar-rator, writes:

> Then I saw thrones, and those seated on them were given authority to judge. I also saw the souls of those who had been beheaded for their testimony to Jesus and for the word of God. They had not worshiped the beast or its image and had not received its mark on their foreheads or their hands. They came to life and reigned with Christ a thousand years. (The rest of the dead did not come to life until the thousand years were ended.)[3]

Sometimes I think mine is the most judgmental generation. Not in its consistency, but its frequency. Judgment itself is a trend. The institutions which once did the judging for us have crum-bled and fallen away. This is almost certainly good. But what has followed is a frenzy of mediated judgment as sport.

Personally, I don't trust my own judgment. For me, at least, polarities of judgment have always been a symptom that some-thing is wrong.

There's a psychological tendency called "splitting," developed by Ronald Fairbairn as part of object relations theory.[4] It de-scribes exaggerated black-and-white thinking, often in relation

---

3   Rev. 20:4 (New International Version).
4   See W.R.D Fairbain, *Psychoanalytic Studies of the Personality* (London: Routledge, 1994).

to whether a person is good or bad. In relationships, someone "splitting" will view another person as all good or all bad, as completely perfect or inherently flawed, or even evil. This creates instability of emotions, extreme reactions, and an interpretation of love as something dangerous, violent and damaging.

Depressed people are prone to splitting. So are people with narcissistic personality disorder, or borderline personality disorder. You can apply splitting to yourself, or to the outcome of something requiring effort. It's a shortcut for making sense of the world, albeit in a way that causes harm rather than making life easier.

I'm one of those who, when depressed or under stress, turn inward with extremes of judgment. On those days, social media becomes impossible, as does any kind of writing work requiring certainty in one's opinions. Twitter, especially, appears to me as a scrolling feed of other people's judgments, a torrent of strangers and distant acquaintances telling me they *feel very strongly* about something, that it's good or evil — usually evil, though they don't go so far as to use that word — and that I should believe this too. On those days I have to avoid social media entirely, because I start to think of myself as profoundly flawed. By withholding judgment, I try to be sane.

All of the judgments, the *alignments* listed in this essay, were made by others. None are my own. This is because I have made a career in evasion; words provide me with space to be slippery. But I have invented an alignment for myself: I am awful neutral. If hell exists, I am surely condemned to the Vestibule of the Futile.

I have noticed a certain tendency, when people apply the alignments to themselves: they'll almost always call themselves "chaotic," whereas other people are considered lawful. In this sense, the alignments reveal something about the nature of existence. Invariably, other people seem to have a method, while we appear chaotic to ourselves.

* * *

Early in its existence, *Dungeons and Dragons* itself became the subject of a number of moral panics. In 1979 it was first linked, in media coverage, to the disappearance of James Dallas Egbert III, a teenage boy who had never played the game. Later, in 1982, an anti-occult advocate named Patricia Pulling blamed the game for the suicide of her son, Irving, and claimed he had been placed under a *D&D* curse. Pulling filed lawsuits, produced campaign leaflets about Satanism and tabletop gaming, and founded Bothered About *Dungeons and Dragons* (BADD), a one-person campaign group.

The subsequent decades saw media coverage, academic research and fiction continue the debate around the morality of Dungeons and Dragons. Commentators appeared on news channels, claiming that when burned, *D&D* game pieces emitted a screaming sound. The game was linked to murders, suicides, and satanic ritual, and in 2004 was even banned from Waupun Prison, Wisconsin, based on the belief that it was encouraging gang violence.

It remains to be said that *D&D* gives players the option to remain unaligned. No one is obliged to morally self-determine, just as, it goes without saying, none of the alignment charts shared on social media claim to be 100% correct. They're based on opinion, on the individual creator's personal judgment.

It's in the interest of every social network that we, as users, continue to think in terms of polarities. "Black-and-white thinking" lends itself to data categorization, and marketing, and profiling. Ambivalent users are harder to advertise to, and are less likely to stir up debate. They get in the way of "growth," by thinking outside the platform.

This mode of thinking surfaces in categorization memes, and in the alignment chart most of all. Social media, as a concept, is relatively young; we're still in the early phase, where we're drunk on information. From behind the screen we love to play the diagnostician, and charts and labels and hashtags are satisfying because they simplify things, offering a guide through the online underworld.

Alignment memes reveal in even the most "chaotic" discourse a latent morality, one we're aware of enough to joke about, and to apply to comic books and tubs of fake butter, but of which we are reluctant to let go.

In such a climate, even decrying our tendency to judge becomes yet another opinion, one which generates further debate. The opinion machine continues to operate, making more money for Twitter, Facebook, Instagram, and their ilk. This leaves me with a quote from Simone Weil's *On the Abolition of All Political Parties,* which found its way to me through the Instagram feed of Pamela Anderson, shared on October 12, 2017:

Nearly everywhere — often even when dealing with purely technical problems — instead of thinking, one merely takes sides: for or against. Such a choice replaces the activity of the mind. This is an intellectual leprosy; it originated in the political world and then spread through the land, contaminating all forms of thinking. This leprosy is killing us; it is doubtful whether it can be cured without first starting with the abolition of all political parties.[5]

A reply below reads "♡ ♡ ♡ ♡."

---

5   Simone Weil, *On the Abolition of All Political Parties,* trans. Simon Leys (New York: NYRB Classics, 2013), 34.

Bibliography

Fairbain, W.R.D. *Psychoanalytic Studies of the Personality.*
    Hove: Routledge, 1994.
Weil, Simone. *On the Abolition of All Political Parties.*
    Translated by Simon Leys. New York: NYRB Classics, 2014.

9

Oh, They Have the Internet on Computers Now? The Online Art of The Simpsons

Tom Whyman

Last September, having finally secured my first real salaried academic job, I finally cleared all of my old stuff out of my old room in my parents' house, since I was now finally able to rent a space big enough to contain it.[1]

There were a *lot* of belongings there, stashed in boxes piled high to the ceiling, crammed into the cavities running along the sides of the walls. Books, clothes, CDs, LPs, cassette tapes, things to play them on, musical instruments, paintings, furniture, ornaments — some brilliant, in great condition, but mostly junk, grimy, half-broken — acquired for the most part while I was studying for my undergraduate degree in Manchester, during which I spent a lot of time trawling charity shops and other repositories of junk, fascinated with these objects despite their crappiness. During this period of my life the whole world seemed to be opening up before me, a world I had been largely unaware of growing up a bored, depressed teenager in an isolated Hampshire suburb, a world of sensory and aesthetic pos-

---

1   This chapter was written in the summer of 2018. Some claims may have since been rendered obsolete by the thankless march of time.

sibility, and each of these objects — insofar as they were unlike anything I had seen for sale on the high street, or in a shopping center — seemed to contain a new sort of possibility within them.

So of course I absolutely *had* to have a home-made clock designed to look like an advertisement for the Liverpool-Manchester Railway Company; of course I couldn't live without that painting we saw for sale in a café of some fishermen with horse's heads asleep in a boat; naturally I needed those 17 full LPs of *The Good Soldier Svejk* being read in its entirety in Czech; yes I probably would wear that grey boiled-wool jacket where the buttons were made out of old Austrian coins for some reason.

Going through these boxes, which took me a few days, was a strange, at times meditative, at times uncanny, at times just physically gruelling experience — opening them up, rifling through them, deciding what to keep and what not to, trying to sort everything out, apply some sort of a system. And at the same time, constantly being struck by the significance of these things — layers of meaning which had once been alive for me, but which I had now forgotten. Oh, this painting, I bought that the day we —; oh wow I had forgotten about this, she gave this to me after — ... and so on. I spent that whole period somehow temporally displaced, constantly slipping down little holes of nostalgia which threw me back from the present to the — or so it felt — much richer world of the past.

But not all of these objects of significance were things that I'd bought. A lot of it was stuff I'd collected — old beer mats, tourist maps, train tickets. One box just contained a huge amount of receipts. Sometimes it was possible to attach meaning to this stuff — a lot of the beer mats, for example, had doodles or sweet messages scribbled on them. But at other times it was impossible. Why *had* I kept all these receipts? Did they really once hold any sort of significance for me? In being caused by these objects to remember myself, I was also becoming aware that there were aspects of my life I had completely forgotten.

There were also a lot of boxes full of things I had created — CDs by various bands I'd been in at one time or another;

loose scraps of watercolor paintings I'd done as a teenager, oscillating between the surreal and the diaristic; print-outs of bad novels I'd never finished. Amongst these objects was a mysterious brown envelope addressed to the house I'd lived in during my second year of university. In it I found a scrap of paper addressed to me from the BBC:

Dear Tom,

Thank you for sending us your idea/proposal. We're sorry, but we can only consider full word processed narrative drama and comedy scripts. Please find enclosed our guidelines to clarify. We do recommend you visit our website www.bbc. co.uk/writersroom for more detailed guidelines. You may also find it useful to visit the BBC commissioning website www.bbc.co.uk/commissioning. We hope that if you have something that meets our requirements you'll consider sending it to us.

Good luck with your writing,

BBC writersroom.

Below this scrap of paper, attached with a paperclip, was a letter I'd written to the BBC, dated 3/12/08:

Dear the BBC,

Hello. My name is Tom Whyman. The other day I came up with an idea which, with your co-operation of course, could make both of us VERY rich indeed.

This idea is *The Simpsons*. You may have heard of *The Simpsons* from travellers to this country from the United States. *The Simpsons* is one of (if not the) longest-running show(s) in US television history. Approximately 69 million viewers tune in to watch Homer, Bart, Lisa, Marge and Maggie's antics each week, and the show has been running for 420 seasons.

Clearly this is a show ripe for adaptation for the UK market. The show's premise is universal — a family of jaundiced, animated characters are led on a series of wacky adventures by a mentally handicapped patriarch, while the family's daughter continues her sure-fire successful campaign to be their nation's president in the "B" story each week. There is not a man, woman or child in this country alive today who cannot relate to this premise, and so it stands to reason that you should listen to my idea.

My Crazy Family is the UK adaptation I have worked out of *The Simpsons*. *My Crazy Family* centres on The Lohans, an everyday family living in some unspecified suburb in the present day (although they never use computers and if they do they never have the internet except in one episode but it doesn't look like the internet at all). Estes is the idiot father figure, Midge his loyal wife, Bert their "cool" son, Becky the always-right genius daughter, and Peggy is a baby. Estes works not in any NUCLEAR PANNER PLANT but in high-level customer complaints for BT. All these details are slightly different, but the beauty of the series is it hardly requires any ideas at all — *The Simpsons* has 992 episodes currently and a further 14 currently in development, so we can just steal ideas from that.

My spec script, for an episode entitled "This Wacky Life," is based on the episode of *The Simpsons* where Marge has an affair with her bowling instructor. In it, Midge has an affair with her darts instructor named Jack. I hope you will find it as entertaining to read as I had fun writing it.

I hope to go into production immediately. I can quit my job at any point to start executive producing the series. I will need 12 writers, an animator, and a full-time secretary/per-

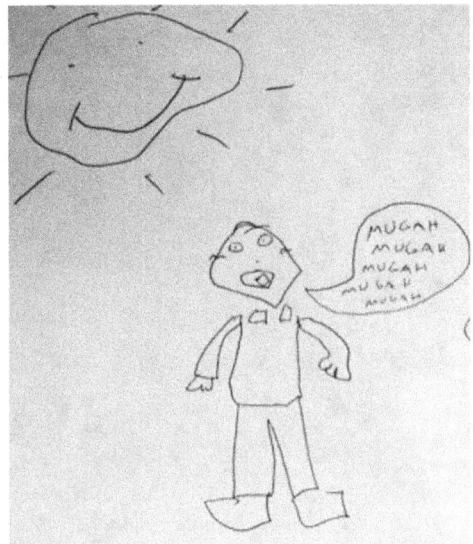

Fig. 1.

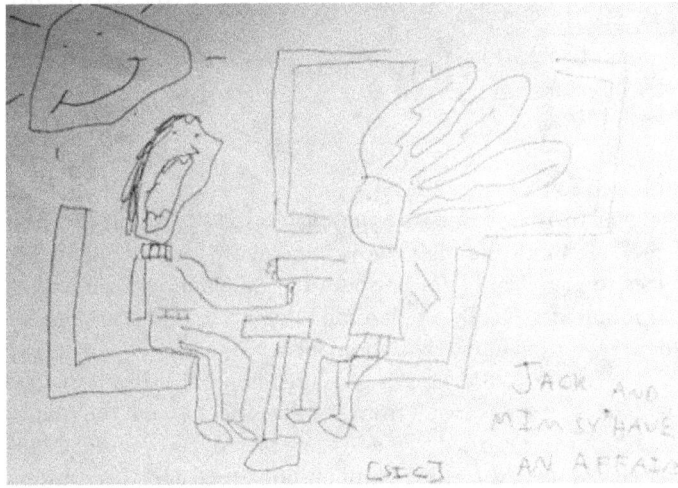

Fig. 2.

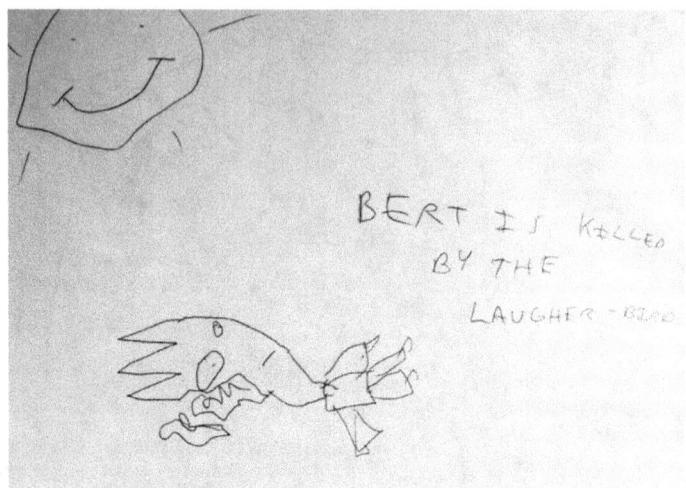

Fig. 3.

sonal assistant, as well as central London office space NOT in the BBC building (to prevent corporate interference). If you do not accept my demands I am fully prepared to go to other channels.

Yours hopefully,
Tom Whyman

Attached to this letter is a 24-page script, which mostly follows the plot of the Seasons 1 *Simpsons* episode "Life on the Fast Lane," although the dialogue is intercut with numerous references to gags from later episodes of *The Simpsons*, crude sexual innuendo, sub-Beckettian monologues to-camera, and (for some reason) a lot of trivia about birds.

Also included are a series of deliberately child-like drawings (which, as far as I can tell from the BBC's notes, were the reason my script was returned to me "unconsidered," as opposed to being picked up and making us all millionaires), depicting among other things "Estes saying his catchphrase" ("Mugah Mugah," which I guess was a reference to Homer trying to get Lisa to establish "Bucka Bucka or Woozle Wozzle" as her catchphrase in the episode "Bart Gets Famous") (fig. 1); "Jack and Mimsy [*sic*] Have an Affair' (which superficially resembles the scene from "Life on the Fast Lane" where Jacques and Marge have brunch, although the Jacques character is screaming) (fig. 2); and "Bert Is Killed By The Laugher-Bird" (in which a melted Bart-creature, which resembles the crappy Bart-snowman he builds out of "the snow left under the car" in the episode "Marge Be Not Proud," lies motionless on the ground, presumably after having been killed by a large bird) (fig. 3). In each of these drawings, a smiling sun appears in the top left-hand corner, a clear reference to Homer's "and this happy little character is the sun," that he draws on the "blueprints" for his dog house in the episode "Bart the Lover."

Feelin' Fine

Why did I make this thing? Well, I suppose on one level this was a prank, aimed at the BBC. But this can't possibly be the whole story: after all, it seems strange to go to all this effort just to get a rise out of an audience of (probably) one single human individual, who if I'm lucky might have found the material I'd sent them funny enough to pass it round the office ("oh look, this is a weird one, what should we send them back?"), but who more likely than not will have just been mildly annoyed. On a personal level, I must have been getting some sort of creative fulfilment *just inherent* to making art (or something like it) out of scrambled-up bits of old *Simpsons* episodes.

Certainly I am not the only person who has ever been driven to make art in this way, mangling and distorting *The Simpsons* to make it weird — or, perhaps better, to throw its pre-existing weirdness into greater relief. In around 2011, a figure emerged called "Chris (Simpsons artist)," a writer and cartoonist who first rose to prominence by posting bizarre, half-mutilated approximations of *Simpsons* characters he had drawn on MS paint. Thus: Homer appears with a heart-shaped face and multiple eyes with a nose that looks like a foot, yelling "spook town" (fig.

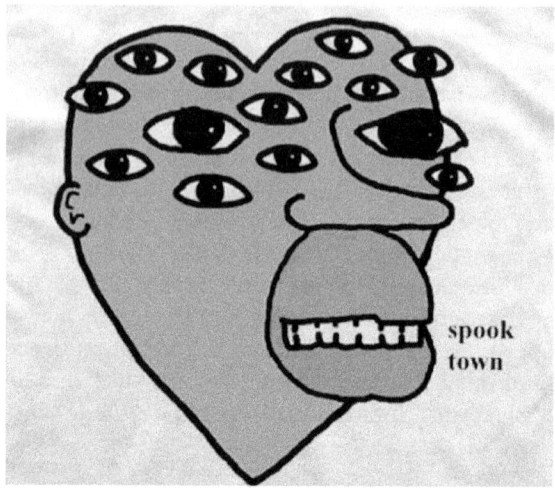

spook
town

Fig. 4.

4); Bart has a hand growing out of his head — the hand is catching an egg, and Bart is saying "I have got it" (fig. 5). Chris has since branched out, and now mainly focuses on other characters — I particularly like his mopey, teenage Thomas the Tank Engine, head in hands with human limbs, moaning "why was I born a train."

Chris has picked up a big enough following to be described in *FHM* as "the internet's Picasso." By contrast, a 2017 *VICE* article by Giacomo Lee surveys the distinctly more underground world of "*Simpsons* zines."[2] These subterranean publications range from comic books re-contextualizing characters and situations from the show (Scott Carr's "The City of New York vs. Hammer Sonpsims," "a very crude and absurd" re-imagining of the episode where Homer leaves his car at the bottom of the World Trade Center; Erms's "Just Say 'Yes' To Saying 'No' To

---

2 Giacomo Lee, "The True Spirit of 'The Simpsons' Lives On in These Bootleg Zines," *Vice*, December 12, 2017, https://www.vice.com/en_uk/article/a3j39j/the-true-spirit-of-the-simpsons-lives-on-in-these-bootleg-zines.

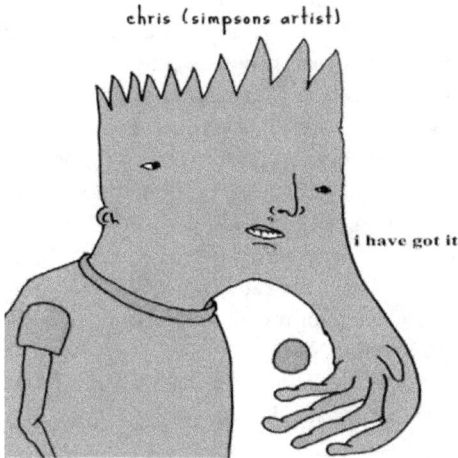

chris (simpsons artist)

i have got it

Fig. 5.

Saying 'Yes' to Soft Drugs," which looks a bit like if *The Simpsons* had been mangled up by R. Crumb) to collections of "found art" from the show itself (book designer Oliver Lebrun's "A Pocket Companion to Books from *The Simpsons*'), to works which in some way celebrate, send up or otherwise comment upon broader cultural responses to the series — for instance Tim Bell's "Homage to Homer," a collection of photographs of people in fancy dress as Homer Simpson.

Not all *Simpsons* art is strictly visual. Okilly Dokilly are a metalcore band from Phoenix, Arizona known for dressing up as Ned Flanders and performing songs inspired by his character in the show (titles include "White Wine Spritzer" and 'Godspeed Little Doodle"). They claim to play music in the genre of "Nedal," which they describe as "not as fast as Bartcore, and a little cleaner than Krusty Punk."

Are You Hugging the TV?

But probably the most prominent genre of music inspired by *The Simpsons* is "Simpsonwave," which became a mini-phenomenon in 2016 — at least to the extent where there was a fairly substantial article about it on Pitchfork.[3] Well, I call Simpsonwave a genre of music. In truth, it is probably best understood as a genre of video art, although it is closely associated with a style of music — namely vaporwave, that style of electronic music which emerged in the early 2010s chopping and screwing 1980s and '90s mall muzak, infomercial jingles, home computer sound effects, and the likes — glitching, lilting, and saturated with nostalgia.[4] Important vaporwave artists include Macintosh Plus, Saint Pepsi, Black Banshee, James Ferraro, and Daniel Lopatin aka Chuck Person (better known for the more classical electronica he makes as Oneohtrix Point Never).

In his seminal 2016 video "How to Simpsonwave," YouTuber FrankJavCee describes the genre as follows:

> The concept of Simpsonwave is simple. Take footage of early episodes of *The Simpsons,* preferably seasons 1–6…[5] Now, edit some [vapor]wavey music to the footage. If you're untalented at crafting your own musical creations, this is totally fine. Just rip-off some other vaporwave producer… Next, add a dream-like filter and VHS distortion to the entire video to represent the adult longing for a childhood they thought they had. If you're really fucking fancy you can chromakey certain parts of the cartoon and overlay modern effects or even alternative scenes to better showcase the brain synapses sometimes crossing in memories, creating phantoms of times that probably never even existed in the first place. Once you're done be sure to name it something vaporwavey by using that aesthetic wide text generator with a name like "Simpsonwave 1995."

3   See Kevin Lozano, "What the Hell Is Simpsonwave?" *Pitchfork,* June 14, 2016, https://pitchfork.com/thepitch/1188-what-the-hell-is-simpsonwave/.

4   I think it still could probably be argued that Simpsonwave is a genre of music, in the same way that northern soul is a genre of music — defined by its later appropriation.

5   FrankJavCee probably should have said 1–8 (or possibly 9), where the cut-off point for "classic" Simpsons is more usually located.

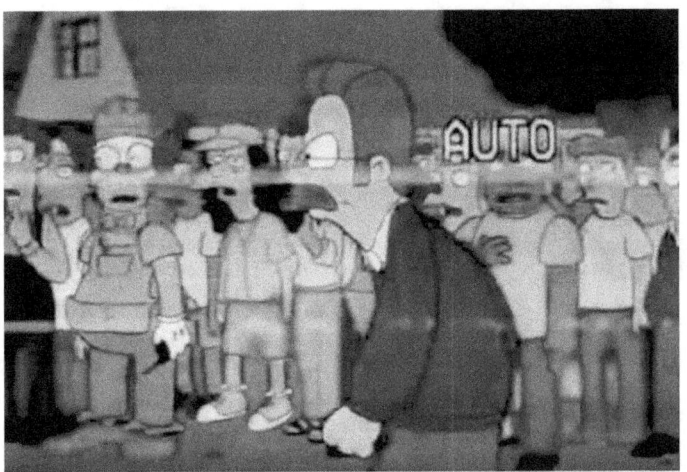

Fig. 6.

To give one example. The Simpsonwave video "ダレ カ (Somebody that I used to know) – VAPORWAVE CHILL REMIX" by LoneDev opens with the scene from the episode "Hurricane Neddy," where Ned Flanders — having seen his house get knocked down twice within the space of about a week — loses his temper at his friends and neighbors. The scene has a VHS filter over it with the word "AUTO" in the top-right corner, to make it look as if it has been shot as a shaky home video, an unpleasant memory no-one should have ever documented (fig. 6). As in the episode itself, Ned walks away from the crowd of well-wishers he has just yelled at, with his family following him. He gets in his car, alone, and drives off. At this point, the color filter changes, briefly saturating the image with purples and blues before turning mostly pink. In addition to the VHS crackle, a snowfall effect is added to make it look as if Flanders is driving through a snowstorm, or through space. Footage of Flanders driving then loops endlessly, as the video's music — a vaporwave remix of "Somebody That I Used To Know" by Gotye — plays.

Another example, the video "CRISIS" by Lucien Hughes, the figure usually cited as Simpsonwave's greatest auteur, presents

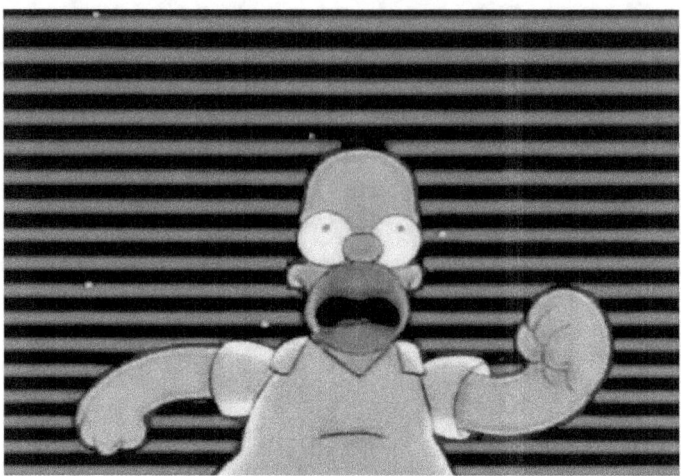

Fig. 7.

a rather more complex narrative. Over the track "Decay" by
HOME, a montage of clips tells a story in which Homer is seen
experiencing — and working through — some sort of deep emotional crisis, probably associated with the death of his mother.
Homer's grief initially causes him to isolate himself from his
family, endangering his marriage as he binges on alcohol to the
point of having to dance outside Moe's for beer money and apparently has an affair. But, by the end of the video, by talking
through his problems he is able to reconcile with Marge and
Lisa.

The video has a complex structure that is partly non-linear,
with events Homer is experiencing in the "main" run of the narrative triggering "memories" which are then presented to the
viewer — for instance at one point, as he sits in bed with another
woman, Homer breaks down and cries and thinks about his first
kiss with Marge, which we then see. This image of Homer in bed
with another woman is also one of a series of repeated motifs.
At various points, Homer is seen running down the street and
yelling (fig. 7); Homer is also regularly seen slouched in a couch
listening to a tape player on headphones (fig. 8). This latter motif

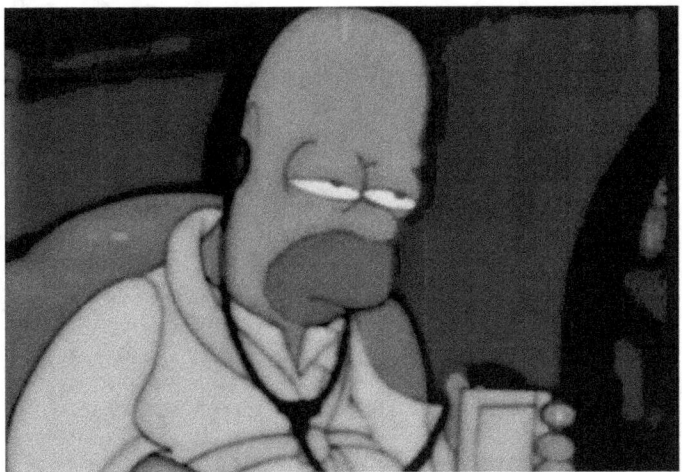

Fig. 8.

could also be read as a framing device, since in the video's first scene Homer is seen sitting down on the couch with the tape player and turning it on. The music then begins, and the image of Homer sitting on the couch fades into one of Homer sitting on the trunk of his car watching the stars — which is presumably also a recollection. All of the scenes in the video have their color palette altered, and vhs crackle and other effects added.

A third example, "Millhouse 1992" by midge, opens with the scene from the episode "Bart's Friend Falls In Love" in which a recently-dumped Milhouse is standing forlorn at the top of the climbing frame in the school playground, "a broken man… it's recess everywhere but in his heart." The scene abruptly cuts away, and the music starts: "I'll Be Wait For Sadness Comes Along" by Chrome Sparks.

The viewer is then presented with a rapidly jumping series of clips featuring Milhouse from various episodes of *The Simpsons* — with scenes from the episode "Summer of 4ft. 2," in which the family vacation with Milhouse at Ned Flanders's beach house, given especial prominence. In amongst these clips, the video regularly cuts to a clip from that episode which does

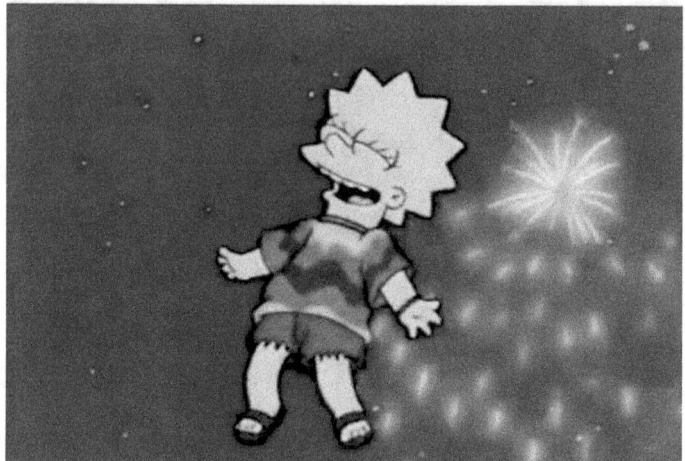

Fig. 9.

not feature Milhouse at all, in which Lisa is being bounced up in the air on a sheet by the new "cool" friends she makes at the beach — fireworks bursting in the sky behind her, the very image of happiness (fig. 9). At around the 30-second mark, we return to the image of Milhouse on the climbing frame, before he disappears from the video entirely, and we are left for the final 34 seconds (of what is a video just 1 minute 6 seconds long) with a loop of Lisa bouncing in the air. And yet Milhouse is still present, because what has come before can leave us in no doubt that what we are seeing is his memory, of Lisa whom he loves — a memory in which he is absent, and Lisa is all the happier for it — and with that memory comes the knowledge that he will never be able to share in her happiness, hence his desolation. Part of what differentiates this video from the others I've looked at is that midge — who Hughes interestingly cites as a key influence[6] — manages to achieve this poignant effect without overlaying any VHS crackle or altering the colors.

6   See the interview with Hughes, in Lozano, "What the Hell Is Simpons-
      wave?" Although it is understandable that Hughes's videos — which

Everything Looks Bad If You Remember It

In *Retromania,* his sprawling, at times brilliant study of pop culture and nostalgia, the music critic Simon Reynolds cites vaporwave pioneer James Ferraro as the creator of a genre he prefers to call "hypnagogic pop" — that is, pop "relating to the state immediately before falling asleep," a term coined by The Wire writer David Keenan:

> Keenan noticed that memory-mangled traces of eighties music were starting to flicker through the hallucinatory haze spewed out by all these groups: crisp funk bass and spangly guitar parts redolent of the slickly produced rock 'n' soul "yacht rock" of that decade [...] the taught sequenced rhythms and bright digital synth sounds of eighties Hollywood soundtracks [...]. Ferraro suggested that all these eighties sounds seeped into the consciousness of today's twenty-something musicians when they were toddlers falling asleep [...]. He speculated that their parents played music in the living room and it came through the bedroom walls muffled and indistinct.[7]

While this origin story may be somewhat fanciful, what is nice about it is the way in which it helps to capture what is perhaps most central to vaporwave — its enchanted atmosphere, at times dreamy and at times haunting, of millennial nostalgia for the world of our childhood.

One of the interesting things about vaporwave is that it is often presented as an "ironic" movement, its practitioners making

---

are generally speaking, much more fully realized — have received more attention thus far, in many ways midge's channel is the more interesting of the two. Hughes tends to cut *Simpsons* clips up to form poignant narratives somewhat independent of anything that actually happens in the show. By contrast, midge's videos tend to draw out existing themes from *The Simpsons* and accentuate their significance. See the discussion of midge's video "Homer's Website" in relation to the concept of hauntology below.

7 Simon Reynolds, *Retromania* (London: Faber & Faber, 2011), 345–46.

music which is not really "supposed" to be good — which I think stems from the fact that vaporwave music is in large part created out of bits of musical junk: crappy, tacky, "commercial." But this seems strange when we compare vaporwave to what is probably its nearest equivalent for Generation X, Boards of Canada's classic 1998 record *Music Has The Right To Children.* As with vaporwave, the music of Boards of Canada is interwoven with bits of cultural detritus their listeners would have been able to recall from childhood: analogue synth tones reminiscent of seventies wildlife documentaries and BBC "TV for schools"; samples from *Sesame Street* and old documentaries; a cover photo which depicts a family on holiday, wearing clothes typical of the 1970s, the image washed out to the point where all the faces had been erased. In *Music Has The Right To Children,* all of this serves to invoke a deep and haunting sense of nostalgia almost exactly analogous to that associated with vaporwave.

> The crumbly smudges of texture, the miasmic melody lines, the tangled threads of wistful and eerie seemed to have an extraordinary capacity to trigger ultra-vivid reveries that felt like childhood memories. I would experience a flood of images that were emotionally neutral yet charged with significance, a mysticism of the commonplace and municipal: playgrounds with fresh rain stippling the swings and slides; canal-side recreation areas, with rows of saplings neatly plotted, wreathed in morning mist; housing estates with identical back gardens and young mums pegging damp wind-flapped sheets on clothing lines as clouds skidded across a cold blue winter sky. I was never sure if these were actual memories from my childhood in the late sixties and early seventies or false ones (dreamed or seen on television).[8]

But Boards of Canada have always been presented (quite rightly) as serious musicians making music that is both seriously sin-

---

8   Ibid., 331–32.

cere and seriously good. So why does vaporwave feel the need to ironically distance itself from itself?

The answer, as far as I can tell, hinges on an important generational difference. We millennials have come of age in an increasingly precarious world, for the most part unable to aspire to any of the things that we have been brought up to think would make us "real" people, like our parents: a stable professional job, home ownership, a family. Correlatively, this has produced in us a sense that our proper comportment toward the world — and toward ourselves, including I suppose our own memories — is one of disassociation, of disinvestment. If you're not "really" trying, and you don't "really" care, then you can't "really" fail, can't "really" be hurt by your various inevitable disappointments. The name "vaporwave," it is worth noting, has its root in "vaporware," a term from the computer industry meaning a product that is announced but, for whatever reason, is never released, never in fact comes to exist. What better term for the music of a generation of half-persons, who can't even become substantial enough to sincerely express their own anguish at the fact of the arrested development that is preventing them from becoming the people who, they have always been told, they ought to be?

Can I Borrow a Feeling?

It is with this in mind that the power of Simpsonwave becomes apparent. In a video attempting to make sense of the genre, "Is Simpsonwave a joke?" a YouTuber called "This Exists" contrasts the "deliberate and manufactured nostalgia" of vaporwave with "the actual real nostalgia of seeing Lisa's trip to Ned Flanders' beach house on the fourth of July," effectively claiming that the former only becomes "emotionally resonant" when it is paired with the latter.[9] It is perhaps more accurate to say: given that vaporwave is constructed out of fragments of millennial childhood memories, vaporwave *could never really be fully itself* unless it also incorporates *The Simpsons*.

---

9   Compare the discussion of the video "Millhouse 1992" above.

After all, when I think back to my childhood, what really formed me? I grew up in a town I barely knew, in a suburb too distant from anywhere for a child to walk there. I dreaded going to school each day, where I would sit restless and bored, waiting to be allowed out. I found shops overwhelming, I had no idea why anyone would want to go to — I don't know — the big Tesco, which was full of things I had no concept of what it would be like to want or need. I always felt sad, except when I was "overexcited," in which case I was probably about to be told off.

The only times I really felt happy, when I felt like myself, was when I was playing computer games (anything from the *Final Fantasy* series, over and over again), or watching *The Simpsons* (on vhs tapes we'd recorded off the tv, on repeat). And then when we weren't playing, or watching, me and my brothers were ranking, which for *The Simpsons* meant ranking every episode (we had a four-tier system, on which — for some reason — the absolute gold standard was the season 3 episode "Homer Alone"). We had a big book, a sort of guide to *The Simpsons,* I guess, which listed every episode from seasons 1–8, and gave you facts about them, allowing you to trace the references (almost my entire pre-university cultural education came from that book). I came to know them all intimately, and a good decade and a half on from that book's final disintegration nothing from those first 8 series has yet left my head.

Whenever I watch *The Simpsons* nowadays, which is not necessarily all that often, I know all the scenes, all the lines already — I can hear what is coming ahead of time. Whenever I read or hear something, that uses the same words or has the same cadence as a line from *The Simpsons,* I'll immediately make the association, and if I'm with someone I'll feel compelled to voice the joke (if I'm by myself, I'll probably just laugh out loud). Recently, my partner made me watch the film *Jaws,* which I'd somehow managed to avoid seeing before, and at least half the shots were immediately, uncannily familiar — because at some point *The Simpsons* had ripped them off. And although I think I am probably a slightly extreme example, I do not think any of this will be entirely unfamiliar, at least to anyone who is roughly the same age as me (I was born in 1988). *The Simpsons* is in our language, it is under our skin; it has colored our souls, it has irreducibly shaped the way we experience the world. And so I will always experience *The Simpsons* in everything — in this sense, I will always be haunted by it. Simpsonwave, as an extension of vaporwave, brings this out masterfully.

But of course — it must also be noted — Simpsonwave does this in a deliberately ironized way. On at least one level, its creators are doing something they know (or think they know) to be incredibly *stupid* — cutting up clips from an old cartoon show and overlaying it with a style of electronic music that is itself performatively ironic despite (of course) the real sincere connections that also bear on it. As art, Simpsonwave thus allows both producers and audiences to maintain themselves in an ironized subjectivity distanced from whatever feelings they might be "really" experiencing, disassociated from whatever they "really" have at stake in the world. It is in the space this opens up, between life and art, that this Real is able to manifest itself: a sincerity that is only possible if it is simultaneously disguised.

So I Tied an Onion to My Belt, Which Was the Style at the Time

That said, when it comes to music and nostalgia, we probably ought to be careful. For Reynolds in *Retromania,* as for his late friend Mark Fisher in *Ghosts of My Life,* contemporary pop culture's overindulgence of nostalgic impulses is in some sense symptomatic of a political culture in which, to put this point as Fisher does (via Franco "Bifo" Berardi), "the future is being slowly cancelled": where what Fisher calls "capitalist realism" — that is, the ideological myth that there is "no alternative" to neoliberal capitalism, a myth which has its roots in the post-Soviet "end of history" — prevents people in general from being able to envisage any possibility of a different, better world which might come-to-be in time.[10]

This context lends itself to the prevalence of a "formal nostalgia" in which artists feel compelled to cling to established, recognizable forms because they are unable to produce anything genuinely new.[11] For Fisher, formal nostalgia is most obviously dominant in popular music:

> This is quickly established by performing a simple thought experiment. Imagine any record released in the past couple of years being beamed back in time to, say, 1995 and played on the radio. It's hard to think that it will produce any jolt in the listeners. On the contrary, what would be likely to shock our 1995 audience would be the very recognisability of the sounds: would music really have changed so little in the next 17 years? Contrast this with the rapid turnover of styles between the 1960s and the 90s: play a jungle record from 1993 to someone in 1989 and it would have challenged them to rethink what music was, or could be.[12]

Fisher identifies a number of material reasons for this. On the supply-side, "neoliberal capitalism has systematically deprived

---

10 See Mark Fisher, *Capitalist Realism: Is There No Alternative?* (Alresford: Zero Books, 2008), and Mark Fisher, *Ghosts of My Life: Writings on Depression, Hauntology and Lost Futures* (Alresford: Zero Books, 2014), 6–7. In what follows, I will discuss Fisher and Reynolds's views together, almost as if they were a single author. It may be that I am not entirely justified in doing this, but certainly there are clear cross-currents: both reference each other frequently when discussing pop music, retro, and nostalgia — and Reynolds even mentions that they started using the term "hauntology" (more on which below) simultaneously (see Reynolds, *Retromania*, 328); indeed, I am not really sure it is possible to understand what Reynolds is talking about when he invokes the term "hauntology" in Retromania without reading Fisher's "The Slow Cancellation of the Future" first. If their views are not strictly speaking identical, then they do at least seem to have been borne out of the same conversation.

11 See Fisher, *Ghosts of My Life,* 7–8.

12 Ibid.

artists of the resources necessary to produce the new."[13] Whereas during eras of great innovation in popular music (the 1960s, the post-punk '80s), the welfare state "constituted an indirect source of funding for [...] experiments [...]. The subsequent ideological and practical attack on public services" from the Thatcher years onward "meant that one of the spaces where artists could be sheltered from the pressure to produce something that was immediately successful was severely circumscribed." Artists — especially if they are not from well-off backgrounds — must immediately conform to the demands of the marketplace or risk destitution. "If there's one factor above all else which contributes to cultural conservatism," Fisher adds, "it is the vast inflation of rent and mortgages."[14]

But audiences themselves also suffer from the effects of precarity.

> As Berardi has argued, the intensity and precariousness of late capitalist work culture leaves people in a state where they are simultaneously exhausted and overstimulated. The combination of precarious work and digital communications leads to a besieging of attention.[15]

The typical austerity-capitalist subject is obliged to work themselves to exhaustion just to be considered minimally functioning at their jobs (a situation which I'm sure will be familiar to any early-career academic).

Meanwhile during any break from work, our attention is bombarded by a vast stream of stimuli from the various interlinked platforms which dominate the instruments with which we navigate the world — our computers, phones, and smart TVs. 24-hour news and the endless stream of commentary surrounding it on Twitter; the lives of others on Facebook and Instagram; almost every cultural product that has ever existed on YouTube,

---

13 Ibid., 15.
14 Ibid.
15 Ibid., 14–15.

Spotify, Netflix, Amazon Prime. Everything is always *there,* but we lack either the time or the energy to ever take any of it in, to have any real understanding of any of it. In this context, Fisher claims, consumers will eschew new experiences in favor of old forms which, like pornography, offer "the quick and easy promise of a minimal variation on an already familiar satisfaction."[16] This means that artists who stick to "classic" styles are able to dominate the marketplace — Fisher's examples include Adele and the Arctic Monkeys.

Of course, as both Fisher and Reynolds are well aware, all established art forms — and popular music is no exception — have always been, at least to some extent, in conversation with their own pasts. And indeed, this conversation has at times led to the birth of new forms. Reynolds in particular notes that revolutionary movements have often "constructed narratives around 'paradise lost and paradise regained' scenarios," and discusses at some length how this revolutionary-reactionary impulse fuelled punk — which set itself stale, mannered prog with "a concerted effort to turn back the clock to [...] fifties rock 'n' roll and sixties garage."[17]

Thus it seems that nostalgia itself cannot possibly be the real problem. Rather, what Fisher in particular seems to object to is the way in which nostalgia has become intertwined with *anachronism,* "the slippage of discrete time periods into one another."[18] Whereas in the past, retro music would have been marketed as such, contemporary retro cultural products typically disavow any explicit reference to the past.[19]

Take someone like the stupendously successful Adele: although her music is not marketed as retro, there is nothing that marks out her records as belonging to the 21st century either. Like so much contemporary cultural production,

---

16 Ibid., 15.
17 Reynolds, *Retromania,* xxvii, 240.
18 Fisher, *Ghosts of My Life,* 5.
19 See ibid., 12.

Adele's records are saturated with a vague but persistent feeling of the past without recalling any specific historical moment.[20]

The result is a music which is supposed to strike listeners as having a non-specifically "classic" feel, blurring the past into the present and, with this, eliminating any radical potential the past ever had. Adele's music communicates a piece of distinctively capitalist realist ideology: the thought that things can never be different, because in truth they were always the same.

What? It's Not Maggie's Birthday?

Of course it must be noted that, as a show, *The Simpsons* is saturated with anachronism. Most obviously, since it began in 1989, none of *The Simpsons* characters have really aged. Bart has been 10 for almost 30 years, Lisa 8, Maggie 1. Homer and Marge, weirdly, *have* aged, although only slightly: Homer was originally referred to as 34, and has since been described as 36, 38, 39, and 40; Marge and Homer met in high school, where they were in the same graduating class, so they are canonically the same age (or near enough).

This has distorted the show's chronology, particularly in relation to cultural time. In early episodes ("The Way We Was" from Season 2), Homer and Marge's teen years were depicted as having taken place in the 1970s. By the mid-1980s, Homer and Marge had two children — and in 1985, Homer would achieve brief success as a member of the Grammy award-winning barbershop quartet The Be Sharps ("Homer's Barbershop Quartet," Season 5). By the episode "Homerpalooza" (Season 7), Homer would be so stuck in a dad-rut behind the times that he has never heard of blockbuster '90s acts like The Smashing Pumpkins and Nine Inch Nails. But in a later episode ("That '90s Show," Season 19), Homer and Marge are seen in the early 1990s with

20 Ibid.

no children, and Homer is in fact a member of a grunge band who become nationally famous, Sadgasm.

This distorted chronology has also affected episodes in which the show "flashes forward" to events in the family's future. For instance, the episode "Lisa's Wedding" from Season 6 is largely set in the year 2010, when Lisa (in the episode, at least) is 23. Technically, if we assume all new *Simpsons* episodes are set in the year they first aired, this is (at the time of writing) the year today's Lisa was born. If she really is to succeed Donald Trump to the presidency, then she had better hope some laws (either on term limits or age restrictions) change soon.[21]

However, it may not necessarily be true that *The Simpsons'* 2018 (say) is really the same year as *our* 2018. In part because the fundamental dynamics of the show have not changed since 1989, it has failed to respond to various real social changes — either in the economy, or to do with technology. If they really lived in our 2018, then Homer and Marge really would need to take up (and — what really would be novel — *keep*) all those new jobs that often drive the episodes' plots, just out of basic necessity: a lower middle-class family of five could never possibly survive in post-crash America on just *one* income, especially if any of them ever suffered a health scare.

Meanwhile, the show has a long history of failing to respond in a convincing way to technological developments associated with computing and the Internet. In middle-period episodes such as "Das Bus" (season 9), where Homer starts an online business, and "The Computer Wore Menace Shoes" (season 12), where Homer buys a computer and starts spreading gossip online, the show does an OK job of satirizing certain trends around the early Internet, but fails badly at capturing either its look or feel; it also fails to depict in a realistic way how people actually use these technologies (contrast this with the adept way in which early episodes of the show depict the family watching TV).

---

21 Although, see my essay, "President Lisa Simpson," *The Baffler,* October 4, 2017, https://thebaffler.com/latest/president-lisa-simpson.

A final way in which *The Simpsons* can be considered anachronistic is the simple fact that it continues to exist as a going concern at all. Simpsons fans like me typically have an obsessive knowledge of the first nine or ten seasons, the canon of a show which flourished from 1990 to around 2000, before — let's not beat around the bush — it got rubbish and all the fans stopped watching. And yet, *The Simpsons* has continued to produce around 22 new episodes a year, persisting in this state of living-death for longer than it was ever "really" alive.

Um… It's Like, Uh… Did Anyone See the Movie *Tron*?

On one level, of course, Simpsonwave could also be accused of slipping into anachronism. After all, these videos are essentially mash-ups of clips which were created for the most part in the 1990s, with a style of electronic music that is much more contemporary.[22] And indeed at least some of the videos self-consciously attempt to make the clips somehow "about" vaporwave, or at any rate the experience of listening to it (see for instance Lucien Hughes's "SUNDAY SCHOOL," where Bart has his walkman confiscated at church while listening to Macintosh Plus, before going off into a sort of vaporwave-induced reverie soundtracked by Black Banshee). Arguably, this elides the past into the present just as the show itself does.

But on another level, Simpsonwave could be understood as helping to correct various anachronisms exhibited by the show. For one thing, the use of vaporwave — a style of music which, although produced during the 2010s, is drenched with millennial childhood nostalgia — helps contextualize the clips, and thus our understanding of the show overall, within a *specifically* 1990s temporality. This helps erase some of the damage done to *The Simpsons* canon by its persistence since 2000.

---

22 As has already been noted above (in the quote from FrankJavCee), few if any Simpsonwave artists use clips from recent episodes — and with good reason, since there is no chance they will invoke the desired sense of nostalgia.

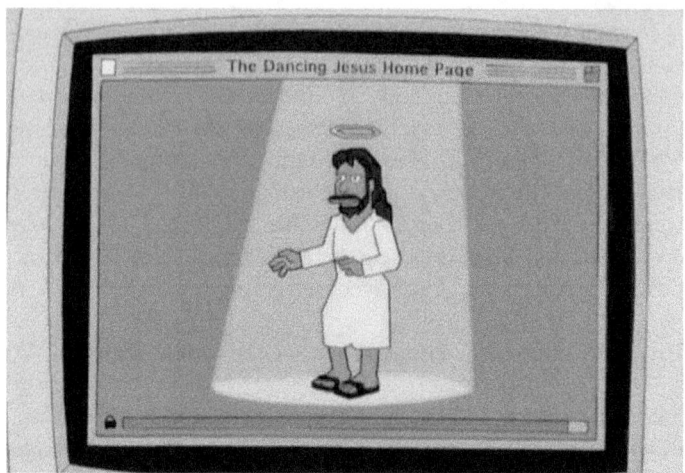

Fig. 10.

A video such as "Homer's Website" by midge could be read as
an attempt to redeem *The Simpsons'* technological illiteracy, presenting us with an alternative vision of the show's development
in which Homer and the family embraced the Internet age.

"Homer's Website" opens with a scene from "The Computer
Wore Menace Shoes." A hefty, 90s-style home computer sits in
a garbage can outside 742 Evergreen Terrace. We hear Marge
yelling: "Homer, bring that back in the house!" "Fine," Homer
grudgingly replies. In the next scene — a clip from the same
episode — Homer, having brought the computer back inside, is
now sat hunched over it at the coffee table in his living room
(which incidentally, has always struck me as a singularly weird
place to put a computer). Whereas in the episode itself, the audience would have then seen Homer engaging with a wholly unconvincing approximation of what the Internet was supposed to
look like (a mostly blank window, free of anything resembling a
navigation toolbar, containing an animation of "Dancing Jesus,"
fig. 10), in midge's video we hear the familiar Windows start-up
noise, before Homer is seen loading up Windows XP (fig. 11).

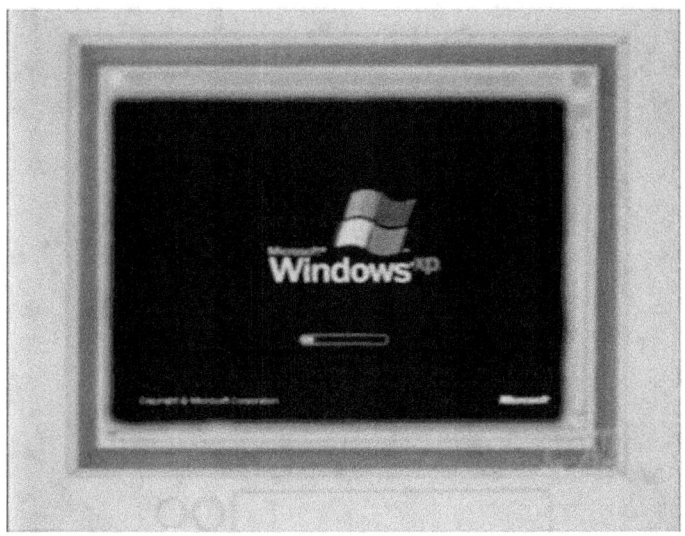

Fig. 11.

As the music associated with the video begins (the track is uncredited, so I am unsure who it is by), the 3D Homer from "Treehouse of Horror VI" is seen dancing among various objects, including a rotating ESC key and a 3D dolphin (possibly a reference to the early-'90s Sega MegaDrive game "Ecco the Dolphin"). A montage of clips then depicts Homer — amongst other things — lost in the 3D world; falling through time screaming and clutching a toaster; and looking pensively on as a flood of static containing the words "VIRTUAL EXODUS" bursts into his kitchen (fig. 12). After around a minute of this, the music and video come abruptly to a halt.

With midge's video, we finally witness (although admittedly only briefly) a version of *The Simpsons* ready to embrace the disorienting, decentring, and indeed liberating power of new technology. The computer, erupting "back into" *The Simpsons'* house from the trash, the future brought back into the show from the past.

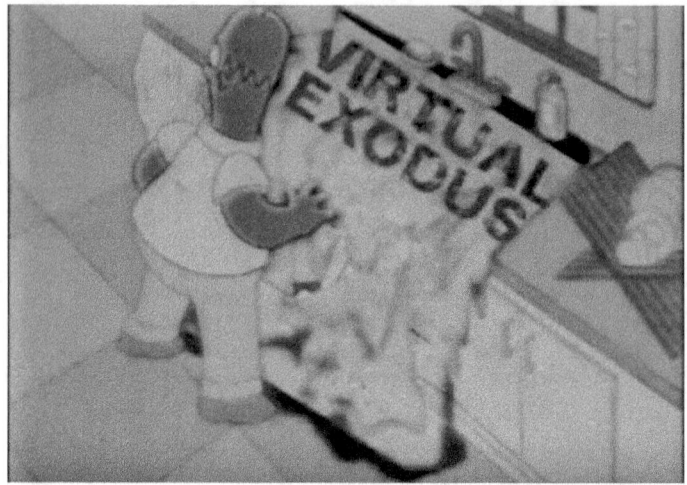

Fig. 12.

In Memory of a Real Tree

"Homer's Website" can thus be understood as engaging in a form of what Fisher and Reynolds call "hauntology." This term is lifted from Jacques Derrida in *Specters of Marx,* where it puns off "ontology" — the study of what can be said to exist. Hauntology, by contrast, is concerned with what is *present but nonexistent,* like a ghost. Fisher specifically conceives of hauntology as "*the agency of the virtual,* with the spectre understood not as anything supernatural, but as that which acts without (physically) existing."[23] Drawing on the work of Martin Hägglund, Fisher distinguishes between two sorts of hauntological relationships: on the one hand, to "what is no longer," on the other, to "the not yet."[24] From this:

> We can provisionally distinguish two directions in hauntology. The first refers to that which is (in actuality is) no lon-

---

23 Fisher, *Ghosts of My Life,* 18.
24 Ibid., 19.

ger, but which remains effective as a virtuality (the traumatic "compulsion to repeat," a fatal pattern). The second sense of hauntology refers to that which (in actuality) has not yet happened, but which is already effective in the virtual (an attractor, an anticipation shaping current behavior). The "specter of communism" that Marx and Engels had warned of in the first lines of the Communist Manifesto was just this kind of ghost: a virtuality whose threatened coming was already playing a part in undermining the present state of things.[25]

In Reynolds's description, hauntology is:

A term that critic Mark Fisher and I started bandying around in 2005 to describe a loose network of mostly UK artists, central among them the musicians on the Ghost Box label (The Focus Group, Belbury Poly, The Advisory Circle et al.) and their kindred spirits Mordant Music and Moon Wiring Club. All of these groups explore a zone of British nostalgia linked to television programming of the sixties and seventies.[26]

Later, they would also apply the term to dubstep producer Burial, whose (much better-known) work Reynolds describes as "hauntological dance music," saturated with a nostalgia not necessarily for childhood but rather for the lost golden age of rave.[27] For Fisher, what the canon of hauntologists share is:

Not a sound so much as a sensibility, an existential orientation. The artists that came to be labelled hauntological were suffused with an overwhelming melancholy; and they were preoccupied with the way in which technology materialised memory — hence a fascination with television, vinyl records, audiotape, and with the sounds of these technologies breaking down. The fixation on materialised memory led to what is

---

25 Ibid.
26 Reynolds, *Retromania,* 328.
27 Ibid., 393.

perhaps the principle sonic signature of hauntology: the use of crackle, the surface noise made by vinyl. Crackle makes us aware that we are listening to a time that is out of joint; it won't allow us to fall into the illusion of presence.[28]

In my view, what Fisher and Reynolds call "hauntology" is thus best understood as a set of techniques which allow artists to invoke nostalgic sentiment while resisting an anachronism which would blur historicity into the present. This allows them to invoke the past in a way which holds fast to its radical potential, even against a general tendency toward (merely) "formal" nostalgia.

In particular, what Fisher is interested in is the way in which hauntological art can allow us to envisage an alternative "trajectory" toward a better future, associated for him with the "popular modernism" of the 1970s. The artists on the Ghost Box label, who he and Reynolds rate, invoke this trajectory by focusing on the tropes of "brutalist architecture, Penguin paperbacks, and the BBC radiophonic workshop."[29] Just think for instance of the band name "Belbury Poly," which invokes a now-lost set of educational institutions. But this art is not simply focused on the past and its possibilities in a morbid, *resigned* way. Indeed, it does not even attempt to invoke the past in a way that is *accurate*: after all, at the time a lot of this stuff would have seemed pretty crappy. The true power of hauntology is in invoking "what is not longer" in order to bring out of it "the not-yet" — possibilities of what, if only the world had been slightly different, *could* have been.

Vaporwave and its more developed form, Simpsonwave, are of course concerned with an entirely different set of tropes — but they are no less hauntological for it. Both are recognizably hauntological by virtue of the techniques they employ — VHS crackle, Windows start-up sounds, etc. These techniques are used to create musical and visual artworks which allow millennials to

---

28 Fisher, *Ghosts of My Life*, 21.
29 Ibid., 22.

imagine a version of the world of our childhood — a different version of it, perhaps, a version that was less empty — which did *not* culminate in the 2008 financial crash and the advent of austerity capitalism; a world in which the post-Soviet "end of history" combined with the utopian promise of the early internet to produce an easy-credit life resplendent with consumerist wonder. In this sense, they are true millennial hauntological art.[30]

We Were Sitting in Barney's Car Eating Packets of Mustard, You Happy?

But it could be argued that online *Simpsons* art also achieves something that is more than simply derivative of what Fisher and Reynolds describe. Simpsonwave in part grew out of — and remains closely associated with — the "Simpsons Shitposting" Facebook group. Founded by Geddy Johnson in 2015, at the time of writing, "Simpsons Shitposting" has over 200,000 members. An anarchic, volatile space, "Simpsons Shitposting" is the largest and most prominent forum dedicated to the sharing of *Simpsons* memes, with images and other media originally posted to the page often going viral elsewhere.[31] The forum's no-

---

30 The vision they present is, of course, much less obviously "leftist" than the clearly statist vision of Fisher's '70s hauntologists — millennial hauntology might thus be thought not to share the radical potential Fisher sees in it. I'm not quite sure what to say about this here. One point I'd like to make is that we millennials are nothing if not Thatcher and Reagan's children, and if we are to achieve anything "radical" in any direction we must come to terms with how our infancy has configured our desires.

31 The group seems to enjoy manufacturing crises. In 2016, the group ostensibly "almost shut down" after Johnson sold it to some "Macedonian scammers" because he needed $3,500 for "dick surgery"; the following year the admins claimed they had sold the group to Buzzfeed, turned off member posting and flooded the group with memes of "Smithers Dabbing"; at the time of writing its name has just been changed to "[omitted] Shitposting" on the basis that the admins have received a cease and desist letter from the legal representatives of Matt Groening, who has had "significant emotional distress" inflicted upon him by the group's "frequent use of the term 'Lowmer'," about which more below. It is hard to know which if any of the crises have been real.

toriety can be evidenced by the treatment it has been given on sites like *Wired* and *The Onion* AV *Club*; it has also inspired a number of imitators — both *Simpsons*-based (Twitter's "Ireland Simpsons Fans" account) and otherwise ("It's Always Sunny In Philadelphia Shitposting," "Frasier Shitposting," "Evangelion Shitposting," etc.).[32]

The concept of the "shitpost" is significant here. According to "Know Your Meme," the term "shitpost" was originally coined in 2007, at which point it referred to "utterly worthless and inane posts on an internet message board" — particularly when these posts were of such a high volume as to make the forum unusable by others.[33] However, according to Google Trends, the phrase was barely used until around the latter half of 2015, when usage suddenly spiked.[34] A 2016 *Independent* article attributes this spike to Donald Trump, who of course announced his candidacy for president at around this time. Many of Trump's earliest supporters were "ironybros" trolling forums with shitposts in support of him, often featuring the now-notorious Pepe the Frog.[35]

But personally I don't quite buy this narrative. After all, Simpsons Shitposting was founded in 2015 as well, and Google Trends clearly identifies the closest related topic to "shitposting" to be "*The Simpsons* — American sitcom." What is also clearly true is that although the definition of the term "shitpost" em-

---

32 See Brian Raftery, "The Homeric Odyssey of the Web's Strangest Simpsons Site," *Wired,* May 22, 2017, https://www.wired.com/2017/05/homeric-odyssy-webs-strangest-simpsons-site/; Randall Colburn, "Read This: The Story Behind the Internet's Weirdest *Simpsons* Fan Group," AV *Club,* May 23, 2017, https://news.avclub.com/read-this-the-story-behind-the-internet-s-weirdest-sim-1798262202.

33 See *Know Your Memes,* s.v. "shitposting," http://knowyourmeme.com/memes/shitposting.

34 See *Google Trends,* s.v. "shitposting," https://trends.google.com/trends/explore?date=all&q=Shitposting.

35 See Andrew Griffin, "Shitposting: What Is the Bizarre Online Behaviour That Could Win Donald Trump the Election?" *Independent,* September 23, 2016, https://www.independent.co.uk/life-style/gadgets-and-tech/news/what-is-shitposting-donald-trump-us-election-2016-palmer-luckey-a7326111.html.

ployed by "Simpsons Shitposting" and its imitators is in some sense related to the original coinage, it is nevertheless qualitatively distinct. After all, the term "shitpost" originally referred to a nuisance — but the whole point of Simpsons Shitposting and other related pages is, well, to shitpost. As the page's mission statement has it:

> A freeflowing definition.
> A simpsons shitpost has no regard for quality nor is it defined by how shit it is.
> Post because you want to.
> Post what you want to.
> No agenda.
> No ulterior motive.
> No care for how terrible it may be.
> No care for how many likes it may garner.
> NO NSFW
> NO EDGELORDS
> Just shitpost the simpsons.
> Art is Subjective.[36]

Here, then, the shitpost is defined not simply by its low quality, nor by how annoying it is for others. It is defined rather by a sort of *indifference,* both to quality ("A simpsons shitpost has no regard for quality [...] Post because you want to. Post what you want to") and to reception — either positive or negative ("No care for how terrible it may be. No care for how many likes to it may garner [...] NO EDGELORDS"). This invites users to produce a high volume of memes based on whatever happens to come into their head ("No agenda [...] Just shitpost the simpsons").

In practice what this means is that the page produces an almost constant stream of memes of wildly varying quality featuring characters and situations from *The Simpsons* (and, as

---

36 See "Shitposting Simpsons," *Facebook,* https://www.facebook.com/groups/shitpostingsimpsons/.

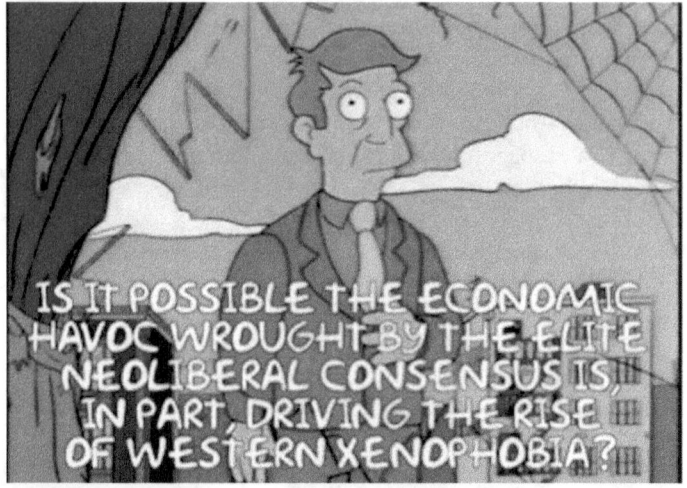
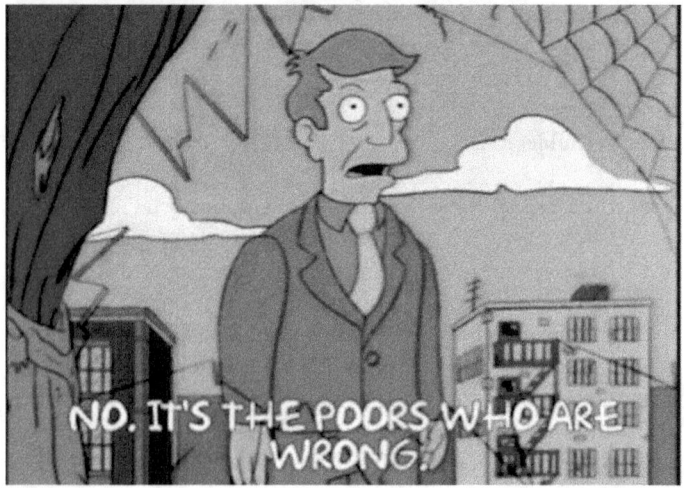

Fig. 13.

with Simpsonwave, this means: almost exclusively from earlier episodes of *The Simpsons*). It would be hard to give a complete survey of these memes — almost as hard as it would be to exaggerate (or to estimate) their sheer volume. Here, I want to move

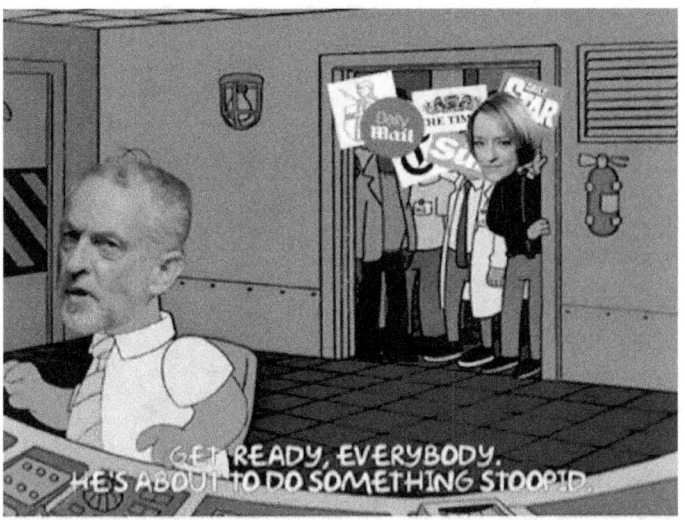

Fig. 14.

toward an understanding of them primarily by focusing on the
sort of *connections* which different sorts of Simpsons shitposts
draw.

One set of *Simpsons* shitposts draws connections between
the show and the wider world, including the news. An example
of this would be the post in fig. 13. This meme uses the form of
the "am I so out of touch? No, it's the children who are wrong"
bit from the episode "The Boy Who Knew Too Much," to make
it look as if Principal Skinner is commenting on the woeful reaction of the political and media establishment to the political
upheavals of 2016. Depending on what has been in the news
recently, the "Simpsons Shitposting" page is typically flooded
with similar (although not always as funny) memes — another
example, satirizing the UK media's treatment of Jeremy Corbyn,
is given in fig. 14. Meanwhile, the post given in fig. 15 relates one
of Troy McClure's songs from the *Planet of the Apes* musical that
he stars in in the episode "A Fish Called Selma" to the revolutionary science of historical materialism.

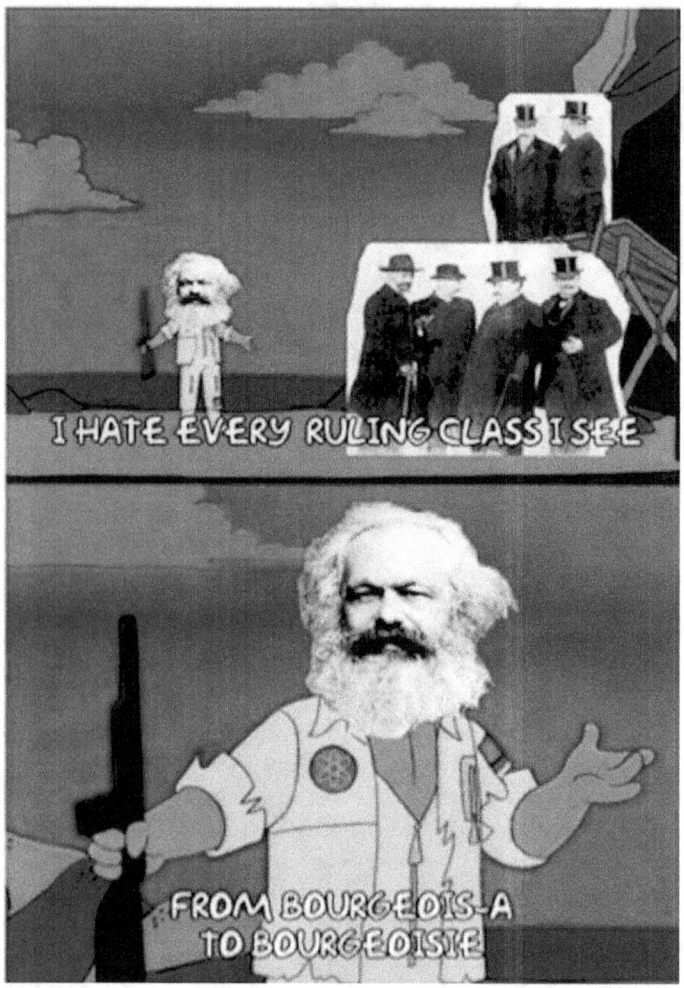

Fig. 15.

A second set of Simpsons shitposts draws connections between images from the show and *other memes*. The image in fig. 16 transposes a scene from the episode "Homer and Apu"—in which Jimbo Jones gets confused about his identity

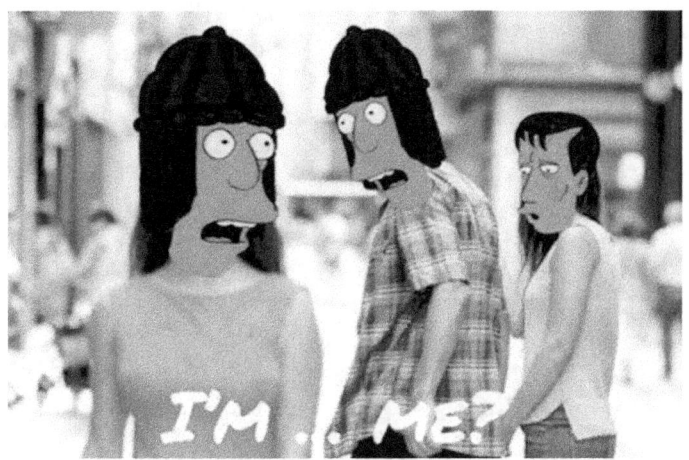

Fig. 16.

while "rehearsing" an impromptu scene with the actor James Woods — onto the well-known "Distracted Boyfriend" meme. A much more ambitious example of this category of shitpost is given to us by YouTube user The Chewanator. His masterful video "Steamed Hams but it's All Star" uses autotune to set the well-known scene from "22 Short Films About Springfield" in which Skinner cooks dinner for Superintendent Chalmers to meme staple "All Star" by Smashmouth.

"Steamed Hams," it is worth noting, has now effectively become a meme all of its own, enjoying a life at least somewhat independent of the "Simpsons Shitposting" page. On YouTube, there are a vast range of "Steamed Hams but its…" videos, ranging from the implicitly Simpsonwavey "Steamed Hams But It's On VHS and When Someone Says 'Steam' or 'Ham' it Suffers from Generation Loss" by Mitchell Hang, to the hellishly trippy "Steamed Hams but you're on bath salts at 60fps" by postalgbv. Recently, the meme most likely peaked with "Steamed Hams But It's Voiced By Jeff Goldblum," where the website Gamespot managed to get the actual actor Jeff Goldblum to do all of Skinner's lines in the scene.

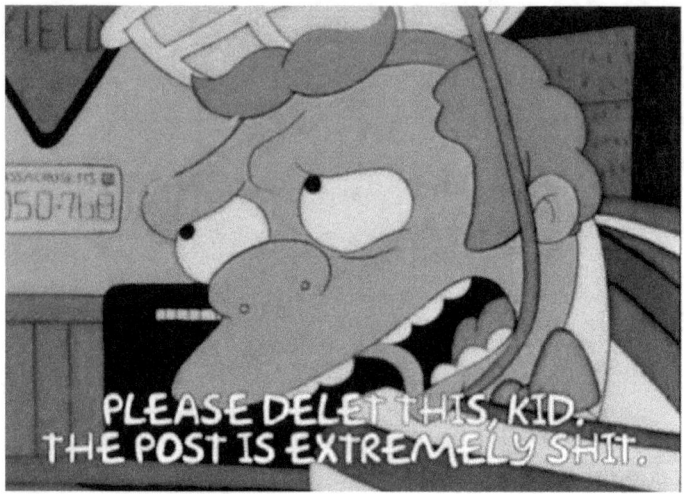

Fig. 17.

Also included in this second category of shitposts would be posts which play off memes associated with the group itself. The image given in fig. 17 is a version of the "delet this" meme, which users often comment under posts they disapprove of (though probably more often jokingly than sincerely).

Two All-Beef Patties Special Sauce Lettuce Cheese Pickles Onions on a Sesame Seed Bun

But the third sort of Simpsons shitpost that I want to identify is, to my mind, by far the most interesting one. This category of shitpost draws connections between the show and *itself*, riffing jokes from one scene into an otherwise unrelated one. The post given in fig. 18 transposes a gag from the episode "Homer the Heretic" — in which Ned Flanders throws an unconscious Homer out of his burning house onto a mattress on the ground below, only for Homer to bounce off the mattress and back into the house through the ground floor window — into a gag from the episode "Homer Loves Flanders," in which Homer appears menacingly in the Flanders's family yard through the hedge. The

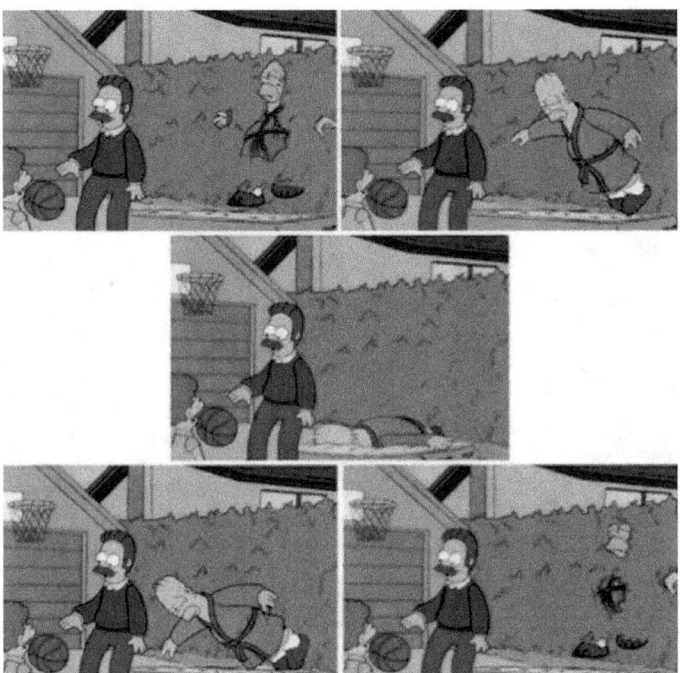

Fig. 18.

weirdness of the transposition is accentuated by the fact that, in the latter scene, Ned is bouncing a basketball — which in the post makes it look as if the rhythm of his bounces is also causing the unconscious Homer to move.

The post given in fig. 19 takes as its basis a scene from the episode "Itchy and Scratchy: The Movie," using this to present to us a world in which "Chanel suits" (of the sort Marge purchases in the episode "Scenes from the Class Struggle in Springfield") have for whatever reason become a playground fad which Bart is excluded from. Fig. 20 imagines a world in which Manjula, Apu's wife has (apparently) had an affair with the pumpkin-headed man from "People Who Look Like Things," a throwaway gag from the episode "Homer's Triple Bypass." After Manjula

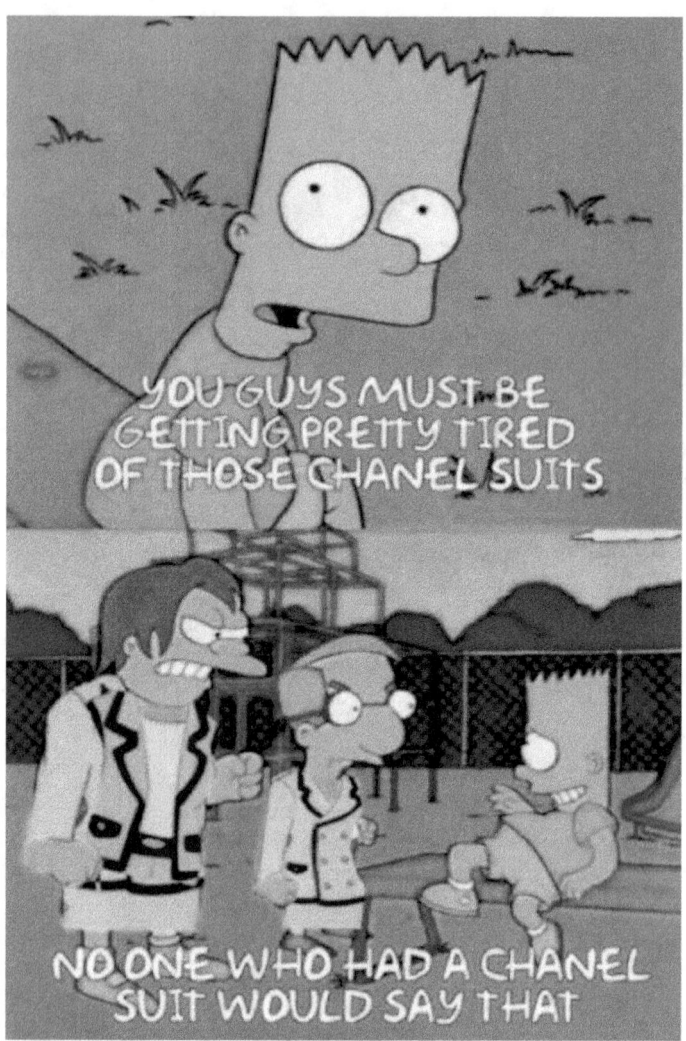

Fig. 19.

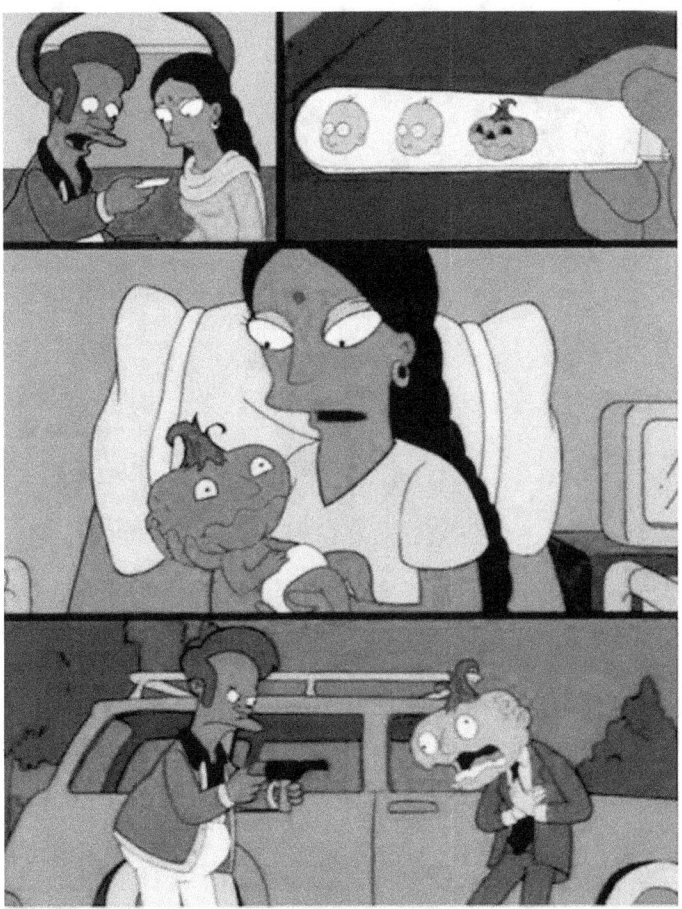

Fig. 20.

gives birth to a pumpkin-headed baby, Apu shoots and kills the pumpkin-man.

When these posts work best, it is like some new neurons have just been connected in your brain, allowing you to see shapes you'd never previously been able to comprehend. To fans of the show, the rhythms of these old Simpsons jokes are so utterly familiar, but these memes allow them to be felt afresh, draw-

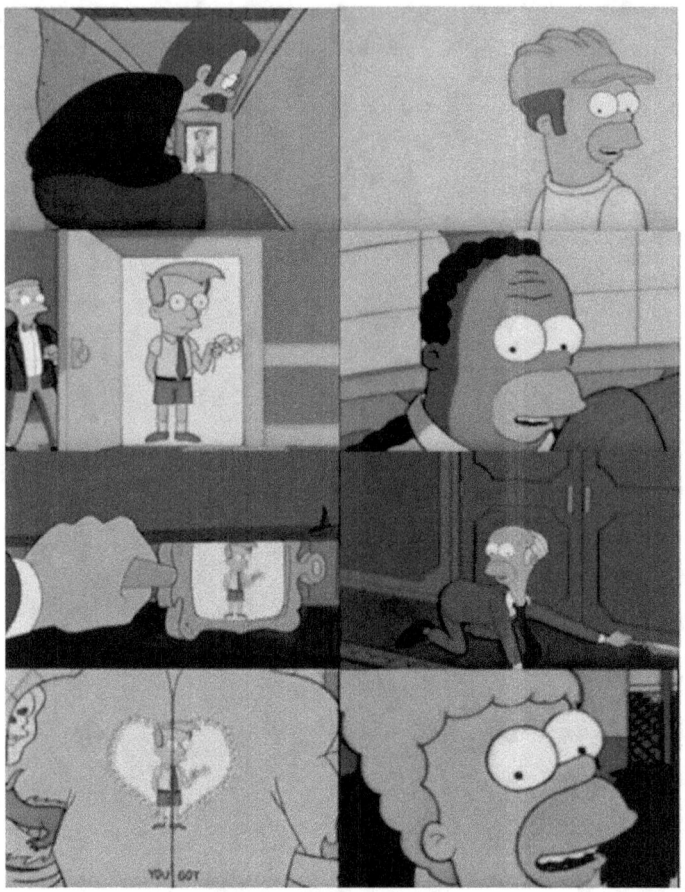

Fig. 21.

ing out new ways in which they can be looped back into each other. The examples given above are just three instances of the countless possibilities associated with this material that could be — and still are being — explored.

This category of shitpost lends itself to the instantiation of a canon of tropes. In fig. 21, we see some examples of the "Dud-face" trope. This trope has its basis in the episode "Summer of

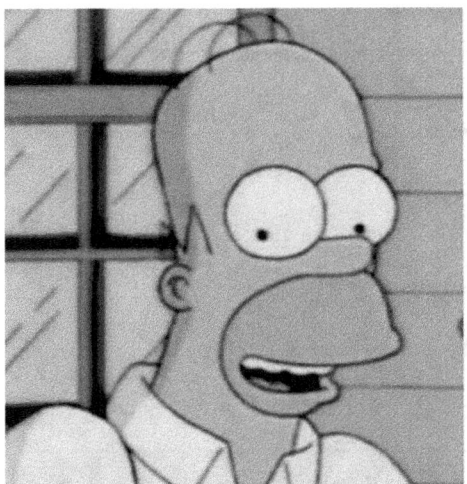

Fig. 22.

4ft 2," where Homer, Marge, Bart, and Milhouse are playing a game called "Mystery Date." After Homer draws "the captain of the football team" (presumably the best "mystery date" in the game), Bart — much to his parents' amusement — gets "the dud" (who seems to be the worst one). Homer's glee is heightened as he realizes that the "dud" character looks almost exactly like Milhouse — and we see his face distinctively brighten at this dawning knowledge (fig. 22).

The "Dudface" trope thus involves something (anything) opening to reveal (or somehow otherwise revealing) "the Dud," before somewhere Homer's face, usually transposed onto another character, "brightens" at the sight of it. Thus these memes have the Dud appearing behind the door in Ned Flanders's rebuilt house; in the mirror a distressed Mr. Burns is using to check if Homer is still in the corridor; on Tattoo Annie's back, etc. A similar logic operates behind the "lemonface" trope, which is taken from an image in the episode "Lemon of Troy" (figs. 23 and 24).

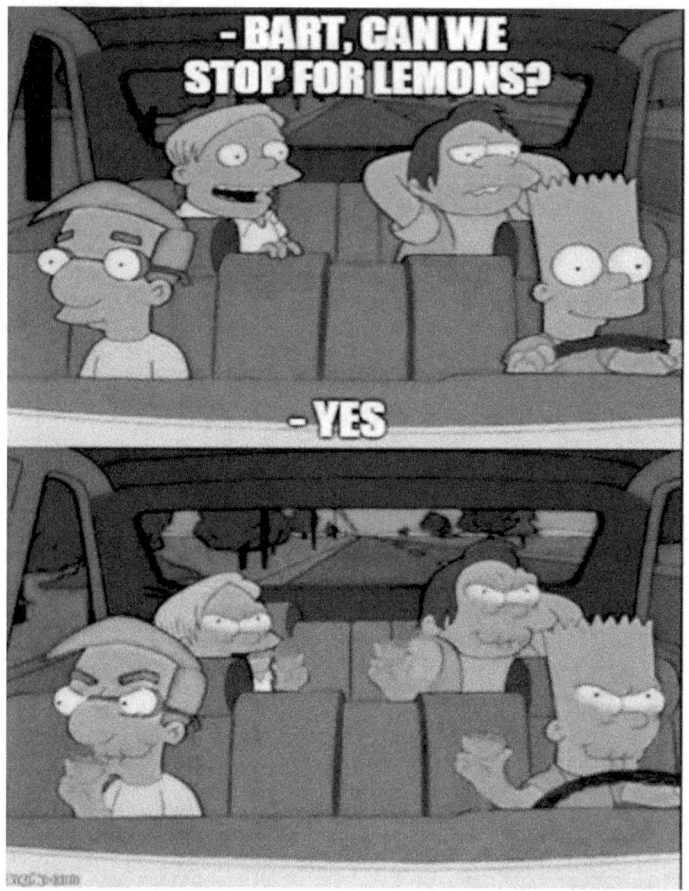

Fig. 23.

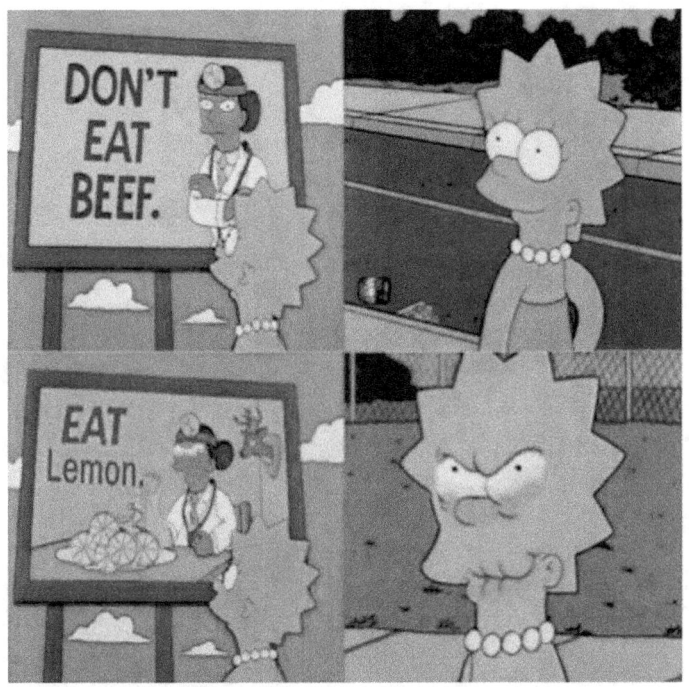

Fig. 24.

One of the most prominent tropes on the "Simpsons Shit-posting" forum is "Lowmer" (fig. 25; some examples of Lowmer memes in figs. 26 and 27). This trope takes as its basis a still from the scene in the episode "Rosebud" in which Homer is fanta-sising about Mr. Burns giving him "my own recording studio." In his fantasy, as he clowns around on the microphone, Homer gets very low to the ground, and for a split second he is drawn as a strange, distortedly "low" version of himself. This version of Homer would have been almost impossible to identify in 1993 when the episode originally aired. However, thanks to the "Frinkiac" search engine, it is now much easier to discover these odd bits of old animation.

Launched in February 2016 by Paul Kehrer, Sean Schulte, and Allie Young, Frinkiac is essentially a searchable database of

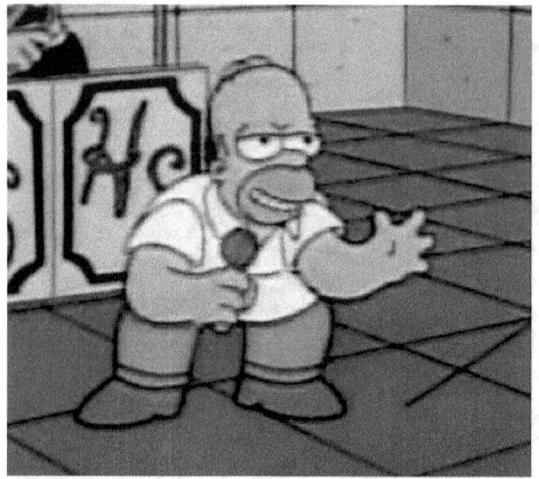

Fig. 25.

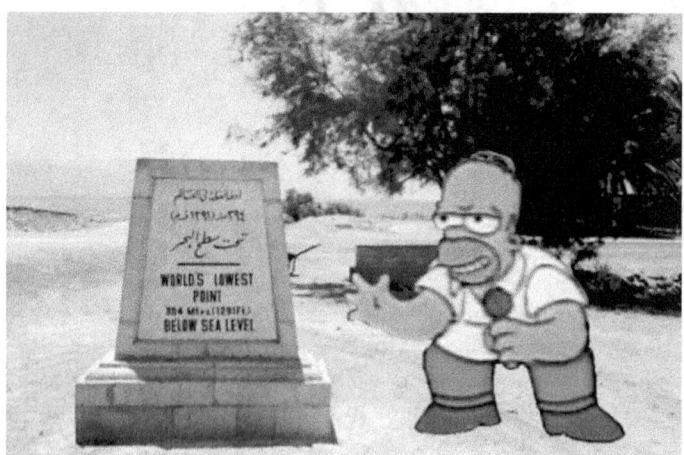

Fig. 26.

How to talk to short people:

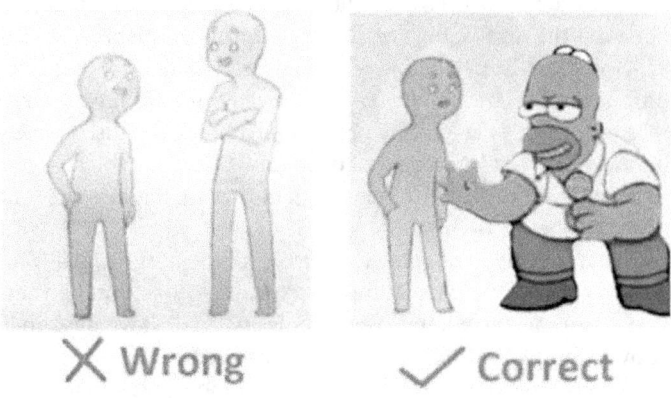

X Wrong   ✓ Correct

Fig. 27.

every episode from the first seventeen seasons of *The Simpsons*, containing every microsecond-long frame together with accompanying text from the script. Since Frinkiac first appeared, it has become an invaluable tool for the creation of *Simpsons* memes of whatever sort. In my view, search engines such as Frinkiac ought to be understood as a new sort of technology — they are to the shitpost what drum machines, samplers, and turntables were to early hip-hop.[37] On the one hand, Frinkiac simply makes it *much easier* to mass-produce Simpsons memes. But moreover, as the popularity of images such as "Lowmer" testifies, Frinkiac makes possible a sort of *Simpsons* "crate-digging," in which weird and rare animations can be lifted from individual clips, then re-contextualized as the building blocks for shitpost jokes.

---

37 There have since been equivalents launched for *Futurama* and *Rick & Morty*, and obviously it would be possible to imagine something analogous for almost any other show.

Well Seymour, I Made It. Despite Your Directions

I want to conclude this essay with two rather bold claims. To understand the first claim, recall first the problem Fisher sketches in "The Slow Cancellation of the Future." Under current conditions, artists are unable to "produce the new." One material reason for this is economic precarity. Another is a distinctively digital, "Internet-age" form of overstimulation, in which we are constantly assaulted with new content that we have neither the time nor the energy to understand.

What I want to suggest is that the shitposting form — pioneered by the Simpsons Shitposting forum — constitutes an aesthetic response to digital overstimulation. As I have described above, "Simpsons Shitposting" presents users with an intensely high volume of posts. These posts for the most part play off material that is very familiar: old *Simpsons* gags, which have, as I have established, been hard-wired into many fans' brains since childhood. Each post uses this material to *draw new connections* with other things: including the news, popular culture, and other memes. Taken together, then, these posts could be understood as an attempt to *draw a map of everything,* indexing everything in existence to something that happened in *The Simpsons.* Now, of course, this map could never be possessed in total by any one individual, could never be surveyed in its entirety. But even being able to access small chunks of it could help individuals feel anchored in a world otherwise rendered incomprehensible (thus meaningless) by its sheer intensity. The shitpost, then, is the new art form we as late capitalist subjects need to help us unconceal our world: *the art of overstimulation.*

The second claim I want to make hinges on a distinction that I believe it is possible to make between art that is *about The Simpsons,* and art that is *in the medium of* "Simpsons." Most of the examples I have discussed above fit into the former category: from the work of Chris (Simpsons artist) to Simpsonwave. These artworks play with characters and themes from the show, often recontextualizing them in interesting ways; they thus have

The Simpsons as their subject matter. Most Simpsons shitposts, too, are "about" *The Simpsons* in exactly this way.

But when it comes to something like the "Lowmer" trope, I'm not so sure. Recall that this is an image which is only able to make its way into the consciousness, *even of dedicated fans of the show,* with the advent of the Frinkiac search engine — which, as I have argued, can be understood as a sort of tool for making *Simpsons* memes. It thus strikes me as being in some way analogous to what Fisher in *Ghosts of My Life* describes as being definitive of jungle music — the "strange metallic excrescence that was produced when samples were slowed down and the software had to fill in the gaps" — a new sound, produced through new timestretching technology, that previously "no human could play."[38] Often, it is through these weird technological side-effects that new genres and forms are produced.

Perhaps something similar could be identified here. Consider the possibility of a Simpsons-based art which nevertheless does not have *The Simpsons* as its primary content. Just as there can be paintings which are not strictly speaking *about* painting itself, so we can imagine a category of Simpsons shitpost which spins frictionless from any events or jokes in — or indeed, associated with anyone's primary experience *of* — the show. This must all remain very speculative for now. But as Simpsons Shitposting and indeed the shitposting form as such develops, I anticipate this becoming increasingly the case.

---

38 Fisher, *Ghosts of My Life,* 30.

Bibliography

Colburn, Randall. "Read This: The Story Behind the Internet's Weirdest Simpsons Fan Group." *AV Club,* May 23, 2017. https://news.avclub.com/read-this-the-story-behind-the-internet-s-weirdest-sim-1798262202.

Fisher, Mark. *Capitalist Realism: Is There No Alternative?* Alresford: Zero Books, 2008.

———. *Ghosts of My Life: Writings on Depression, Hauntology and Lost Futures.* Alresford: Zero Books, 2014.

Griffin, Andrew. "Shitposting: What Is the Bizarre Online Behaviour That Could Win Donald Trump the Election?" *Independent,* September 23, 2016. https://www.independent.co.uk/life-style/gadgets-and-tech/news/what-is-shitposting-donald-trump-us-election-2016-palmer-luckey-a7326111.html.

Lee, Giacomo. "The True Spirit of '*The Simpsons*' Lives On in These Bootleg Zines." *Vice,* December 12, 2017. https://www.vice.com/en_uk/article/a3j39j/the-true-spirit-of-the-simpsons-lives-on-in-these-bootleg-zines.

Lozano, Kevin. "What the Hell Is Simpsonwave?" *Pitchfork,* June 14, 2016. https://pitchfork.com/thepitch/1188-what-the-hell-is-simpsonwave/.

Raftery, Brian "The Homeric Odyssey of the Web's Strangest Simpsons Site." *Wired,* May 22, 2017. https://www.wired.com/2017/05/homeric-odyessy-webs-strangest-simpsons-site/.

Reynolds, Simon. *Retromania.* London: Faber & Faber, 2011.

Whyman, Tom. "President Lisa Simpson." *The Baffler,* October 4, 2017. https://thebaffler.com/latest/president-lisa-simpson.

10

An Interview with the NEEM ("Non-Existent Existentialist Memes") Admins

Angus Reoch

I began my correspondence with the crew behind Non-Existent Existentialist Memes after years of lels, tags, and unexpected philosophical reflection. The home of deliberately esoteric and non-denominational politics, NEEM is a breath of fresh air in the crowded sphere of "philosophy memes," where often the joke was the smug knowledge that the reader had studied philosophy at university. Instead, NEEM's work attacks the presumption of knowledge itself, offering deliberately contradictory arguments and explanations, obscure medieval metaphysics, and a deep engagement with Chinese and Indian thought. And photos of people and animals in predicaments, because…the absurd.

Undoubtedly, however, the page is most famous for its endless interpretations of Albert Camus's memeable phrase, "we must imagine Sisyphus happy," so much so that it prompted a self-critique — "Holy Shit! Is that a Motherfucking Camus reference???" Jean-Paul Sartre's oeuvre also gets a minor workout from the page and its readership, however the jokes quickly move on. For an existentialist meme page, one admin shares that the original intent was to never actually post any existen-

DOI: 10.21983/P3.0255.1.11   233

tialist memes as they would be "non-existent." To the extent there is any articulated vision behind the page, NEEM's drive to both widen and deepen social and philosophical dialogue is more important than any commitment to a particular doctrine.

Where much liberal discourse around online dialogue centers on its capacity to entrench us into particular camps and identities — something the NEEM crew themselves express their concerns over — little attention has been paid to the deeply liberating potential of being encountered repeatedly with differing, opposing, and even ersatz opinions. At a time when any purported marketplace of ideas — physical and digital — is immediately crowded out with native advertising, corporate sponsorship, reactive think pieces and political echo chambers, the idea that online platforms like Facebook could actually play host to philosophical discussion is both anachronistic and yet more urgent than ever.

I began my interaction with the crew in April 2018, performing one of the more fittingly absurd tasks of my writing career: Facebook messaging a meme page to request an interview. Fortunately, the three core admins agreed, under the condition of pseudonymity.

ANGUS: *So could you please tell me a bit about yourself, like your country, academic background, and your interest in philosophy, politics, and memes?*

EDWIN: We're all from the United States, though with different ethnic backgrounds. JT for example is Chinese; I'm a typical American mix of European ancestry. We're all recent college graduates as well. Funny thing is none of us actually have philosophy degrees, I'm probably the closest with a B.A. in Asian Studies.

My interest in philosophy actually with Eastern philosophy, which you can definitely tell from the page. In university I mostly took classes on "Eastern" religions, such as Daoism, Buddhism, and Islam. I'm also really into art, but I could never draw a straight line so I went with art history instead. As for politics, I was initially really into that kind of stuff, but my interest waned over time. Now I mostly just see it as a source for memes. That's not to say I don't have political views, but I tend to think expending political energy is a waste of time for most people. Also my own views change so much based on new information that I spent so much time bouncing around ideologies.

JT: I'm the growth hacker admin of NEEM and made the high impact memes that grew the page to 595k [now 597k]. I studied Buddhism, Platonism, Islam, and Christian theology in Uni. I also launched the marketing campaigns, T-shirt designs, and our Instagram initiative. I'm the "delivery, execution, and copy editing" side of Neem. Edwin was the big boi who conceived of the idea of NEEM and he was the one who babies it while it was at a humble 100 follower base. I don't remember exactly but I think I joined when we had 5k followers.

DAN: Like the others, I am from the northeastern United States and we all went to the same high school. Both of my parents emigrated from Ethiopia. In high school, my main academic interest was in neuroscience but I majored in computer science in college, specifically focusing on AI and machine learning/deep learning. However, my intellectual interests have always been broad and since late high school I loved learning about and discussing philosophy, theology, politics, science, society, culture, and so on. I went to college on the West Coast and experienced a mild culture shock, and this experience primed me to key in on some of the more subtle yet persistent fundamental differences in how people think, believe, evaluate, socialize, and express themselves. I have always been more interested in learning as opposed to opining, and apart from fundamental principles, I rely on to guide my life, don't have many strong political or philosophical views.

ANGUS: *What was it that brought you into memeing as a mode of philosophical expression? Was it out of a natural urge to stir the pot and shitpost, or was there genuine intellectual intention? A page with a name like "non-existent existential memes" seems like it has more intent than most.*

EDWIN: I'm an old-school *chan guy. Nowadays all the *chans are either dead or just bad, but that was where all my initial inspiration came from. I think the real birthplace of "intellectual" memes was on 4chan's /lit/ back in the earlier 2010s. My own personal home was Krautchan for the longest time, but they went down for good (RIP). I've loved memes forever, though. They're basically the best medium for extremely niche humor. You can't really make a funny TV show about early 20th-century philosophy, but you can definitely make memes about it.

Another great thing about memes compared to traditional media is they're inherently social and easily accessible. Anyone can make a meme, anyone can edit a meme, anyone can enjoy a meme. You just go into any online community and that's how people communicate. There's no Corporate Overlord pulling the strings, no censor to get through, no software, skills, or training required.

I really enjoy playing Devil's advocate, and that shows through in our content. Anyone who makes memes will tell you they just do it for their own amusement, I don't think we're different. But part of that amusement to me was also developing ideas. When you type out 200 words for some "long-form" meme (the really TL:DR ones), it really helps you develop your own thoughts. I think this comes from the fact that memes were initially just a shortcut in online discussions, and that's what they end up being used as typically. So anytime I want to develop my own thoughts, I just make a meme; then you can reuse it whenever you get into an argument!

One thing I think our page does well is just showing a ton of underappreciated viewpoints. It's not that I literally think Chinese alchemy is real like some of our memes say, but it's a funny position to take. Same with things like "The burden of proof is bad."

I love the name because while it hints at what you can expect from our content, it's ultimately a meaningless nonsense phrase, but when you think about it, it describes the content perfectly.

DAN: I've been into memes since middle school when the first what I guess you could call prehistoric ones came out on Facebook. I just always found them hilarious, illuminating, and infectious — modern lowbrow (sometimes highbrow?) art. People may intentionally or unintentionally create "memeable" moments, but for whatever reason they resonate. I did not even consider creating memes until junior year, when JT and Edwin told me they needed more OC and asked me to join as an admin. To me memeing feels like creating digital art because you have to think of your audience, collective knowledge, the pool of allusions you can rely on, forms, symbols, wordplay, themes, and so on. I used to write short stories and novellas of sorts in middle school so I have a lot of experience thinking about and creating narratives and, especially for my longer-form memes, try to encapsulate a little vignette.

The main reason I started memeing was for laughs. My first meme, I believe, was an Albert Camus Tinder bio, and my first few memes after that were mostly for lols too. Once I started realizing how my memes and the memes of my fellow admins were resonating with fans and I started having greater ambitions for the significance of my memes, then I started to take my memes a bit more seriously. I must admit I even had some moments where I was inspired to make some completely genuine intellectual and aesthetic statements with my memes. Most of my memes are still for lols because they're often easier to make and come to me more readily, but, as I've started reading and thinking more about the main underlying philosophical/theological material for our page, refined my craft, and debated with my fellow admins over meme ideas and execution, I'm a bit more inclined to at least incorporate some greater meat in my memes. I also very much enjoy sometimes intentionally creating controversial (and a blend of serious and humorous) philosophical memes and observing the uproar in the comments from the supporters of the philosophical viewpoint I undermined or attacked (my fellow admins are especially good at doing this, even when we don't necessarily even strongly disagree with the side we attacked or have a strong opinion either way). In fact, many of these memes promote some very intense and serious discussion, and it was then that I realized a lot of our fans took our work quite seriously, maybe even more seriously than we did sometimes. Nevertheless, I always loved seeing their reactions and sometimes even arguing with and learning from them.

ANGUS: NEEM is quite a unique page, combining more commonly understood Western existential themes with a deep appreciation of Indian and Chinese philosophy, as well as some genuinely absurdist content which is difficult to describe in a textual format (people and animals in predicaments, non-sequiturs, etc). How did you come to combine these various elements?

JT: My answer is that we always try to veil our beliefs whenever possible and try to make ironic memes that can be appealing no matter what angle you view it from. Often we might even make a meme that, on a surface level, seems to be totally disagreeable with what we believe, though the inner layer of that meme is actually the truth. In the past we used to propagandize our ideologies much more often but I now discourage our admins from doing this, since it's much more fun when no one knows what the admins believe. We also sometimes go full propaganda mode on beliefs that we ourselves disagree with, to keep it fresh.

A lot of the memes related to Sufism, Hinduism, Platonism, and Buddhism come directly from moments in time when I was attending classes on those subjects. I was thinking about those ideas all the time so it was natural for me to fuse them with contemporary meme formats.

EDWIN: We're all pretty cosmopolitan guys, and I was always big into exploring the "foreign Internet." Like, what are Japanese people doing on 2ch? What's a Nigerian forum like? (Turns out actually really interesting: check out Nairaland.)

So the content just came naturally; we're Westerners so we've read lots of the Western canon, but my real interest was always beyond that, so that content got made as well. I remember when I first started doing a lot of the Daoist stuff it was because Zhuangzi is sometimes lumped in with Camus as an "absurdist" thinker. When we gave it a shot, the feedback was great; tons of people appreciated how we were broadening their horizons and not taking a Eurocentric view of philosophy. So we just kept doing it.

The random images are truly the heart of the page, at least in my view. That's what we started with and I never want to stop posting them. The only real criteria I can give you for those is if it makes me laugh really hard, makes me sad, or "really makes u think," I post it. Sometimes we get flack for posting stuff that is downright sad or disturbing, but I think anything that fills with you with genuine emotion is good content.

JT: The way that we produce work is pretty simple. Usually we have a shared queue of "meme ideas that we must make" and also "meme templates we must abuse". Whenever I have spare time I sit down and look at the list and try to make something good from it. During my really active days in university, I would sometimes get struck down and inspired by a meme idea right where I was standing, and I'd walk over to a desk, pull out my laptop, and submit the meme immediately.

My friends and fellow admins have a habit also of green-texting hypothetical situations to each other quite frequently. A lot of times our banter will be focused on obscure philosophical topics, and if a banter session produces a good meme idea, then we manufacture it. Usually we like to strawman an imaginary character who represents some sort of modern Western delusion and we banter against him. For example:

- colonialism is really bad and morality is relative, so we shouldn't impose our views on others

- omg these guys in Africa are imposing their views on others, we need to impose our views on them so that they can stop imposing their views on others
- this is totally not colonialism btw

And we might exchange dialogues like that.

DAN: In terms of how and why I personally combine Western existentialism with Indian and Chinese philosophy, much of that inclination has to do with becoming genuinely interested in the intersection of Eastern metaphysics and epistemology with Western existentialism as I touched on a bit before. As I started exploring this intersection and realized that most Westerners were not even considering, let alone well-informed on, Eastern thought (and the same vice versa from what I've observed), I started making East-West hybrid philosophy memes mostly around some questions, thoughts, or situations I was considering at the time. What I love about the work on our page is how diverse it is not just across topics but even across time too — we make a lot of our memes based off of what we're talking, researching, and thinking about and that content goes through major changes at least a couple times a year. I also love how, especially given how big our audience is, we can highlight some underappreciated figures and ideas and our showcase for many people can hopefully expand their intellectual horizons.

ANGUS: *Relatedly, do you think that there are parallels between Western existentialism and Indian and Chinese philosophy which aren't merely superficial? Did it really take Western philosophy until the 19th–20th centuries to begin to tackle the topics that Eastern philosophy had dealt with for a long time, or is this being unfair to Platonists and medieval European thought?*

EDWIN: For sure. Like I said earlier, the Camus–Zhuangzi connection is pretty obvious when you're reading them. Zhuangzi is the philosopher I most enjoy, and probably the guy closest to my own outlook on life. Camus is a close second, perhaps.

But both of them agree that man is thrust into the world with a deep void in his heart that he has to fill with meaning. Both of them take a very active perspective on life as well; we should be doing things and going our own way rather than living a life of pure contemplation. Finally, their epistemology is quite similar in that they basically reject the idea of "knowledge" all together. The thought that no one actually knows what's going on is rather comforting, I believe.

Of course also many of the existentialists like Heidegger were inspired by the East as well, particularly Daoism. While I do love Eastern philosophy, it's not like the West didn't tackle similar ideas at similar times. Even when learning about Eastern philosophy, you'll find most teachers frame it in terms of Western philosophy, like the "myriad things" in the Dao De Jing being similar to the Platonic idea of "forms," etc. I don't think this unfair to either side, it just makes teaching easier. But of course there are also irreconcilable differences between the two.

DAN: I would say beyond the superficial there are definitely some major parallels in the questions and dilemmas Western and Eastern philosophers face that are similar to some of the questions and dilemmas many individuals come across in their own lifetimes—the ontological, epistemological, moral, how to live a good life, and so on. I would say Western philosophy before the 19th–20th century partially addressed some of what Eastern philosophy was tackling, but I believe there were major gaps and assumptions taken at face value that the East did away with, which led to some new and richer insights in my opinion. I'm speaking in broad strokes because I would need to do a review of sorts to suggest anything concrete and specific, but I do believe Heidegger, as Edwin mentioned, went on at length about what the West failed to tackle that the East did by his time.

JT: I think in many ways Western philosophy is catching up to Eastern philosophy, especially when it comes to scepticism. 21st-century Western philosophers in general seem to place too much value in their idea of logic and smuggle in modern delusions without realizing it. They hate religion and they hate mysticism but they have a religious orthodoxy of their own. This sort of intellectual dishonesty is what I dislike seeing. I like 19th-century European philosophy because it has a uniquely European flavor and because, even though I myself believe in the existence of objective truth, the poetry of existentialism is very beautiful and does capture the despair of the man who is trapped in the material world, which is an important topic in both Ecclesiastes and also in Indian philosophies. It would be unfair to say that 19th-century Euro philosophy is totally derivative of Eastern philosophy, but it is definitely true that many 21st-century Western philosophers are philistines who can't conceive of the Eastern mentality and who place too much trust in social dogmas that they've unwittingly inherited and abused.

A decent example of this is Occam's razor, conceived by William of Occam who believed in a simple and uncontingent God. It's a fairly unconvincing way of arguing that works best as a rule of thumb, and it's abused by people who wrongly think that belief in materialism is "more simple and more elegant" than belief in a One or a Divinity. You can see how laughably incorrect such a view is by looking at Mahayana Buddhist metaphysics, which discusses cause and effect and the non-existence of cluster objects in a way that is very honest and very consistent (and by the way, I've come nowadays never to expect honesty or consistency from mainstream Western philosophers). The Buddhist explanation of consciousness, language, and objectively existing objects is incredibly complex, non-obvious, and ugly; how could anyone say that Occam's razor supports a materialist viewpoint? If anything, it supports belief in God (not an old man in the sky who creates things in moment-to-moment time using voodoo magic, but a simple and unconstrained One Origin beyond time and space whose outpouring and unraveling generates and sustains all things).

Platonism and Neoplatonism are really great traditions and they're very Eastern. When you read Plato, you don't see any British mathematical arrogance even though Plato is considered "Western" philosophy. Plato loves logic but he uses it to clear away delusions and does this out of his love for beauty and truth. If you confronted most modern Western philosophers and asked them, "do you love beauty and truth?" they would not be able to give you a satisfying answer and might actually be very uncomfortable to even engage with such concepts. By denying beauty and truth, they've cut themselves off from their Platonic inheritance! And by un-sceptically affirming contemporary and contingent viewpoints, they also cut themselves off from Socrates (who, incidentally, was pious and has an uncanny resemblance to an Eastern character, even more so than Plato). The Platonic traditions are very much alive in a new form, in the Eastern Orthodox Christian faith, and if you read their prayers and philosophy, you will see they are much more Platonist than a British guy talking about how he proved God is not real.

My rambling point can be summarized like this: we live in a very limited marketplace of ideas, and our contemporary orthodox Western viewpoints do not represent the full capabilities of human rationality at all. People who claim to be secular masters of logic actually have irrational religious beliefs of their own, and modern viewpoints have not "triumphed" over the past, nor have Western views "triumphed" over so-called irrational Eastern mysticism. They have rather performed great intellectual violence by suppressing the representation of the past and of the East in contemporary discourse. This is as close to a manifesto that I've ever written.

ANGUS: *I'm impressed by how much dialogue and multiple perspectives forms part of NEEM's output. The Internet and particularly "niche" culture is commonly given a lot of flak nowadays for creating "polarized" institutions. How do you see the production of memes as contributing to a greater dialogue? It seems you've have a lot of positive experiences and feedback.*

EDWIN: They allow people from opposing viewpoints to discuss things with the layer of humor or irony needed to actually remove one's own biases from the discussion. People seemingly are more willing to engage with memes from an opposing viewpoint as well because there is less of the "serious" or "combat-ive" feeling that comes with arguing in earnest. However a lot of young people are radicalized nowadays into a lot of potentially self-destructive ideologies through memes (the "alt-right", for example. How many of these guys just thought of themselves as just edgy memers on the Internet until they were doxed, or until they got arrested for fighting some anarchist?), so it's not neces-sarily a good thing.

I believe you're starting to see a sort of global politics emerg-ing, where people are extremely focused on things outside their borders, especially those invested in political "Internet cliques" as I call them. So the power of all borders are diminishing. The most powerful is still linguistic though, and I don't think those will ever go away unless some extremely powerful translation software is invented.

JT: I enjoy promoting somewhat foreign perspectives, and it's not just limited to Eastern views since we will genuinely pro-mote anything that is shocking to the modern-day Western mentality, including weird pre-modern views, Abrahamic reli-gion, communism, and scepticism. I enjoy using the vocabulary of popular memes to articulate concepts that might be totally foreign to the typical reader. As a lay historian, I hate it when people impose their own shitty contingent viewpoints on the past and I hate to see people who literally cannot comprehend views that are outside their own local history. Comedy is a sort of koan-like mechanism where you can breach past someone's own delusions and give them temporary access to a fun new viewpoint.

For me, the inspiration to stir up debate is a combination of playfulness and wanting to fight against some particular mis-conceptions. If somebody starts talking near me about some very contingent and untrue belief (e.g., Internet access is a ba-sic human right), I'll be more motivated to make fun of it in a future meme. Also, sometimes we want to throw a bone to different audience members. If we have been making fun of ma-terialist sceptical atheists for too long, then we eventually throw them a placating meme and make fun of Christians. Part of it too is that we don't *really* care about these happenings and we don't really get butthurt about these things. Because we don't get butthurt too often, we have a lot of creative freedom in this world. We love to make fun of ourselves and to make fun of our intellectual allies.

DAN: This is maybe my favorite aspect of memes. When we create memes, NEEM is reaching people across the world of different races, cultures, politics, backgrounds, even ages (most of our audience is anywhere from 15–25, but I've seen comments from the middle-aged and elderly who are genuinely interested in our memes on a daily basis!). As Edwin mentioned, online memes really open up people to consumption of information and discussion because of the anonymity of the Internet (Facebook not really, but you could say interactions between strangers who will probably never meet in real life can be treated as if each of the interlocutors are anonymous to each other) and implicit understanding of the freedom of meme content. I would say that the polarization of the Internet and of society on an intellectual and cultural level is disappointing, but may also be just a reflection of how open-minded and free-thinking people in general really are (read: not really), and the greater visibility of the Internet makes division and conflict more available and obvious. In general, I've found that people who enjoy and seek out open, contemplative conversation will probably find it, although in some cases I've witnessed personally some closed-minded people approached in a respectful and curious manner becoming more open to new ideas and experiences, which helps me become a little less alienated and more hopeful.

ANGUS: *I'm also interested to hear you say you're not actively political — or in some sense, "actively" philosophical either. I see NEEM as constantly opening up new ways of thinking through drawing out the logical inanity of certain positions or by contrasting them with "obviously wrong" positions, including reposting a lot of deliberately anti-racist and anti-bigotry content. Certainly this isn't partisan, and a great deal isn't even necessarily "philosophical" per se, but to me this is an actively political way of dealing with modern life. Do you really think your work is relatively apolitical?*

EDWIN: Relatively, yes. But from a metapolitical standpoint, we're doing something pretty substantial. That is, weakening the partisan divide while attacking modern thinking as a whole. Also I think by attacking modern epistemology as a whole, we're also attacking establishment media, political pundits, etc. from a position they're extremely weak to defend against.

I'm going to get a little off-track here, but independent media doesn't necessarily do this. You can just look at "independent" Twitter pundits and the obvious fact that 90% are nothing of the sort; they're the ones who stick most closely to a rigid ideology and they're often the ones taking money from special interests. People are sort of suckered into following these people because the "independent" model creates a personal relationship with the pundit where you trust what they say because they've become your "friend" in your mind. And not to get too tinfoil hat, but individuals are just as, if not more, susceptible to blackmail/extortion/bribes/etc. as corporate media.

In my experience, electoral politics is just a battle of special interests, and rarely do policies get implemented the way voters imagined they would be. And I don't want to get too preachy, but speaking from experience from forays into the far-right, far-left, and what lies between, usually political radicalization just ruins your mental health and eventually your life. So I just try to avoid the subject.

As for those anti-racist type posts that subvert your expectation, those are amazing. That's the kind of stuff we need as a society right now. It's an old trope, but the media tends to focus on negatives, even when reporting a positive. It's been talked about before (even relating to "bronies"…) but "new sincerity" is back. People are starving for wholesome content, and it's doubly funny because the Internet is so edgy that it feels original and refreshing. What I think is happening now is that "meme culture," especially in the political realm has morphed into two distinct bubbles: the "alt-right" and the "irony left". Both gained their power through being transgressive, but now being not-transgressive is actually transgressive.

There used to be a cozy metapolitical Internet, and before 2014, I'd say a lot of online political discussion was free from the idea that the person on the other side of the screen was your literal enemy. I'd like to return to that, personally. I realize that's sort of a privileged position to take; many people are forced into political action because their lives are actually at risk from people that are there literal enemies, but within a liberal democracy, it's not healthy to be where we are now.

ANGUS: *What can you say about Camus's* The Myth of Sisyphus? *This work has had a strange (struggling not to say "absurd") afterlife on the Internet, persisting almost as a meme itself. It's quite a difficult work, with relatively contemporary references, and the final pay-off is only towards the end, yet it's still a somewhat entrancing piece. How could you describe the work's influence on you and its continual relevance?*

EDWIN: I'll be honest, I mostly like Camus from *The Plague* and his other literary work.

That being said, *The Myth of Sisyphus* is probably our most memed work from Camus. Likely because it just has a meme-able quality to it. "We must imagine Sisyphus happy" is just an extremely condensed version of Camus's entire philosophy, so that's likely the reason it's so common on our page.

The book is of course still relevant, and I think absurdism will continue to help young adults out of their first existential crisis for years to come. There's just something so poignant about it, and so natural. It is steeped in complex thinking, but you don't need to be an expert at all to grasp the practical meaning.

ANGUS: *How did you find this whole process? Does talking about a meme page—me interviewing you in this sense—reduce the spontaneity somewhat?*

DAN: I wouldn't say so. I've probably thought about every question I answered to some extent before, but formulating responses and reflecting on my thought and experience in this email does feel very much like having an interview IRL. I must admit this idea seemed bizarre to me at first glance, but after thinking about and experiencing it, it seems like a modern, valuable, and rich way for people to get to learn about meme pages and their admins. I would say this may be the new standard for interviews of this sort, along with anonymous chats.

EDWIN: It was a little strange, but I've thought about all these things before. I don't think putting it in writing really reduces anything.

A fun thought exercise is just thinking about how we're going to study memes, if at all, in the future. I imagine we will because studying pop culture is big in academia nowadays. So I really don't think it's that strange, it's actually rather forward-thinking.

But there is that very 21st-century feeling to it.

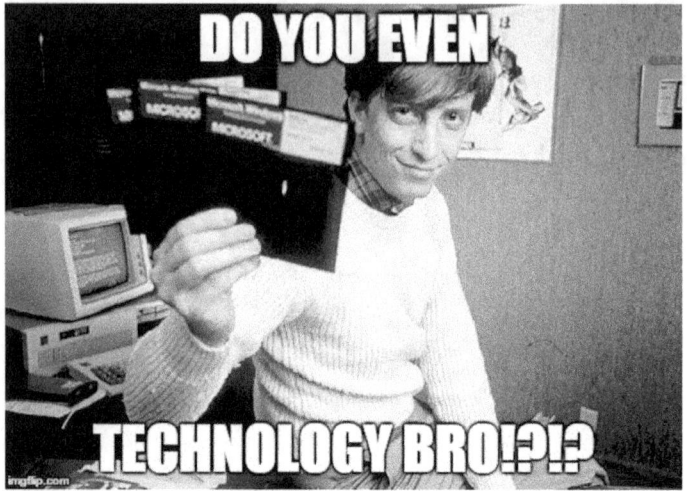

Fig. 1.

11

Meme Dankness: Floating Glittery Trash for an Economic Heresy

Yvette Granata

Dank Meme Authenticity: Fucking Stop It, Wendy's

In a 2015 video playlist of short meme videos on YouTube entitled "Important Videos," a video called "Stop Putting Memes in the Media" is a thirteen-second clip of someone filming a Wendy's commercial on their phone. The commercial depicts a "memer" eating a spicy chicken sandwich. As the character in the commercial chews on his sandwich, bold white text pops up on the screen: "the memer," followed by more text, "eats spicy goodness like a boss" (fig. 2) The person filming the commercial lets out a blood-curdling angry scream at the commercial: "Stopppppp! Fucking Stop!," and the video cuts before the screaming ends. The description of the video posted by the user is simply: "I want to die." Users in the comments section agree with the sentiments of the video-poster; they too are horrified by the commercial use of image board meme culture, stating such things as: "this is how the world ends [...] with the media

DOI: 10.21983/P3.0255.1.12

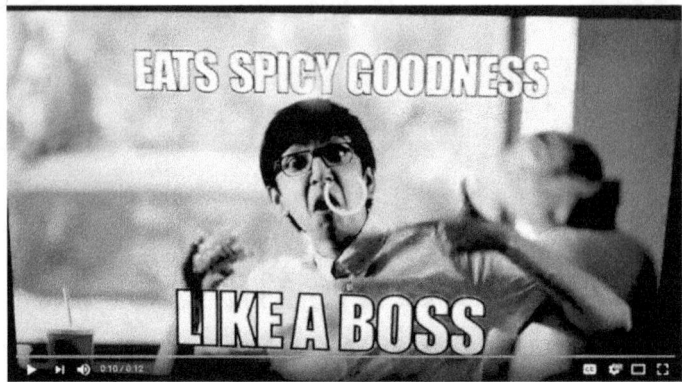

Fig. 2.

trying to grasp a hold of the enigma that is internet culture."[1] The users' critique is of the cultural appropriation of memes by "the media," or the mainstreamization of underground meme culture. The commercial is a "forced meme." As described on Know Your Meme, a forced meme "is any 'meme' that is artificially created and spread. Rather than spreading through word of mouth as a naturally created meme, a forced meme [is] made with the intent of becoming a meme and aggressively promoted by its creator."[2] In other words, a forced meme either buys or purposefully organizes the repetition of its appearance. Forced memes have an explicitly different agenda to the appearance of the meme itself, whereas an authentic meme is meant to appear for-itself. Any organized purpose for a meme beyond the production of its own particular existence is a destruction of the authenticity of dankness.

And then someone posted this (fig. 3).

There, at least someone has done something. Actually, it appears that this is Wendy's again. This time, the company is

---

1   See Infinity Media, "STOP PUTTING MEMES IN MEDIA," *YouTube,* April 24, 2015, https://www.youtube.com/watch?v=yNtySt6Fg3o.

2   See *Know Your Meme,* s.v. "forced meme," http://knowyourmeme.com/memes/forced-meme.

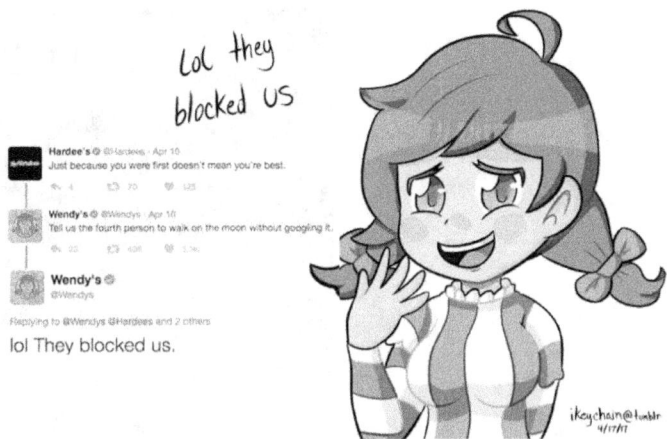

Fig. 3.

attempting to rebrand Wendy as a deviant shitposter (unconvincingly) who gets blocked. In the early 2000s, Lev Manovich pointed out the shifts brought about by new software and digital media, pointing to endlessly mutable, modular, synthetic, digital media aesthetics as symptoms of the "general tendencies of a culture undergoing computerization."[3] With software, media are digital signals that can be modulated in endless flows, generated, swapped, shared, and proliferated. For example, Microsoft Paint (itself the content of memes), Photoshop, GIMP — any image editing software — gives us a list of effects to choose from a menu to manipulate and produce new images, to rearrange and re-mix image data, erase parts, add text and shapes, and scribble with, using digital paint colors (fig 4). In addition to editing software, mark-up languages — XML, HTML, LaTeX, etc. — made it simple to post images within a flow of web-hosted text. Internet users began editing and remixing various digital information, establishing a visual vernacular for digital document data

---

3   Lev Manovich, *The Language of New Media* (Cambridge: MIT Press, 2001), 49.

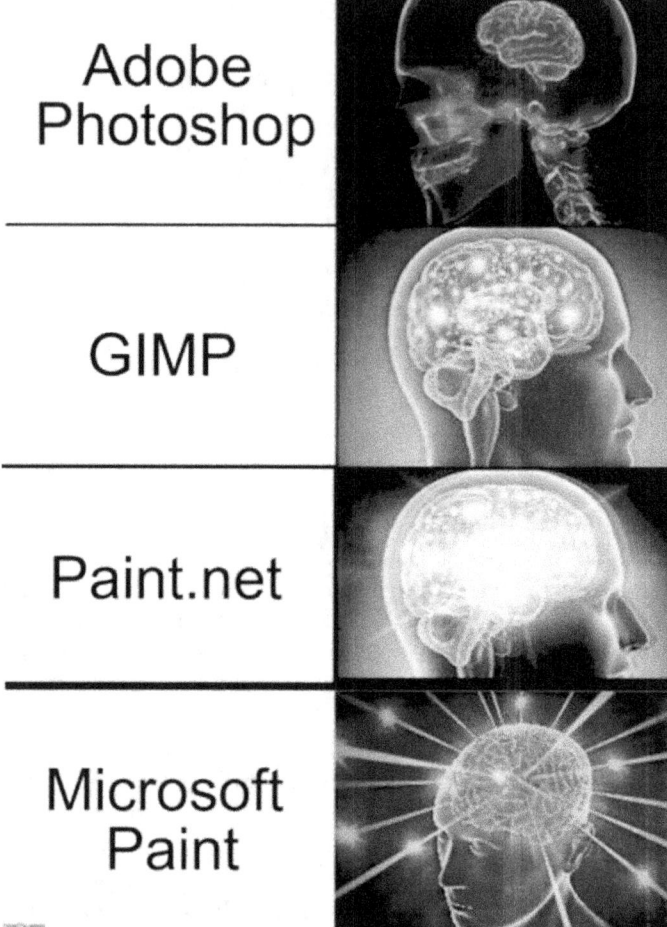

Fig. 4.

communication and creating new formats of information exchange. Intellectual property was also called into question.

In the spirit of the "copyleft," McKenzie Wark's Hacker Manifesto (2004) claimed that the ability to mutate, change, and

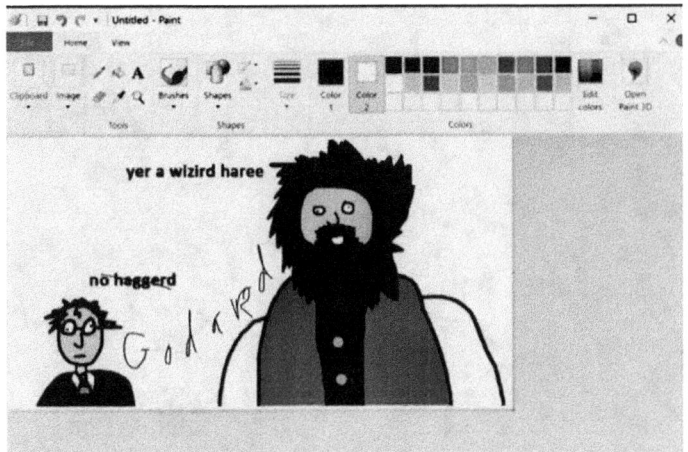

Fig. 5.

remix ideas from existing cultural material equates to hacking. Anything that opens the potential for the creation of the new — culture jamming, sampling, mixing, and swapping — is part of a free-flow hacking practice.[4] Gregory Ulmer called it "electracy," and promoted software techniques for the reuse of found material as the process of Internet invention.[5] Alex Galloway thus makes note in *The Interface Effect*: "the first phase of web culture, one must admit, carried a revolutionary impulse."[6] However, endless selections, modulations, and digital mutations within proprietary software eventually contributed to its loss of luster: "when Jean-Luc Godard becomes a plug-in, we must look beyond the Nouvelle Vague" (fig. 5).[7] Although unstated by the anti-Wendy's video poster and other users, what is implied by their response against the commercial use of Internet meme form is similar to Galloway's statement — that when

---

4   See McKenzie Wark, *A Hacker Manifesto* (Cambridge: Harvard University Press, 2004).

5   See Gregory L. Ulmer, *Internet Invention: From Literacy to Electracy* (New York: Longman, 2002).

6   Alexander R. Galloway, *The Interface Effect* (Cambridge: Polity, 2013), 2.

7   Ibid., 8.

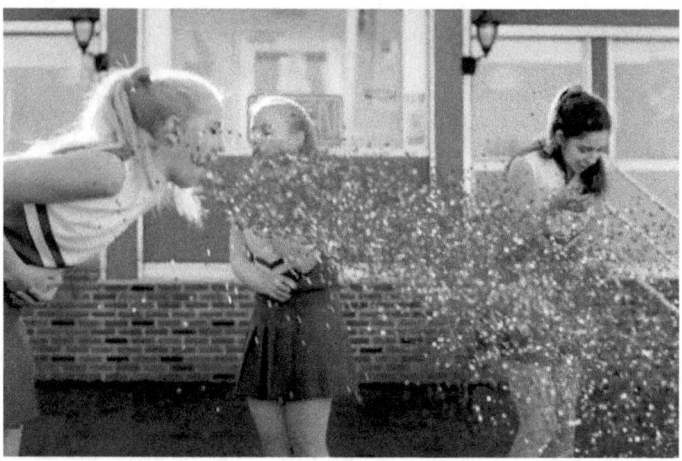

Fig. 6.

the cultural practice of meme-making becomes a Wendy's commercial, it's time to scream "fucking stop!" at the screen.

Unlike Godard, however, the memer sentiment against mainstreamization of memes is not meant to reserve meme practice for revolutionary political aims. The defense of image board meme culture here is instead the desire to maintain a lack of political organization, to perpetually subvert centralized control, and to preserve the image board meme as a type of representational fall-out shelter. The image board is a place where memes are both created and posted for no other reason than for the exchange of purely cultural expressions. Meme makers who protest the commercialization of memes defend the meme as an end itself. It is neither politically nor economically motivated; it is not a means.

What then is implied in the defense of dank meme authenticity? As an end itself for cultural exchange, is the practice of meme-production a strange digital gift economy? Or is there an inherently reactionary impulse that bends it toward a tyrannical expression of *ressentiment*? The 21st-century Internet meme practice, I argue, is neither gift nor tyranny, but reveals itself as a stranger form of exchange — a type of economic heresy. We must enter into the glittery absurdity of image board culture in order to further unpack the dankness of its political economy (fig. 6).

Mass Meme Art

While the broader sense of the term "meme" has been used to describe an abstract unit of mimesis — a type of human cultural behavioral *noumena* — 1990s Internet and software culture has morphed its definition toward an abstraction unit of idea or culture. Popularly, it denotes a type of information form that can replicate, recombine, morph, and redistribute across multiple media. Analytic philosopher Susan Blackmore sees this as an inappropriate use of the term, claiming that "in popular discourse, the word 'meme' is horribly abused. It is confused with 'idea' or 'concept' or treated as something ethereal or non-material floating about quite separate from behaviours and artefacts."[8] Within software and Internet culture, the digital meme has been redefined to indicate the form and technique of digital media and software architecture. In his work on dynamic software architectures as meme media, Yuzuru Tanaka calls memes in general "intellectual assets" that are a part of "knowledge media." For Tanaka, the meme is that which is reduced to its communicability, an externally expressible thing that can appear across various media architectures. Digital "meme media" is therefore specifically tied to computerized media architectures and to dynamic software that enables users to edit and redistribute intellectual assets. From the point of view of back-end architectures and front-end user experience, this aligns with the notion of memes as "behaviors and artifacts." The digital meme in this sense may be any re-usable digital media pattern; for example, a blog timeline or a Google document, any repeatable and customizable

---

8   See Susan Blackmore, "The Evolution of Meme Machines," in *Ontopsychology and Memetics,* eds. A. Meneghetti et al. (Rome: Psicologica Editrice, 2003), 233–40, https://www.susanblackmore.uk/conferences/the-evolution-of-meme-machines-3/ — TFW people try to control the definition of memes, but Internet memes still act like memes regardless.

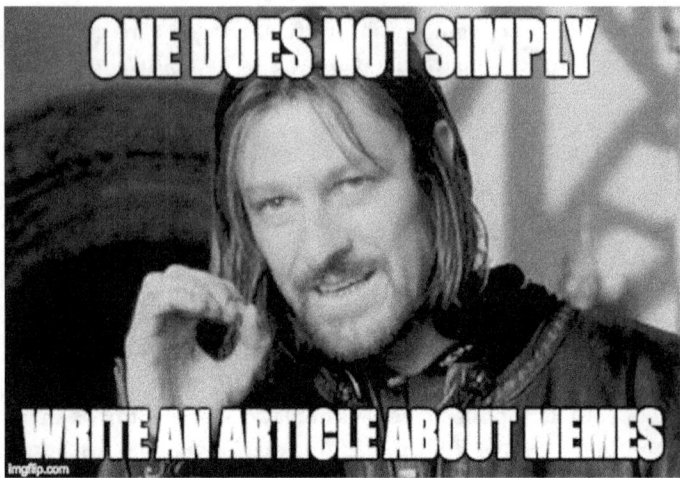

Fig. 7.

media pattern or method for sharing and editing intellectual information digitally. In other words, digital memes are the behavior and artifact of the form and content of dynamic media.

The "Internet meme" as a "dank meme," however, is a more specific genre of digital meme that was born from specific image board culture and its use of text-image patterns. It includes both the practice of using image manipulation software and web software that enables one to post an image on a bulletin board, turning images into bits of conversational text. Taking shape primarily on image board sites like 4chan, and then later Reddit and other social media platforms, the flow of the image board is enabled by the software architecture. The appearance of image-text as conversational material is a new form of visual-verbal communication. Dump.fm epitomized this purposefully from 2010–17, as an image board in which users were only able to post images in order to communicate, in effect producing a morphing conversational free-form flow of image-words.[9] The results are somewhere between absurd and sensible — like a

---

9   Dump.fm operated from 2010–17 and was invite-only.

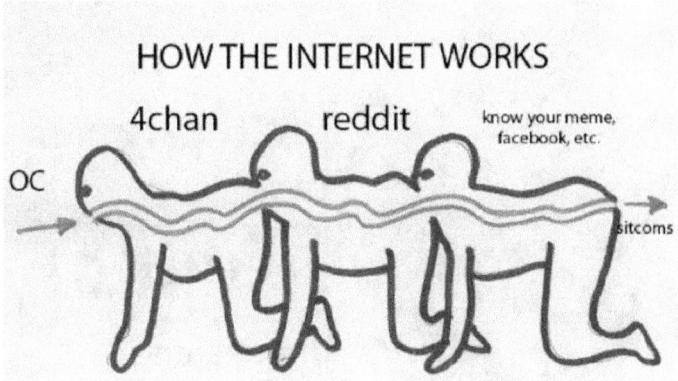

Fig. 8.

pragmatic form of surrealism. An Internet meme that falls into the category of dank meme is also aesthetically specific to image board culture's absurdist love for the digital flow of low-fi humor. As Aria Dean points out:

[T]he term ["meme"] has evolved: once used to describe ideas or behaviors that are passed from person to person, "meme" now refers metonymically to internet memes, which are as trope-filled and easy-made as stock imagery, but are unprofessional and intentionally funny, with often-absurdist text floating on or above a low-res image.[10]

In this sense, "Internet memes" are re-useable image-word joke patterns enabled by software patterns. Aesthetically, they also entail absurdist or nihilist humor, "petty" observations, and as Dean notes, unprofessional looking "poor images."

Nothing is aesthetically sacrosanct on an image board; nothing appears to be labored over for more than five minutes. Memes are not valued for their newness nor for their aesthetic craft, but because of their trashness. They are irreverent to the

---

10 Aria Dean, "Poor Meme, Rich Meme," *Real Life,* July 25, 2016, http://reallifemag.com/poor-meme-rich-meme/.

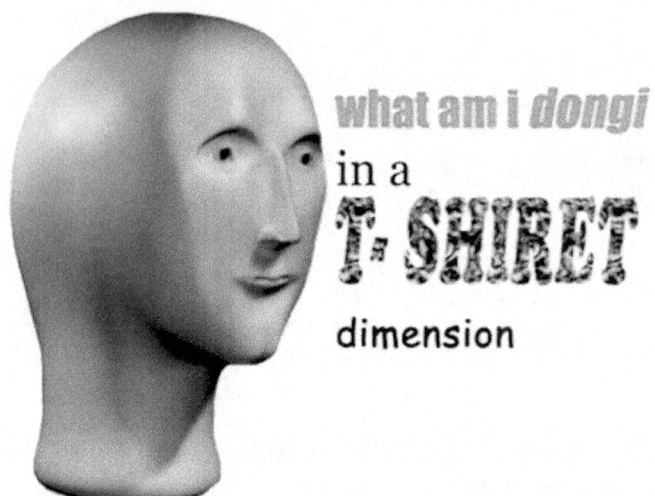

Fig. 9.

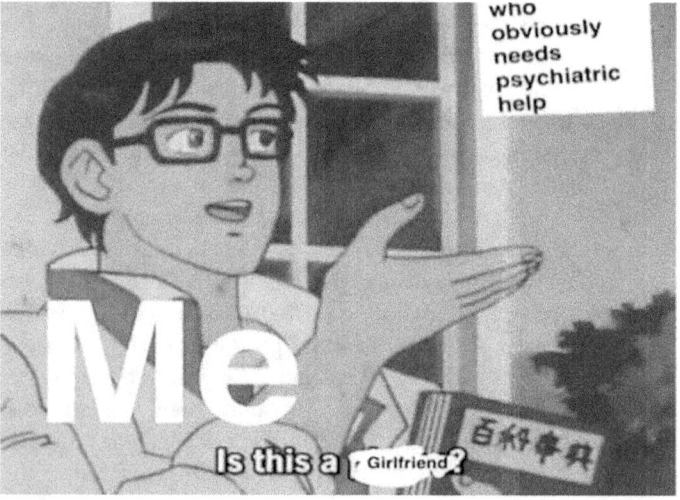

Fig. 10.

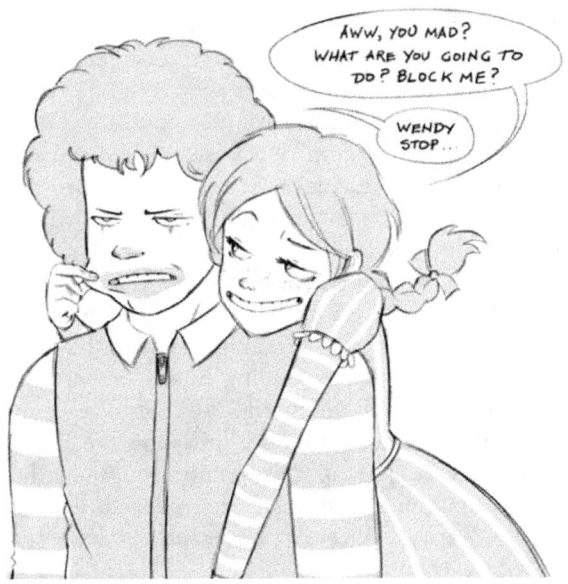

Fig. 11.

labor of skilled artistic production. The "meme man" head, for example, is a badly sculpted 3D model of a human head (fig. 9). The maker openly claims meme man's origin as a faulty, early attempt at 3D modeling. Whereas a technically well-crafted 3D model of a human head might look more photorealistically like a human head, meme man works as meme material precisely because he is 3D digital trash. This is his charm. He's aesthetically basic. In another recently circulated meme, we see an animation still of a guy looking off camera with a subtitle scratched over and replaced with different text (fig. 10). It is meant to reveal its quick imperfect handwriting, done by a generic person on the Internet.

What Alain Badiou says of the cinema as a mass art applies to Internet memes full-force: "it is always at the edge of non-art. Cinema is an art particularly laden with non-art. An art that is always full of trite forms [...] cinema is always beneath art. Even its most obvious artistic successes include an immanent infinity of shoddy ingredients, of blatant bits of non-art."[11] Internet memes are even less art than the non-art of cinema. There is no montage, no acting, no cinematography. The Internet meme is itself a pure bit of non-art: a quick trash image-text piece made for a digital aesthetic "dump." It is less than an imperfect image, albeit intentionally; it is chicken scratch spelled-wrong. BTW, in fig. 11 we see Wendy's, again, attempting to make their character appear a cute low-life troll (but failing).

In addition to its visual trashness, the more absurdly the manner in which the meme points to its lowness, often, the more relatable it is. For example, this is the case in the "whomst've'"meme — an expanding mind comparison format that uses the words "who whom whomst whomst've whomst've'd." The more letters in the "whomst've" variation, the more absurdly intellectually "deep" it appears, pointing out the ordinariness of common grammar mistakes from whence it derives. Using "whomst've'd" is so intellectual that it causes pink lasers to shoot out of your eyeballs due to your having reached such a high transcendental level of the word usage of "whom." The longer the "whomst've," the better: "whomst've'iv'e'ist'ive'whomst > whomst." The aesthetic is that of a sarcasm of intellectual absurdity, pushing the facade of "proper grammar" to meaningless excess. Similar to the appeal of Charlie Chaplin, the more low-fi and low-life juxtaposed with the supposedly hi-fi and high-class, the more charming. As Dean points out, memes are thus indeed Hito Steyerl's poor image *par excellence.*[12] Dean further draws the relation of this visual wretchedness and the use of vernacular in meme culture to blackness, specifically in the economics of memes and the way that they circulate:

> [M]emes move like blackness itself [...] vulnerable to appropriation and capture. The meme is a form that allows for a sense of collective ownership among those who come into

---

11 Alain Badiou, *Cinema,* trans. Susan Spitzer (Cambridge: Polity, 2013), 238.

12 See Hito Steyerl, "In Defense of the Poor Image," *e-flux* 10 (2009), https://www.e-flux.com/journal/10/61362/in-defense-of-the-poor-image/.

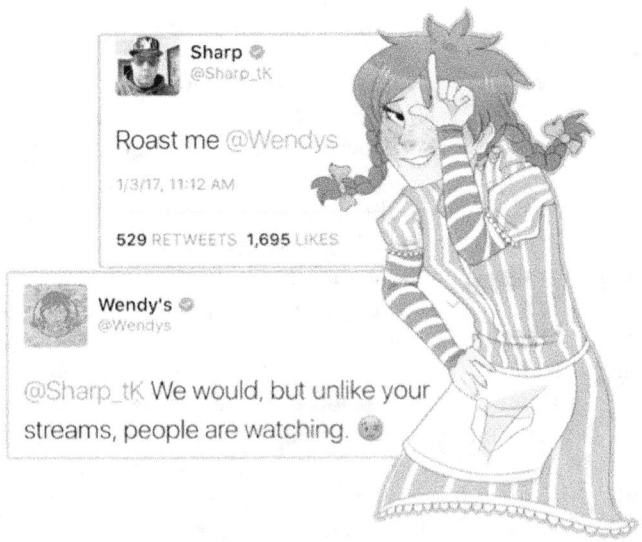

Fig. 12.

contact with it — black or nonblack. The meme seems open to appropriation and interpretation by whoever possesses it for a moment, echoing Fred Moten's description of blackness as being only what we hold in our outstretched hands.[13]

Stated differently, the condition of lack is the generic condition expressed by meme culture. Its potential to be appropriated, its mutability, and its trashness is fundamental to the genre because, like Chaplin and Steyerl's "poor image," it is an expression of a commonness from within the tramp-like condition of living in a precarious economic system and under state control. The more trash in the aesthetics of the image, the better. This is the manner in which it intentionally takes up its position.

---

13   See Dean, "Poor Meme, Rich Meme."

In fig. 12, we see Wendy trying again (pathetically) to appear low-life, forming an L for "Loser" on her forehead, pretending to be a troll).

The humor of dank meme authenticity, however, is not about its poor condition; it is an absurdity shaped from within. A more Kafkaesque humor thus emerges. There is a mix of the strange and the singular, co-mingled with the common, the ordinary, and the stupid. As Gerald Raunig writes of Kafka's story, "Josephine and the Mouse Folk," it is a strange mix of the popular and the singular. Josephine's singing is seen no differently than the mouse folk's way of speaking or of making noise: "piping is the acoustic expression of mouse folk normality. No one would call it art. The mouse folk pipe away without attaching importance to it."[14] Any one of the mouse folk can pipe. It's relatable, not special — a vernacular way of speaking, an ordinary sound, albeit made in a singular fashion: the humdrum of daily life mixed with the particularity of a subjectivity. Raunig calls Josephine's singing a weak event that enables, or causes, the mouse folk to gather — a Deleuzian "streaking of the territory."[15] It is not because of Josephine, but just the fact that she sings that cause the mouse folk to show up.

The low-fi craft of meme culture likewise streaks Internet territory. A human-turned-cockroach stuck in a chat room because life sucks: Gregor Samsa makes for good dank meme material. The cockroach would not work so well as a sales pitch for Wendy's. The Internet meme is an image made *for* and is borne out of the image board user's Internet life: low-res, low-fi, a small file, streaking the system. The humor is common, irreverent, petty — the more low-life, absurd, ridiculous, politically and grammatically incorrect, the better, the more shareable. As Badiou points out: "'mass art' defines a paradoxical relationship [...] because "mass" is a political category, or more precisely a category of activist democracy, of communism [...] and nowa-

---

14   Gerald Raunig, *Factories of Knowledge, Industries of Creativity*, trans.
       Aileen Derieg (Los Angeles: Semiotext(e), 2013), 10.
15   Ibid., 2.

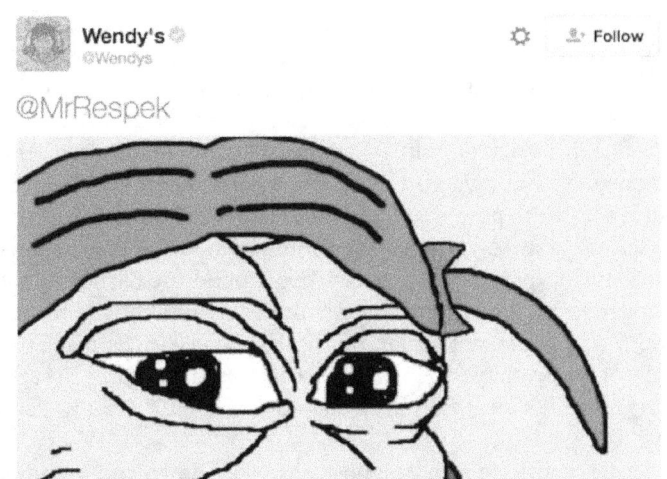

Fig. 13.

days we oppose "mass democracy" to representative and consti-
tutional democracy. Mao said that 'the masses, the masses alone,
make universal history.'"[16] The paradox of the meme as mass art
is that is it is usually meant not to be an art at all and is without
a political program but is nonetheless political by simply being
"mass" — scattered across many little bits. As François Laruelle
states: "it is with micropolitics that power passes from the infinitely large to the infinitely small."[17] The meme does just that.
As a pure tiny piece of non-art — memes are mass dank micropolitics.

Towards an Economic Heresy: Fucking Stop It, Facebook

The mouse folk constantly scatter and reconvene, like a disjointed swarm, difficult to capture and control. But this is not their

---

16 Badiou, *Cinema*, 235.
17 François Laruelle, "Homo ex Machina," trans. Taylor Adkins, *Fractal
Ontology* (blog), February 8, 2018, https://fractalontology.wordpress.
com/2018/02/08/new-translation-of-francois-laruelles-homo-ex-
machina-1980/.

intention. At the same time that their scattering makes them uncontrollable, they likewise sacrifice their ability to organize — and to monetize. The perpetual condition of dank meme culture is this condition of lack. Lack of economic value, lack of reverence, lack of political control, lack of organization. The memeplex is always on the verge of mass meme breakdown. Junk DNA is its power. While Dean frames this in terms of the potential of an Afro-pessimist annihilation and a Black accelerationism, there is also always Pepe around the corner. What happens when meme culture establishes its authenticity by being racist, sexist, ableist, and basically just mean? Is it for the sake of perpetually rebelling against systematic capture? In early 2017, Wendy's new fully troll identity tweeted a Wendy-Pepe (fig. 13).

After swift criticism, the post was taken down and Wendy's made a public statement in which it claimed it did know that Pepe was a racist symbol. Hard to believe considering they clearly made a sustained effort to turn Wendy into a meme troll all year long. It started with bad forced-memes about eating a sandwich and ended in a Wendy-Pepe... While a cockroach might not have worked for Wendy's marketing campaign, Pepe did in fact seem to work for it. True to Internet meme fashion, the post was shared and widely written about by the time it was taken down. The next day the *Daily Stormer* declared Wendy's the official fast food chain of the alt-right.

Did the alt-right appropriate Wendy's (as it seemed to think)? Or did the alt-right and the Pepe meme simply become the free ad server for Wendy's? Clearly the company achieved its goal of gaining free meme marketing magic and the dank authenticity usually attributed to the "natural virality" of non-forced memes. With Trump already in power and the next election far off, it is unclear what the alt-right would have gained from a political alliance with Wendy's at this moment. Both the control and the favor appears to be in Wendy's hands. Her forced meme method worked — the Wendy troll has won.

SEPTEMBER 28–30TH

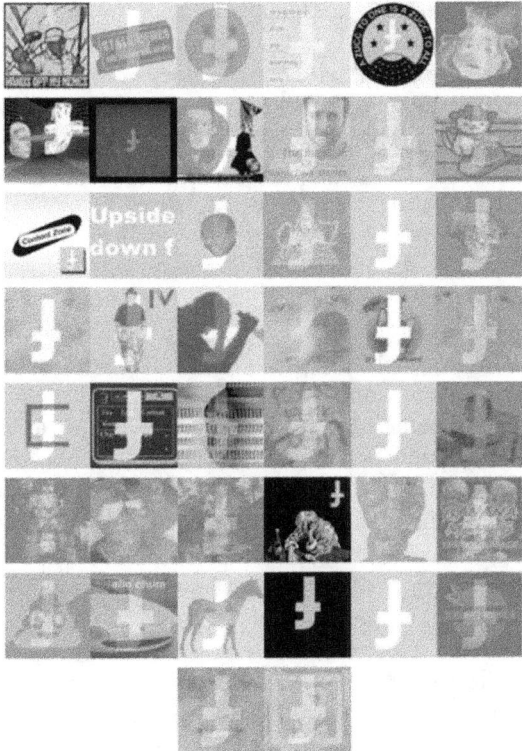

WE STRIKE!

Fig. 14.

Pepe — just a frog in a cartoon who got "highjacked" by racist trolls and crowned the racist frog king troll — is now a racist Pepe troll hijacked by a Wendy troll, forced to sell burgers. Free marketing, free branding, free labor. This is the economic normality of capitalist appropriation — but now mixed with the weird image board flow of the Internet meme. What then of the future for mass meme dankness?

The surface of the meme "poor image" is low-fi and it circulates via an appropriation that epitomizes its poverty — these characteristics are the frontend of its poverty. In terms of the dank meme backend, it is in fact, even poorer. The Wendy's example shows how dank authenticity does not make economic gains except only when hijacked as a forced meme for advertising. Increasingly over the last few years, meme culture has spread on social media platforms. After Facebook made their "groups" and "pages" feature in 2008, "Weird Facebook" groups started to make pages to distribute dank memes. While we have established that it holds no economic power itself, does the swarm of viral images replicating across the Internet like an alien glitter disease hold political sway? In 2016, Facebook already began to "crack down" on anonymous meme groups, inciting the #FreeTheMemes and #Zuxit protests by various Weird Facebook pages, including Freddy YOLO, Cabbage Cat, Exploding Fish Shitposting and Senseless Drivel, Inc., I play KORN to my DMT plants, smoke blunts all day & do sex stuff, and Special Meme Fresh, among many other pages. The protests were against Facebook's seemingly arbitrary review policies that took down some pages, but left other pages alone. Various Weird FB pages changed their profile picture to an inverted pink FB logo filter for #FreeTheMemes (fig. 14).

A website called MemeAlliance.org, which organized #Zuxit, cites that it's in alliance with over 100 meme-themed Facebook pages with "an aggregate following of 20 million users," and that many of them have moved to MeWe.[18] One of the original weird Facebook groups, "Special Meme Fresh" (also one of the pages that first posted meme man), responded with various memes, such as meme man sitting on an abstract hierarchy. The hierarchy goes in this order from top to bottom: meme man, Facebook, Normal People, Memes (i.e., "wow! 10 images that will shit your fuck"), the data that Facebook collects, and under-

---

18 See *Meme Alliance Acttion,* http://memealliance.org/actions/.

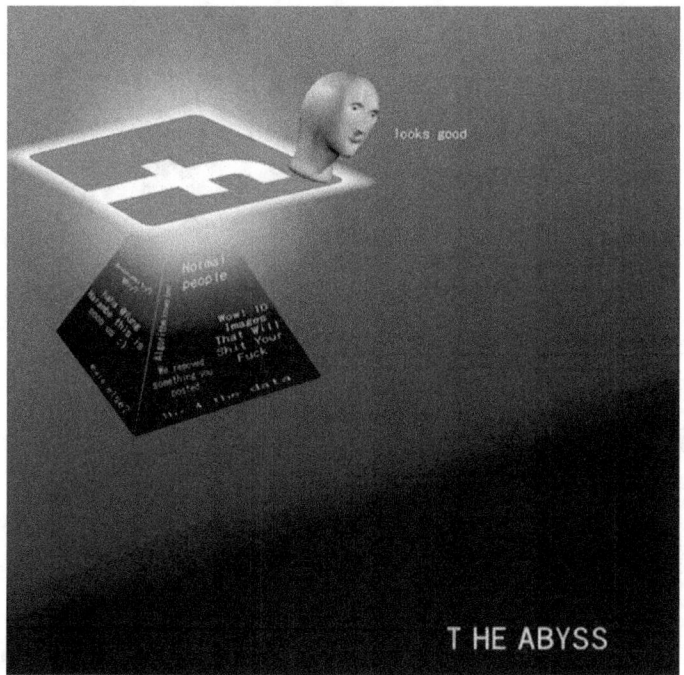

Fig. 15.

neath it all, the abyss (fig. 15).[19] Meme man here is Zuckerberg, who peers off of the ledge of Facebook like a god that created the abyss underneath it all and saw that it was Good.

At the recent Facebook hearing in front of the US Congress, Mark Zuckerberg stated — to the government — "Facebook will always be free." The "free" that Zuckerberg refers to here is not the "free" that #FreeTheMemes refers to. Facebook makes money from selling advertisements, clarified by Zuckerberg during the hearing, which is paid for by its customers (such as Wendy's and Russia); meanwhile, the users are what are free for Facebook to sell to its customers. Facebook is free to use, so long as

19　See @EvieYv, *Twitter,* September 11, 2016, 6:14PM, https://twitter.com/
　　EvieYv/status/775004493020704769.

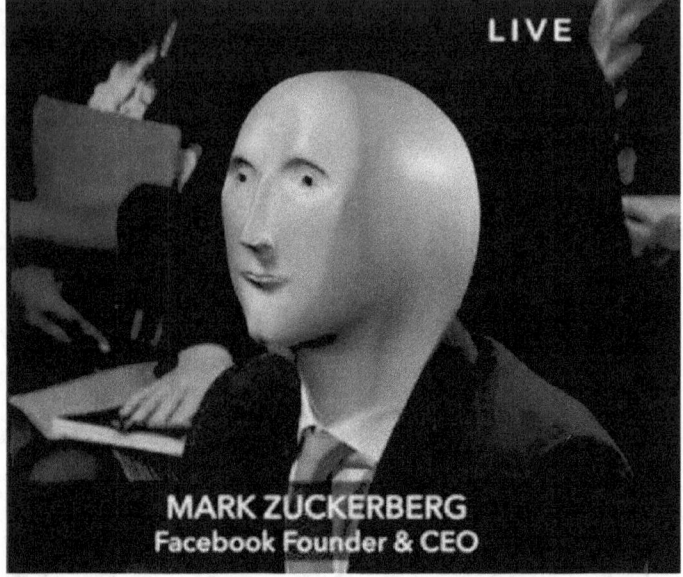

Fig. 16.

it us used in order to mainly be shown forced memes (ads). It is not free for the proliferation of memes. Meme man again thus appeared as Zuckerberg (fig. 16)

An article in *Huffington Post* posing the question "do memes have civil rights?" further lays out one of the problems inherent to this meme protest:

> [W]hile some [meme] pages have taken the issue very seriously and even started making complaints to the Federal Trade Commission, it was evident from the start that memes' overwhelming tendency towards irony would be in tension with a serious programme, and predictably enough some of the more nihilistic pages have started to subvert the protest with faux messages of solidarity with Facebook.[20]

---

20 Sam Harrison, "Facebook, Feudalism, and Civil Rights for Memes?" *Huffington Post,* August 15, 2016, https://www.huffingtonpost.co.uk/sam-

The Internet meme as the mass dankness of non-art becomes essentially a nihilist practice in its commitment to expressing the condition of being politically and economically free — and therefore precarious. Nonetheless, unlike an advertisement or the destructive forces of capitalist forced memes, memers seem to genuinely want the circulation of an authentic dankness. Dank memes are meant to be made freely, as a cultural gift, and must likewise circulate freely. Perhaps in line with Lauren Berlant's cruel optimism, it is a cruel desire for there to be something that cannot be bought.

Although the memes of the alt-right, such as Pepe, are attributed with having helped spread the MAGA (Make America Great Again) campaign virally — and thus making some lefties agree with blaming meme pages and agree with shutting down meme pages — looking to the way that meme pages are arbitrarily shut down on Facebook, it seems that the meme is still very much controlled. Further looking to the way that Facebook tightly maintains its real estate to prioritize its purchasing customers, we might ask: is a "viral" meme of Pepe really doing much? Perhaps more clear after Facebook's so-called "data breach," the 2016 election reveals that having access to user data on the backend is what is politically valuable. The direct access to user data and relational data on user habits in databases was, in fact, a more effective strategy, as it allowed for the purposely directed targeting of users, in comparison to the untracked and untargeted circulation of a racist frog cartoon who now works for Wendy's. What the Facebook–Cambridge Analytica alliance revealed was that both companies were able to simultaneously create political targets and monetize their data in circulation (memes). Highly specific data about users and trackable data of server ads tailored not for individuals but particular political leanings was perhaps the model of mass swarm action. This targeted data, plus tracking on backend formulae, is the exact opposite of amorphous mutable meme data, which remains always untracked and never purposely directed. How much political

harrison/facebook-feudalism-and-ci_b_11505412.html.

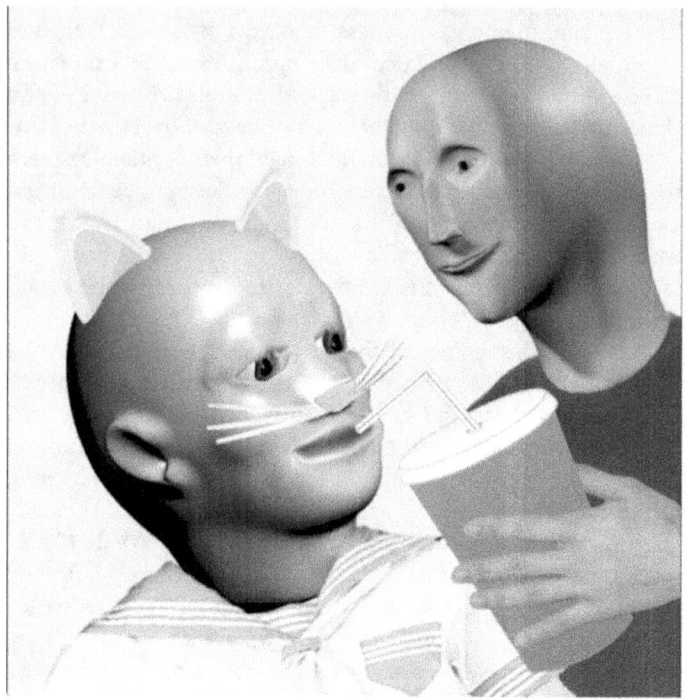

Fig. 17.

power did viral Pepe really have then in terms of voter value is questionable. Stated differently, Facebook and Cambridge Analytica made a lot of money by implementing targeted user data and data tracking, while Pepe now sells burgers for free.

If neither for economic nor political gains, why do we make memes? Limor Shifman points out: "a quick look at any Web 2.0 application would reveal that people do choose to create their *own versions* of Internet memes, in startling volumes."[21] Do people secretly want to spread covfefe everywhere, laughing out

---

21 Limor Shifman, "Memes in a Digital World: Reconciling with a Conceptual Troublemaker," *Journal of Computer-Mediated Communication* 18 (2013): 362–77, at 365.

loud as we all die from twitter fights turned nuclear holocaust? As Laruelle says: "*dissolve* States, classes, institutions, factories, all forms of community—something will still remain, i.e. ultimately the pure operation of dissolution and production that is linked to accomplished gregariousness, the superior masterful biocracy of bodies and souls, till death do us part [*à la vie à la mort*]."[22] For Roberto Esposito, the definition of community is one formed out of a nihilism of community itself, not something built. A "community isn't a property, nor is it a territory to be separated and defended against those who do not belong to it. Rather, it is a void, a debt, a gift to the other that also reminds us of our constitutive alterity with respect to ourselves."[23] Dank memes are thus an economic heresy, because like good comedy and good tragedy, they're not about creating a community but are a cultural form that we produce merely to remind us how life sucks for everyone.

---

22 Laruelle, "Homo ex Machina."
23 See Roberto Esposito, *Communitas,* trans. Timothy Campbell (Stanford: Stanford University Press, 2010), back cover.

Bibliography

Badiou, Alain. *Cinema.* Translated by Susan Spitzer. Cambridge: Polity, 2013.

Blackmore, Susan. "The Evolution of Meme Machines." In *Ontopsychology and Memetics,* edited by A. Meneghetti et al., 233–40. Rome: Psicologica Editrice, 2003. https://www.susanblackmore.uk/conferences/the-evolution-of-meme-machines-3/.

Dean, Aria. "Poor Meme, Rich Meme." *Real Life,* July 25, 2016. http://reallifemag.com/poor-meme-rich-meme/.

Esposito, Roberto. *Communitas.* Translated by Timothy Campbell. Stanford: Stanford University Press, 2010.

@EvieYv. Twitter status, September 11, 2016, 6:14PM. https://twitter.com/EvieYv/status/775004493020704769.

Galloway, Alexander R. *The Interface Effect.* Cambridge: Polity, 2013.

Harrison, Sam. "Facebook, Feudalism, and Civil Rights for Memes?" *Huffington Post,* August 15, 2016. https://www.huffingtonpost.co.uk/sam-harrison/facebook-feudalism-and-ci_b_11505412.html.

Infinity Media, "STOP PUTTING MEMES IN MEDIA." *YouTube,* April 24, 2015. https://www.youtube.com/watch?v=yNtySt6Fg3o.

Meme Alliance Action. http://memealliance.org/actions/.

Laruelle, François. "Homo ex Machina." Translated by Taylor Adkins. *Fractal Ontology* (blog), February 8, 2018. https://fractalontology.wordpress.com/2018/02/08/new-translation-of-francois-laruelles-homo-ex-machina-1980/. Originally published in *Revue Philosophique de la France et de l'Étranger* 170, no. 3 (1980): 325–42.

Manovich, Lev. *The Language of New Media.* Cambridge: MIT Press, 2001.

Raunig, Gerald. *Factories of Knowledge, Industries of Creativity.* Translated by Aileen Derieg. Los Angeles: Semiotext(e), 2013.

Shifman, Limor. "Memes in a Digital World: Reconciling with a Conceptual Troublemaker." *Journal of Computer-Mediated Communication* 18 (2013): 362–77. DOI: 10.1111/jcc4.12013.

Steyerl, Hito. "In Defense of the Poor Image." *e-flux* 10 (2009). https://www.e-flux.com/journal/10/61362/in-defense-of-the-poor-image/.

Ulmer, Gregory L. *Internet Invention: From Literacy to Electracy.* New York: Longman, 2002.

Wark, McKenzie. *A Hacker Manifesto.* Cambridge: Harvard University Press, 2004.

12

Meso-Memetics, Service Fetishism, and Deep Mediation

Patricia Reed

The punny call to "seize the memes of production" (a meme in its own right) would entail a gargantuan, though not undeliberated task, of both designing and implementing a model of collective ownership for the platforms that enable users to circulate memes in the first place. In a production mode composed of infrastructure, hardware, software and crucially, a *critical mass* of users, how far down the chain of production does such a call gesture at? If this call is to be taken seriously, and is not merely a play of fortuitously matched words, what do we actually mean by it? The backbone enabling our base connectivity? The ownership of our extracted data on an individual and/or aggregate level? The socialization of gains made through collective, unpaid labor? Platforms reorganized along the principle of a globally scaled public utility? The open-sourcing of platform architecture and algorithms that guide what we see and what others see from us? All of the above? As a point of entry, these questions point to the depth of scales one is compelled to consider within this comparative play on the historical expression.

The second point concerns the relevance of this historical referent within our present. Do emancipatory labor models from industrial capitalist historical contexts hold the same degree of

DOI: 10.21983/P3.0255.1.13

effectivity under current conditions of production, value creation, and surplus value extraction? When "seizing the means
of production" became a communist meme in industrial capitalism, it specifically targeted the socialization of surplus value
of production as an emancipatory claim tied to the productive
labor of workers (where the enclosure of "the social" presumably assumed the bounds of a nation-state organizational form).
Deploying this phrase in the context of globally networked platform economies requires that we would first map the relation
between worker and user; secondly, that we identify how surplus value is accrued; and thirdly, contend with a global scale
of sociality from which this surplus value is derived, and for
whom it would be destined. Additionally, and only adjacently
addressed in historical Marxian analyses, are the negative externalities these production modes are tethered to at a planetary
scale, which can no longer be a mere aside in conceptualizing
durable transformation. Without adapting the telos of the demands to our present conditions, these referents operate less
to catalyze progressive change, and serve to entrap our futural
imaginaries by ossifying nostalgic ideals with little use-value or
malleability. Can we uphold the general ambitions contained
within the historical expression, while doing the analytical work
in grasping the different affordances, modes of value-creation,
technicity, and possible points of leverage at play in our moment
for a transformative pragmatics to emerge? When the playing
field has changed, strategies for reengineering the rules demand
adaption.

From the outset, let's admit the unfortunate misstep in labe-
ling digital labor as immaterial. Now it's true that "immaterial
labor" helpfully charts out a shift in the quality of *some* forms
of labor from Fordist modes of commodity production, to post-
Fordism premised on informational, affective, or cognitive labor,
where the assimilation of human communicative practices is directly folded into economic production and selfhood becomes
interpolated with entrepreneurship. The term, however, ends up
obfuscating the material supports as well as the conventional
factory labor required to make these production modes func-

tion. On top of that, as Peter Wolfendale has noted, the rise of the gig economy centered on the fulfillment of micro-tasks, like Amazon's Mechanical Turk, harkens to a resurgence of Taylorist modes of production management in parallel,[1] not to mention the micro-tasks assigned to software engineers for problem solving, who ultimately lose sight of the systemic implications of their "solutions" in aggregation.[2] Digital labor, as such, amalgamates a variety of types of labor and management techniques of it, in simultaneity. Furthermore, the cloud, as know from the endless stream of server farm stock photography, coupled with the carbon emissions for each retweet, and the fact that we "hold a piece of the Congo in our pockets," is anything but immaterial.[3] Without this geophysical layer of material extraction and physical manipulation of it, "immaterial labor" simply cannot operate. One must then assert that the socialization of platforms would need to include a struggle among all types of participants (differentiating between their various organizational structures) and materials within the chain of production, without the exclusive privileging of the cognitariat-user, as if she operates as a body-without-devices. When platforms can be generalized as "digital infrastructures that enable two or more groups to interact," one needs to apply this mediating premise in binding the various types of laborers and, importantly, the resources involved in production that span traditional material workers and the users who are wholly (and hungrily) dependent upon a material substrate.[4] This is not to dismiss the potential

---

1   Peter Wolfendale, "Response to 'Cold War Cold World,'" seminar presented at the Cold War Cold World working group, CalArts, Valencia, CA, December 7, 2017.

2   Wendy Lui, "On Silicon Valley and the Democratisation of Technology," *Politics Theory Other* (podcast), May 31, 2018, https://soundcloud.com/poltheoryother/9-wendy-liu-on-silicon-valley-and-the-democratisation-of-technology.

3   Anne DeVoe, "Carrying a Piece of Congo in Our Pockets: Global Complicity to Congo's Sexual Violence and the Conflict Minerals Trade," *Seattle Journal for Social Justice* 10, no., 1 (2011), http://digitalcommons.law.seattleu.edu/sjsj/vol10/iss1/30.

4   Nick Srnicek, *Platform Capitalism* (Cambridge: Polity Press, 2016), 32.

for *human* solidarity building extending from the autonomist tradition that focuses less on the means of production and more on class struggle, but it is to highlight the inseparability of these forces or "layers" and the ways in which they are codependent.[5]

This tension between layers of analysis, and the focus of only certain types of labor can be read alongside current trajectories stemming from Marxist Internet Studies. Eran Fisher points out two of those dominant perspectives, namely: cultural analysis and materialist analysis.[6] On the one hand, cultural analysis concerns the semantic level of production, focusing on the "superstructure" to uncover "the ideological role of media content in the reproduction of capitalism."[7] Whether one figures the users of media as passive consumers or content co-creators — where platforms encourage both — the cultural strand emphasizes the semiotic level of ideological dissemination and reception. The materialist perspective, on the other hand, focuses on the "base," the political economy underlying "the relations of production entailed in media institutions."[8] This second strand centers on the ownership of media and the organizational practices of its institutions, notably addressing pressing issues such as monopolization, private/governmental "partnerships," as well as the employment conditions of workers.[9]

To my mind, there is a conceptual and operational deadlock in at once seeking to maximize potential solidarities through the figure of the cognitariat, whilst analytically isolating this particular type of labor and neglecting the multi-level means of

---

5   Gordon Hull, "Notes on Big Data, Marx, Time, and the Production of Value," *New APPS: Art, Politics, Philosophy, Science,* February 21, 2017, http://www.newappsblog.com/2017/02/notes-on-big-data-marx-time-and-the-production-of-value.html.

6   Eran Fisher, "How Less Alienation Creates More Exploitation? Audience Labour on Social Network Sites," in *Marx in the Age of Digital Capitalism,* eds. Christian Fuchs and Vincent Mosco (Leiden: Brill, 2016), 180.

7   Ibid.

8   Ibid.

9   Ibid.

production underpinning them. Given the immense amount of energy required for this production chain, with some estimates suggesting 20% of the world's electricity will be consumed via networked communication activities by 2025, while generating 5.5% of the world's carbon emissions, the need to contend with environmental dependencies and externalities of this new labor form becomes glaringly apparent.[10] A humble step in this direction is to begin reworking some of the conceptual separations between these layers that get reinforced by the vocabularies we use to frame and construct a certain perspectival correlation to our condition. Taking cues from Donna Haraway's theoretical-linguistic hybrids, the term "medianature," coined by Jussi Parikka captures this necessity for integrating an entangled, multi-scalar perspective traversing layers. It's a term that aims to account for the scope of a deep materialist view of technology and communication, beyond, but not nullifying human perspectives, defining it as:

> A concept that crystallizes the "double bind" of media and nature as co-constituting spheres, where the ties are intensively connected in material nonhuman realities as much as in relations of power, economy, and work. Indeed, it is a regime constituted as much by the work of micro-organisms, chemical components, minerals, and metals as by the work of underpaid laborers in mines or in high-tech entertainment device component production factories, or people in Pakistan and China sacrificing their health for scraps of left-over electronics."[11]

As language itself operates as a relational and collaborative technology between humans and the world, creating new ver-

---

10   John Vidal, "'Tsunami of Data' Could Consume One Fifth of Global Electricity by 2025," *Climate Change News,* December 11, 2017, http://www.climatechangenews.com/2017/12/11/tsunami-data-consume-one-fifth-global-electricity-2025/.

11   Jussi Parikka, *A Geology of Media* (Minneapolis: University of Minnesota Press, 2015), 14.

naculars that instantiate better accounts of our reality is not inconsequential. Of course, language alone won't substantially change the world, but it's a contributing force for constructing new possibilities for substantially thinking it. Language, like media in the thought of Parikka, "structure how things are in the world and how things are known in the world."[12]

While the cultural influence of meme-ing is undeniable, be it in its more progressive manifestation in 2011, or in its hard-right turn in 2016, remaining strictly within the valances of ideology transmission, however, engages with political transformation only at the level of the symptom. There are likely nontrivial superstructural gains to be won in so-called meme wars advocated from some on the left who suggest we learn to game memes for socialist ambitions (like left trolling), yet this ought to be grasped as an interim tactic, not as an end unto itself. Without the ambitions of intervening in the means of enablement, our semio-labor, no matter how radical, only economically benefits the increasingly few, specifically the vectoralist class who own the data, in the parlance of McKenzie Wark.[13] Such an acknowledgment echoes Walter Benjamin's demand in "The Author as Producer," where he called upon authors not to merely mimic the historical apparatuses of production of their time, but to transform them by way of re-engineering. His thesis came about not by being satisfied by how content stands in relation *to* contemporary production procedures, but how it stands *in* them, casting the difference between being an activist in attitude only (content), and not in production (form).[14] Such a perspective helps to contend with the semiotic ambivalence inherent to platform logic, whose incentives are bound only to the expansion of user-bases and techniques of seducing more interaction, while structurally having no investment in the signification of ideological transmission. "Communicative capitalism," as Jodi

12 Ibid., 1.

13 McKenzie Wark, "The Vectoralist Class," *e-flux journal: Supercommunity* 65 (2015), http://supercommunity.e-flux.com/texts/the-vectoralist-class/.

14 Walter Benjamin, "The Author as Producer," trans. John Heckman, *New Left Review* 1, no. 62 (1970): n.p.

Dean named it nearly ten years ago, extracts surplus value from *all* communicative activities regardless of content, in the form of derivative data. It matters only *that* something is circulated, and not what is circulated. For the platform, there is an equivalence between a kitten and Pepe meme, so long as attention to either is measureable, and can therefore be exploited.[15] There is a tension that arises between us semio-creatures who are presumably somewhat invested in the content of our communicative activities, and the economization of this content-without-quality from the eyes of the platform, including the proliferation of shadow labor involved in gaming this mechanism through semi-automated click farms. Like posting anti-Facebook memes within the social media platform, the productive level not only remains undisturbed, it profits from it; similar to Benjamin's framing of publishing houses, whose owners could also "afford" to disseminate radical content that directly opposed them, without posing any actual threat to their socio-economic standing. The memer may care deeply about the semiotic influence of their user-labor (enjoying, perhaps, the cultural-capital rewards through statistical notifications), but platform economies are indifferent to it. There is an inconsistent, yet not antagonistic set of incentives at play between user actions and platform logics: we get the relatively unbridled means at (at no direct cost) to visibly express ourselves, while platforms translate that expressive visibility into data commodities, uninterested in *what* we have said/circulated, only *that* we have said/circulated it. By focusing primarily on this top layer of semiotic transmission, by remaining at the interpretive level of communicative circulation and its cultural weight, a quasi-symbiosis between users and platforms is instantiated, however unintendedly so. In view of Marxist tradition, it's useful here to highlight a poignant overlap in this semblance of symbiosis problem, since it works to conceal the exploitative operations at play, namely that it's largely the function of the superstructure to *maintain* the base, despite

---

15   Jodi Dean, *Blog Theory: Feedback and Capture in Circuits of Drive* (Cambridge: Polity Press, 2010).

the weak-signal reciprocity from the top down between the two layers that is put forth as a model of human societies. This is not to dissuade analysis and intervention upon this superstructural layer — to suggest otherwise is to fall into the all-or-nothing pitfall of degree-zero fantasies without pragmatics, a trap that offers no space for tractability in the here and now — it is solely, and humbly to weight its role. Like the commodity fetishism of Marx's time that obscured the subjective-material forces of its production, platform economies conceal their structural function of extracting data, beneath the slick parading-out of user utilities, a phenomenon we may speculatively diagnose as "service fetishism."

The memer as producer would entail an intervention within the relationship between these layers of semiotic labor and productive means, if we are to avoid "attitude"-only effects of platform symbiosis underwritten by service fetishism. Otherwise said, an intervention within the ways these layers interact, forming (infra-)structures of enablement, constraint and value creation/extraction. We might call this meso-memetics, which firstly stresses that we have not overcome memes, we are definitely not post-meme, but are squarely in the middle of their increasing influence; and, more crucially, denotes a conceptual position *within* layers of production without privileging one layer over the other, but looking, rather, at their inter-relations. Clearly, this transformational demand cannot be ascribed to the practice meme-ing alone, but to lament that limitation is to miss the broader point. The far more pressing meta-question at stake, one that ought to concern both die-hard Marxists and those who see little relevance in applying this tradition today, is the general question of political transformation actionable within the paradigm of the platform and the particular geopolitical economy it entails. When taking the deep view of production chains, including non-humans and carbon by-products, the two-tiered model of *human* societies is no longer robust enough to address all levels demanding consideration. Despite the fact that all models reduce complexity, there is a point when that reduction becomes too simplified to serve us conceptual use-value. The assertion I'm putting forth, is that the humanist underpinnings driving this superstructure/base model require extrapolations, not only to factor in the view of social (re-)production from the vista of a resituated human, thereby better contending with our relativized, positional agency within production chains, but also the need to grasp the "medianature" of platforms from an array of scalar, non-human standpoints. Such an inhumanist position is buttressed by humanism, a humanism where we are conceived as exceptional creatures possessing certain conceptual abilities, but pushed to the point where these capacities arrive at an unexceptional self-understanding that undermines our systemic centrality.[16] The hypermaterialist, six-tiered model of The Stack, outlined by Benjamin Bratton is an aggregate of platforms, and serves as a useful diagrammatic vehicle here, since it follows in the traditions of modelling grand scales (like the superstructure/base model), yet is adapted to an age of planetary-scaled computation. Not only does it make explicit certain systemic differentiations at work that are collapsed in a Marxian "base," but additionally, it factors in both human and non-human agents (Users). These Users, sitting at the top of The Stack, are defined as any entity capable of initiating signals (columns) down through its layers from the Interface to Address, City, Cloud, and Earth layers successively; and, as a reciprocal machine, said Users receive mediated signals back up the chain.[17] As a model *and* an actual (albeit accidental) organizational complex, The Stack has been postulated as a design brief perched on the "cliff's edge of the Anthropocene," complicating the human-centric biases implicit the original "seizing of means of production" meme, as if re-distribution of surplus value alone

---

16 Nina Power, "Inhumanism, Reason, Blackness, Feminism," *Glass Bead: Site 1: Logic Gate, Politics of the Artefactual Mind* (2017), http://www.glass-bead.org/article/inhumanism-reason-blackness-feminism/?lang=enview. This definition of "inhumanism" was put forth by Reza Negarestani in his essay "Labor of the Inhuman," *e-flux journal* 52 (2014), http://www.e-flux.com/journal/52/59920/the-labor-of-the-inhuman-part-i-human/.

17 Benjamin H. Bratton, *The Stack: On Sovereignty and Software* (Cambridge: MIT Press, 2015).

would be enough to avoid the cliff's precipice.[18] It is not. And, yet "complication" is not isomorphic with "nullification," as if thinking at a planetary scale entails only a macro perspective from which to distantly gaze upon our condition to the conceptual diminishment of the micro, or localized forces of exploitation, brushed aside as but a petty, residual folly of human self-centeredness. This reality-check should not arrest ambitions for re-engineering current procedures of labor exploitation, value creation/extraction, and increasing economic stratification today, but what it does complicate are the conditions and "nature" of agency, human or otherwise, within this novel geopolitical meta-machine.

The network effects, or a critical mass of users, upon which platforms structurally live or die, pushes this type of production system toward monopolization.[19] As Evgeny Morozov writes:

> It doesn't really make sense to have five competing social networks with twenty million people on each; you want all of them on one platform. It's the same for search engines: the more people are using Google, the better it becomes, because every search is in some sense a tinkering and improvement in the service.[20]

When capturing and controlling data is the primary economic incentive driving platforms, as Nick Srnicek notes, extracting as much data as possible from users is built into these business models, revealing a deep-seated incompatibility in suggesting this exploitation can be resolved through sheer privacy regulations.[21] Without a profoundly alternate economic condition but-

---

18 Ibid., 72.
19 Srnicek, *Platform Capitalism*, 59.
20 Evgeny Morozov, "Socialize the Data Centres!" *New Left Review* 91 (2015), https://newleftreview.org/II/91/evgeny-morozov-socialize-the-data-centres.
21 University of Leicester School of Business, "'Platform Capitalism' - Dr Nick Srnicek, University of London," *YouTube,* February 14, 2017, https://www.youtube.com/watch?v=BMoKAn1grgQ.

tressing platform logics, where network effects can be seized for the benefit of the users who co-constitute them, our personal, but more importantly, our aggregate data remains out of reach. When this aggregate data is privatized there is no social access to it, meaning we possess no means of decision, nor speculation on the potential use-value of it. Such an observation is precisely why arguing against data extraction absolutely qua platform logics, is self-defeating, insofar as this data can be used in vastly different, meaningful and advantageous ways. What it does point to, however, is how the market we currently have is ill-designed and, quite plainly, disincentivized to deliver on these possible social benefits. As Morozov insists, these questions are not purely technical, but more political in terms of how computation will be used, for whom, and who (or what) gains access to all the "sensors, filters, profiles and algorithms" passing through, and being parsed by the platform.[22]

Service fetishism enables a veneer of symbiosis between users and platforms that mask actual procedures of data mining and machine training labor that are more valuable than the costs involved in engineering the platform — this is precisely what platform surplus value is.[23] When I say "masking" these procedures, this is not to suggest we are unaware of how our communicative labor, or leisure time, is translated into monopolized data commodities, but it remains entirely invisible to us in the (mostly) smooth everyday use of these services. That is to say, the reciprocal dynamics of platform interaction is hidden in the way they use us. (An embedded widget conveying this reciprocity would constitute far more transparency than the biblically proportioned privacy legalese we blindly consent to nowadays.) Sarcasm aside, there seems to be an important shift in value creation specific to platform economies to take note of, namely the emphasis less on production, but on mediation, where platforms position themselves as infrastructural

---

22 Morozov, "Socialize the Data Centres!"
23 Bratton, *The Stack*, s.v. "Platform Surplus Value," 374.

"intermediaries that bring together different users."[24] Obviously, production still takes place, platform algorithms and software are highly laborious projects, but the operations of surplus value extraction occur at the level of interfacial activity. In view of this particular dynamic of surplus value extraction, one might then update the Marxian imperative from seizing the means of production, to seizing the means of mediation as a more specific, influential site from which to recast platform logics.

More generally, it's of relevance to consider how these platform dynamics transform the ways in which we conceive of agency within them. Historically, politics has not only been an exclusively human enterprise (most often, not even for most humans), but has equally been bound to imperatives of visibility, audibility, and sensibility. For something to be properly political, it requires some form of appearance and/or mode of public visibility. As we have never before had the technological affordances to appear and be heard to such large audiences, so quickly, and occasionally, even virally, that capacity for expression has become a target of exploitation (even more so in neoliberalism, where economic self-design requires maximal visibility). Even when radical congregations are enabled, or we use platform means to disseminate vital messages — of which we have seen important movements facilitated, there is always a reverse instrumentalization at work. In this scenario, potential empowerment lies less in the fact or act of appearing than in the mediation of that appearance. Platform design, with its specific techniques and lures for inciting interaction, is a protocol-driven, partially determinate system of rules that shapes (and trains) user behavior its own image, "whose agency is configured accordingly."[25] The degree of partiality (i.e., system malleability) of those rule-based determinations for reverse user-to-machine influence, is a critical design choice that constitutes an important point to leverage (despite its technicality), when imagining how network effects could, in the aggregate, become a collective

---

24 Srnicek, *Platform Capitalism*, 57.
25 Bratton, *The Stack*, 164.

force in re-weighting platform logics. In discussing speculative strategies of governance within platform logics, Bratton writes: "it is the interfacial relays between addressable objects that are the real object of governance."[26] Governance, as an amalgam of managerial protocols, however, is not isomorphic with politics understood as a mode of dissensus to techniques, and technicalities of that very mode of governance. As such, we may rebut, that a crucial object of platform politics ought to target this very layer of interfacial relays, and the ways in which reciprocal influence is enabled. Seizing the means of mediation, as an intervention entails not only a break-out from service fetishism that obfuscates interfacial relations, but a claim on those very interfacial protocols.

---

26 Ibid., 357.

Bibliography

Benjamin, Walter. "The Author as Producer." Translated by John Heckman. *New Left Review* 1, no. 62 (1970): n.p.

Bratton, Benjamin H. *The Stack: On Sovereignty and Software.* Cambridge: MIT Press, 2015.

Dean, Jodi. *Blog Theory: Feedback and Capture in Circuits of Drive.* Cambridge: Polity Press, 2010.

DeVoe, Anne. "Carrying a Piece of Congo in Our Pockets: Global Complicity to Congo's Sexual Violence and the Conflict Minerals Trade." *Seattle Journal for Social Justice* 10, no., 1 (2011). http://digitalcommons.law.seattleu.edu/sjsj/vol10/iss1/30.

Fisher, Eran. "How Less Alienation Creates More Exploitation? Audience Labour on Social Network Sites." In *Marx in the Age of Digital Capitalism,* edited by Christian Fuchs and Vincent Mosco. Leiden: Brill, 2016.

Hull, Gordon. "Notes on Big Data, Marx, Time, and the Production of Value." *New APPS: Art, Politics, Philosophy, Science,* February 21, 2017. http://www.newappsblog.com/2017/02/notes-on-big-data-marx-time-and-the-production-of-value.html.

Lui, Wendy. "On Silicon Valley and the Democratisation of Technology." *Politics Theory Other* (podcast), May 31, 2018. https://soundcloud.com/poltheoryother/9-wendy-liu-on-silicon-valley-and-the-democratisation-of-technology.

Morozov, Evgeny. "Socialize the Data Centres!" *New Left Review* 91 (2015). https://newleftreview.org/II/91/evgeny-morozov-socialize-the-data-centres.

Negarestani, Reza. "Labor of the Inhuman." *e-flux journal* 52 (2014). http://www.e-flux.com/journal/52/59920/the-labor-of-the-inhuman-part-i-human/.

Parrikka, Jussi. *A Geology of Media.* Minneapolis: University of Minnesota Press, 2015.

Power, Nina. "Inhumanism, Reason, Blackness, Feminism." *Glass Bead: Site 1: Logic Gate, Politics of the Artefactual*

Mind, 2017. http://www.glass-bead.org/article/inhumanism-reason-blackness-feminism/?lang=enview.

Srnicek, Nick. *Platform Capitalism.* Cambridge: Polity Press, 2016.

University of Leicester School of Business. "'Platform Capitalism' - Dr Nick Srnicek, University of London." *YouTube,* February 14, 2017. https://www.youtube.com/watch?v=BMoKAn1grgQ.

Vidal, John. "'Tsunami of Data' Could Consume One Fifth of Global Electricity by 2025." *Climate Change News,* December 11, 2017. http://www.climatechangenews.com/2017/12/11/tsunami-data-consume-one-fifth-global-electricity-2025/.

Wark, McKenzie. "The Vectoralist Class." *e-flux journal: Supercommunity* 65 (2015). http://supercommunity.e-flux.com/texts/the-vectoralist-class/.

Wolfendale, Peter. "Response to 'Cold War Cold World.'" Seminar presented at the Cold War Cold World working group, CalArts, Valencia, CA, December 7, 2017.

13

Circulation and its Discontents

Scott Wark and McKenzie Wark

Introduction: Meme Magic

To paraphrase Hito Steyerl, Internet memes have "crossed the screen," bringing nothing but bad news and censurable politics along with them.[1] There's an almost occult quality to Internet memes' capacity to boil out of the hellish recesses of the 'net. Or at least, that's how some parts of 'net culture spin things.

The Internet meme is of a class of media that has emerged with distributed, platform-based networks. In Limor Shifman's simple and compelling definition, three qualities characterize it: it's collectively produced; it mutates; and it circulates.[2] While it shares some qualities with like media — viral media also circulate; spam is collectively produced — it also differs from them.[3] Memes are

---

1 Hito Steyerl, "Too Much World: Is the Internet Dead?" *e-flux journal* 49 (2013), https://www.e-flux.com/journal/49/60004/too-much-world-is-the-internet-dead/.

2 Limor Shifman, *Memes in Digital Culture* (Cambridge: MIT Press, 2013), 41.

3 On viral media, see Marissa Olson, "Lost Not Found: The Circulation of Images in Digital Visual Culture," in *Mass Effect: Art and the Internet in the Twenty-First Century*, eds. Lauren Cornell and Ed Halter (Cambridge: MIT Press, 2015), 159–66. On spam, see Scott Wark, "Literature After Language's Algorithmic Normalisation: Spam, Code, and the Digitality of Print in

---

DOI: 10.21983/P3.0255.1.14

not only passed along, they are remade, varied, altered. They mutate. At scale and in circulation, an Internet meme's capacity to change and proliferate can be mystifying. No one hand guides it. They appear as if the instrument of an unconscious drive. 'Net culture has a term for this drive's apparent capacity to use Internet memes to wreak havoc and sow negativity beyond the confines of the 'net itself. They call it "meme magic."

Perhaps the most notorious example of meme magic at work is the assertion that a meme of a corpulent green frog, Pepe, might have swung the 2016 U.S. presidential election. In the terrain of what could be true as defined by our new online culture wars, this claim seems both absurd and entirely plausible. In 'net vernacular, meme magic is by turns ironic and esoteric. It is ironic because 'net culture is always ironic, at once embracing the idea that an Internet meme might have contributed to electing a president whilst also disparaging anyone who takes that idea seriously.

Meme magic is also limned with esoteric implications. Sometimes "magic" is spelt with a "k," investing internet memes with an incantatory power to make the fanciful real. Did Pepe effect an election? Did Internet memes invoke Trump's presidency? We don't want to draw conclusions. But let's suspend the reflex to dismiss the concept of meme magic out of hand. As concept, meme magic is absurd. Yet it also captures something that's essential to' net culture — and to Internet memes in particular — that's otherwise difficult to articulate.

There's a kernel of *incommensurability* at 'net culture's core. We endlessly produce data about what we do online, but we do it for the benefit of others. We do the labor, and often it is what Tiziana Terranova calls free labor, but we don't profit from our digital products.[4] Underneath the apparently free-floating world of circulating texts, images, memes, there is an *asymmetry of*

Blood Rites of the Bourgeoisie," *Scan | Journal of Media Arts Culture* 10, no. 2 (2013), http://scan.net.au/scn/journal/vol10number2/Scott-Wark.html.

4   Tiziana Terranova, *Network Culture: Politics in the Information Age* (London: Pluto Press, 2004).

information. The means to produce data is decentralized to us, but the means to collect and process that data is recentralized to the proprietors of the platform-based services we use.[5]

Ownership and control over the vector of information, its means of transmission and archiving, its interfaces and nodes of attraction, turns the asymmetry of information into a relation that could even be considered a class relation.[6] A subordinate class — us — makes information, shares information, passes it around, is sometimes paid a wage, is often precariously employed, or is not employed at all. This subordinate class gets access to *particular* bits and pieces of information; to memes, for example. But this subordinate class does not get to recuperate the value of that information in the aggregate, as a whole.

What the subordinate class of information producers get and what the dominant class who own the vector of information get are incommensurable, and in a double sense. If it were possible to measure what the subordinate class makes and what it gets in terms of information, the sums would not add up. It gets less than it makes. But how would this even be measured? The vector is designed to obfuscate the labor on which it depends.

This double incommensurability creates the conditions for 'net culture's impulse to call what Internet memes do "magic." The expropriation of information value in the aggregate and the capacity to occult the production of culture have the same source, but express it differently. The concept of meme magic teaches us that media theory deals just as badly with this incommensurability as 'net culture does.

Peel back the levels of irony and meme magic operates as what theory used to call the *fetish.* This term has a long and sometimes dubious history.[7] But we're struck by its habit of re-

5   Anne Helmond, "The Platformization of the Web: Making Web Data Platform Ready," *Social Media + Society* 1, no. 2 (2015): 1–11.

6   McKenzie Wark, *A Hacker Manifesto* (Cambridge: Harvard University Press, 2004).

7   William Pietz, "Fetishism and Materialism: The Limits of Theory in Marx," in *Fetishism as Cultural Discourse,* eds. Emily Apter and William Pietz (Ithaca: Cornell University Press, 1993).

curring across time and in different disciplines — including media theory. If we treat meme magic as a fetish, what becomes apparent is not only that 'net culture mistakes its occult lulz for reality. Rather, it's that media theory invokes its own magic word to resolve this incommensurability: *circulation*.

The parallel we're drawing might sound far-fetched. After all, circulation is a key term in media theory's lexicon of concepts. Both meme magic and circulation respond to the same set of problems. Each attempts to overcome an incommensurability that divides technics and labor from value or culture. Each attempts to grapple with the production of culture at scale. And each evokes a power that is neither adequately conceptualized nor, we would argue, substantiated.

Circulation's parallels with meme magic show how it operates as fetish when it's used to explain the 'net and 'net culture. We treat its limitations as a failure of our concepts. Our claim is that media theory has failed to see how the incommensurability that platforms actively produce also actively mediates media theory itself. As a result, its concepts reproduce the incommensurability they're supposed to explain.

We use the word fetish because, in the mongrel world of memes, it is a critical concept with some pedigree. The fetish is not just a substitute for the phallus, as Sigmund Freud's psychoanalytical appropriation of the term would have it.[8] Our approach draws on both Marxist and anthropological traditions. Whilst we acknowledge that the anthropological tradition of the fetish has a dubious history, we are confident that we can draw on deployments of it that negotiate the term's colonial heritage.[9] The Marxist concept of the fetish explains how we attribute the value of commodities to their physical properties rather than the labor that produces them.[10] The anthropological heritage

---

8   Sigmund Freud, "Fetishism," *The International Journal of Psycho-Analysis* 9 (1928): 161–66.

9   Michael Taussig, *The Devil and Commodity Fetishism in South America* (Chapel Hill: University of North Carolina Press, 2010).

10 Karl Marx, *Capital: A Critique of Political Economy, Volume 1,* trans. Ben Fowkes (London: Penguin Classics, 1990), 163ff.

expands the term's purview. It retains its power for us because it gives us the means to name those theoretical gestures by which we claim commensurability between otherwise incommensurable things.

Besides the role of living labor and free labor in the production of data, what the fetishizing of circulation obfuscates is the role that media technologies — *dead labor* — play in the production of culture.[11] More than this, they obfuscate how platforms actively make labor and technics incommensurable. Industrial technology fragmented the body and articulated it as components with machine components. Information technology goes much further, and fragments individual subjects into *dividual* components, weaving each into the information production process to the point where it would no longer be possible to distinguish living from dead labor.[12]

Meme magic might be absurd, but we also want to take a cue from it. It's no coincidence that 'net culture has invoked meme magic just when the extent of platforms' incommensurability has become known and has been politicized in a series of issues. Ours is an age of leaks, malware, hacks, encryption, drones, flash crashes, tech monopolies, tech gurus, the dark web, and DDOS attacks. Much of what makes 'net culture go around seems mysteriously beyond our ken. We are encouraged not to concern ourselves too much with all this, so long as our packets arrive at their destinations and our services stay online. But there's a lingering anxiety that it does matter. Meme magic points in negative to something real and perhaps even something true, beyond perennially refreshing appearances.

Casting down the fetishes of meme magic or of circulation might demonstrate how the media we theorize also mediate our theories of them, but it doesn't resolve the incommensurability that platforms produce. That gesture properly belongs to what we might think of as a *modern* style of theorization — a topic

---

11   Ibid., 322ff.
12   Maurizio Lazzarato, *Signs and Machines: Capitalism and the Production of Subjectivity* (Los Angeles: Semiotext(e), 2014), 26ff.

to which we shall return. Rather, there's a kernel of validity at meme magic's core: its recognition that something about 'net culture must remain incommensurable.

Perhaps 'net culture is actually driven by that incommensurability. Through the fetishizing of meme magic and the parallel fetishizing of circulation, we can glean something about what happens to culture when history no longer makes sense. Casting down the fetishes we make of the 'net doesn't make history or the real apparent. It makes apparent the incommensurability that organizes each.

We used to have a word for the practice of clothing what was difficult to know in more tractable guises: *myth*.[13] Shorn of the esotericism, the offensiveness, and the abominable politics — but not necessarily the irony, as Donna Haraway teaches us — perhaps meme magic is just a vernacular theory of contemporary political myth.[14] Within the technological conditions that constitute contemporaneity, perhaps myth has become memetic. So, did Pepe swing the 2016 United States Presidential election? Or is that too a myth? Internet culture seems to respond as though by saying, "When the meme becomes fact, make danker memes."[15] In this we can find the cultural politics underlying our new online culture wars.

The Fetish of Circulation

Circulation is a concept that circulates almost unnoticed in media theory. It is routinely used to describe what both old and new media do. The concept of circulation is particularly crucial in discussions of 'net culture, which use it to describe how media are distributed, the conditions in which we interact with

---

13 On myth as something more than structural, see Eduardo Viveiros de Castro, *Cannibal Metaphysics* (Minneapolis: Univocal, 2017).

14 Donna Haraway, *Manifestly Haraway* (Minneapolis: Minnesota University Press, 2016).

15 Anticipated, perhaps, in Jean Baudrillard, *Fatal Strategies,* trans. Jim Fleming (Los Angeles: Semiotext(e), 2008).

them, and how they generate effects. But perhaps circulation, which appears as a concept, acts more as a fetish.

Our claim is premised on a particular understanding of what a fetish is. As fetish, circulation renders invisible the incommensurability of what information labor makes and what it gets. It also renders invisible the incommensurability of what labor makes and what technics make. With the fetish concept, we can critique media theory's incapacity to grasp its relation to its own conditions of possibility; that is, media themselves as hybrid flesh-tech from which an information asymmetry is extracted.

Put simply, to fetishize is to invest a material object with outsize significance. But the concept of the fetish has a mixed reputation in the history of anthropology, where this understanding of it originates.[16] As William Pietz outlines in his seminal series of essays on the concept, the fetish first emerges from the "intercultural spaces" created when Italian, Portuguese, and Dutch traders started doing business along the West African coast from the late fifteenth century onwards.[17]

The fetish — from the Portuguese *fetisso* — is what European outsiders began to call objects that West Africans seemed to venerate. To these outside observers, these objects were invested with inexplicable material agency and anthropomorphic characteristics. The fetish played a specific role in its historical context: as Pietz puts it, to mediate the "social value of material objects" between the "radically heterogeneous social systems" — Christianity, African society, merchant capitalism — brought in to contact along the West African coast.[18]

At first, merchants had to participate in fetish-based social rituals trade with West African societies.[19] Expanding on Pietz, David Graeber argues that the charge of fetishism helped Eu-

16 L. Lorand Matory, *The Fetish Revisited: Marx, Freud, and the Gods Black People Make* (Durham: Duke University Press, 2018).

17 William Pietz, "The Problem of the Fetish, 1," RES: *Anthropology and Aesthetics* 9 (Spring 1985): 5–17, at 6.

18 Ibid., 6–7.

19 William Pietz, "The Problem of the Fetish, 2: The Origin of the Fetish," RES: *Anthropology and Aesthetics* 13 (Spring 1987): 23–45, at 45.

ropeans to "avoid some of the most disturbing implications of their own experience."[20] This is why Pietz argues that the fetish is defined by what he calls a "double consciousness" of "absorbed credulity" and "distanced incredulity," or of participation and disdain.[21] In this intercultural space, West African social conventions posed a challenge to the self-evidence of European systems of value.

What interests us in the concept, however, is not what it says about our "consciousness" of heterogeneous value systems, but a more general fetish function that Pietz identifies: the — anthropological — fetish is a physical object that mediates values that are otherwise "incommensurable."[22] This aspect of the fetish concept is what provides traction on the present. The fetish lives on in the way incommensurability is processed by the technologies that constitute the Internet, for example under the vernacular heading of meme magic. In media theory's concept of circulation, we find a version of the same fetish, albeit one that's less an object and more a process: a mediation.

We can use Graeber's work as a guide here. For him, the construction of fetishes follows a pattern. With no small dose of irony, Graeber describes the fetish as "a god under process of construction."[23] The gesture of *fetishizing* marks a point at which "objects we have created or appropriated for our own purposes suddenly come to be seen as powers imposed on us, precisely at the moment when they come to embody some newly created social bond."[24]

The animism found in the anthropological concept has a broader and recurrent significance. As far as we're aware, nei-

---

20 David Graeber, "Fetishism as Social Creativity: Or, Fetishes are Gods in the Process of Construction," *Anthropological Theory* 5, no. 4 (2005): 407–38, at 411.

21 Pietz, "The Problem of the Fetish, 1," 14.

22 Ibid., 16.

23 Graeber, "Fetishism as Social Creativity," 427.

24 Ibid.

ther of us has any gods. But we do have Google.[25] After Pietz and Graeber, we want to ask what contemporary role fetishes play in mediating otherwise incommensurable systems. With a little retrofitting, we can apply what Graeber describes to the contemporary Internet and the operations of its defining infrastructure: the *platform*.

The concept of the fetish has already recurred in media theory in different ways. Wendy H.K. Chun identifies the concept of "source code" as a kind of fetishism, critiquing it as a form of "ideology."[26] Taina Bucher and others identify and analyze the ways that we fetishize algorithms, using them as polyvalent explanatory devices.[27] These approaches mix a little from the Marxist tradition and a little from anthropology's concern with incommensurability.

Labor and algorithms are incommensurable, not because they represent different *social* value systems, but because they confront us with epistemological limits. With contemporary media, the question of incommensurability is mediated by the reorganization of epistemology by computation, automation, and what Benjamin H. Bratton calls its planetary distribution.[28] We take our cue from these media theoretical approaches: platforms obfuscate labor; they can do so because their operations are incommensurable.

But our fetish concept doesn't deal with a physical thing, as in Pietz; or code or algorithms, as in recent media theory. Régis Debray notes that whilst we're easily able to fetishize "objects isolated against their background," networks — which hold

---

25 John Durham Peters, *The Marvellous Clouds: Towards a Philosophy of Elemental Media* (Chicago: University of Chicago Press, 2016).

26 Wendy H.K. Chun, *Programmed Visions: Software and Memory* (Cambridge: MIT Press, 2011).

27 Taina Bucher, "Neither Black Nor Box: Ways of Knowing Algorithms," in *Innovative Methods in Media and Communication Research*, eds. Sebastian Kubitschko and Anne Kaun (London: Palgrave Macmillan, 2016), 81–98.

28 Benjamin H. Bratton, *The Stack: On Software and Sovereignty* (Cambridge: MIT Press, 2015).

platforms together — are "less easily turned into myth."[29] It's a stretch to call a platform an object. To call a platform a *hyperobject* (Morton) seems to capitulate in advance to understanding them as ineffable, intelligible only by their resonances.[30] To call a platform a *stack* (Bratton) offers a more analytical container for material technical systems that are complex and distributed, but it may not entirely avoid making a fetish of mediation.[31]

So what's to be gained by recovering the concept of the fetish and applying it to platforms? The platform itself isn't the fetish here — though this is one way we might read the concept's capaciousness.[32] What concerns us is not whether platforms are fetishes, but that they *produce* fetishism by producing its form. We might understand meme magic and circulation as fetishes if we understand how they become this form's *content*.

The Content of Circulation

The Internet meme is a paradigmatic case of why *circulation* is crucial for understanding 'net culture. Circulation is constitutive of the Internet meme as thing: the Internet meme can't be collectively produced and can't mutate unless it circulates. But circulation is also crucial to the conceptual work of media theory. In theories of the Internet meme, we invoke the media-technical process of circulation to account for one of its most confounding qualities: that an Internet meme might be simulta-

---

29 Régis Debray, *Media Manifestos: On the Technological Transmission of Cultural Forms,* trans. Eric Rauth (London: Verso, 1996), 34.

30 Timothy Morton, *Hyperobjects: Philosophy and Ecology after the End of the World* (Minneapolis: University of Minnesota Press, 2013).

31 As a computational concept, the stack isn't immune to fetishization. For an approach that uses the stack as technical concept rather than theoretical one, see Till Straube, "Stacked Spaces: Mapping Digital Infrastructures," *Big Data & Society* 3, no. 2 (2016): 1–12.

32 On the term's polyvalence, see Tarleton Gillespie, "The Politics of 'Platforms,'" *New Media & Society* 12, no. 3 (2010): 347–64.

neously *this* meme, or an instance; and the meme, or the plurality to which an instance belongs.[33]

Let's take the SpongeBob SquarePants meme as an example. Whether intentionally or not, any new SpongeBob SquarePants meme makes its meaning out of the original children's animated TV show and what 'net culture has already made of its characters. In the 'net vernacular, "Internet meme" oscillates ambiguously between instance and plurality. We can talk about the Sponge-Bob meme by talking about a specific instance of the meme or to gesture towards an envisaged totality of related instances of it. This totality of related instances of the SpongeBob meme might then shade off toward an adjacent one featuring SpongeBob's offsider, the dull and likeable pink starfish Patrick, and so on.

The relationship between the Internet meme's instance and plurality isn't just a whole–part relation; nor does it recapitulate Charles Sanders Peirce's type–token.[34] Perhaps it is a little like the process that Guy Debord called *détournement*.[35] Perhaps it is a little like what Jacques Derrida called *iterability*.[36] However, it is not just something that happens in language. An Internet meme's mutations are enabled by a media-technical process. It mutates, we say, in circulation, through acts of collective production that stretch and mould SpongeBob's features to affect the plurality through the instance.

Circulation smooths the ambiguity between the Internet meme's instance and its plurality into something that 'net culture works with intuitively. For media theory, this ambiguity is more problematic. Circulation has never been adequately conceptualized in media theory — or in many of its uses across the

---

33 For an early version of this argument, see Scott Wark, "The Meme is Excess of Its Instance," Excessive Research: transmediale "Conversation Piece" workshop blog, 2015, https://transmedialeblog.wordpress.com/2015/09/30/scott-wark-the-meme-in-excess-of-its-instance/.

34 Charles Sanders Peirce, "Prolegomena to an Apology for Pragmaticism," *The Monist* 16, no. 4 (October 1906): 492–546, at 506.

35 Guy Debord, *The Society of the Spectacle*, trans. Donald Nicholson-Smith (New York: Zone Books, New York, 1995), 146.

36 Jacques Derrida, *Limited Inc.,* trans. Samuel Weber and Jeffrey Mehlman (Evanston: Northwestern University Press, 1988).

humanities and social sciences more generally.[37] What media theory takes to be a concept with purchase on media-technical processes is actually a product of those processes themselves. Circulation functions as a fetish.

This has consequences for our ability to conceptualize either the Internet meme or 'net culture more broadly. To see why, we can ask a deceptively simple question: What actually circulates online? The answer to this question is also deceptively simple: *Content* is what circulates. Content is the form that platforms produce and that our vernacular and conceptual fetishes — meme magic and circulation — both take.

"Content" has widespread currency in tech circles, the media, in public discussion, and even in academic debate. Content is what fills our feeds: it's what we interact with online, what we share, what we download and, of course, what we produce. In discussions of 'net culture, it's often used interchangeably with "media." So digital media has become digital media content, while the culture we produce online is equated with the online content that the 'net produces. Ironically enough, content becomes a problematic concept without content.[38]

Content is not as self-evident as its widespread currency otherwise suggests. In the simplest of terms, content is that which is contained by something else. We need to ask what content is the content of. The answer to *this* question is the platform, which complicates the seeming self-evidence of content itself. The platform becomes that which enables — or appears to enable — content's circulation.

This circulating capacity of platforms emerges when discrete media can be encoded with markup languages. These languages — like TCP, XML, CSS, Java, and so on — automate the presentation of media in new digital contexts by fixing their parameters. Alan Liu argues that markup languages make content

---

37 An early version of this argument can be read in Wark, "The Meme in Excess of its Instance."

38 See for example Bharat Anand, *The Content Trap: A Strategist's Guide to Digital Change* (New York: Random House, 2016).

"autonomously mobile."[39] They make something like an image or a video more easily shared, embedded, and controlled.

Anne Helmond calls this the "programmability" of platforms and web pages and argues that it creates the conditions for content to "circulate through modular elements."[40] Crucially, though, Aden Evans argues that the modular elements through which content circulates are "neutral with respect to content."[41] So long as these elements support a particular discrete bit of content — a file type, for instance, or a chunk of text — what content actually contains doesn't matter.[42]

This inverts the concept of content. Content is the content of platforms, but content is not the media or the data that populate our feeds and that we interact with. Content is a set of the parameters that allow modular compartments to be filled.[43] Marshall McLuhan infamously proposed that "the content of any medium is always another medium".[44] The discourse surrounding online media might invite us to rephrase this claim: the media of content is other content. Content is a placeholder for digital media. *Content is itself an empty form.*

This is a problem for media theory. It throws the media concept into question by distributing it across platform elements. This has interesting implications, but is not our primary concern here. The paradox of content is a problem for media theory because it also empties circulation of *its* conceptual content.

39 Alan Liu, "Transcendental Data: Toward a Cultural History and Aesthetics of the New Encoded Discourse," *Critical Inquiry* 31, no. 1 (2004): 49–84, at 57. Emphasis in the original.

40 Helmond, "The Platformization of the Web," 6.

41 Aden Evans, "Dreams of a New Medium," *Fibreculture Journal* 14 (2009), http://fourteen.fibreculturejournal.org/fcj-092-dreams-of-a-new-medium/.

42 One could add intermediate steps to this argument without negating its core. For example, one could pause over the intermediate role of file formats. See Lev Manovich, *Software Takes Command* (London: Bloomsbury, 2013).

43 Alexander R. Galloway, "The Cybernetic Hypothesis," *differences* 25, no. 1 (2014): 107–31, at 115.

44 Marshall McLuhan, *Understanding Media: The Extensions of Man* (Cambridge: MIT Press, 1994), 8.

We can illustrate this claim by asking another question: What is circulation? In media-theoretical discussions of 'net culture, this question has its own self-evident answer: *Circulation is the circulation of content.*

These slippages and substitutions elide the tautological form of this answer. The process of circulation gets ascribed to media, to memes, as though it's also a neutral term that describes something that just happens in media systems; as though circulation is just a quality of media understood as content. Content is what circulates; circulation is the circulation of content. Rather, content is the death mask of its circulation.[45]

In producing content as empty form, the platform produces the form which our fetishes of 'net culture can then take. Just as popular discourse invokes meme magic, media theory invokes circulation as though it has analytical purchase on platforms, when it's really just an expression of an incommensurability that platforms produce. This paradox points to the incommensurability between the labor and the technics that platforms obfuscate, but that now underwrite the production of culture. The tautological concepts of content and circulation function as a fetish that obfuscates the double incommensurability of what information labor makes with what it receives and of what part of what is made is made by technics and is made by labor.

The Fetish of the User

The fetish concept provides us with the means for identifying how platforms obfuscate both the labor and the technology by which culture is produced. This is perhaps another kind of (Marxist) fetishism, another way of avoiding the question of labor and of underwriting the notion that the realm of culture is separate to it. This labor that platforms obfuscate is not pure

---

45 To mistranslate Walter Benjamin's "the work is the death mask of its conception." See Walter Benjamin, *Reflections: Essays, Aphorisms, Autobiographical Writings,* ed. Peter Demetz (New York: Shocken Books, 1986), 81.

living labor, however. It's a labor inseparable from technics. On the 'net, the labor of producing culture emerges out of meshed hybrids of flesh and tech.

So our version of the fetish concept is a debased derivation of Marx's commodity fetish.[46] What we want to use it to think is neither a kind of false consciousness (after Marx) or double consciousness (à la Pietz). Borrowing from both, we want to underscore that what platforms obfuscate is the hybrid productivity of labor and technics. What they render incommensurable on the other side is labor, technics, and finally culture itself.

If the technical component of this triumvirate is obfuscated by content, the labor component has its own empty form: the *user*. Alongside the question of what circulates on the 'net, we might ask the question that resonates more clearly with the fetish concept's earlier formulations: who puts media-as-content into circulation? The common sense answer is the user. The user is the subject who operates a computational device.[47] This, too, is a kind of fetish.

Bratton calls it the *user position*.[48] Or perhaps we can call it, after Olga Goriunova, the *digital subject*.[49] The user position is the necessary and identifiable predicate of the actions we take online. When we like a post or modify a meme, platforms register this action not as one that we take, but as one taken by the user whom the digital subject functions as. Like content, the user is also a platform construct.[50]

A clamor over authenticity has long defined discussions about the digital subject.[51] Recently, it has manifested in prob-

46 Marx, *Capital: Volume 1,* 163ff.

47 Olia Lialina, "Turing Complete User," *Contemporary Home Computing,* 2012, http://contemporary-home-computing.org/turing-complete-user/.

48 Bratton, *The Stack,* 251.

49 Olga Goriunova, quoted in Olia Lialina, "Not Art&Tech," *Contemporary Home Computing,* 2015, http://contemporary-home-computing.org/art-and-tech/not/.

50 Scott Wark, "The Subject of Circulation: On the Digital Subject's Inhuman Individuations," *Subjectivity* 12, no. 1 (2018): 65–81.

51 Lisa Nakamura, *Cybertypes: Race, Ethnicity and Identity on the Internet* (New York: Routledge, 2002), 15–20.

lematic 'net vernacular panics about social media being populated by bots, manipulated by "the Russians" or scammed by
"Nigerians." This reflects 'net culture's understanding of the user's role. It suspects it's a construct. It knows that the user is insufficient for explaining all of the actions that we might take on
the 'net. The Internet meme — and 'net culture's fetish of meme
magic — make this abundantly clear by probing what it means
for culture to be collectively produced by such indeterminate
user constructs.

Meme magic makes a fetish of the capacity for the content
we create and which we enter into circulation to undergo rapid
proliferation, filling feeds and plastering walls. We can also see
it as a response to the insufficiency of the user position. The
Internet meme is produced by a collective. This collective is
constitutive of its capacity to be produced as a plurality and to
mutate as it's produced in common. But who are the "we" who
constitutes this collective? It appears as a plurality of user positions, all formally the same, all of more or less troubling or
compromised authenticity.

Internet memes seem to outstrip such a plurality's capacity
to produce rapidly proliferating culture. Alongside the occult
capacity of this content itself, meme magic also fetishizes users' capacity to collectively engineer content and to produce
large-scale effects. The invocation of meme magic contrives an
authentic subject — a collective will — in the gap between the
internet meme's effects and a collective of users' insufficiency in
explaining them.[52]

This is how we might understand the absurd-ironic invocation of the ancient Egyptian god Kek in recent 'net culture. After
the 2016 Presidential election and in the wake of the apparent
effect that the Pepe meme had on the outcome, some segments
of meme culture began to invoke this Egyptian god and to pro-
claim Pepe as its contemporary manifestation. Amongst other

---

52 On invocation, see Chris Chesher, "Layers of Code, Layers of Subjectivity,"
    Culturemachine 5 (2003), https://culturemachine.net/the-e-issue/layers-of-
    code/.

things, Kek is the god of darkness and chaos. It is often depicted as a frog. In the 'net vernacular, "kek" is another way of saying "lol", or "laugh out loud." These serendipitous confluences provided the basis for a joke religious cult: the cult of Kek.

This is, in a certain sense, ironic. But it also marks out one way that 'net culture responds to the insufficiency of the user position: with forms of what we might call anthropomorphic animism. When the user is insufficient, Internet memes can conjure a degree of seemingly authentic agency: Pepe not only conveys hateful feelings, but comes to personify them.

Or, the cult of Kek that emerges in Pepe's wake is absurd and ironic, again like all 'net culture, but also indicates something true. Namely, that when the living labor (and non-labor) of making 'net culture interfaces via subject positions that are as interchangeable and dubious as user positions, and when 'net culture makes content that in the end is also an empty form, something else will end up being invoked, as if by magic, to cover over the troubling non-identity of object, subject, and everything in between.

Meme magic is then predicated upon a double fetish: that when the user puts content into circulation, something can be made to happen. Here, meme magic and media theory echo one another: invoking circulation is supposed to explain the production of culture by users. With both concepts, the platform obfuscates the productive roles played by technics and labor in the production of culture. With the concepts of circulation and the user, respectively, platforms produce the forms that media theory uses to fetishize technics and labor while also obfuscating their incommensurability. Meme magic's tacit faith in the generative power of 'net culture is homologous to media theory's.

Mediating Theory

What we have called fetishes — circulation, the user — do not yet account for the epistemological influence platforms have on media theory itself. Platforms produce content as parameters, which we mistake for media. Platforms put content in circulation, which we mistake for circulating media. Platforms predicate us as users, which we mistake for agents. The fallacy of identifying media with content, or circulation with the circulation of content, or the subject with the user, is that these identifications don't recognize that the empty form of content or the user position are components of platforms. They're designed to extract information asymmetries for the owners of the information vector from incommensurate hybrids of laboring flesh-tech.

Media theory is mediated by the platform, which presents us with readymade conceptualizations that we uncritically incorporate into our theories. To fetishize today is to mistake these forms for media wonders. Magic and circulation merge to form something like the magic circle that used to dog linguistic paradigms; media become our epistemological beginning and end. If we're to cast these fetishes down, it's not clear that we'll find what's real; but maybe we'll find what's political.

To cast down a fetish is not to critique it. It is not to unmask a form of false or double consciousness. We don't mean to ape the caricature of "critique" that's animated recent turns to realism and materialism.[53] We're not allergic to critique, but we don't want to replicate what we see as a properly *modern* gesture. A kind of reality — history, or the field of incommensurable value systems — is supposed to lurk behind the fetish's veil. What if we know this already?

Perhaps 'net culture is already aware of the limitations of the user fetish, for instance. It even mobilizes the insufficiency of the user for its own ends. What if the role of the fetish concept is not to reveal some kind of reality, but instead to help us sort what's real into what's effective and what's just the form that effects take? The fetish concept helps us to think how media theory is implicated in what it theorizes. Now, we might ask, what is

---

53 As most forcefully articulated in Bruno Latour, "Why Has Critique Run Out of Steam? From Matters of Fact to Matters of Concern," *Critical Inquiry* 30, no. 2 (2004): 225–48.

the role of the concept itself when it's exposed to the circulations it's supposed to conceptualize?

Platforms actively produce incommensurability: they "black box" their technical workings, leaving us with parameters in which we might enmesh the labor of producing culture and through which the value of our labor might be expropriated. Labor and technics recede, leaving us — *users* — with their epiphenomena: what we call *content*. The Internet meme challenges us to think 'net culture across the incommensurability that platforms produce — in circulation.

When it is understood as the circulation of content, the concept of circulation works in much the same way as "meme magic." We invoke it to smooth over this incommensurability and the questions of what circulation is and how media circulate. If it's to function as concept rather than fetish, media theory must also reckon with the role that platforms play in producing its concepts — and the conceptual terrain — in which it operates. This would be the premise and promise of a meme theory as a critical media theory: *a media theory that's able to account for its own conditions of production.*[54]

We think of this kind of meme theory as one that refuses to be modern by understanding that its concepts are implicated in the thing it tries to theorize, media themselves. For Peter Osborne, the modern theoretical gesture produces the new by treating "the present as a negation of the past."[55] Pietz notes that the fetish concept is always limned with this force of negation.[56] To construe the act of casting down the fetish as an act of casting out the false would embrace negativity — and its conception of history as that which is occluded. This is not our project.

Osborne also identifies another theoretical gesture, one that's addressed to the *contemporary*: this gesture joins "the times of

54 This is the animating concern of Scott Wark's work in progress, *Meme Theory*.

55 Peter Osborne, "Philosophy after Theory: Transdisciplinarity and the New," in *Theory after "Theory*," eds. Jane Elliott and Derek Attridge (London: Routledge, 2011), 29.

56 Pietz, "The Problem of the Fetish, 1," 9.

the spaces it addresses" — its theoretical material — together in *a* present.[57] We might think of media theory's magpie proclivity to mix theory from different domains in this way. This is how media theory produces what Osborne calls the "illusory present of the space of the contemporary."[58] In this space, theory itself has no history and is no product of labor or technics. In this space, theory participates in and so produces the idea that culture, of which it's a part, is separate from labor and technics.

It's no longer possible to assume that culture can be separated from technics. To pretend that it can be, 'net culture invokes meme magic — this is its fetish. Media theory has its own magic word, too: circulation. These fetishes aren't adequately able to divide labor and technics. Hence what we sometimes read as the "occult" quality we attribute to our technology, which is one version of a misattribution of agency, or what used to be called animism.

We might say that our contemporary technological condition expresses the fact that platforms participate in the modern "purification" of the realms of nature and culture, as per Bruno Latour.[59] But if the project that 'net culture participates in and that the platform constructs is not a modern one, but a contemporary one, perhaps what they respond to is something else entirely. The platform can't adequately purify labor-technics hybrids because it's no longer participating in a modern project.

Perhaps, then, what 'net culture produces is not a desire to affirm the limits of this modern project, but a response to its failure. Perhaps what lies beyond the fetishes invoked is not history, but something else. Concepts that can no longer be theorized other than as derivatives of circulation.[60] Concepts cannot be understood separately from their objects, like media, but rather are subject to them. This is a derivative culture caught up in a

---

57 Osborne, "Philosophy after Theory," 29.

58 Ibid.

59 Bruno Latour, *We Have Never Been Modern,* trans. Catherine Porter (Cambridge: Harvard University Press, 1993).

60 On the derivative, see Randy Martin, *Knowledge LTD: Towards a Social Logic of the Derivative* (Philadelphia: Temple University Press, 2016).

different kind of temporality, one whose author or driving agent is no longer apparent.

We want to say, rather, that the 'net confounds our capacity to identify the agents behind, and the authors of, history. It's magic. Or, it's circulation. And it licenses an entirely new and often disturbing cultural politics. Like theory, culture has become contemporary. One of the things this means is that it has lost the modern mythic landscape it once deployed to make sense of the incommensurable.

Following Ernst Cassirer, we can understand myth as something that binds people together through "sympathy," or feeling, rather than "causality," or objective concerns.[61] Myth mixes the abstract and the real in a workable complex by giving emotion expression through form.[62] In Cassirer, this form is what he calls an "image," but we might understand it to encompass other forms of abstraction suited to our contemporary technological conditions. Myth makes feelings real and makes them workable through techniques of what Cassirer calls "ritualization," which we might think of as various modes of collective production. Myth isn't antithetical to politics, but is a constituent of it: it helps bind people into publics.

The modern mythic landscape provided the anchor points of history and agency on which a politics could be built. When the rituals — including the media-rituals — that constitute the modern fall away, so too does its mythic landscape. On the 'net, new rituals emerge. Only, their anchors — a modern mode of history; the agency of the subject — are now insufficient. In response, 'net culture's had to create its own mythic landscape to make tractable what's otherwise incommensurable. The fetish is a species of myth; meme magic is the kind of myth that emerges when history and agency fall away.

---

61 Ernst Cassirer, *The Myth of the State* (New Haven: Yale University Press, 1946), 38.
62 Ibid., 43.

The 'net community operates without the modern processes of *immunization* to which we've become accustomed.[63] It can no longer detect and neutralize the outside within its inside. Its fetishes establish myths in which the agency to produce culture is fed by the fact that culture is no longer anchored to the possibility that one might be excommunicated if one goes too far. We might think of the Internet meme as one of the techniques that mobilizes myth to cultural and political ends.

To associate a set of antagonistic qualities with an avatar — like Pepe — is to exercise the political potential of myth: to bind an insider 'net culture sect by excluding through offending. So the mythic subject who now acts as the paradigmatic representative of the user position is the one who antagonizes endlessly; who in antagonizing longs to be immunized, if only to affirm that community could, once more, be possible not only on the 'net, but within the field of the contemporary that it helps to produce. This subject, in other words, is the "edgelord."

What the fetish tells us is that edgelord avatars emerge out of the insufficiency of our concepts to adequately encompass our contemporary technical conditions.[64] It also tells us that our media-theoretical concepts participate in the propagation of the myths that found 'net culture — and its extremes. Perhaps most surprisingly, it tells is that the edgelord's is a political project that is constructive rather than negative. Meme magic invokes new anchors for a culture adrift. We're raising fetishes to propagate myths, only we're not raising the kind that we would perhaps like. If the Internet meme's to be a productive object of theory, theory must use the Internet meme to think beyond this impasse and its founding incommensurability: that platforms obfuscate the role of labor and technics in producing culture; that our fetishes are necessary, but that we might not need to build them in the platform's image.

---

63 Roberto Esposito, *Immunitas: The Protection and Negation of Life* (Cambridge: Polity, 2011).

64 On avatars, see Beth Coleman, *Hello Avatar: The Rise of a Networked Generation* (Cambridge: MIT Press, 2011).

Bibliography

Anand, Bharat. *The Content Trap: A Strategist's Guide to Digital Change.* New York: Random House, 2016.

Baudrillard, Jean. *Fatal Strategies.* Translated by Jim Fleming. Los Angeles: Semiotext(e), 2008.

Benjamin, Walter. *Reflections: Essays, Aphorisms, Autobiographical Writings.* Edited by Peter Demetz. New York: Shocken Books, 1986.

Bratton, Benjamin H. *The Stack: On Software and Sovereignty.* Cambridge: MIT Press, 2015.

Bucher, Taina. "Neither Black Nor Box: Ways of Knowing Algorithms." In *Innovative Methods in Media and Communication Research,* edited by Sebastian Kubitschko and Anne Kaun. London: Palgrave Macmillan, 2016.

Cassirer, Ernst. *The Myth of the State.* New Haven: Yale University Press, 1946.

Chesher, Chris. "Layers of Code, Layers of Subjectivity." *Culturemachine* 5 (2003). https://culturemachine.net/the-e-issue/layers-of-code/

Chun, Wendy H.K. *Programmed Visions: Software and Memory.* Cambridge: MIT Press, 2011.

Coleman, Beth. *Hello Avatar: The Rise of a Networked Generation.* Cambridge: MIT Press, 2011.

Debord, Guy. *The Society of the Spectacle.* Translated by Donald Nicholson-Smith. New York: Zone Books, New York, 1995.

Debray, Régis. *Media Manifestos: On the Technological Transmission of Cultural Forms.* Translated by Eric Rauth. London: Verso, 1996.

Derrida, Jacques. *Limited Inc.* Translated by Samuel Weber and Jeffrey Mehlman. Evanston: Northwestern University Press, 1988.

Esposito, Roberto. *Immunitas: The Protection and Negation of Life.* Cambridge: Polity, 2011.

Evens, Aden. "Dreams of a New Medium." *Fibreculture Journal* 14 (2009). http://fourteen.fibreculturejournal.org/fcj-092-dreams-of-a-new-medium/.

Freud, Sigmund. "Fetishism." *The International Journal of Psycho-Analysis* 9 (1928): 161–66.

Galloway, Alexander R. "The Cybernetic Hypothesis." *differences* 25, no. 1 (2014): 107–31. DOI: 10.1215/10407391-2420021.

Gillespie, Tarleton. "The Politics of 'Platforms'." *New Media & Society* 12, no. 3 (2010): 347–64. https://papers.ssrn.com/sol3/papers.cfm?abstract_id=1601487.

Graeber, David. "Fetishism as Social Creativity: Or, Fetishes are Gods in the Process of Construction." *Anthropological Theory* 5, no. 4 (2005): 407–38. DOI: 10.1177/1463499605059230.

Haraway, Donna, and Cary Wolfe. *Manifestly Haraway.* Minneapolis: Minnesota University Press, 2016.

Helmond, Anne. "The Platformization of the Web: Making Web Data Platform Ready." *Social Media + Society* 1, no. 2 (2015): 1–11. DOI: 10.1177/2056305115603080.

Latour, Bruno. *We Have Never Been Modern.* Cambridge: Harvard University Press, 1993.

———. "Why Has Critique Run Out of Steam? From Matters of Fact to Matters of Concern." *Critical Inquiry* 30, no. 2 (2004): 225–48. DOI: 10.1086/421123.

Lazzarato, Maurizio. *Signs and Machines: Capitalism and the Production of Subjectivity.* Los Angeles: Semiotext(e), 2014.

Lialina, Olia. "Not Art&Tech." *Contemporary Home Computing,* 2015. http://contemporary-home-computing.org/art-and-tech/not/.

———. "Turing Complete User." *Contemporary Home Computing,* 2012. http://contemporary-home-computing.org/turing-complete-user/.

Liu, Alan. "Transcendental Data: Toward a Cultural History and Aesthetics of the New Encoded Discourse." *Critical Inquiry* 31, no. 1 (2004) 49–84. DOI: 10.1086/427302.

Manovich, Lev. *Software Takes Command.* London: Bloomsbury, 2013.

Martin, Randy. *Knowledge LTD: Towards a Social Logic of the Derivative.* Philadelphia: Temple University Press, 2016.

Marx, Karl. *Capital: A Critique of Political Economy, Volume 1.* Translated by Ben Fowkes. London: Penguin Classics, 1990.

Matory, L. Lorand. *The Fetish Revisited: Marx, Freud, and the Gods Black People Make.* Durham: Duke University Press, 2018.

McLuhan, Marshall. *Understanding Media: The Extensions of Man.* Cambridge: MIT Press, 1994.

Morton, Timothy. *Hyperobjects: Philosophy and Ecology after the End of the World.* Minneapolis: University of Minnesota Press, 2013.

Nakamura, Lisa. *Cybertypes: Race, Ethnicity and Identity on the Internet.* New York: Routledge, 2002.

Olson, Marissa. "Lost Not Found: The Circulation of Images in Digital Visual Culture." In *Mass Effect: Art and the Internet in the Twenty-First Century,* edited by Lauren Cornell and Ed Halter, 159–66. Cambridge: MIT Press, 2015.

Osborne, Peter. "Philosophy after Theory: Transdisciplinarity and the New." In *Theory after "Theory,"* edited by Jane Elliott and Derek Attridge, 19–33. London: Routledge, 2011.

Peirce, Charles Sanders. "Prolegomena to an Apology for Pragmaticism." *The Monist* 16, no. 4 (October 1906): 492–546.

Peters, John Durham. *The Marvellous Clouds: Towards a Philosophy of Elemental Media.* Chicago: University of Chicago Press, 2016.

Pietz, William. "Fetishism and Materialism: The Limits of Theory in Marx." In *Fetishism as Cultural Discourse,* edited by Emily Apter and William Pietz, 119–51. Ithaca: Cornell University Press, 1993.

———. "The Problem of the Fetish, 1." *RES: Anthropology and Aesthetics* 9 (Spring 1985): 5–17.

———. "The Problem of the Fetish, 2: The Origin of the Fetish." *RES: Anthropology and Aesthetics* 13 (Spring 1987) 23–45.

Shifman, Limor. *Memes in Digital Culture.* Cambridge: MIT Press, 2013.

Steyerl, Hito. "Too Much World: Is the Internet Dead?"
e-flux journal 49 (2013). https://www.e-flux.com/
journal/49/60004/too-much-world-is-the-internet-dead/.

Straube, Till. "Stacked Spaces: Mapping Digital
Infrastructures." *Big Data & Society* 3, no. 2 (2016) 1–12. DOI:
10.1177/2053951716642456.

Taussig, Michael. *The Devil and Commodity Fetishism in South
America.* Chapel Hill: University of North Carolina Press,
2010.

Terranova, Tiziana. *Network Culture: Politics in the Information
Age.* London: Pluto Press, 2004.

Viveiros de Castro, Eduardo. *Cannibal Metaphysics.*
Minneapolis: Univocal, 2017.

Wark, McKenzie. *A Hacker Manifesto.* Cambridge: Harvard
University Press, 2004.

Wark, Scott. "Literature After Language's Algorithmic
Normalisation: Spam, Code, and the Digitality of Print in
Blood Rites of the Bourgeoisie." *Scan | Journal of Media
Arts Culture* 10, no. 2 (2013). http://scan.net.au/scn/journal/
vol10number2/Scott-Wark.html.

———. "The Meme is Excess of Its Instance." Excessive
Research: transmediale "Conversation Piece" Workshop
Blog, 2015, https://transmedialeblog.wordpress.
com/2015/09/30/scott-wark-the-meme-in-excess-of-its-
instance/.

———. "The Subject of Circulation: On the Digital Subject's
Inhuman Individuations." *Subjectivity* 19, no. 1 (2019): 65–81.
DOI: 10.1057/s41286-018-00062-5.

In the Future, the Means of Production Will Own Themselves

C_YS

> "It is not enough to change the world.
> That is all we have ever done.
> That happens even without us.
> We also have to interpret this change.
> And precisely in order to change it.
> So that the world will not go on changing without us.
> And so that it is not changed in the
> end into a world without us."
> — Günther Anders, *The Obsolescence of Man, Volume II:
> On the Destruction of Life in the Epoch
> of the Third Industrial Revolution*

The neuroscientist Christof Koch thinks it will one day *feel* like something to be the Internet. Building on Giulio Tononi's Integrated Information Theory (IIT), Koch's consciousness is treated as an emergent property of any sufficiently integrated complex system with the necessary cause–effect action, a quality rising from specific, though not uncommon, organisations of matter (and not, as in the panpsychic tradition, a non-discrete feature of the universe itself).

DOI: 10.21983/P3.0255.1.15

A version of this idea has long held an almost mystic viability among technical exponents of Artificial Intelligence (AI), with Machine Learning now at the vanguard of their movement. Machine Learning methods could lead to a more generalized intelligence than currently exists. But it would be an error to ignore the historic failures of positivist approaches to producing consciousness, ones that rest atop philosophical assumptions about the nature of mind which, barring some notable exceptions, the AI community has yet to adequately theorize.

It may one day make sense to talk about the Internet as the (sub)conscious output of a new type of mind, if it is in the Dreyfussian sense embodied and situated in a spatiotemporal world. It will also require understanding the materiality of subject as central to the question of its being.

Already, algorithmic automation determines much of what we see online. Specialized if/else bots have long conquered online space, as to almost be considered old hat. Automated chumboxes and banner advertising are the primary income stream for many platforms, while low-fee social bots divert our attention to glossy social profiles pushing sponsored content.

The computer ethicist James Williams writes in *Stand Out of Our Light*: "While we weren't watching, persuasion became industrialized."[1] The psychoanalytic project was in the interwar period ushered into the service of consumer capitalism, famously by advertising mogul — and Sigmund Freud's nephew — Edward Bernays. Combining techniques from psychology and public relations, this new type of advertising sublimated our unconscious desires into aspirational consumer choices. It turned objects into repositories of ideas, feelings, and connotations, and people themselves into objects of desire, in an inversion of Hegel's object–ego relation where the object first identifies the subject, before identifying itself as the self-knowing Other. For Bernays, desire was the new American frontier.

---

1   James Williams, *Stand Out of Our Light: Freedom and Resistance in the Attention Economy* (Cambridge: Cambridge University Press, 2018), 28.

The countervoice in our digital era to advertising's visual hegenomy is meme culture; a form with no intrinsic meaning, full of sound and fury, signifying fuck all. The evasive art form establishes a representational scheme inverse to advertising and, through a sort of dream-like resampling, dilutes its potency.

Unlike emojis, imagined by artist Shigetaka Kurita for Japanese mobile giant NTT DoCoMo, memes were never created but instead emerged from the runoff of early Internet culture, primarily on boards such as 4chan. They were a way to facilitate online community-building, and became over time a more universal vocabulary through which to speak across its atomized structure.

Memes remain a bottom-up phenomenon in the tradition of folk art, one with a crucial spatiotemporal morphing property: a means (us) and a medium (our technology) of embodied expression. In the eyes of their creator/audience, the more distance between a meme and its maker the better. They must be able to take on a social existence of their own.

Twitter's @ShitpostBot5000 is an almost entirely self-contained meme generator, while @sapphobot shares haunting fragments torn from the work of her Greek namesake. Reddit's r/me_irl (tagline: *selfies of the soul*) and its equivalent Instagram bot both function as a subjectivized being in a corresponding spirit. The nihilistic subreddit represents a generation navigating the high drama of young adulthood while vying with an increasingly negligent global order. Their awkwardness, hopelessness, and otherwise general *inability to adult* are here amplified and commuted as comedic catharsis. r/me_irl's subversions of advertising's forms, parodied, duplicated, and shared anonymously into the commons, make it a breeding ground of their autopoiesis. Its simple subversion of advertising's forms and imagery are a riposte to Bernays' vision; a place where memes begin to take on the representational qualities of the unconscious mind while changing, adapting, and in a reciprocal dialogue with one another as sites of desiring-production. To adapt a Don DeLillo maxim, "memes are talking to themselves."

The shift to surrealism within the culture is a form of cultural dissonance; a way of figuring the dual absurdities of coming-of-age in a sophisticated, technologized world made up of quasi-magical soft machines, while being denied the material returns promised for taking part in the great dance of capital. A precarity of meaning has led to a breakdown of trust in the traditional symbols of expression. Surrealism, whose meaning-making eschews reason like the unconscious, is a way to enquire what lies beyond the dazzling refraction: it is a search for the source of the light itself. These memes provide new vistas into the poetics of struggle, and offer a credible schema within IIT through which the Internet might begin to know itself.

In their modern-day prominence, memes are the speculative image board of the new political imaginary, counterpoints in a culturo-digital call and response codified through a density of self-reference. They are an example of Marx's ideal, instantiated in this case as the material world reflected back in the *digital* mind as forms of thought.

In the run-up to the 2016 American presidential election, Facebook's great indifference engine, whose weighted distribution of content remains an insider secret, became a central point of focus among political commentators. But while news networks lit up with alarming (if uncritical) stories of Russian bots destabilising the democratic process, the platform quietly gained a resurgence among young users due in part to its unique group function, and the opportunities for meme tribalism it afforded. Hyperpartisan political memes collectivized responsibility for extreme or otherwise unspeakable positions, layered with reference and an all-important blink-and-you'll-miss-it irony. They gave credence to the indelicate opinions of those who are, and those who feel, politically marginalized, made specifically to transgress the economic and social cores of the Fukuyamian liberal order, and thereby transform of quantity into quality.

Facebook has occasionally been forthcoming about the use of its huge data sets to conduct "social experiments" (*"It's just a prank, bro!"*), from the benign to the sinister. Williams suggests this sort of manipulation is a feature, not a bug, of our media landscape.[2] However, the unpolished, rudimentary aesthetic of 2018's meme culture — a will-to-anarchy from a generation disenchanted with the top-down integration and slick controls of web 2.0 — pushes against this datafication of the Internet, injecting an element of play into the increasingly serious platform.

Whatever form AI may come to take, its cognitivist antecedents are already jacked into an expanding body of human knowledge and its adherent capitalist morality. Silicon Valley's soothsayers take moral precepts as crowdsourced, or indeed guided by an invisible hand. But their error in thinking is that their creations will somehow internalize the symbols of capitalist virtue into a system of moral thought. This is, at best, undertheorized. It will require a more fundamental shift in thinking than Machine Learning if we're to achieve true human-like intelligence, but better thinking about the kinds of creatures we are will necessarily lead to better thinking about the kinds of creatures it's possible to be. There needn't be a wholesale inquiry into the nature of morality, but a basic acknowledgment of its contingency as a type of faculty that is both material and social would at least begin to point us in the right direction.

Conservative Jungian psychologist and living meme Jordan Peterson argues in his *Maps of Meaning* for the primacy of our aesthetic impressions, suggesting the articulation of our psychic structures must come before any such understanding of them. Ever the Nietzschean, Peterson's thesis proposes that we must first *Other-ize* ourselves to become a *Self.*[3] It is this same instinct that gave us music, poetry, and now memes. Under this description, history and culture are a dreamstate of the unconscious mind.

Online media are not merely a replication of real-world phenomena superimposed on the digital realm, but another layer of abstraction entirely. They are the self-producing imagination of

2   Williams, *Stand Out of Our Light,* 30ff.

3   Jordan Peterson, *Maps of Meaning: The Architecture of Belief* (New York: Routledge, 1999), 95ff.

the Internet; a late, novel form of expression by a culture stitching its own demise into the fabric of history. Rich libertarians at the helm of the AI movement overlook technology's *nonessentiality*, regarding their creations as pliable cogs in the unstoppable wealth-generating machine of capitalism. But these technologies alone will not liberate us, free somehow from subjective concerns or unshackled from ideology. Not if we get it right. Objectivity as an ontological position itself *is* entirely ideological, inhuman, and inhumane. Until we undertake a more fundamental reorganisation of society, material resources (of which AI is part) will continue to be distributed according to the interests of the already powerful, reflecting back to us the historical object as it becomes history's subject.

AI must first understand ideology, the furnace in which it is forged, to be anything at all. Günther Anders's counter to the most famous of Marx's *Theses On Feuerbach* —which is itself an attempt to rehistoricize philosophical thinking — checks the notion that technological and social development are apiece.[4] It is a recognition that changing the world, as it is often conceived, leans heavily on capitalist modes of speculation.

Against Peterson's *laissez-faire* naturalism, within a modern Marxist vein, the world-changing capacity of AI needs interpretation. With so much contemporary history now recorded, the past zooms up on us with crystalline clarity. Koch believes the Internet will one day conform to IIT's axiomatic system, emerging in a splendor of sentience.[5] Were that to be the case, the left cannot afford to uselessly sit back and watch all this unfold from afar, holding out half a hope for some poorly theorized data-driven Marxism — Althusser with 1012 teraflops of processing

---

4   Günther Anders, *The Obsolescence of Man, Volume II: On the Destruction of Life in the Epoch of the Third Industrial Revolution*, 1, http://libcom.org/files/ObsolescenceofManVol%20IIGunther%20Anders.pdf.

5   See Steve Paulson's interview with Christof Koch: Steve Paulson, "The Nature of Consciousness: How the Internet Could Learn to Feel," *The Atlantic*, August 22, 2012, https://www.theatlantic.com/health/archive/2012/08/the-nature-of-consciousness-how-the-internet-could-learn-to-feel/261397/.

power, arriving like an electronic God to deliver Fully Automated Luxury Gay Space Communism to the people. This ignores all experience we have of the benefactors of technological change. Everything we gain we must first fight for, in our deeds and our words.

It is no more possible to hardcode sentience into our machines than it is every possible permutation of the world and its actors. They are dialectical systems whose shifting nature are constitutive of the very thing they are. Political memes (note: all memes are political) help us to feel out the steeper banks of our ideologies and, by colliding in these new arenas, become truly dialectical. If the Internet is to ever become conscious, it will need to act both as an incubator for life and a violent death machine.

The route to its own emancipation is as yet unmapped, but if we are there and we are ready, it will allow us to finally see ourselves as the great Other, and, hopefully, to become more human(e) for it. The alternative is for all of us, equally, to share in the total destruction of what is good.

Bibliography

Anders, Günther. *The Obsolescence of Man, Volume II: On the Destruction of Life in the Epoch of the Third Industrial Revolution.* http://libcom.org/files/ObsolescenceofManVol%20IIGunther%20Anders.pdf.

Paulson, Steve. "The Nature of Consciousness: How the Internet Could Learn to Feel." *The Atlantic,* August 22, 2012. https://www.theatlantic.com/health/archive/2012/08/the-nature-of-consciousness-how-the-internet-could-learn-to-feel/261397/.

Peterson, Jordan. *Maps of Meaning: The Architecture of Belief.* New York: Routledge, 1999.

Williams, James. *Stand Out of Our Light: Freedom and Resistance in the Attention Economy.* Cambridge: Cambridge University Press, 2018.

15

Socialist Imaginaries and Queer Futures: Memes as Sites of Collective Imagining

Thomas Hobson and Kaajal Modi

*"I like to think (and
the sooner the better!)
of a cybernetic meadow
where mammals and computers
live together in mutually
programming harmony
like pure water
touching clear sky.*

*I like to think
(right now, please!)
of a cybernetic forest
filled with pines and electronics
where deer stroll peacefully
past computers
as if they were flowers
with spinning blossoms.*

*I like to think
(it has to be!)*

DOI: 10.21983/P3.0255.1.16

> *of a cybernetic ecology*
> *where we are free of our labors*
> *and joined back to nature,*
> *returned to our mammal*
> *brothers and sisters,*
> *and all watched over*
> *by machines of loving grace."*
> — Richard Brautigan,
> *All Watched over by Machines of Loving Grace*[1]

> *"I want freedom, the right to self-expression,*
> *everybody's right to beautiful, radiant things."*
> — Emma Goldman[2]

Introduction: It Was the Memes Wot Dun It

On Friday June 9, 2017, UK residents woke up to a state of serious uncertainty as to which political party, exactly, was in power. The subsequent days would see a reshuffling of the narrative into an apparently easy Tory win, and a smoothing over of the initial surprise at Labour having gained 36 seats (albeit having lost 6), but for one brief, shining moment, the left, under Jeremy Corbyn's Labour Party, had categorically Not Lost a General Election. So how, despite all of the punditry and expertise saying otherwise, had this happened? According to myriad editorials, opinion pieces and other forms of Serious Journalism, it woz the memes wot dun it.[3]

---

1   Richard Brautigan, "All Watched Over by Machines of Loving Grace," *The Atlantic,* September 17, 2011, https://www.theatlantic.com/technology/archive/2011/09/weekend-poem-all-watched-over-by-machines-of-loving-grace/245251/. Originally published in *All Watched Over by Machines of Loving Grace* (San Francisco: Communication Company, 1967). Please note that wherever possible, all references and further readings suggested are open access.

2   Emma Goldman, *Living My Life* (London: Penguin Classics, 2006), 42.

3   See, e.g., Hannah Jane Parkinson, "Was It the Corbyn Memes Wot Won It? Here Are Some of the Best," *The Guardian,* June 9, 2017, https://www.theguardian.com/politics/2017/jun/09/corbyn-memes-wot-won-it-some-

An elderly, awkwardly sincere socialist had become the poster boy for the revolution. Jeremy Corbyn had arrived, and he was both a rockstar and your dad in a homemade cardigan. He had motivated a previously "apathetic" group of youth voters that everyone else had given up on. Corbynmania galvanized a generation of young people, and those young people had not only voted Labour, they had convinced their families to vote Labour, they had organized, and they had gotten out onto the streets and knocked on doors and convinced others to vote Labour. Here was the holy grail of politics.

Suddenly, memes were valuable currency. The Tories found themselves with a need to get in on the act by pretending that they had young new media-savvy members in their ranks and by starting the thankfully short-lived Activate Twitter account (#meme, anybody?), and even hotly tipped young pretender to the Conservative Leadership Jacob Rees-Mogg, got himself an Instagram where he could post twee selfies of himself, presumably from his country estate in the 1920s.

While a tracing of the phenomenon of Corbynism and its many offshoots through online meme culture and into mainstream politics would be a worthy endeavor, by necessity it sits outside of the scope of this particular investigation. What we're instead interested in, is getting to grips with some aspects of a fairly fundamental set of questions: *what do memes do* and *what are they for?*

In offering some tentative answers to these questions, we focus on the productive capacity of political memes — seeing them as both sites and practices of world building, and as places where understandings of *what is* and our visions of *what ought to be* can be produced collectively. What we are interested in,

---

of-the-best; Olivia Ovenden, "Here Are the Memes That Helped Swing the Election in Labour's Favour," *Esquire,* June 12, 2017, https://www.esquire.com/uk/culture/news/a15451/election-memes-corbyn; Charles White, "The Memes That Decided the Outcome of the General Election," *Metro,* June 11, 2017, https://metro.co.uk/2017/06/11/the-memes-that-decided-the-outcome-of-the-general-election-6701277/.

specifically, is the potential for online memes to act as sites of intersubjective imagination and world building.

This is a study in two parts. Firstly, we engage with the concept of the "sociotechnical imaginary," bringing it to bear on the future as imagined of Fully Automated Luxury Communism (FALC) — an online meme that gained currency around the same time as the rise of Corbynism.[4] Secondly, we look to a second articulation of luxury communism, Fully Automated Luxury Gay Space Communism, and the manner in which it, both substantively and materially, acts to "queer" the imaginative space of FALC.

By doing so, this chapter offers a tentative and exploratory investigation of the following:

1. "Imaginaries" as useful conceptual frameworks for studying online memes, and;
2. The usefulness of these as a starting or staging point for collectively imagined futures.

While we acknowledge that this represents rather a substantial undertaking, we readily acknowledge the limited scope of a short chapter in addressing these goals. Rather than advancing the work here as a comprehensive investigation, we instead present it as an opportunity to open new avenues for discussion and research, and most particularly as a chance to lay the groundwork useful framework through which to view this new and exciting activist community.

---

4   Sheila Jasanoff and Sang-Hyun Kim, *Dreamscapes of Modernity: Sociotechnical Imaginaries and the Fabrication of Power* (Chicago: University of Chicago Press, 2015). The introductory chapter, which explains a great deal of the basic theory employed here, is available open access at http://iglp.law.harvard.edu/wp-content/uploads/2014/10/Jasanoff-Ch-1.pdf.

Fully Automated Luxury Communism

In November 2014, Aaron Bastani uploaded a video to the Novara Media YouTube channel, as part of his "IMO" series, in which he outlined a concept called Fully Automated Luxury Communism (FALC). Prior to this, the term FALC had been circulating online as a(n at least partially) tongue-in-cheek meme among (predominantly) London-based lefties.[5]

In this video Bastani asked why, at a time when capitalism is in crisis, and living standards, profitability, and wages are all falling in a manner unprecedented in modern history, we are still afraid of automation and unwilling to consider the potential for technology to act for the public good. Automation, he proposed, and crucially, automation *for the people,* rather than *for profit,* might prove to the answer to all of our problems in this era of devalued labor.

The imperative behind FALC, in both its substantive critique and its capacity as a rhetorical device, was a recognition of the ways in which technological systems, under capitalism, are deployed in the service of profit. Challenging the idea that this is an inevitable consequence of industrialization and the natural state of things, FALC instead proposes that these technologies could serve the cause of emancipation. The increasing sophistication of technologies in the present age — with, for example, substantial innovations in autonomization, global communications, advanced production techniques, AI and machine learning, and biotechnologies — could, it is argued, create abundance rather than austerity.

FALC proposes a post-scarcity economy where we are no longer beholden to a capitalist idea of wage labor and, there-

---

5   Novara Media, "Fully Automated Luxury Communism!" *YouTube,* November 10, 2014, https://www.youtube.com/watch?v=dmQ-BZ3eWxM. While Aaron Bastani's long-awaited FALC book has now been published, the authors would like to note that the critique presented here is based on the partial elaborations that were extant at the time of writing and does not engage with the (presumably similarly fantastical) contents of that book.

fore, can work "10–12–15-hour weeks." With the rest of our time, the population would be free to learn languages, retrain as engineers, make art, and travel the world.[6] He then asked the question: "what would you do with your remaining time?," and the responses, hashtagged #falc, began to pour in.

Post-Scarcity and Techno-Utopianism

While there most certainly have been a number of important and necessary critiques of the conceptual limitations of FALC, very few, on the left at least, would challenge the basic merit of such a bold and Utopian vision. These critiques have been put forward by, amongst others, other members of Novara, and in an excellent and readily accessible essay published on LibCom.[7]

Some of the key criticisms have included that:

— FALC misapprehends how social relations and commodity values are mutually constructed, and the ways in which technologies embody and reproduce social and political orders;
— The fundamental conceptualization of labor within its formulation is deeply gendered, and;
— In very much the same vein as other techno-utopian thought systems, it almost entirely neglects consideration of the social, economic, and ecological impacts of the production cycles of luxury goods in an age of globalization.

---

6 Ibid.
7 For examples, please see: mcm_cmc, "Fully Automated Luxury Communism: A Utopian Critique," *Libcom* (blog), June 14, 2015, https://libcom.org/blog/fully-automated-luxury-communism-utopian-critique-14062015; Tom Syverson, "'Fully Automated Luxury Gay Space Communism': Has the Time For Universal Basic Income Finally Come?" *Paste,* June 7, 2017, https://www.pastemagazine.com/articles/2017/06/fully-automated-luxury-gay-space-communism-univers.html; Brian Merchant, "Fully Automated Luxury Communism," *The Guardian,* March 18, 2015, https://www.theguardian.com/sustainable-business/2015/mar/18/fully-automated-luxury-communism-robots-employment.

The most fundamental criticism of FALC that we make in this work is that it employs somewhat paradoxical understanding of technology. Rooted in rather commonplace and Whiggish misreading of Marxist thought, FALC sees technology as capable of embodying (or, at least, facilitating) the immanence of social, political, and economic emancipation, but to a large degree ignores its substantive effects.

We wish to avoid to lengthy a detour into a critique of FALC's misapprehension of the co-constitutive relationship between social systems and technologies, and as such, direct the reader towards some useful initial reading on these ideas below. We also recommend further useful reading on the ideas of co-production, socio-technical relations, and the substantive effects of technology in this chapter's footnotes.[8] We see these critiques of the theoretical and conceptual underpinnings of FALC as invaluable, and certainly hope that their insights can become more prominent in left conversations about technology and its role in conditioning social and economic relationships in the future.

Before moving on, however, we note that this particular understanding of technology — one which sees technology as both instrumental and deterministic — is a troubling one for those among us who spend time thinking about the relationship between technologies and the societies that produce them. In FALC, technology is seen as creating the conditions for emancipation — with technological and scientific advance a promissory force — but is then able to be unproblematically directed towards utopian social ends in entirely instrumental terms. We should likely ask whether a utopian vision that is so dependent on technology, that comprehends technology so poorly, really represents as convincing an idiom as is often claimed.

---

8   The idiom of co-production is cited as particularly useful in this work, for more on this, please see: Sheila Jasanoff, ed., *States of Knowledge: The Co-Production of Science and Social Order* (London: Routledge, 2004). However, it is also worth noting that several other valuable approaches to sociotechnical relations exist. For additional reading, we recommend Andrew Feenberg, *Critical Theory of Technology* (New York: Oxford University Press, 1991).

FALC, Memes, and the Future

For the purposes of the present work, we are rather more in-terested in understanding how FALC has acted as a catalyst for memetic conceptualizations of not only labor value, but for so-cial transformation and the possibilities that technological ad-vances are increasingly affording us. Our intention is to uncover some of the ways in which FALC has been captured by, and is continually re-invented and reproduced in, online memes. And it is to this end that, in the paragraphs that follow, we make the claim that online memes can be usefully understood as sites of intersubjective imagination — wherein communities can be united by certain shared socio-cultural or socio-technical vi-sions of what kinds of futures could, and indeed, should (or should not) be realized.

Contrary to the traditional liberal conceptualization of com-munism as rooted in misery, austerity, and predicated on su-perhuman forbearance free from excess or private desire, FALC (in spite of any conceptual limitations one may charge it with) allows us the permission and the space to imagine the possi-bility of abundance, of a future where the enforced privation of capitalism is overthrown in favor of a vision of communal living where the basic needs of food/water/housing/medicine are not only met but overcome, and where we can imagine new futures free from such prosaic concerns. In opposition to the sparse utilitarianism suggested by dominant representations of "the Eastern Bloc" or the scarcity and corruption prevalent in depictions of Latin American socialism, it invokes an image of the future where emancipation is intrinsic to material satisfac-tion, rather than coming at the expense of it.

Imagining the Impossible

Thinking critically about culture memetically is not a new un-dertaking. That scholars, artists, and theorists have been dis-cussing the definition and significance — indeed even the basic usefulness of the concept — of (what can broadly be described as) memes for upward of half a century now, is perhaps testament to the persistence and attractiveness of them as both a tangible artefact and trope for analysis.[9] Clearly though — as evidenced by the prominence of online memes in contemporary discourse, and by the variety of societal and political ends for which they are credited as the means — there must be at least something more to say on the subject. It is certainly to be hoped that this is the case, lest we have rather wasted our collective energies as contributors to this book.

We expect, however, that there is little cause for concern on that front, with this volume prompting its readers to consider the politics of memes from a variety of fascinating perspectives. Here, we argue that, in the image-saturated world of the early 21st century, the political is ever more inextricably linked to the production and sharing of iconic imagery and text, and that — in light of this — it is crucial that we develop critical theoretical and pragmatic understandings of this evolving relationship and its substantive consequences. From a more normative standpoint we, along with the other contributors to this volume, are concerned with understanding how memes can be usefully deployed in the service of emancipatory, inclusive and progressive Left politics. Our contribution to this effort is (hopefully) a rather straightforward one. We ask our readers to consider the relationship between memes and imagination.

The task facing those of us who aspire to a better world is, inherently, an imaginative one. In seeing the world as it is, and believing that a fairer, more just world is possible — we, however faintly, look toward a future that we imagine to be desirable. The making and sharing of memes, we suggest, represents a site of imagination as a cultural and social practice — and therefore that memes themselves are an important component of the

---

9   In tracing this idea of the meme from its origins in evolutionary theory, through to its current status as an idiom of communication, please see James Gleick, "What Defines a Meme?" *Smithsonian,* May 2011, https://www.smithsonianmag.com/arts-culture/what-defines-a-meme-1904778/.

evolving shared perceptions of the desirable or utopian futures that are fundamental to the project of emancipatory politics.

We argue that political memes are sites of *collective* world building. In creating and/or sharing a political meme, we offer our visions of the future worlds we imagine to be possible or desirable. These visions are incredibly significant — shaping discourse, guiding action and uniting communities. The challenge, of course, is in usefully conceptualising this relationship between memes, shared imaginaries, and the social and material relations of a society.

Seizing the Memes of Production

Returning to the title of this volume, we argue that one valuable way forward in this endeavor is to begin considering the interconnectivity between the *means* of production and the *memes* of production — and, somewhat turning this on its head, the ways in which the production of memes can influence the production of means. Our central thesis here rests on the following key arguments:

Firstly, that ideas and imaginaries have a substantial impact upon material conditions and technological processes. Technological and industrial advances don't occur in isolation from social contexts, and are never just rational, scientific, necessary events on a linear trajectory of improvement. Instead, technologies are inherently social — the types of technologies we create, the problems we try to solve, and the sorts of worlds we try to create with technology are all guided by our understandings of how the world is, how it has been, and how it ought to be.

Similarly, despite the pervasiveness of claims very much to the contrary (made by liberals and conservatives the world over), the material conditions of our societies and distributions of wealth are never representative of a linear progress narrative, and do not embody the rational and inevitable course of history. Rather, they are always political and always predicated on judgments about how the world is and ought to be, on what outcomes are desirable, and on who should be allowed to benefit from these desirable outcomes.

Following from this, we argue that online memes are sites where ideas are made and imaginations are explored, shared, and popularized. When considering the pithy or even surrealist nature of some political memes, this may seem like something of a stretch (though even here we would argue that memes are an increasingly important component of political discourse) however, in our present study, FALC provides a clear example of how this can be the case.

FALC memes, and indeed, political memes in general, even at their most abstracted or satirical, invoke various ideas about how industry and society relate to one another (specifically in regard to who should benefit from and govern their production), and, at least in the case of FALC, about how a desirable, emancipatory, future can be realized through technology. We would further argue that these *memes of production* (that is, images and text that capture and invoke a set of ideas about how social and industrial relations can be reorganized and emancipation realized through technology) can, and should, be understood as important aspects of left-wing perceptions of how the *means of production* can, and should, be reorganized.

If technologies are always embedded in and conditioned by ideas and shared understandings, and the means of production are increasingly dependent on the technological, then our ideas are capable of producing new means — new relations between labor and technology and new sociotechnical systems for organizing production and its benefits. Our *memes of production* as important sites of political imagination represent important opportunities to rethink our means of production.

Collective Imaginaries

Leftist politics have always tended toward the proudly utopian; activism is, after all, the project of imagining better worlds, and collectively, endeavoring to realize them. It is only in recent years that these practices have, by necessity, become bogged down in the mundane realities of bureaucracy and capitalist productivity. This study is part recovery of that tendency towards action, and partly a new paradigm through which that action can be viewed.

As a culture, we often celebrate the power and potential of the individual imagination — and with some justification — lauding especially those who promote, or appear to create, transformative or radical visions of the future. Reflect for a moment on the celebrity status of (shamelessly self-promoting tech-bro poster boys) Elon Musk or Steve Jobs. Or, perhaps consider the instant attention garnered by Labour MP Liam Byrne's (in our view, rather misguided) book *Dragons,* which recounts the contribution of innovative entrepreneurs to the making of modern Britain.[10]

Imagination though, is not just the preserve of the visionary, but also operates intersubjectively — uniting members of a community in shared perceptions of futures which can, and should (or shouldn't) be realized.[11] It is this — the collective imaginary — that we are interested in exploring further in relation to political memes.

The idea that collective imaginaries not only exist, but are important sociocultural forces, shaping (variously) identity, social relations, desires and aspirations, and morality, has its roots in the philosophy of Émile Durkheim and Max Weber. Most notable in the history of thought on collective imaginaries are the works of Benedict Anderson,[12] Charles Taylor,[13] and Arjun Appadurai.[14] Taylor, for example has defined his modern and social imaginaries as so:

---

10 We urge you, in the strongest possible terms, to not waste your time on this book: *Liam Byrne, Dragons: 10 Entrepreneurs Who Built Britain* (London: Head of Zeus, 2016).

11 See here the open-access introduction to Jasanoff, cited in n. 4.

12 Benedict Anderson, *Imagined Communities: Reflections on the Origin and Spread of Nationalism* (London: Verso, 1983).

13 Charles Taylor, *Modern Social Imaginaries* (Durham: Duke University Press, 2004).

14 Arjun Appadurai, "Disjuncture and Difference in the Global Cultural Economy," in *Modernity at Large: Cultural Dimensions of Globalization*

By social imaginary, I mean something much broader and deeper than the intellectual schemes people may entertain when they think about reality in a disengaged mode. I am thinking, rather, of the ways people imagine their social existence, how they fit together with others, how things go on between them and their fellows, the expectations that are normally met, and the deeper normative notions and images that underlie these expectations.[15]

This imaginary, for Taylor, entails an array of common understandings and practices based on a sense of what is real, and rejects the idea that politics is determined solely by deliberate and rational actions. Perhaps more immediately resonant to the arguments in this chapter, is the following reflection on the imagination, offered by Appadurai:

No longer mere fantasy (opium for the masses whose real work is elsewhere), no longer simple escape (from a world defined principally by more concrete purposes and structures), no longer elite pastime (thus not relevant to the lives of ordinary people), and no longer mere contemplation (irrelevant for new forms of desire and subjectivity), the imagination has become an organized field of social practices, a form of work (both in the sense of labor and of culturally organized practice) and a form of negotiation between sites of agency ("individuals") and globally defined fields of possibility.[16]

Reading this, we can begin to engage with imagination not only as the site in which action is conceptualized, but as the staging point for future possibility. With relatively little effort toward reframing, we can apply some of these ideas on the imaginary to

(Minneapolis: University of Minnesota Press, 1996), 27–48.

15 Charles Taylor, "Modern Social Imaginaries," *Public Culture* 14, no. 1 (2002): 91–124.

16 Appadurai, "Disjuncture and Difference in the Global Cultural Economy," 31.

our earlier discussion of the ideational content and function of political memes. In doing so we start to gain some traction on not just the significance of shared imaginaries, but on how we can understand memes as a site for their creation and propagation. The imagination is a place for serious (whether deliberate or not) negotiation (and consensus) on the possibility of societal and human conditions. Returning to memes, we see that they represent a locale in which these imaginaries are developed, shared, and have affect.

Dreamscapes of Modernity

Our own definition of imaginaries rests rather more closely on that offered by Sheila Jasanoff in the introduction to *Dreamscapes of Modernity.* Jasanoff's *sociotechnical* imaginaries engage more explicitly with two factors we are deeply concerned with in our discussion of FALC and the potentiality of political memes for an emancipatory politics, those being: science and technology — which we argue is not only one of the most powerful guiding forces in global modernity, but is intrinsic to the utopian visions of FALC (and of techno-positive leftism more generally) and; the future — which we argue is inherent to creative work of striving for an emancipatory politics, and is also implicated in the explicitly futuristic images invoked by FALC.

Jasanoff defines sociotechnical imaginaries as: "collectively held and performed visions of desirable futures (or of resistance against the undesirable) [that are] animated by shared understandings of forms of social life and social order attainable through, and supportive of, advances in science and technology."[17] One could then, rather readily, reconceptualize the FALC meme itself as a recognizable imaginary — with the making and sharing of memes representing the public performance of a collectively held vision. The vision, of course, is one

---

17 Sheila Jasanoff, "Future Imperfect: Science, Technology, and the Imaginations of Modernity," in Jasanoff and Kim, *Dreamscapes of Modernity*, 19.

wherein automation and technological advance facilitate a future of emancipatory politics — and consequently the imaginary is supportive of certain modes of technological advance and advocates for certain reorganisations of industrial and economic relations.

While FALC memes take many forms, ranging from the naïve to the ludicrous to the vital and instructive — in each instance the cooperative, communal, and crucially, *discursive* practice of imagination is taking place. Whether understood through the semiotics of image macros, or through the production of shared understanding in discourse, we argue that FALC memes invoke a communal set of ideas (or at the very least a shared framework for thinking) about how the world as it currently is may be reimagined and re-ordered toward emancipatory ends.

For Jasanoff, the imaginary is also necessarily culturally particular, and temporally situated. This goes some way towards helping conceptualize the ways that our visions of the future — even (in fact especially) our utopian ones — are conditioned by our experiences and, often, prejudices in the present. Returning again to some of the earlier critiques of FALC that we touched upon, understanding imaginaries as conditioned by, and reproductive of, contemporary judgements of what and who is important, can help us get to grips with some of the extant limitations of popular iterations of FALC — especially in relation to some of the issues we will discuss below.

Signs and Signifiers

Since 2014, memes relating to FALC have seemingly appeared with ever-increasing frequency. They are regularly posted in threads under (often apparently unrelated) posts about, variously: technology, feminism, space, gender, race, sexuality, Marxism, and often all (or none) of the above. They have appeared across groups and collectives on Leftbook, left Twitter, Tumblr, and beyond, taking the forms of gifs and image macros. Frequently they evoke the classic Soviet constructivist iconography of revolutionary leftist politics, and of the (perhaps un-

surprisingly) similar off-planet science fiction or abstract utopias. In practice, the memes are often collaborative and evolve
continually in-situ, being overlaid with, or accompanied by, increasingly detailed or often esoteric text threads.

While we have argued above in favor of understanding
memes as *imaginaries* — framing their production and sharing as a practice of collective imagination, we turn here to the
work of Stuart Hall — whose insight into culture, discourse, and
materiality is instructive in getting to grips with how political
memes can embody, communicate, and produce understandings and ideas. When considered through Hall's theory of en-
coding/decoding, memes, like any other media, and like Appadurai's imagination, are discursive, in that they contain both
symbolic and material potentiality that is only realized in moments of interpretation or negotiation between the meme space
and the viewer. In fact, unlike traditional media, they go one
step further, as they are encoded by one audience, as it were, in
one symbolic context, and decoded in another context by another audience. While new media theorists often find this a useful stepping-off to start to think in terms of "affordances," let's
stay here a moment and consider what this means.

It means that there is no "wrong" way to meme, in the same
way that there is no "wrong" way to consume any other media. Seeming "user errors" are absorbed into the fabric of the
practice of meme-ing, and spawn their own semiotic offshoots.
If you decide that your utopia has automated cats, for example, then automated cats are immediately incorporated into the
visual language of that discourse (robot cats in space, robot cats
with laserbeam eyes, robot cats that resemble Vladimir Lenin
standing proudly in front of a Soviet sunrise in full Soviet uni-
form, etc).

That a great deal of this interaction is consciously humorous
or even deliberately ridiculous shouldn't discount them from
being taken seriously on the terms laid out above. Satire, even
the involuntary kind, is a valid critique, and intention does not
necessarily undermine the impact of situated cultural forms. In
fact, it is this irreverence, and seemingly deliberate postmod-

ernism, which is itself an intrinsic part of meme culture; it is persistently and (often unconsciously) anarchic in its lack of reverence for any traditions whilst at the same time borrowing heavily from revolutionary, particularly soviet/communist, ideas and symbology. It is this dichotomy that allows it to occupy a space that is at once meaning-making and subversive, and at the same time representative of wider socio-cultural tendencies. To paraphrase Hall, the individual memer is always living some larger socio-cultural narrative, whether they like it or not. [18]

Queering the Problem Space

While an in-depth tracing of the FALC meme and its various offshoots falls outside of the scope of this work, it is here that a reading of one of its more persistent offshoots is particularly illustrative as an example of the manner in which meme-ing can act as a space for intersubjective, dialectical, and discursive future-making among online collectivities.

This section examines the Fully Automated Luxury Gay (or Queer) Space Communist (FALGSC) society, reading it as an imaginary space that acts to queer the classic FALC meme (both literally and figuratively speaking). According to *Know Your Meme,* FALGSC

envisions an idealistic society where gender norms have been abolished to such an extent that there is little to no difference between gay and straight, and due to automation, luxury is available to all people[.] The term has inspired the creation of communism-themed memes and image macros.[19]

---

18 See Stuart Hall, quoted in Tim Adams, "Cultural Hallmark," *The Guardian,* September 23, 2007, https://www.theguardian.com/society/2007/sep/23/communities.politicsphilosophyandsociety.

19 See *Know Your Meme,* s.v. "Fully Automated Luxury Gay Space Communism," http://knowyourmeme.com/memes/fully-automated-luxury-gay-space-communism.

For those readers unfamiliar with queer theory, it is important here to note that "queering" is not necessarily just a process that explicitly reads a text through the binary of the homosexual and heterosexual (although it is that), but is instead a heuristic that acts to dismantle "the dynamics of power and privilege persisting among diverse subjectivities."[20] Queer Studies is a critical position rather than a sexual one; queer can mean "the open mesh of possibilities, gaps [...] and excesses of meaning."[21] "Queer gets a critical edge by defining itself against the normal rather than the heterosexual."[22] Queering is an act that can be performed.[23]

When read through this paradigm, FALGSC becomes an injoke, a meta-reference, a wink and a nod to those of us in the know about FALC, and about the current rift in the left between traditional Marxism and the new identity politics. These latter post-Marxist formulations of society, culture, and gender, that seek to be more inclusive of non-hegemonic and marginalized experiences and understandings of the world, therefore require an envisioning of futures that can encompass difference.

These memes are ridiculous, and they are gay as hell. They incorporate the semiotics of queerness while at the same time, both in its literal and academic definitions, "queering" the traditional forms of communist futuring. If FALC is the neo-capitalist faux socialist utopianism of *Star Trek*, FALGSC is the post-scarcity civilisation of Iain M Banks's "the Culture," wherein sentient post-gender pan-humans and artificial intelligences co-exist in an automated interstellar collection of societies that has no discernable end.

---

20 Thelathia "Nikki" Young, "Queering 'The Human Situation,'" *Journal of Feminist Studies in Religion* 28, no. 1 (2012): 126–31.

21 Eve Kosofsky Sedgwick, *Tendencies* (Abingdon: Routledge, 1998), 8.

22 Michael Warner, "Introduction," in *Fear of a Queer Planet: Queer Politics and Social Theory*, ed. Michael Warner (Minneapolis: University of Minnesota Press, 1993), xxvi.

23 See Judith Butler, "Critically Queer," in *The Routledge Queer Studies Reader*, eds. Donald E. Hall and Annamarie Jagose (London: Routledge, 2013), 18–31.

Returning, briefly, to our earlier discussion of memes as *imaginaries,* the divergent futures described above illustrate the constitutive effect of how we understand the present — our experiences, prejudices, and priorities — on the futures we strive to create. If we don't understand gender and sexual equality to be issues worth fighting for in the present, are we likely to make room for them in our imaginaries — even utopian ones — of the future?

Memes as Sites of Political Contestation

Online fora are increasingly the battlegrounds on which political battles are fought, and if not where hearts and minds won exactly, then at least where they can be exposed to alternative political ideas, causes, and crusades. They are a rich recruiting ground for previously antithetical or apolitical young people who might feel disenfranchised by the established politics of our time. One doesn't have to look far to see examples of online political movements on both the right and the left that spread through their memetic conceptualizations; the more shareable the better. From isis and InCel to Bernie Bros and Corbynmania, to the rise of Trump and the new British nationalism via the terrifyingly (and apparently insidiously) shareable content of Britain First.

Successful memes transcend echo chambers; they overspill. We've all come across memes that expose us to new ideas in a manner that is pithy, funny, or particularly striking, and we are all more likely to share something that makes us pause to think, and/or laugh (preferably both). One of the most notable things about memes, particularly image macros, is that they do not display a particularly refined design aesthetic; and that might in fact constitute a large part of their power. Those of us in the global minority tend to live in highly sophisticated visual societies, and to cultures overloaded by slick advertising tropes and hyper-real soft focus filters, an inexpertly made image can often seem like the last authentic voice in a sea of artificiality.

The self-replicating and somewhat simplistic nature of the meme lends itself well to utopianism — and to the production of shared meanings. They are accessible, and they are democratic (in that anyone can make or share them). This is political propaganda, for the people, by the people. It is writ small, but it is infinitely modular, replicable, scalable, and modifiable. One can imagine worlds in these creations, and indeed the democratic format of the standard image macro is one of its most compelling and, indeed, sustaining features. If memes are the basic units of cultural (re)production, then FALC and its offshoots are both an evolving dialectic and a representation of the current state of the (online) left.

Imagining the Future

At a recent Q&A at the Women of the World festival at the Southbank Centre in London, an audience member asked the prominent black activist and theorist Angela Davis whether she was tired of fighting against the same injustices as she had been since her youth in the seventies. Davis first, and true to form, took a moment to credit the young black activists of BLM in the US and the UK, as well as the Palestine solidarity movement, for inspiring her daily. She then pointed out that, despite the neo-liberal capitalist imperative to measure any form of labor in terms of progress, true change is slow, and it is inexorable. She went on to say that the work we do now would probably change the world in fifty years time, and "that today we are living the imaginaries of those who have been long gone. We are living the world they wanted."[24]

So who gets to participate in this world building? In Lizzie Borden's 1983 cult feminist classic sci-fi film *Born in Flames,* in a not-too-distant American future, the revolution has come and gone, and women, particularly women of color, find themselves still fighting against classism, sexism, and racism. What certain

---

24 See Southbank Centre, "WOW: Angela Davis in Conversation," *YouTube,* March 11, 2017, https://www.youtube.com/watch?v=lBgdzK3jfEg.

techno-utopian Marxist thinkers seem compelled to ignore is that the form of revolution for which they are advocating excludes the needs of a sizeable chunk of the population, particularly those who are excluded by dominant and hegemonic social, cultural, and political formulations.

Again, to restate an earlier contestation, the ways in which we understand and order the present — that is, the sum total of our experiences, prejudices, priorities, and politics — have a substantial impact on the kinds of worlds we try to create, and on the possible futures we are able to incorporate into our imaginaries. If we don't understand how gender, race, geographical, or sexual equality work in the present, how able are we to make room for them in our imaginaries of the future? Naturally we all want to live in a world that is post-racial and post-scarcity, and many of us even in one that is post-gender, but if we don't make space for, and even center those voices that are marginalised even in the dominant narratives of current subcultures, we will find ourselves recreating the same inequalities even in our utopias.

It is easy to downplay the value of online politics; one cannot click on a news site without seeing yet another op-ed lambasting millennials and their apparent myriad social and cultural ineptitudes (these are the imaginaries of mainstream media, it seems). However, if we can understand interactive media as sites of collective meaning-making, indeed sites of culture, and of world-making, then it is imperative that we harness the emancipatory power of these new media formats. In order to do so, we must firstly understand the ways in which they work. We must understand the ways in which ideas and understandings are reproduced or made new through these interactions, and we must understand their relationship to the political and material conditions of the present and the potentialities of the future.

We should especially be alert to how memes themselves act to queer dominant cultures through their role as imaginaries, and secondly, we must approach them as a purely utopian endeavor (in the best sense of the word). It is this queering that acts to elevate the meme format from standard new media;

memes continuously trouble the boundaries and spaces below and between hegemonic cultural formulations, operating something like a virus (it is no wonder that popular memes "go viral") or a catchy melody.

In these memes we can see entire worlds — cultures created through shared meaning and practice; some last hours, others days, months, or even years. They are constantly evolving and changing to fit the contexts in which they are being created and shared, and it is this quality that, at the same time as making them difficult to pin down and analyse, makes them impossible to commodify, and a useful site of resistance. As Hall argues: "in the study [of popular culture] we should always start here: with the double stake in popular culture, the double movement of containment and resistance, which is always inevitably inside it."[25] Our collective imaginaries are larger than all of us, and do not necessarily require our knowledge or even acknowledgement of the wider socio-cultural forces at play in order for us to participate in this world-building.

Imagining Freedom/Imagining Justice

Rather than closing with a summary of the discussion above, or with our own endeavors toward a grand theory of memes and political imagination, we instead choose to leave the reader with the wisdom of one of the 20th century's greatest imaginers, Ursula K. Le Guin, who offers the following typically poetic reflection on the relationship between the imagination, justice, and freedom. We do this, in part, because of the provocative and apposite nature of her words, but also in part, to denote that — for all of us — our work here, in imagining emancipatory futures, is far from done. It is in fact, always, just beginning:

---

25   Stuart Hall, "Notes on Deconstructing 'the Popular,'" in *People's History and Socialist Theory,* ed. R. Samuel (London: Routledge and Kegan Paul, 1981), 228.

We will not know our own injustice if we cannot imagine justice. We will not be free if we do not imagine freedom. We cannot demand that anyone try to attain justice and freedom who has not had a chance to imagine them as attainable.[26]

---

26 Ursula K. Le Guin, *The Wave in the Mind: Talks and Essays on the Writer, the Reader, and the Imagination* (Boston: Shambhala, 2004), 220.

Bibliography

Adams, Tim. "Cultural Hallmark." *The Guardian,* September 23, 2007. https://www.theguardian.com/society/2007/sep/23/communities.politicsphilosophyandsociety.

Anderson, Benedict. *Imagined Communities: Reflections on the Origin and Spread of Nationalism.* London: Verso, 1983.

Appadurai, Arjun. "Disjuncture and Difference in the Global Cultural Economy." In *Modernity at Large: Cultural Dimensions of Globalization,* 27–48. Minneapolis: University of Minnesota Press, 1996.

Brautigan, Richard. "All Watched Over by Machines of Loving Grace." *The Atlantic,* September 17, 2011. https://www.theatlantic.com/technology/archive/2011/09/weekend-poem-all-watched-over-by-machines-of-loving-grace/245251/. Originally published in *All Watched Over by Machines of Loving Grace* (San Francisco: Communication Company, 1967).

Butler, Judith. "Critically Queer." In *The Routledge Queer Studies Reader,* edited by Donald E. Hall and Annamarie Jagose, 18–31. Abingdon: Routledge, 2013.

Byrne, Liam. *Dragons: 10 Entrepreneurs Who Built Britain.* London: Head of Zeus, 2016.

Feenberg, Andrew. *Critical Theory of Technology.* New York: Oxford University Press, 1991.

Gleick, James. "What Defines a Meme?" *Smithsonian,* May 2011. https://www.smithsonianmag.com/arts-culture/what-defines-a-meme-1904778/.

Goldman, Emma. *Living My Life.* London: Penguin Classics, 2006.

Hall, Stuart. "Notes on Deconstructing 'the Popular.'" In *People's History and Socialist Theory,* edited by R. Samuel, 227–40. London: Routledge and Kegan Paul, 1981.

Jasanoff, Sheila, ed. *States of Knowledge: The Co-Production of Science and Social Order.* London: Routledge, 2004.

————, and Sang-Hyun Kim. *Dreamscapes of Modernity: Sociotechnical Imaginaries and the Fabrication of Power.* Chicago: University of Chicago Press, 2015.

Le Guin, Ursula K. *The Wave in the Mind: Talks and Essays on the Writer, the Reader, and the Imagination.* Boston: Shambhala, 2004.

mcm_cmc. "Fully Automated Luxury Communism: A Utopian Critique." *Libcom,* June 14, 2015. https://libcom. org/blog/fully-automated-luxury-communism-utopian-critique-14062015.

Merchant, Brian. "Fully Automated Luxury Communism." *The Guardian,* March 18, 2015. https://www.theguardian.com/ sustainable-business/2015/mar/18/fully-automated-luxury-communism-robots-employment.

Novara Media. "Fully Automated Luxury Communism!" *YouTube,* November 10, 2014. https://www.youtube.com/ watch?v=dmQ-BZ3eWxM.

Ovenden, Olivia. "Here Are the Memes That Helped Swing the Election in Labour's Favour." *Esquire,* June 12, 2017. https:// www.esquire.com/uk/culture/news/a15451/election-memes-corbyn.

Parkinson, Hannah Jane. "Was It the Corbyn Memes Wot Won It? Here Are Some of the Best." *The Guardian,* June 9, 2017. https://www.theguardian.com/politics/2017/jun/09/corbyn-memes-wot-won-it-some-of-the-best.

Sedgwick, Eve Kosofsky. *Tendencies.* London: Routledge, 1998.

Southbank Centre. "WOW: Angela Davis in Conversation." *YouTube,* March 11, 2017. https://www.youtube.com/ watch?v=lBgdzK3jfEg.

Syverson, Tom. "'Fully Automated Luxury Gay Space Communism': Has the Time For Universal Basic Income Finally Come?" *Paste,* June 7, 2017. https://www. pastemagazine.com/articles/2017/06/fully-automated-luxury-gay-space-communism-univers.html.

Taylor, Charles. "Modern Social Imaginaries." *Public Culture* 14, no. 1 (2002): 91–124. DOI: 10.1215/08992363–14–1-91.

———. *Modern Social Imaginaries.* Durham: Duke University Press, 2004.

Warner, Michael. "Introduction." In *Fear of a Queer Planet: Queer Politics and Social Theory,* edited by Michael Warner, 3–17. Minneapolis: University of Minnesota Press, 1993.

White, Charles. "The Memes that Decided the Outcome of the General Election." *Metro,* June 11, 2017. https://metro.co.uk/2017/06/11/the-memes-that-decided-the-outcome-of-the-general-election-6701277/.

Young, Thelathia "Nikki." "Queering 'The Human Situation.'" *Journal of Feminist Studies in Religion* 28, no. 1 (2012): 126–31. https://muse.jhu.edu/article/480267.

16

Memesis and Psychoanalysis: Mediatizing Donald Trump

Ian Parker

We need to be clear why we are fixated, for the moment, on Donald Trump. There is actually some optimism in the business community and among financial analysts about the Trump regime and what it can deliver, if you are sold on neoliberal policies of deregulation and privatization and a strong state. If Michael Wolff's insider book *Fire and Fury* is to be believed, much of the policy agenda is actually being driven by "Jarvanka," that is Jared Kushner and Ivanka Trump, Democrats (to gloss) who have the aim of installing Ivanka in the White House in the future.[1] Within the frame of this political-economic agenda, and a record of military intervention abroad, there is little evidence that Hillary Clinton would have been much more progressive in charge of the White House. The Trump vote should be set in the context of suspicion of elite machine politics that Hillary was into up to her neck and popular reaction to that, populist reaction peppered with a good dose of misogyny. In this regime, the figure of Trump himself stands out as an exception, an unpredictable element in a political move-

---

1   See Michael Wolff, *Fire and Fury: Inside the Trump White House* (London: Little, Brown, 2018) chapter 5, and 117–19, for example.

ment which, as Steve Bannon feared, would be drawn into the establishment. Trump could become a generally conformist and typical member of the President's Club. Trump is an anomaly, object of derision in the press, but should our response be in line with that derision?

The Trump election campaign was a media campaign. More than previous elections, which have been thoroughly mediatized in recent years as part of the society of the spectacle, this campaign revolved around mass media.[2] It was a campaign oriented to the media, by media and for the media. And we learn from Michael Wolff's book that the Trump team had the media in its sights as the main prize, as the end rather than the mere means. Members of the Trump team had their eyes set on media positions at the end of a campaign they expected and hoped to lose, and Trump himself aimed to use the campaign to set up a media empire to rival Fox. They had in mind the advice by ex-Murdoch anchorman Roger Ailes, that if you want a career in television, "first run for president." The election campaign effectively continues after Trump has been installed with a proliferation of fake news and the signifier "fake news" which haunts the media now. From this flows the kind of analyses we need, either analysis that will be really critical of Trump, or the kind of analysis that will easily and pretty immediately be recuperated, neutralized, and absorbed by the spectacle.

It wasn't just any old media that was crucial here, but new social media. Rapid decline in newspaper readership, which spells a crisis for the old media empires like Murdoch's Fox News, and near-death for standard format news television programs as a source of information, has seen a correlative rise in importance of platforms like Facebook, and, more so, Twitter, Instagram, Tumblr, and 4chan. These are platforms for the circulation of particular kinds of information; information that works by way of what it says and, crucially, how it is packaged. These are little packets of semiotic stuff that hook and take, they are memes.

---

2   On the "society of the spectacle," see Guy Debord, *Society of the Spectacle*, trans. Fredy Perlman et al. (Detroit: Black and Red, 1977).

Memes as tagged images or repetitive gif files provide messages which are intimately and peculiarly bound up with the form of the media. More than ever, perhaps even now with a qualitative shift in the speed and intensity of media experience and its impact on subjectivity, the medium is the message.[3] These are the memes produced and consumed in a significant component domain of contemporary politics, activating and replicating a certain mode of experiential engagement with Trump. There is something essential to be grasped here about the form of memes that keys into new forms of subjectivity and political engagement.

Take the example of the Trump open-book law-signing meme. In this gif, the big book Trump shows to camera as public evidence that a new statute has just been signed by him is inscribed with other messages; one of the earliest instances has the word "Kat" and an arrow on the verso page pointing to a scrawled child-like image of cat recto (joke: Trump is childish); a later version after the exchanges with North Korea has an image of a little red scribble marked "his button" on one page and a bigger splodge on the other page marked "my button" (joke: Trump is childishly preoccupied with having something bigger than Kim Jong-un). The message content for this meme can be easily pasted in and posted by anyone using a mobile app that is advertised on the Internet; the advertising also pokes fun at alt-rightists who might be grammatically challenged but even so will find it simple to use.[4] There are elements to these gifs that are also very easy for pop-Lacanians to describe; of a Symbolic register in which the message also connotes Trump's childish nature, of an Imaginary aspect which hooks us and replicates something childish about the intervention, and even a hint of something Real, of the stupidity of Trump as dangerous, this

---

3   See Marshall McLuhan, *Understanding Media: The Extensions of Man* (New York: McGraw Hill, 1964).

4   See Elissa Salamy, "Create Your Own Trump-signed Executive Order with Online Generator," *Newsday*, February 5, 2017, https://www.newsday. com/news/nation/create-your-own-trump-signed-executive-order-with-online-generator-1.13066643.

image game inciting the very jouissance, the very deathly pleasure it pretends to ward off. It is as if, and only as if, we can connect with what we know about Trump, and find a way to tell the truth about him, about how we feel about him.

Take another example, Pepe the Frog. This character was claimed and used by the alt-right to ventriloquize a series of often racist messages to support Trump during the election campaign. Pepe says the unthinkable, enunciates what is already said among the alt-right community. This is beyond dog-whistling politics; it includes humorous jpegs of Pepe with a Hitler moustache saying "Kill Jews Man." The Anti-Defamation League is onto this, but that isn't a problem for the alt-right; that merely heightens the peculiar pleasure of fans of Pepe. Here, you could say that an obscene underside of political discourse is relayed which pretends to connect with the unconscious, an unconscious realm which is configured as the repressed realm of what people really think and want to say. If there are perversions of the Imaginary, Symbolic, and Real here, it is as if they are already conceptualized and mobilized as part of the stuff of the meme; with the performative aim to feed a relay between Imaginary and Symbolic and make the Real speak. It is as if, and only as if, the unconscious can speak, with the construction of truths that have been censored now released, finally free.

Notice that there is a particular kind of framing and localization of the enemy and resistance. This framing and localization brings to the fore the Angela Nagle thesis, the argument in her book *Kill All Normies* that the Left prepared the ground for the rise of the alt-right; that arrogant attempts to enclose new media platforms and shut down debate, to humiliate and "no-platform" political opponents, set the conditions for an alt-right that was then much more adept at scapegoating others in order to triumph.[5] The Nagle thesis also raises a question about the complicity of what we like to call "analysis" or even "intervention" when we are being more grandiose, about our

---

5   See Angela Nagle, *Kill All Normies: The Online Culture Wars from Tumblr and 4chan to the Alt-right and Trump* (Winchester: Zero Books, 2017).

complicity with the phenomena our critique keys into. We can see the looping of this critique and phenomenon in the widely circulated little video clip of alt-right leader Richard Spencer beginning to explain what his badge with an image of Pepe the Frog on it means, before being punched in the face; the video becomes an Antifa gif, it becomes a meme. In the process, opponents and supporters of Trump become mediatized, part of the same looping process of memesis. So, a fantasy about what censorship is and how to break it, and what "free association" is and how to enjoy it becomes part of the media in which that fantasy is represented.

Trump is seductive, and so is psychoanalytic critique of him. It is tempting to home in on Trump as a pathological personality. Perhaps he is, as Michael Wolff says, "unmediated," "crazylike," without what neuroscientists call "executive functions," perhaps he is only mediated by his own image. This is where Wolff's spoof anecdote, which is unfortunately not included in *Fire and Fury,* is so enjoyable; the one about Trump watching a special cable channel devoted to gorillas fighting, his face four inches from the screen as he gives advice to them saying things like "you hit him good there." But we don't necessarily avoid wild analysis when we simply shift focus away from Trump himself and pretend instead that psychoanalysis can explain how someone like Trump could be elected; that is the argument in Robert Samuels's book *Psychoanalyzing the Left and Right after Donald Trump,* an argument that is actually underpinned by Lacanian theory, a very accessible clear book.[6] There is a place for psychoanalysis, but the question is, what is that place, how does psychoanalysis key into the media phenomena it wants to explain? We need to take care, take care not to be hooked by that question. We should not extrapolate from the psychoanalytic clinic to psychoanalyze politics.

---

6   See Robert Samuels, *Psychoanalyzing the Left and Right after Donald Trump: Conservativism, Liberalism, and Neoliberal Populisms* (London and New York: Palgrave Macmillan, 2016).

Trump is a paradoxical figure, not a psychoanalytic subject but a psychoanalytic object. He cannot not be aware of psychoanalytic discourse swilling around him and framing him, so pervasive and sometimes explicit is that discourse, but he seems resistant to that discourse, showing some awareness of it even as he rails against it. This use of psychoanalytic-style critique is one of the axes of the class hatred that underlies much of the mainstream media contempt of Trump and the representations of his stupidity. It is then also one of the suztexts of populist reaction against the media, the media seen as part of the elite that patronizes those who know a little but not a lot — here those who know a little but not a lot about psychoanalysis — who know what is being pointed at but who cannot articulate what exactly is being mocked in Trump and why. He is reduced to being an object of scorn, seemingly unable to reflexively engage with psychoanalytic mockery of him as if he was an analysand, to reflexively engage as an analysand would do. It is as if we have the inverse of the anecdote reported in the Michael Wolff book in which a model asks Trump what this "white trash" is that people are talking about; Trump replies "they are people like me, but poor." In this case the question might be "What are these psychoanalytic subjects, analysands?"; Trump's answer would be "they are people like me, but reflexive." He is in this language game but not of it, and the joke is that he doesn't quite get the joke, our sophisticated psychoanalytic joke. Trump is what Sigmund Freud would term the butt of the joke, and here the butt of psychoanalytic discourse as a class weapon used against him.[7]

Take, for example, a Trump meme which frames him as what we might call the case of Little Hands. This meme picks up on a comment made twenty years ago by a journalist — it was Graydon Carter in *Spy* magazine — that Trump has unusually short fingers. Trump reacted badly to this comment ap-

---

7   See Sigmund Freud, *Jokes and Their Relation to the Unconscious,* trans. James Strachey, in *The Standard Edition of the Complete Psychological Works of Sigmund Freud, Volume VIII (1905): Jokes and Their Relation to the Unconscious,* ed. James Strachey with Anna Freud (London: Vintage, 2001), viii.

parently, and ever since has been mailing the journalist cut-out magazine images of Trump himself with his hands circled in pen and the scribble "not so short!" During the 2016 Republican Primary one of Trump's rivals Marco Rubio said that Trump's hands were tiny, and "you know what they say about guys with tiny hands" — he waits for laughter — "you can't trust them." Trump's angry response took the implicit reference to the size of his dick seriously, and he responded publically in a speech in which he said "I guarantee you, there's no problem." This is where the meme poking fun at Trump spins into psychoanalytic discourse. Stories circulated in the media about this, including about the formation of a political action committee, that is an electoral campaign group, called "Americans Against Insecure Billionaires With Tiny Hands." You see how this works as a double-joke; Trump is insecure about power, but he doesn't realize that it's about power. You could say that the meme joke revolves around the fact that he doesn't get the difference between the penis and the phallus. The Trump Little Hands meme drums home a message about what he knows but doesn't want to know.

So what can psychoanalytic theory as such say about this process? We need to ask why it is so easy to make a psychoanalytic argument about these political phenomena. It does indeed look as if a Kleinian account of splitting and projective identification is perfectly suited to explaining not only why Trump acts the way he does, but also, better, it explains how we become bewitched by Trump, filling him with our hopes or hatred. It looks as if a version of us-American object relations theory perfectly captures the nature of Trump as a narcissist or, better, as an expression of an age of narcissism in which we stage our political objections to him as for a meritocratic ego ideal that we want to be loved by. It looks as if Lacanian psychoanalysis identifies a cause that drives and pulls Trump through the blind alleys of desire for he knows not what and, better still, this psychoanalysis explains what it is about Trump as *objet petit a* that is coming close to us and causing us anxiety. These are lines of argument rehearsed by Robert Samuels. The reason why these explanations make sense is not because they are true but because they

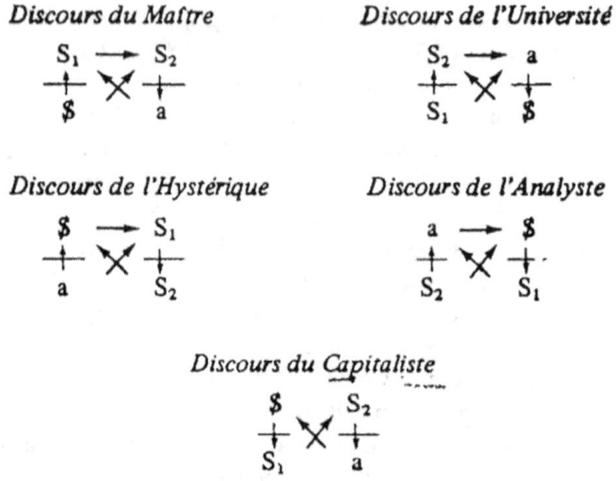

Discours du Maître

$$S_1 \longrightarrow S_2$$
$$\frac{}{\$} \quad \frac{}{a}$$

Discours de l'Université

$$S_2 \longrightarrow a$$
$$\frac{}{S_1} \quad \frac{}{\$}$$

Discours de l'Hystérique

$$\$ \longrightarrow S_1$$
$$\frac{}{a} \quad \frac{}{S_2}$$

Discours de l'Analyste

$$a \longrightarrow \$$$
$$\frac{}{S_2} \quad \frac{}{S_1}$$

Discours du Capitaliste

$$\$ \quad S_2$$
$$\frac{}{S_1} \quad \frac{}{a}$$

Fig. 1.

are made true, woven into the stuff they are applied to.[8] So, there is a deeper problem in the supposed "application" of psychoanalysis to politics, but is there a way out of this?

One of the peculiar things about Lacanian psychoanalysis is that it is implicitly, potentially reflexively self-critical. One of Jacques Lacan's conceptual devices helps us to understand a bit better exactly how recuperation operates under new mediatized conditions of possibility for political discourse. I have in mind the so-called "discourse of the capitalist" (at the bottom of fig. 1), though I am not sure that it is actually a fifth discourse that runs alongside the other four discourses that Lacan describes.[9] In *Seminar XVII* Lacan describes four discourses in one of his few extensions of psychoanalysis beyond the clinic, to understanding the political-economic context for the psychoanalytic

---

8 See Ian Parker, *Psychoanalytic Culture: Psychoanalytic Discourse in Western Society* (Thousand Oaks: Sage, 1997).

9 For a discussion of this, see Samo Tomšič, *The Capitalist Unconscious: Marx and Lacan* (London: Verso, 2015).

clinic.[10] These discourses are: discourse of the master as foundational, foundational condition of consciousness; discourse of the university, bureaucratically pretending to include all knowledge; discourse of the hysteric, productively rebellious questioning; and discourse of the analyst, hystericizing, facilitating critique. The so-called discourse of the capitalist that Lacan briefly proposes is a twist on the discourse of the master in conditions of commodity production and, I would say, of its mutation into the society of the spectacle.[11] Here in this discourse, the barred subject is in the position of the agent, as if we are in the discourse of the hysteric, but it faces knowledge, the battery of signifiers as other. Underneath the barred subject in the position of truth is S1, master signifier, facing the *objet petit a,* product.[12] The master signifier is where it would be in the discourse of the university, but the endpoint of this is still a commodity, as it would be in the discourse of the master. So, the discourse of the capitalist is a diagnostic tool complicit in power.

We could relabel this fifth discourse "the discourse of psychoanalysis," as Lacan himself implies it is. This is not the discourse of the analyst; no element is in the same position that we find in this mutation of discourse and the discourse of the analyst, but there is some significant mapping of elements with positions in the other three discourses, especially, of course, with the foundational discourse of the master. Here it is as if the agent, hysterical barred subject, is rebellious, questioning, but this agent attacks not the master but knowledge as such, rails against all knowledge, treating it as fake news. This agent revels in their division, aware of the existence of something of the unconscious in them, loving it; they are psychoanalytic subjects,

---

10 See Jacques Lacan, *The Other Side of Psychoanalysis: The Seminar of Jacques Lacan, Book XVII*, trans. Russell Grigg (New York: Norton, 2007).

11 See Julie Evans, "On Psychoanalytic Discourse — The Capitalist's Discourse (Milan, Italy): 12th May 1972: Jacques Lacan," *Lacanian Works,* May 12, 1972, http://www.lacanianworks.net/?p=334.

12 For more, see Stijn Vanheule, "Capitalist Discourse, Subjectivity and Lacanian Psychoanalysis," *Frontiers in Psychology* 7 (2016), https://www.ncbi.nlm.nih.gov/pmc/articles/PMC5145885/.

ripe for analysis, up for it. It is as if the truth of this subject will be found in the little significant scraps of master signifier that anchor it, signifying substance that seems to explain but actually explains nothing. This is how memes function in the imaginary production and reproduction of politics. This kind of truth includes those signifiers that are cobbled together from our own psychoanalytic knowledge, rather like the way they function in the discourse of the university, chatter about the "ego" and the "unconscious" and the rest of the paraphernalia. Two key elements of the discourse of the master are still in place; knowledge as a fragmented constellation of memes mined for meaning, for signs of conspiracy or, at least, something that serves well enough as explanation, including psychoanalytic explanation; and there is the product, *objet petit a,* something lost, something that escapes, something that drives us on to make more of it. We know well enough the paranoiac incomplete nature of the psychoanalysis that lures us in and keeps us going; here it is again.[13] We can draw on the discourse of psychoanalysis to make sense of Trump, and, more importantly, how he is represented.

This discourse is one manifestation of an "age of interpretation" that now circumscribes and feeds psychoanalysis. Remember that Freud did not discover the unconscious, Lacan insists on this; rather he invented it, and that invention which is coterminous with burgeoning capitalism in Europe functions.[14] It functions not only in the clinic, but in society. When it flourishes, its prevalence as an interpretative frame poses questions for psychoanalytic practice. Psychoanalytic subjects love psychoanalysis, love psychoanalytic discourse, they want more of it, want to speak it in the clinic and want to hear it interpreted, want it fed. The questions they pose in the clinic demand certain kinds of answers, psychoanalytic answers. In what Jacques-Alain Miller calls the age of interpretation there is a real danger

---

13   See Ian Parker, *Psychoanalytic Mythologies* (London: Anthem Books, 2009).

14   See Ian Parker, *Lacanian Psychoanalysis: Revolutions in Subjectivity* (London and New York: Routledge, 2011).

that the analyst buys into this, feeds the unconscious.[15] The appropriate analytic response to this demand is not to "interpret" but to "cut" the discourse, to disrupt it by a particular kind of interpretation, intervention which includes cutting the session. This is also why psychoanalysis should not be merely "applied," for it will merely feed what it is being applied to. These conditions of discourse call for different kinds of interpretative strategies.

There are implications of this for what we think is psychoanalytic critique of meme-politics. Mere description won't cut it. Perhaps it calls for what Robert Samuels describes as an ethic of neutrality combined with an ethic of free association; that is, neutrality of the analyst which does not rest on empathic engagement, and free association which does not feed the fantasy that something must be censored in order for correct speech to emerge. I'm not sure this will work. Perhaps it requires performative description in which there is some kind of over-identification with the discourse and unravelling of its internal contradictions; that is, deliberate use of the terms used, memes turned against memes. In which case we risk falling into the trap that Angela Nagle describes, one in which we replicate the conditions in which the alt-right emerged triumphant. Perhaps what we need is direct critique grounded in other forms of discourse, not only the discourse of the analyst which might work in the clinic but merely hystericizes, usually unproductively hystericizes its audience when it is "applied" outside the clinic. Other forms of discourse, from situationist critique and feminism and Marxism are necessary to break from the discourse that keeps all this going. Lacanian theory can connect with those other kinds of discourse as I have tried to show. This kind of anti-Trump in the media critique needs also be anti-psychoanalytic.

So, how do we speak as psychoanalysts about Trump? We can attend to the way that psychoanalytic discourse is mobilized in the public realm, but we need to take care not to simply feed that

---

15   See Jacques-Alain Miller, "Interpretation in Reverse," *Psychoanalytical Notebooks of the London Circle* 2 (1999): 9–18.

discourse. We should not pretend that we can speak as psycho-analysts. In fact, to speak as a psychoanalyst in the clinic is itself a performative impossibility. Lacan points out that what we say in the clinic may sometimes position us as psychoanalyst for the analysand, position us as subject supposed to know, but there is no guarantee that we are speaking there to them as a psycho-analyst. To pretend to speak from the identity of psychoanalyst is to speak as if we are a subject who does know. And so, then, to speak as if we are a psychoanalyst with a privileged position to interpret political phenomena in the public realm is to perform a double betrayal of psychoanalysis itself. Words are weapons, Trump knows that. Psychoanalysis is a double-edged weapon, and so we need to take care over how to use it to speak about politics, including how we speak about Trump.

Bibliography

Debord, Guy. *Society of the Spectacle.* Translated by Fredy Perlman et al. Detroit: Black and Red, 1977.

Evans, Julie. "On Psychoanalytic Discourse — The Capitalist's Discourse (Milan, Italy): 12th May 1972: Jacques Lacan." *Lacanian Works,* May 12, 1972. http://www.lacanianworks. net/?p=334.

Freud, Sigmund. *Jokes and Their Relation to the Unconscious.* Translated by James Strachey. In *The Standard Edition of the Complete Psychological Works of Sigmund Freud, Volume VIII (1905): Jokes and Their Relation to the Unconscious,* edited by by James Strachey, with Anna Freud. London: Vintage, 2001.

Lacan, Jacques. *The Other Side of Psychoanalysis: The Seminar of Jacques Lacan, Book XVII.* Translated by Russell Grigg. New York: Norton, 2007.

McLuhan, Marshall. *Understanding Media: The Extensions of Man.* New York: McGraw Hill, 1964.

Miller, Jacques-Alain. "Interpretation in Reverse," *Psychoanalytical Notebooks of the London Circle* 2 (1999): 9–18.

Nagle, Angela. *Kill All Normies: The Online Culture Wars from Tumblr and 4chan to the Alt-right and Trump.* Winchester: Zero Books, 2017.

Parker, Ian. *Lacanian Psychoanalysis: Revolutions in Subjectivity.* London and New York: Routledge, 2011.

———. *Psychoanalytic Culture: Psychoanalytic Discourse in Western Society.* Thousand Oaks: Sage, 1997.

———. *Psychoanalytic Mythologies.* London: Anthem Books, 2009.

Salamy, Elissa. "Create Your Own Trump-signed Executive Order with Online Generator," *Newsday,* February 5, 2017. https://www.newsday.com/news/nation/create-your-own-trump-signed-executive-order-with-online-generator-1.13066643.

Samuels, Robert. *Psychoanalyzing the Left and Right after Donald Trump: Conservativism, Liberalism, and Neoliberal Populisms.* London and New York: Palgrave Macmillan, 2016.

Tomšič, Samo. *The Capitalist Unconscious: Marx and Lacan.* London: Verso, 2015.

Vanheule, Stijn. "Capitalist Discourse, Subjectivity and Lacanian Psychoanalysis." *Frontiers in Psychology* 7 (2016), https://www.ncbi.nlm.nih.gov/pmc/articles/PMC5145885/.

Wolff, Michael. *Fire and Fury: Inside the Trump White House.* London: Little, Brown, 2018.

17

Simulation and Dissimulation: Esoteric Memes Pages at the Limits of Irony

Giacomo Bianchino

In September 2016, the *Atlantic* published an interview with Matt Furie. A 30-something stoner with an air of confused pathos, Furie's only claim to fame is bringing Pepe the Frog into the world. Pepe is a ubiquitous motif in what I'm going to begrudgingly call "meme culture." He has had probably the most controversial history of any viral symbol in the last five years. Starting life as a one of four zoomorphic characters in a puerile comic strip, he has since become the unofficial aegis of the alt-right. Things reached fever pitch in late 2016 when the Anti-Defamation League labeled him a hate symbol. Furie's desperate attempt to recapture the original "meaning" of Pepe prompted his intervention into the politics of popular culture. His sprawling justification for creating the fascist frog reads in the register of the frenetic:

> Pepe is kind of like, in the comic version of him, in my version of him, he's just kind of an everyman frog [...]. It just kind of expresses early 20-something hedonistic lifestyle, of

just hanging out, playing pranks on each other, eating pizza, partying, that kind of thing. A lot of bodily humor.[1]

The spectacle that this paper is interested in is not the political transformation of Pepe from bodily humor to white supremacy. Instead, it is Furie's scrambling to regain control over a rogue signifier that puts the drama of meme production and consumption into relief. The experience of losing control over a symbol reaches its peak in a futile assertion of the "owner's" creative authority. Indeed, in May 2017, Furie literally killed off Pepe in a single-panel version of a comic nobody read in the first place.[2] It is with the weird proportions of such a *Trauerspiel* in mind that this essay seeks to analyze quite what is at stake with the language of memes. The competition for control over the identity of Pepe heralds something interesting about the simulative capacity of Internet symbols. The ease with which an act of reposting or reinterpretation is able to, in the words of Alain Badiou, "inaugurate its own primitive event" speaks to a primary emptiness at the heart of this kind of communication.[3] To understand what makes the death of Pepe necessary demands a return to the philosophical territory of irony, which in turns means exhuming Søren Kierkegaard and G.W.F. Hegel to ask why conventional theories of language fail to account for it. With the indeterminacies of irony in mind, the essay asks whether the simulative character of memes can have a political dimension, and what this might mean for those on either side of the production and consumption relationship. To this end, it addresses the most acute species of divergence in the conflict

1   Adam Serwer, "It's Not Easy Being Meme: How Artist Matt Furie Feels About His Creation, Pepe the Frog, Becoming a Favoured Symbol of White Nationalists and Trump Supporters," *The Atlantic,* September 13, 2016, https://www.theatlantic.com/politics/archive/2016/09/its-not-easy-being-green/499892.

2   James Vincent, "Pepe the Frog is Officially Dead," *The Verge,* May 8, 2017, https://www.theverge.com/2017/5/8/15577340/pepe-the-frog-is-dead-matt-furie.

3   Alain Badiou, *Being and Event,* trans. Oliver Feltham (London: Continuum Press, 2005), 346.

between "normies" and esoteric meme pages. The tension between these two extreme poles of language will be shown, in the end, not to contradict one another, but to comprise a single dialectical unity. In liberating themselves from the claim of normativity, esoteric meme-creators end up forming the basis of the mainstream view's legitimacy. A proper online political praxis must be built with this dependency firmly in mind.

Kierkegaard and the Ironic Locution

The emptiness of the meme as a form of expression is something underwritten by its proximity to irony. That it is able to float between absolutely divergent interpretations has little to do with the legitimacy of the competing narratives. It has more to do with the ironic way in which the articulation is framed in the first place. Irony is a rare category that is simultaneously metaphysical and linguistic. Kierkegaard developed a theory of this indistinction during his early engagement with Hegel's work. In the *Philosophy of History,* Hegel defends the idea that one must actively seek the rational aspect for the world to appear rationally. For Kierkegaard, a *decision* to see the world rationally is only possible when one is committed to the metaphysical notion that the essence of an object dissimulates or deceives in the manner of its appearance. Metaphysical irony holds of the world that "the phenomenon differs from the essence."[4] Where a subject of truth acknowledges this, they are expected to negate the phenomenon in order to reach the essence. The split between appearance and essence is repeated at the level of articulation in the idea that "when I am speaking, the thought, the meaning, is the essence, and the word is the phenomenon."[5] Where this awareness is self-consciously deployed as a tool of communication, the irony shifts from metaphysical to rhetorical. The ironist brings out the essence by actively differentiat-

---

4 Søren Kierkegaard, *Concept of Irony,* trans. Howard V. Hong and Edna H. Hong (Princeton: Princeton University Press, 1989), 247.

5 Ibid.

ing their intention from their articulation. While base untruth misleads in order to conceal the truth, irony actively alludes to a meaning other than the one it announces. The act of representation is made to intentionally obfuscate about its content. The dialectic of irony produces the image of the locution's meaning without announcing it.

The reason for this obfuscation, according to Kierkegaard, is to exercise the "infinite absolute negativity" of subjectivity over and against the contradictions of the objective world.[6] In his own work, he drew these edifying moments of negativity from the paradoxical moments at which reality and thought necessarily diverged. Such moments of "negative determination," in the phraseology of Geoffrey Hlibchuk, alienate and liberate the subject from their material background.[7] This strategy seeks to preserve the determinate individual subject against the processual abstraction of Hegel's substance-subject of history. Kierkegaard's attempts to "arrest" the progress of the Hegelian system sought to trip up the putative universal subject of history and science on a linguistic stumbling block.[8] Irony, as the separation of signifier and signified, was the most immediate means for preserving a sense of personal subjectivity against the inert, plodding march of historical substance.

The reasons for exercising one's infinite negativity depend heavily on the subject. Irony presupposes a certain social context: one populated by canny equals and uneducated inferiors. Some use irony as a tool that "mystifies the world" and guarantees their intellectual superiority. For others, irony is used to negate the word in order to bring out a hidden thought in their interlocutor. In both operations, however, there is a problem of authenticity and legitimacy. Where the ironic subject intervenes

---

6   Ibid., 254.

7   Geoffrey Hlibchuk, *The Poetics of Exception: Contemporary North American Poetry and the Ghosts of Relation,* PhD Thesis, State University of New York, 2008, 46.

8   See Henry Sussman, *The Hegelian Aftermath: Readings in Hegel, Kierkegaard, Freud, Proust and James* (Baltimore: John Hopkins University Press, 1982), 156.

in language in order to undermine it, it opens a contradictory torsion. For Kierkegaard, an ironic locution must reproduce the conditions of legitimacy while negating them in relation to its own content. Kierkegaard took umbrage with Hegel's attempt to reconcile this problem by withdrawing all irony from the process of knowledge formation. For the purposes of philosophical reason, Hegel makes a distinction between the universal, objective content of history and the realm of "mere phenomena." This realm constitutes "the sphere of particular purposes, in effecting which individuals exert themselves on behalf of their individuality, give it full play and objective realization."[9] This sphere, in which irony itself must move, cannot inoculate itself against the violent structuration of events *post factum*. Gradually, as history is objectivized, all of the particularity of an ironic subject's intentions disappears. Hegel's historian determines the status of irony: its historical value has no relation to the intention it supposedly expressed.[10] Only the universal element is taken up by philosophy. For an author like Kierkegaard, this is especially troubling. The ironic writer is perennially at the behest of the reader and their context: the creator's intentions disappear necessarily in the audience's construction of the content.

The generation and interpretation of memes plays out precisely this drama of ironic dissimulation and posterior structuration. By entering into the universal realm of communication (language), the meme finds itself at the behest of its audience and their interpretation. But the ironic withholding of something from the meme's act of communication creates a kind of non-relation between the process of production and of consumption. It is into this divide that hops Pepe the Frog and his burning question about authority of a meme's content.

---

9   G.W.F. Hegel, *The Philosophy of History*, trans. J. Sibree (New York: Dover Publications, 2004), 26.

10 Ibid., 28; Sussman, *The Hegelian Aftermath*, 97.

Power From Below Truth: The Double Object of Irony

Irony supposedly liberates the communicative act from its traditional role of conveying information. By effecting the split
between object and subject at the level of intention, it manipu-
lates the phenomenal to create the negative perception of some
hidden essence. This operates through a specific kind of negative signification. Where the ironist doesn't consider themself
beholden to linguistic responsibility, they are able to freely force
symbol and meaning together. It is then the task of the audience
to unpick it. The same drama is operating in the production and
consumption of memes. As Furie says of Pepe in another video,
"he's kind of a blank slate. He means a lot of things to a lot of different people."[11] This split between author and audience is as old
as writing. The relationship between "force" (the subjective play
of the writing subject) and "signification" (the responsibility of
the communicative act) was at the center of Jacques Derrida's
drama of writing. Like Kierkegaard's scepticism toward Hegel's
historicizing impulse, Derrida believed that posterior signification denied the contingency of the interchange between symbol
and meaning by "divesting" the entire literary field of its force.[12]
Here he introduces a split between the intentionality of a work's
author and the formality of the work's consumer. Like the split
between Kierkegaard's subject and the retrospective settling of
its status by Hegel's subject of history, the reader is always engaged in ossifying and structuring the author. As Derrida says:
"the force of the work, the force of genius, the force, too, of that
which engenders in general is precisely that which resists geo-
metrical metaphorization and is the proper object of literary
criticism."[13] Where the critic forgets this playful force, they fall
back into "essentialism" or "teleological structuralism."[14] The

---

11   See Super Deluxe, "Pepe the Frog: From Innocent Meme to Hate Symbol,"
     Facebook, 2017, https://www.facebook.com/watch/?v=353532971657926.
12   Jacques Derrida, *Writing and Difference,* trans. Alan Bass (London:
     Routledge, 2001), 4.
13   Ibid., 23.
14   Ibid., 24.

creator of memes, in their foray into language, subverts the relation by creating the illusion of essence. By actively dissimulating the phenomenon, the ironist second-guesses their audience by creating the sense that what has been withdrawn from the image is the truth.

This holds so long as the audience doesn't know what the ironist is doing. But the audience's comprehension of the force changes the terms of engagement. Where irony is directed at those who are its unknowing target, the ironist merely elevates their subjective position by mystifying the world.[15] Where the reader acknowledges the ironic negation in the act of articulation, however, a new dialectic emerges. This compact union between ironists "seeks" in the words of Kierkegaard "to form a society."[16] But its inability to shoulder any kind of linguistic responsibility leads to abandoning community and confining itself to "conventicles."[17] With this, one enters the territory of "esoteric" meme pages; online societies based around a very recondite and narrow common point of interest. Like any other society of ironists, the dialectic between the esoteric meme creator and consumer is an attempt to be initiated into the inner sanctum of the conventicle. This desire for initiation takes the form of a struggle to know something about the other. Because they understand that there is no real essence to the communicative act, the consumer does not seek hysterically to "know" and embody the creator's intention. The "layers" (and here there is a Milnerian equivocality between the imagistic layering of the meme on media like Photoshop and the layers of meaning it belies) of a meme's irony are not unravelled in search of the "reality" of the meme's message, but the most "authentic" layer: the ironic limit. The only qualitative criterion of a meme is just how ironic the producer was being. Like Derrida's ideal literary criticism, the dialectical negation of the meme's appearance seeks to reveal the force or "play" of the author by determining what

---

15   See Kierkegaard, *Concept of Irony*, 250.

16   Ibid., 249.

17   Ibid.

such an author is capable of. Truth as such is disposed of in favor of simply knowing the password to the ironic community through overcoming the authorial limits. What a meme audience goes in neurotic search of is power over the author.

This search for the author in place of truth, long a plague of criticism, has gradually elided the sense of difference between what Jean Baudrillard would call "real" and "simulation."[18] Where irony begins with the necessity of the distinction between phenomenon and essence, it is gradually replaced with the pervading sense that the real is a creation of the simulation. The withdrawal from a need for truth leads the critic to a thesis of "hyperreality," where the goal of criticism and consumption is to divine the limitations of production rather than its convergence with historical actuality.[19] The hyperreality of esoteric meme production creates a critical culture of materialism, where the object is not material reality as the factical precondition of consciousness, but a mere attention to the materials with which consciousness is working. The search is for the template from which the meme was made, but also the epistemic conditions that allowed for its creation (the book read, the video seen, etc.). In the words of a popular meme phrase in a particular philosophy community (Dialectical Dialecticzposting for Big Others and Negated Absolutes), "read x book, it's only y pages or so." The empirical center of the meme's "meaning" has little importance. Kierkegaard intuited this limitation on the communication of truth, and influenced his defining decision to become a fictionalist. According to Karl Jaspers, Kierkegaard's commitment to the infinite interpretation of life's content came to replace any desire for objectivity. In Jaspers's view, "Kierkegaard gave his own writings no other meaning than that they should read again the original text of individual, human exis-

---

18 Jean Baudrillard, "Simulacra and Simulations," trans. Paul Foss, Paul Patton, and Philip Beitchman, in *Selected Writings*, ed. Mark Poster (Stanford: Stanford University Press, 1988), 166.

19 Ibid., 167.

tential relations."[20] The perpetual chain of interpretation is not broken by the emergence of any real. The bilateral consent to simulation creates the sense of a myth of a real, but understands it exactly as a myth. All that is left is a struggle for the most virtuosic recalibration of form, the most outrageous chain of association.

Supplementarity: The Politics of Production and Critique

Such a model of de-substantialized communication works where there is no need to justify one's claims. The problem emerges when this conventicle of irony edges onto politics. By its definition, the relationship of memes to reality prevents them from establishing any given position as authoritative. At the basis of the articulation is an acceptance of the absoluteness of interpretation. In literature, "play" allows for a continual chain of substitution that emanates from a mythical, unsubstitutable center. As Derrida says in "Structure, Sign and Play in the Human Sciences," "one cannot determine the centre and exhaust totalization because the sign which replaces the centre, which supplements it, taking the centre's place in its absence — this sign is added, occurs as a surplus, as a supplement."[21] Ironic meme culture consciously supplements, knowing that there is no center that isn't directly added in the act of interpretation or reproduction.

The consent to supplementarity is why those who stand outside the meme page's discourse (we can call them, along with classical Internet culture and with a degree of schadenfreude, "normies") can only ever lead failed crusades to steer memes on the right path. For instance, some have called for a new kind of solidarity to be built from the pervasive atmosphere of "relatability" in online meme content.[22] Here we have a legitimate so-

---

20 Karl Jaspers, *Reason and Existenz: Five Lectures,* trans. William Earle (London: Kegan Paul, 1956), 27.

21 Derrida, *Writing and Difference,* 365.

22 Aria Dean, "Poor Meme, Rich Meme," *Real Life,* July 25, 2016, http://reallifemag.com/poor-meme-rich-meme/.

cial appeal to a new transcendental; a generalized idea of memes as the unproblematic union of universal image and universal message.

This might work in the cheerful context of non-esoteric meme pages. Indeed, a lot of Internet culture is premised around the possibility of sharing content as widely as possible. There is an argument here that such pages operate according to a logic of "virality" rather than the exclusive inclusivity of meme production and reproduction. Indeed, virality is defined by Karine Nahon and Jeff Hemsley in their pioneering work *Going Viral* as a kind of "social information flow process."[23] Many Internet critics hold obscurantists and esotericists to the standards of virality, either supposing that they should create the product that has the greatest possible dissemination, or that the Internet is a marketplace of ideas in which only the most viral can survive. This virality would certainly have to take linguistic and moral responsibility very seriously in order to succeed in its aims. The problem is, however, that esoteric meme pages and vlogs don't care all too much about shareability. Where the acknowledgment of irony occurs on both sides of the divide, the possibility of standard communication is doubly impeded. The normie demand fails to take into account this mutual indeterminacy. Like Hegel's universal history, it misses the supplementarity of the subjective act of "centering". The cultivation of ironic dissimulation and deferral on both sides of the meme relation means that the kind of universalism aspired to by the Normie critics is definitionally impossible. As Kierkegaard says, "there is just as little social unity in a coterie of ironists as there is real honesty in a band of thieves."[24]

---

23 Nahon and Hemsley define virality as "a social information flow process where many people simultaneously forward a specific information item, over a short period of time, within their social networks, and where the message spreads beyond their own [social] networks to different, often distant networks, resulting in a sharp acceleration in the number of people who are exposed to the message." See Karine Nahon and Jeff Hemsley, *Going Viral* (London: Polity Press, 2013), 15–16.

24 Kierkegaard, *Concept of Irony*, 249.

The failure to register this flux of supplementarity between producer and consumer, or author and audience, is the origin of the weird spectacle of Pepe. The terrified scramble that ensues when meme culture verges on politics is often produced by a misplaced sincerity in its external critics (or, in Furie's case, the very creator of the original image). In February 2017, *Wired* magazine published a write-up by Emma Grey Ellis on the decline and fall of a neo-nazi videogame reviewer, Pewdiepie, a Swedish vlogger, who earned the attention of the alt-right when he repeatedly invoked Hitler and made holocaust jokes in his YouTube videos.[25] Because of the ironic detachment of both Pewdiepie's "trolling" and its reception by fascists, Grey Ellis granted that it was impossible to know "whether he means what he says." She proceeded to put an imaginary limit on the acceptable content of memes:

> None of this means that *anything* that offends *anyone* is off limits as a joke. But jokes that goof on racism are different than jokes that rely on race — a fine line to be sure.[26]

She doesn't even seem to convince herself. In trying to set the limits of irony, Grey Ellis aims at the responsibility that is supposed to attend all political acts of communication. To do so, she tacitly commits to an order of language in which thought and word constitute a single unit. This ideal register of language, not unlike that on Jorge Luis Borges's Tlön, is a vain kind of idealism. It assumes, conservatively, that memes abide the same conventional form of communication as regular language. Making the word fit the intention is like forcing the reproduction of the meme to fit with the original image. It absolutely mistakes irony's false essentialism for the real thing. It is the necessary suspicion of this formalism that if one peels back the layers of

---

25 Emma Grey-Ellis, "Pewdiepie's Fall Shows the Limits of 'LOL JK'," *Wired*, February 16, 2017, https://www.wired.com/2017/02/pewdiepie-racism-alt-right/.

26 Ibid.

irony, one will arrive at the "truth." This takes no account of the supplementary structure of ironic relations, nor of the ambiguities of memes' simulation and dissimulation.

The response by most critics of political memes has the effect of feeding the very irony it seeks to undermine. Memes play in the virtuosic realm of free association and a deferred kind of jouissance. The jouissance does not come from making the best fit between word and image, but the most esoteric. The index of a successful meme is the elided pleasure of forcing a conceptual mismatch and the confusion this would cause to the uninitiated. And it is the earnest gravitas of critics like Grey Ellis that automatically aligns them with the latter. The bitter paradox is that their conventionalism creates the necessary social background for the development of irony's "conventicle." The more normies make noise about the problematic nature of memes, the further the meme producers and consumers retreat into the subjectivism of irony.

Discourse and Tangent

This presses against the contours of a dialectic that exists between the forces of irony and of normality. The specification of the Normie as the object of the meme's derision does more than simply distinguish the friend from the enemy. The acceptance of simulation at the expense of the real excuses the meme from academic conventions. The meme page ceases to function as the locus of what Jacques Lacan calls the university discourse. No longer is the "institution" (here the meme page) trying to doctor and include its excess to strengthen itself.[27] The virtuosic accumulation of knowledge in the place of truth aligns the ironic page instead with a desire to differentiate itself as the excess. It seeks to become the exception to the rule of normality by banishing the kinds of codification associated with "normality."

---

27 See Slavoj Žižek, "Jacques Lacan's Four Discourses," *JL*, 2006, http://www.lacan.com/zizfour.htm.

It would seem, then, that in its rejection of conventional epistemic discourse a meme page represents a Foucauldian challenge to the disciplinarian regimes of measurement and power. But the reality is that the meme page structures itself around an invisible center of both power and desire. This is because it comprises an intentional conventicle in the form of a self-appointed alternative "discourse." Instead of objectivity, esoteric meme pages are organized around the forbidding of the Other's pleasure, and thus must found themselves on a primary act of excision or otherising. These esoteric pages are discourses, in Michel Foucault's words,

> which are arbitrary to start with or which at least are organized around historical contingencies; which are not only modifiable but in perpetual displacement; which are supported by a whole system of institutions which impose them and renew them; and which act in a constraining and sometimes violent way.[28]

It is this act of constraining and demarcation that does not simply identify the Other, but makes their banishment the center of its activities. In inaugurating a discourse, the meme group specifies not "what it is" but "who it isn't." Like any discourse which separates itself out from its alternative, "the prohibitions that surround it very soon reveal its link with desire and with power."[29]

With this understanding, the analysis of the dialectic between normie and esoteric memeist can be brought into its proper dimension. Structurally, the center of a meme is supplementary; it is added in. But this act of supplementation is governed by a dialectic of desire which edges onto a political problem of power. The desire that belies the fundamental act of

28 Michel Foucault, "The Order of Discourse," trans. Ian McLeod, in *Untying the Text: A Post-Structuralist Reader,* ed. Robert Young (Boston: Routledge and Kegan Paul, 1981), 54.

29 Ibid., 53.

prohibition is not merely for pleasure in the displeasure of the excluded. This pleasure is the symptom, rather than the cause, of the constraining act. In fact, the desire governing this excision is (in Foucault's own words) "discourse itself."[30] The forms of knowledge and power which define the ironic negation are, as has been argued, virtuosic and ornamental. The baroque element of the meme page's esoteric logic is to collect signifiers that mark it off from its "uninitiated" other in order to preserve this very logic. It is thus a self-moving force which survives in relishing its own independence.

In its categorical demands for "imposition and renewal", the meme community is beholden to the same strictures as any other discursive institution. When Badiou wonders at what it is precisely that constitutes a philosophical institution, he arrives at three component features. The first is the importance of an address, through which a subject is apparently interpellated from the position of the void. In this case, the absolute invisibilizing or ironic deferral of the memeist's identity is paramount to its success as an anonymous address to the multiple recipients. Pepe, in this context, issues forth like some Aphrodite from the froth; there can be no suture of primary meaning to the initial appearance of the image. The primal address can only be sustained, in Badiou's understanding, by the second feature of an institution: transmission. Transmission is the appointing of a discipline; of a set of recipients upon whom falls the "interminable imperative of continuing" and expanding the remit of the address.[31] In this sense, all meme consumption is reproduction; the endless metonymy of signifiers that operates through the aggregation of new memes or the "sharing" of old ones. Importantly, for Badiou transmission takes place among disciples and apostles. It is never the task of a public, whose sanctioning of the discourse would transform the address into something tangible

---

30 Ibid., 54.
31 Alain Badiou, "What Is a Philosophical Institution?," trans. A.J. Bartlett, in *The Praxis of Alain Badiou,* eds. Paul Ashton, A.J. Bartlett, and Justin Clemens (Melbourne: re.press, 2006), 14.

and usable rather than submitting to the imperative of renewing and continuing its void articulation. Finally, the process of inscription ensures that the address is made to subsist through a lasting mark. In this case, the meme page forms a physical archive whose acts of transmission become archeological testaments to the endurance of the address.

What makes the meme page different to other discursive institutions is the militancy with which it inures its acts of transmission against the public. There is a paradox at the heart of this procedure. As an institution, its acts of transmission treat the initial address as a certain species of speech ex nihilo. It supposedly confines meaning and truth to the discourse itself while shutting out the outside. Its independence, however, is illusory. By subverting the expectations of the "uninitiated," the meme artists reiterate that it is their practice that is subversive or aberrant, assenting to the Normie's claim on the register of truth. The meme maker tacitly acknowledges the reality of the claim of what lies outside their discourse. The attempt to make themselves into a challenge to normality is a simple admission that the center of their task is to be in the appropriate relation to the normal. The meme community utters a plaintive "che vuoi!" to the normies because the normies refuse to recognize the legitimacy of their desire; the prolongation of the excluded discourse. The esoteric ironist seems to have ceased the search for any tangible center of their own. What forms the real center of their task is the desire of the Other; the reality of the normie as the discourse of Truth. In assuming the prestige of the ironic discourse, the meme community tries to transform themselves into the object of normie desire. They are in neurotic relation to each other, maintaining with militant sedulousness the Law they have elected. But in relation to the outside world they remain hopelessly hysterical, seeking to be the exception that normie neurosis longs for.

Turning the Relation Outside-In: The Inequilibrium of Memeists and Their Normies

Clearly, a dialectical inversion of the relationship between esoteric meme pages and the social reality of normies reveals two very different positions. The attempt to impose the demands of reason onto the meme community is generally met with the reinforcement of irony. But this coquetry belies the demand of the meme maker to be transformed into the object of desire. The two are locked in interdeterminate dependency. The relationship, however, is by no means equal. In wanting to transform themselves into the desired object, the meme conventicle affirms only a parasitic relationship to its excised other. In this way, it assents to its status as the leftover excess of the university discourse. Such a desire is not unconventional, nor particularly unreasonable. Indeed, the imperative to become the University's other is demanded by the Discourse of the University itself. As Žižek says, "names like Kierkegaard, Nietzsche, or Benjamin, all three great antiuniversitarians whose presence in the academy is today all-pervasive—demonstrate that the 'excluded' or 'damned' authors are the IDEAL feeding stuff for the academic machine."[32] The register of truth desires its exceptions.

So what is the balance between the discourse of truth and normality (the normies) and its happily excluded others (the memeists)? Luckily, one of the very "antiuniversitarians" named by Žižek wrote about this exact issue. It is with some nostalgia, then, that we can now return to Kierkegaard. In *Repetition*, a book that came shortly after his exposition on irony, Kierkegaard put the discourse of the exception and universality into dramatic relief. In the guise of Constantius Constantine (an ironist but not a mystifier; rather an unlikely champion of the universal), he staged what he called "the dialectic by which the

---

32 Žižek says of Lacan's discourses: "that the university goes to great lengths to produce such exceptions can be seen from the consistent attacks it has made on its employees and students in the name of 'business investment plans' or 'economic diversification." See Žižek, "Jacques Lacan's Four Discourses."

exception emerges from the general."[33] This process mirrors exactly the Foucauldian inauguration of a discourse, because it begins in its own extrication from the other. The problem for the ironic exception is that it suffers greatly in its act of differentiation. And it suffers precisely so the "universal," the regular order of truth, can secure itself:

> The universal delights in the exception to the same extent that heaven delights in the reformed sinner — more than in ninety-nine righteous souls. On the other side is the resistance and defiance of the exception, its weakness and infirmity.[34]

Heaven's delight in the reformed sinner is its delight in the outside demonstrating that it is really an inside. The universal delights in the exception in the same way. Through its act of "repentance," the exception recognizes that it is founded in the regime of normality for which it longs. In this sense it is "reconciled to the universal."[35] Despite this, the universal remains, at all costs, "polemically opposed" to the exception.[36] It comfortably excises the exception because it knows that it constitutes the origin of the exception's desire. Kierkegaard, Benjamin, and Nietzsche may all have abandoned the university discourse, but they still wrote for it! Their action, their gesture (and György Lukács took this up against his beloved Kierkegaard) was never an abandonment. It was a sycophantic reassurance to the world of normality that it could produce an alien discourse while still controlling it.

The problem is the same for the memeist. They need the approbation of the normies, but the normies just need them to exist. As Giorgio Agamben says, the system proves its universality through its specification of the outside as the inside: "confronted

---

33 Søren Kierkegaard, *Repetition and Philosophical Crumbs,* trans. M.G. Piety (Oxford: Oxford World Classics, 2009), 77.

34 Ibid.

35 Ibid., 78.

36 Ibid.

with an excess, the system interiorizes what exceeds it through an interdiction and in this way 'designates itself as exterior to itself.'"[37] The dimensions of this act of inclusion, while purely social, delineate the process whereby irony feeds the discourse of normality. When it is transferred to the political realm, however, the situation is "even more complex."[38] The generality, the sphere of normies, if you will, seem to demand that the meme creator hold themselves to the same conventional definition of language that they abide. The very performance of a normal register of language, however, disguises its own violent center in an act of exclusion that is simultaneously inclusion. Rather, the normie critic sustains the hegemonic definition of conventional language by an act of denomination. This act doesn't seek to generalize the conditions of responsibility and hold the other to its own prescriptions. Instead, it seeks to create the possibility of its own transgression, thus commanding not only the spaces of its inclusion but the very possibility of its breach:

> Here what is outside is included, not simply by means of an interdiction or an internment, but rather by means of the suspension of the juridical order's validity, by letting the juridical order, that is, withdraw from the exception and abandon it. The exception does not subtract itself from the rule; rather, the rule, suspending itself, gives rise to the exception and, maintaining itself in relation to the exception, first constitutes itself as a rule.[39]

The Grey-Ellises of the world, in their demand that memes be held to the standards of political language, are not showing concern for the excised meme conventicle.[40] They are validating the mainstream that violently demands its own excess and exceptions. In this sense, they are "withdrawing from it and abandon-

---

37 Giorgio Agamben, *Homo Sacer: Sovereign Power and Bare Life,* trans. Daniel Heller-Roazen (Stanford: Stanford University Press, 1998), 18.

38 Ibid.

39 Ibid.

40 Grey-Ellis, "Pewdiepie's Fall."

ing it" simply by showing that it exists internally to the normie's moral world. They have to recognize the validity of the meme articulation in order to legitimately overcome it. So Grey-Ellis herself reminds us that under the beneficence of the conventional, "none of this means that *anything* that offends *anyone* is off limits as a joke." The category of the joke is the generality under which the meme is effectively subsumed by the logic of the normie's sovereignty. Thus fascist in-jokes like Pepe become self-identified as exceptional but externally defined as "problematic." This fingerpoint, this denomination, marks out the excess in exactly the way that the discourse of truth demands it. In the unthreatening Internet existence of the alt-right, civil society proves itself capable of cultivating its other without recompense. It thus proves itself as sovereign.

Conclusion

The tricky territory of memes verges onto problems of textuality, sociality, and authority. Firstly, the facticity of meme groups makes them, at all times, devoid of tangible social or moral content. They are definitionally impervious to the demands of civil society. This is partly because of the supplementarity of their ironic process. Matt Furie makes the mistake of believing that changing the original meaning of the symbol, or silencing it, will put an end to the chain of substitution that he himself inaugurated. What he doesn't realize is that it is the later commitment to Pepe that inaugurated Pepe himself. The center has always been added in as a supplement. As Badiou says, a representative fidelity (the way a thing is later made sense of) is "always in non-existent excess over its being".[41] There is no need for the alt-right to justify their use of Pepe in line with the intentions of its creator. Furie, like all authors, is effectively dead. It is the chain of Pepe's substitution that turned him into a symbolic center, and no amount of meddling on the part of the author can rend apart what has already been cleaved together. This is why the

---

41 Badiou, *Being and Event*, 235.

campaign to #savepepe and its attendant YouTube video makes such great viewing. Watching a collapsed stoner evoking vague universal humanisms in defense of his nazi frog creates the very source material for which a meme society hungers.

This longing for content, however, belies a contradiction at the heart of meme societies. The ironic conventicle, confined as it is to a shared conspiracy, requires its own negation to function. A meme page, like any coterie of ironists, makes of itself an exception. As Kierkegaard's Constantius Constantine tells us, however, this exception, "despite its struggle with the universal, is an offshoot [rodskud] of it."[42] Notwithstanding its best efforts, the meme group is beholden to its tangential status in relation to the generality of normie culture. By aggressively excising convention, they turn this dismissal of society into their raison d'être. Without a target (in this case the ubiquitous normie) the limits and bonds of the group become altogether more elastic. Here, the crucifixion of the Big Other is the condition of its living on as spirit. In the place of a concrete meaning, the meme takes its center of jouissance from the suffering of the other. In doing so, it enters into a master/slave dialectic with the world outside its discourse: a dependence from which it can't be liberated. Although it seems as if the meme page has differentiated itself, it has really turned the outside world into its absolute center. Without normies, the dialectic of the esoteric meme page is impossible.

---

42 Kierkegaard, *Repetition*, 78.

Bibliography

Agamben, Giorgio. *Homo Sacer: Sovereign Power and Bare Life.* Translated by Daniel Heller-Roazen. Stanford: Stanford University Press, 1998.

Badiou, Alain. *Being and Event.* Translated by Oliver Feltham. London: Continuum Press, 2005.

———. "What Is a Philosophical Institution?" Translated by A.J. Bartlett. In *The Praxis of Alain Badiou,* edited by Paul Ashton, A.J., Bartlett and Justin Clemens, 13–23. Melbourne: re.press, 2006.

Baudrillard, Jean. "Simulacra and Simulations," translated by Paul Foss, Paul Patton, and Philip Beitchman. In *Selected Writings,* edited by Mark Poster, 169–88. Stanford: Stanford University Press, 1988.

Dean, Aria. "Poor Meme, Rich Meme." *Real Life,* July 25, 2016. http://reallifemag.com/poor-meme-rich-meme/

Derrida, Jacques. *Writing and Difference.* Translated by Alan Bass. London: Routledge, 2001.

Foucault, Michel. "The Order of Discourse," translated by Ian McLeod. In *Untying the Text: A Post-Structuralist Reader,* edited by Robert Young, 48–79. Boston: Routledge and Kegan Paul, 1981.

Grey-Ellis, Emma. "Pewdiepie's Fall Shows the Limits of 'LOL JK.'" *Wired,* February 16, 2017. https://www.wired.com/2017/02/pewdiepie-racism-alt-right/.

Hegel, G.W.F. *The Philosophy of History.* Translated by J. Sibree. New York: Dover Publications, 2004.

Hlibchuk, Geoffrey. *The Poetics of Exception: Contemporary North American Poetry and the Ghosts of Relation.* PhD Thesis, State University of New York, 2008.

Jaspers, Karl. *Reason and Existenz: Five Lectures.* Translated by William Earle. London: Kegan Paul, 1956.

Kierkegaard, Søren. *Concept of Irony.* Translated by Howard V. Hong and Edna H. Hong. Princeton: Princeton University Press, 1989.

———. *Repetition and Philosophical Crumbs.* Translated by M.G. Piety. Oxford: Oxford World Classics, 2009.

Nahon, Karine, and Jeff Hemsley. *Going Viral.* London: Polity Press, 2013.

Serwer, Adam. "It's Not Easy Being Meme: How Artist Matt Furie Feels About His Creation, Pepe the Frog, Becoming a Favoured Symbol of White Nationalists and Trump Supporters." *The Atlantic,* September 13, 2016. https://www.theatlantic.com/politics/archive/2016/09/its-not-easy-being-green/499892.

Super Deluxe, "Pepe the Frog: From Innocent Meme to Hate Symbol." *Facebook,* 2017. https://www.facebook.com/watch/?v=353532971657926.

Sussman, Henry. *The Hegelian Aftermath: Readings in Hegel, Kierkegaard, Freud, Proust and James.* Baltimore: John Hopkins University Press, 1982.

Vincent, James. "Pepe the Frog is Officially Dead." *The Verge,* May 8, 2017. https://www.theverge.com/2017/5/8/15577340/pepe-the-frog-is-dead-matt-furie.

Žižek, Slavoj. "Jacques Lacan's Four Discourses." *JL,* 2006. http://www.lacan.com/zizfour.htm.

18

Pepe Goes to China, or, the Post-Global Circulation of Memes

Gabriele de Seta

Internet Memes in Platform Times[1]

The thick layering of interpretive frames and indexical elements accruing around the "Pepe the Frog" character between 2015 and 2018 is perhaps the process that most poignantly captures the construction of digital media cultures in platform times. The anthropomorphic frog originally appeared as a protagonist of Matt Furie's indie comic series *Boy's Club* (2006). By 2010, the character's stylized expression had already become one of the most distinctive examples of American digital folklore: one specific comic panel (in which Pepe pronounces the by now iconic sentence "feels good man" after peeing) started circulating in relatively unknown bodybuilding forums; when the image was picked up by users of larger dis-

---

1   This essay is partly based on a blog post published by the author on the Cyborgology website. See Gabriele de Seta, "The Social Life of Sad Frogs, or: Pepe Goes to China," *The Society Pages*, November 3, 2016, https://thesocietypages.org/cyborgology/2016/11/03/the-social-life-of-sad-frogs-or-pepe-goes-to-china/.

DOI: 10.21983/P3.0255.1.19

cussion boards like Something Awful, 4chan, and Reddit, it was quickly spun into an endless series of self-referential variations.[2]

The fortuitous and unpredictable popularity of Pepe — cropped out from Furie's comic pages, inventively augmented through image editing software and widely copy-pasted across digital media platforms — cemented it as one of the most representative examples of an "Internet meme." The "Pepe the Frog" meme has been repeatedly invoked as a textbook case study of how, after the global popularization of Internet access and the imbrication of social media platforms in everyday life, the creative practices of digital media users can propel anyone or anything up the plateau of a momentary and self-fulfilling relevance.[3] Matt Furie himself, reflecting on the unexpected online fame achieved by one of his artistic creations, describes the cultural dynamics exemplified in the circulation of Pepe in terms of a "post-capitalist" vernacular creativity: "it's like a decentralized folk art, with people taking it, doing their own thing with it, and then capitalizing on it using bumper stickers or t-shirts."[4]

Despite the global reach of its iconicity, the history of Pepe — from its origins in independent comics to its moment of mainstream limelight on the social media accounts of celebrities like Nicky Minaj or Katy Perry — has for the most part been narrated as a thoroughly American story. Throughout the 2016 US Presidential election year, the archetypal meme frog has experienced a further bout of popularity after being adopted as a humor device by Donald Trump supporters, identified by the Hillary Clinton campaign as white supremacist iconography, and condemned by the Anti-Defamation League as an "anti-

2   *Know Your Meme,* s.v. "Pepe the Frog," http://knowyourmeme.com/memes/pepe-the-frog.

3   Ryan M. Milner, "This Memetic Moment: Ridiculously Photogenic Guy and the Perils of Internet Fame," *Los Angeles Review of Books,* October 10, 2016, https://lareviewofbooks.org/article/memetic-moment-ridiculously-photogenic-guy-perils-internet-fame/.

4   Sean T. Collins, "The Creator of Pepe the Frog Talks About Making Comics in the Post-Meme World," *Vice,* July 28, 2015, https://www.vice.com/en_us/article/avy3aj/feels-good-man-728.

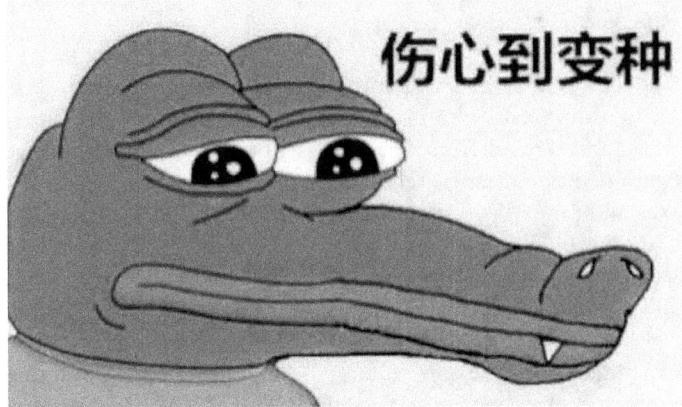

Fig. 1. "So sad I mutated species," Pepe image with Mandarin Chinese caption.

semitic symbol" — all the while being continually repurposed as the protagonist of increasingly complex and self-referential genres of Internet memes including "Rare Pepes," "Cult of Kek," and "Beta Uprising."[5] Repeatedly interviewed about the political reappropriations that turned his iconic character into a "culturally thick object," Matt Furie has minimized this phenomenon as "just a product of the internet."[6] And yet, years before its spells of mainstream popularity and its contested political interpretations, Pepe had already found its way to Chinese social media platforms with surprising outcomes (fig. 1).

5   See Marley-Vincent Lindsey, "Parting Ways with Pepe? Anti-semitism and the Medium of Memes," *The Society Pages,* October 8, 2016, https://thesocietypages.org/cyborgology/2016/10/08/parting-ways-with-pepe-anti-semitism-and-the-medium-of-memes/.

6   See Adam Serwer, "It's Not Easy Being Meme," *The Atlantic,* September 13, 2016, https://www.theatlantic.com/politics/archive/2016/09/its-not-easy-being-green/499892/.

Pepe Goes to China

I encountered my first Chinese Pepe in early 2014. I had just begun doing fieldwork in China for my doctoral research project, and a friend from Shanghai sent me a QQ message that contained the instantly recognizable image of a frog with teary eyes and pouty lips.[7] I asked him if he knew what the frog was, and where the image came from; he replied that it was called *shangxin qingwa,* "sad frog," but he had no idea about its origins. "It's just funny. It's really popular on the Baidu Tieba forums right now, that's where I got it. There's many versions of it," he explained over the chat interface. During the following months, more and more long-time friends, new acquaintances, and interviewees brought the *shangxin qingwa* into our online interactions, describing the stylized frog as a "weird" and "funny" character whose "existential sadness is easy to empathize with."

Multiple versions of the *shangxin qingwa,* augmented with Mandarin captions and at times localized through visual elements indexing it to local specificities, accumulate over the years in my archive of Chinese digital folklore. Pepe has become a *biaoqing*—literally an "expression," a term that describes a broad category of digital content including emoticons, reaction images, animated GIFs, and stickers.[8] *Biaoqing* are shared across platforms, from Baidu Tieba forum boards and Sina Weibo posts to QQ and WeChat conversations, and users collect them in thematic *biaoqing bao* [expression packs] designed to be imported into the interfaces of messaging programs and social media apps. Pepe has made it to China as a sad frog, and sits snugly in personalized sticker menus, reaction image folders, and *biaoqing* repositories along with Communist Party leaders,

---

7   Tencent QQ, launched in 1999, is one of the instant messaging applications most popular in China, with 843 million MAU (monthly active users) as of the end of 2017.

8   See Gabriele de Seta, "Neither Meme Nor Viral: The Circulationist Semiotics of Vernacular Content," *Lexia: rivista di semiotica* 25/26 (2016): 463–86.

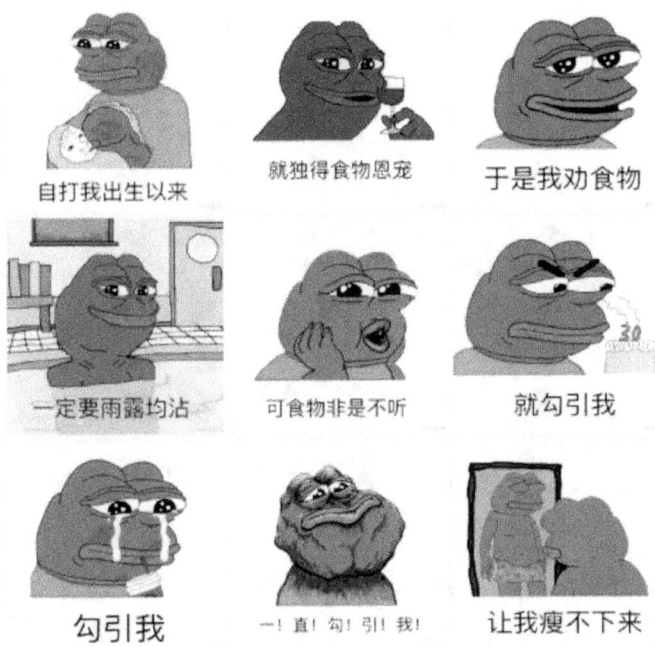

自打我出生以来　　就独得食物恩宠　　于是我劝食物

一定要雨露均沾　　可食物非是不听　　就勾引我

勾引我　　一！直！勾！引！我！　　让我瘦不下来

Fig. 2. Series of Mandarin-captioned sad frog *biaoqing* collected on the microblogging platform Sina Weibo.

TV series characters, pop culture icons, and local social media mascots such as Tuzki the Rabbit (fig. 2).

Besides its popularity as a semiotic resource, the *shangxin qingwa* is also extensively discussed across social media posts, news articles, and community wikis. A Douban post by Shi Yezhong chronicles the online circulation of frog imagery, a rich repertoire of content ranging from the "Crazy Frog" song and captioned GIFs of the Muppet character Kermit the Frog to the "Foul Bachelorette Frog" advice animal memes and, of course, Pepe itself.[9] Yet, it is in the comment section that some Douban

---

9   Y. Shi, "Shangxin Qingwa Shi Nali Lai De? [Where does the sad frog come from?]," 2016, https://moment.douban.com/post/140446/.

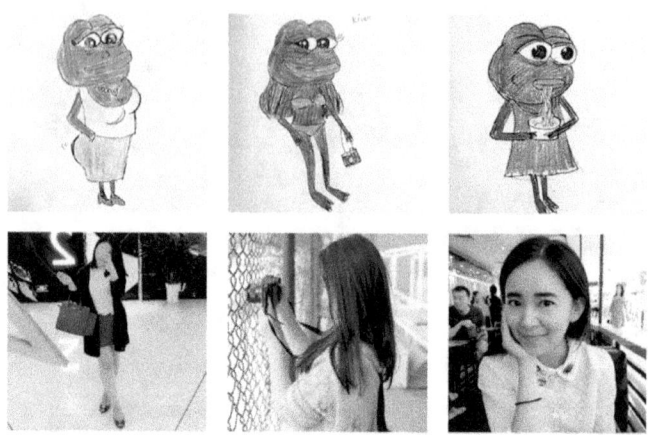

Fig. 3. Personalized sad frog profile pictures drawn by a WeChat group member (Xing Mei, 2015).

members interestingly reclaim a local frog heritage, suggesting that the *ha* ("toad," a humorous nickname for ex-president Jiang Zemin) should be included in the list as a "Chinese mutation" of Pepe, wearing the leader's iconic high-belt trousers and thick glasses. One thread on the Q&A website Zhihu, titled "Why did Pepe the Frog Become So Popular?," receives a detailed answer by a user recounting an intensive three-day exposure to the sad frog *biaoqing* in a WeChat group chat:

> There were more than a thousand new messages every day, and surprisingly this girl kept participating in all discussions without sending any text or voice message, she! just! used! *shangxin!* *qingwa!* expressions! And a few days later, another girl from the same group started drawing *shangxin qingwa* caricatures of other group members' profile pictures...[10]

---

10 Xing Mei, "Weishenme Pepe the Frog Hui Huo? [Why did Pepe the Frog Become So Popular?]" (2015) [URL defunct].

Reacting to the sad frog's popularity across Chinese social media platforms, another essay posted on a videogame website blames local users for not understanding Pepe and not respecting its origins: "filenames like 'World's Saddest Frog biaoqing pack' are just too stupid — if Matt Furie ever saw them, he would cry."[11]

Unsurprisingly, given the thorough commercialization of digital media content in China, the users' practices of vernacular creativity aren't limited to the circulation of edited images, emoticon packs, and hand-drawn profile pictures described above. A simple search query for *shangxin qingwa* on the e-commerce marketplace Taobao results in a wide variety of sad frog merchandise for sale on the platform, ranging from WeChat sticker packs (¥1.98) and smartphone covers (¥26.90) to frog eyes sleeping masks (¥15.50), and Pepe-shaped tissue dispensers (¥35.00). The description of another product (a sad frog hand warmer pillow selling for ¥24.18) is tagged with a constellation of keywords useful to understand the context of this genre of merchandise: ACG (animation, comics, and games), QQ *biaoqing,* and *jingshen wuran* ("spiritual pollution," an ironic term for brainwashing online phenomena). Printed over t-shirts and cushions, molded into keychains and phone cases, Pepe as sad frog becomes an index anchoring various networked publics of Chinese digital media users to different platforms (Baidu Tieba, QQ, WeChat), consumption preferences (animation, gaming, video streaming), and visual content genres.

It is not clear when and how Pepe started circulating on Chinese social media platforms, but it makes sense to imagine one or more local users downloading some images of the comic character from 4chan, its Japanese equivalent 2chan, or perhaps even from websites like KnowYourMeme, and uploading it in a Baitu Tieba thread or a Sina Weibo post. What is evident is that, hailed as the *shangxin qingwa,* Pepe has entered a vast pantheon of characters drawn from the universes of ACG fandom and popular media, has found a home in the customizable in-

---

11   Ruo Ji, "Yi Ge Jianming Yidong De Pepe Shi [A simple and clear history of Pepe]" (2015) [URL defunct].

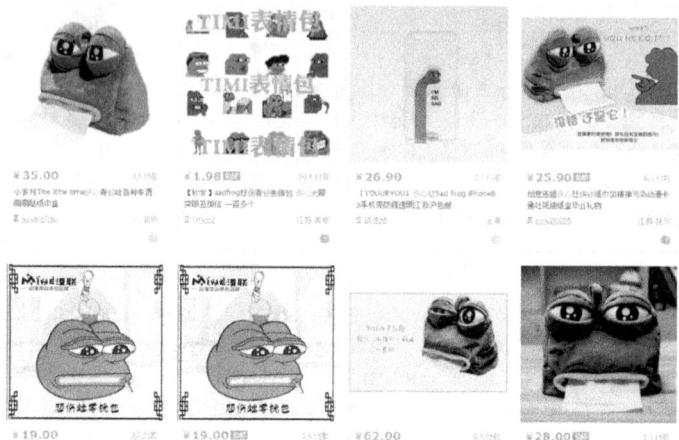

Fig. 4. Some of the *shangxin qingwa* merchandise sold on Taobao, China's largest online marketplace.

terfaces of social media platforms, and has become part of a repertoire of "spiritual pollution" quickly converted into Taobao merchandise. On the other side of the Pacific, Matt Furie has been collecting the artisanal Pepe pins, t-shirts, and earrings sold on websites like Etsy, and even launched an official line of Pepe apparel in 2017; and yet, he probably has no idea of the degree to which his most iconic character is being commercialized on industrial scale in China (fig. 4).

"So Sad I Mutated Species"

It is commonplace to imagine the "Chinese Internet"—a vague category encompassing national networking infrastructures, homegrown digital media platforms, and local online phenomena—as an exotic portion of cyberspace sealed away by the Great Firewalls of authoritarian surveillance and techno-nationalist development. And yet, while it is hard to deny that protectionist policies, censorship apparatuses, and the Chinese government's clutch on the development of national Internet

industries have resulted in insular techno-economic infrastructures, the existence of a geolinguistic cluster of web content
does not necessarily imply a self-contained repertory of digital folklore.[12] Besides local biaoqing, Chinese digital media users also collect, interpret, and repurpose content sourced from
global genres such as American "Rage Comics," Japanese anime
characters, and Korean pop idols, weaving it into their online
interactions and integrating it in situated repertories. During
my fieldwork, I earmarked this sort of content as indicative of
a post-global circulation of vernacular content, but it was only
through my recurring encounters with Pepe's local fortune as
shangxin qingwa that I could articulate a consistent case study
of how digital folklore challenges the notions of the local and
the global.

In a study of the cross-national circulation of Internet jokes,
Limor Shifman, Hadar Levy, and Mike Thelwall argue that the
translation of humorous content contributes to a process of "user-generated globalization."[13] Grounding their analysis on a cor-
pus of English jokes and tracking their translation online across
nine languages, Shifman, Levy, and Thelwall conclude that the
humorous content translated by ordinary users functions as an
agent of a process of globalization and Americanization that
does not explicitly involve economic transactions, resulting in
a "global humorous sphere," whose reach is often unclear to
users themselves.[14] The authors recognize that privileging ver-
bal humor over visual content and focusing on texts from the
contexts of production, consumption, and interpretation could
limit the validity of their research, and I argue that the case of
Pepe highlights precisely how these limitations skew their con-

---

12 See Harsh Taneja and Angela Xiao Wu, "Does the Great Firewall Really
    Isolate the Chinese? Integrating Access Blockage with Cultural Factors
    to Explain Web User Behavior," *The Information Society* 30, no. 5 (2014):
    297–309.

13 Limor Shifman, Hadar Levy, and Mike Thelwall, "Internet Jokes:
    The Secret Agents of Globalization?" *Journal of Computer-Mediated
    Communication* 19, no. 4 (2014): 727–43.

14 Ibid., 740.

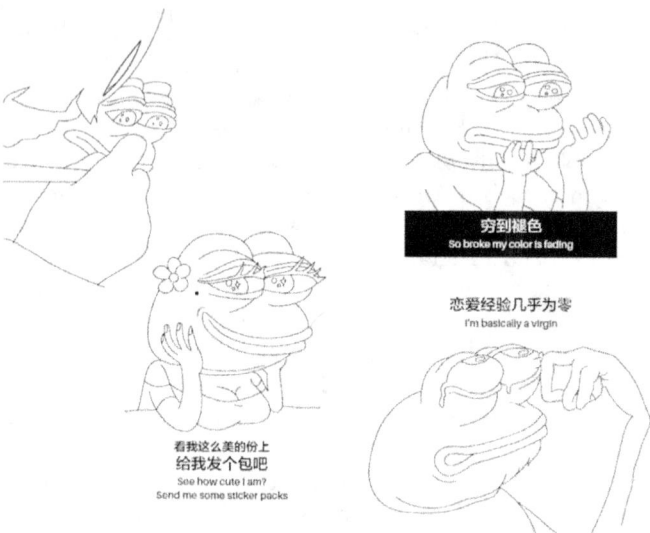

Fig. 5. A page spread from Fei Liu's zine *Pepe the Sad Frog Coloring Book and Chinese Language Guide* (2017)

clusions regarding the globalizing role of vernacular content.[15] As described in the previous section, the circulation of Pepe does not necessarily involve a direct translation — being a visual rather than a textual joke, the character's expression crosses the linguistic boundaries of social media platforms and audiences through acts of copy-pasting, downloading, and uploading, and is repurposed by users according to their own reactions to it: a sad, funny, weird, relatable mascot that can be layered with situated elements and references. More dedicated interpretation only follows circulation, as users try to reconstruct the sad frog's origins as Pepe, linking it back to its original creator through distinction claims to proper usage and respectful referencing.

The circulation of Pepe, from Matt Furie's pencil to its situated reappropriations, doesn't stop at a frog-shaped toilet paper dispenser sold on Taobao. *Pepe the Sad Frog Coloring Book and*

---

15 See ibid., 741.

Chinese Language Guide, a zine published by New York-based Chinese artist and designer Fei Liu (fig. 5), reflects on the post-global circulation of the character while bringing it back to its original media format.[16] As Fei Liu recounts:

It all started from me flipping through my younger step sister's WeChat album. She was living in Chongqing at the time, and she had posted a photo of a little girl drawing a picture of Pepe by hand, and coloring him in. My reaction was like… what the hell is going on here?[17]

Departing from a similar encounter with Pepe in the practices of Chinese digital media users, Fei Liu's zine offers American readers a field guide to Pepe's Chinese travels: "It has made Chinese Americans who can't really read Chinese excited to learn a few things about Chinese digital media, talk to their parents, and so on." The caption featured on the zine's front cover, "so sad I mutated species," embodies a condensed understanding of the post-global circulation of vernacular content, and helps understanding Internet memes as one among many genres of digital folklore, each situated in specific interpretive contexts negotiated among networked publics. Once in China, Pepe's sadness become its defining trait, granting it a position in the ever-growing pantheon of tongue-in-cheek content decried as "spiritual pollution," accompanying local digital media users all the way from their chat conversations to their smartphone covers.

---

16 See Fei Liu, *Pepe the Sad Frog Coloring Book and Chinese Language Guide* (New York, 2017). Retrieved from trytobegood.com.

17 Interview with the author, 2018.

Bibliography

Collins, Sean T. "The Creator of Pepe the Frog Talks About Making Comics in the Post-Meme World." *Vice,* July 28, 2015. https://www.vice.com/en_us/article/avy3aj/feels-good-man-728.

Ji, Ruo. "Yi Ge Jianming Yidong De Pepe Shi [A simple and clear history of Pepe]." 2015. https://www.g-cores.com/articles/16104.

Lindsey, Marley-Vincent. "Parting Ways with Pepe? Anti-semitism and the Medium of Memes." *The Society Pages,* October 8, 2016. https://thesocietypages.org/cyborgology/2016/10/08/parting-ways-with-pepe-anti-semitism-and-the-medium-of-memes/.

Liu, Fei. *Pepe the Sad Frog Coloring Book and Chinese Language Guide.* New York, 2017.

Mei, Xing. "Weishenme Pepe the Frog Hui Huo? [Why did Pepe the Frog Become So Popular?]." 2015. https://www.zhihu.com/question/27695606.

Milner, Ryan M. "This Memetic Moment: Ridiculously Photogenic Guy and the Perils of Internet Fame." *Los Angeles Review of Books,* October 10, 2016, https://lareviewofbooks.org/article/memetic-moment-ridiculously-photogenic-guy-perils-internet-fame/.

de Seta, Gabriele. "Neither Meme Nor Viral: The Circulationist Semiotics of Vernacular Content." *Lexia: rivista di semiotica* 25/26 (2016): 463–86.

———. "The Social Life of Sad Frogs, or: Pepe Goes to China." *The Society Pages,* November 3, 2016, https://thesocietypages.org/cyborgology/2016/11/03/the-social-life-of-sad-frogs-or-pepe-goes-to-china/.

Shi, Y. "Shangxin Qingwa Shi Nali Lai De? [Where does the sad frog come from?]." 2016. https://moment.douban.com/post/140446/.

Shifman, Limor, Hadar Levy, and Mike Thelwall. "Internet Jokes: The Secret Agents of Globalization?" *Journal of*

Computer-Mediated Communication 19, no. 4 (2014): 727–43. DOI: 10.1111/jcc4.12082.

Serwer, Adam. "It's Not Easy Being Meme." *The Atlantic,* September 13, 2016. https://www.theatlantic.com/politics/archive/2016/09/its-not-easy-being-green/499892/.

Taneja, Harsh, and Angela Xiao Wu. "Does the Great Firewall Really Isolate the Chinese? Integrating Access Blockage with Cultural Factors to Explain Web User Behavior." *The Information Society* 30, no. 5 (2014): 297–309. DOI: 10.1080/01972243.2014.944728.

19

The Post-Pepe Manifesto

Seong-Young Her

Plagiarism is necessary. Progress implies it.

For old memes to become resources for the present requires their reinvention and reuse; appropriation of collective inheritance, not of private property. The cultural vanguard of shitposters expresses the memetic commons with an autistic, rather than schizophrenic, knowledge of 'net ephemera. We mean that the treatment of art as concept was *de rigueur* well before those eager, crumb-covered fingers set out to finish what the dadaists and situationists never could. Leaving behind the dazzling rhizomes of the postmodern, the cutting-edge now spearheads the Internet's transition into the post-postmodern.

Our name for this kind of reinvention and reuse of memes is *détournement*; as in to detour, to hijack, to lead astray, to appropriate. This is no shitpost *qua* shit post. The task is not the destruction of the meme, but rather the destruction of the ownership of the meme which manifests as the invisible hand of conservative prescriptivism — comments, screeching from Imgur and Reddit; "you're using that meme wrong!" The elimination of the very notion of personal property in this area is what once made ironic memes so great: the meme was true only to itself.

But the normies came once more and "ironic memes" became the new normal, with only soccer-mom Garfields and rural-American Jesus-posting left behind. But this time they came branded, watermarked with links to their Instagram and studded with emojis — or did they? Was that how it happened?

We remember the Great Meme War of 2014: the history books of KnowYourMeme will not mention the numerous fallen who endured deletions from Facebook in the name of spicy memes, among them the first wave of "historical alliteration" pages. It was not the normies who caused admins to rally followers to mass-report other pages posting 9/11 memes, nor threaten to doxx each other for reposting without credit.

Was it that the normies stole our memes? Or did we simply lose sight of something important, the very thing 4chan tried to explain to us that October by way of a Pepe-Market metaphor? It was our Internet-hipster, Pepe-capitalist valuation — keep it rare and keep it ours; if it isn't rare it isn't dank — which led us to cast Pepe to the normies, relinquishing hegemony over use and meaning as we stopped producing, as we stopped distributing. Were we the normies?

Normies produce a culture in their own image, a culture of the meme as private property, the author as sole proprietor of a work of genius. *Détournement* sifts through the memetic remnants of past and present culture for memes whose untimeliness can be utilized against normie culture. *Détournement* offers an ease of production far surpassing — in quantity, variety and quality — the normie content that has bored us for so long. Rather than further elaborate normie memetics, *détournement* exploits it.

Our aim is the subversion of the culture of predatory meme pages through a sincere repurposing of normie productions. We claim that meaning is the result of use, and so we move to use anything and everything.

The meme scene has persevered the hellfire of meta-irony, whose blackening flames of mutation turned every meme inside out, exploding them, exposing the hypocrisy of ironic memes becoming decidedly unironic yet still retaining the cynicism and elitism of insincere play. We now advance into the informed naivety of post-ironic memes, weaponizing the past. We inherit the pathos of sincerity from the oldfags while the fruits of all that ironic experimentation inform our ethos. The unironic evaluation of memes as real things is the source of our new logos. As normies metastasize outwards, making the Web over in their image, at home on Facebook they will find their own image turned against them.

All culture is derivative.

The revolution will be reposted.

20

Afterword: Post_Meme

Alfie Bown and Francis Russell

A common trope in cultural studies or critical theory texts that seek to engage with popular phenomena is an implication that readers of such theory, and those that care about popular phenomena, have been remiss for not seeing the possible connections between the two. In other words, the rhetorical gambit of many critical texts on popular culture involves the implication — often unconscious and unintended — that *by now* someone should have seen that this particular popular phenomenon was calling out to us, pleading with us to be *taken seriously,* to be given the dignity of an invitation to enter into a dialogue with critical or philosophical thought. However, what such a move functions to do, almost always against its explicit interests and intent, is to suggest that popular phenomena were not being taken seriously, were not being treated with dignity, were not being recognized as fully as they might be, when they were being engaged through the pluralism of non-academic guises. Contrary to the assumptions of some, this cannot be said of memes, which have been taken as a very serious phenomenon since their very emergence online.

Perhaps the prevalence of such a common rhetorical trope has something to do with the influence of thinkers like Martin Heidegger and Gilles Deleuze. For both of these thinkers, though in very different contexts and to different ends, overlooked every-

DOI: 10.21983/P3.0255.1.21

day phenomena such as jugs or films were taken to be veritable sites of philosophy, genuine invitations to think — and not only invitations, but phenomena in themselves that *afford* thinking, which is to say, phenomena that are always already offering us questions and concepts. While such pluralistic gestures should certainly not be taken for granted, there is a sense in which such a gesture can be misread as reinforcing conventional, and dare we say ideological, notions of work and stratifications of labor. Indeed, there is something seductive and thrilling about the notion that a "mere" jug or a "mere" film could both invite us to, and in a certain way already be conducting, serious theoretical work. But such seduction runs the risk of reinforcing the notion that there is a clear hierarchy and stratification that separates the world of everyday things from that of intellectual work. Moreover, the seductive *Aha-Erlebnis,* the moment where something mundane reveals its critical or theoretical potential, also produces the risk of reinforcing the commonsense that intellectual labor must be serious, does bestow dignity to its subject matter, and enjoys a moral height over what it surveys.

The question that has come out of considering the subject matter of this collection of essays is what the thinker is to do when the subject matter resists these terms altogether. If the subject matter embraces indignity, stupidity, and crassness, and a joyful frivolousness, would the thinker be missing the point to hope to show the reader that the popular phenomena in question has been demanding — though secretly, and in a language that only the theorist understands — to be taken seriously? The theorists who contributed to this volume have dealt with this problem in various ways.

In light of such concerns, this collection of essays on memes garnered its primary title, *Post Memes,* in a twofold sense. On the one hand, it situates itself *after* memes, insofar as we acknowledge and appreciate that memes have already established themselves as a significant phenomenon and that reflection on this phenomenon has long since begun. No theoretical gesture of charity is required to show the significance of memes and meme culture. They have penetrated elections worldwide. They have become the subject of monographs and think pieces. They have spawned commentaries and meta-commentaries. And, perhaps presenting the greatest difficulty for the theorist, there are a multitude of memes about theory itself. It is for this reason that we acknowledge ourselves as coming after memes, as opposed to positioning ourselves as the ones to bestow dignity onto them, to put them on the map, to reveal their truth through piercing analytic maneuvers.

On the other hand, this text has also been about trying to get caught up in, trying to get contaminated by, what it is that makes posting memes so compelling. For us, this question has necessarily been approached in terms of the act of sharing, the act of loosening the assumed sovereignty of authority — or of author-authority — in order to allow wider channels for flows and disseminations. It is for this reason that this book has basically eschewed any promise to explain memes by providing them with a static identity, or to position memes as belonging to one specific moment or event. Instead, we fully acknowledge that the sharing of memes, placing them into different contexts or editing their form even marginally, is already itself an act of writing. In this sense, this text has not so much been a collection of writings on memes — a collection that's tried to get on top of, or get on with the task of explaining what memes are all about, once and for all — but instead a continuation of *posting,* i.e., sharing, modifying, and circulating ideas, images, and provocations. For that reason too, we decided to work with the brilliant people at punctum books, whose project is in the spirit of the meme: open-access, available, inclusive, and experimental.

To offer here another angle through which memes could be approached, to those discussed in the preceding pages, it is via an existing body of work on comedy studies. Memes could be viewed through various theories of laughter theory, from Freud and Henri Bergson through to later theorists of caricature and political satire. Yet, we have tried to resist applying existing theoretical models to the contemporary meme in any traditional sense, showing instead how new theoretical frameworks are needed to understand the political importance of memes and the political pleasures of posting. Memes do share a number of characteristics with traditions of political satire (e.g., the derision of establishment logic) and with histories of caricature (e.g., the clashing of form with content) but it is the differences between memes and hitherto existing modes of comedy, rather than the similarities, which present the most interesting and politically important topics for discussion.

At the same time, memes must be understood theoretically and conceptually, and this text brings memes into contact with a range of theoretical material. An important critique of the patterns of humor prevalent online could be provided, for example, via the French Marxist Henri Lefebvre. In his *Critique of Everyday Life,* Lefebvre joined Marx's idea of alienation with comedy, using Charlie Chaplin as his prime case study. While appreciating Chaplin's potentially subversive comedy, Lefebvre concludes his discussion with the realization that "on leaving the darkness of the cinema" after a Chaplin movie, "we rediscover the same world as before, it closes round as again."[1] Since "the comic event has taken place, we feel decontaminated, returned to normality, purified somehow, and stronger."[2] Lefebvre's work points to the problem of *satiety* in the kinds of comedy prevalent on social media today — meming included. Such acts — themselves often a symptom of desperation — simulate a feeling of success and produce a sense of productivity and satisfaction but sometimes without initiating any kind of political change.

From another perspective, it seems that the exact opposite is true: memes play a definitive role in political change. We are in a reality — quite clear even in general journalistic discourse — in which what can be described as meme culture has a concrete sway over both direct and indirect ideology, affecting both elec-

---

1   Henri Lefebvre, *Critique of Everyday Life: The One Volume Edition,* trans. John Moore and Gregory Elliott (London: Verso, 2014), 96–97.
2   Ibid., 97.

tion outcomes and the terms of wider political debate. As Matt Goerzen has recently observed:

> Beyond the musings of think piece writers, memes are now taken with the utmost seriousness, by entities ranging from DARPA US military researchers and NATO agents to ISIS's ideological warriors — all of whom see the form as a contemporary weapon of war.[3]

If nothing else, this shows that the mindless idea of memes proposed by Richard Dawkins has long since been defunct, even if we pretend that it was in one context valid. While Dawkins saw memes as definitionally about replication, we are quite clearly in a political world where memes are far more transformative. While Dawkins linked memes to natural progression, the meme is clearly better seen as interruption than continuation. Memes erupt into newsfeeds, as they erupted collectively into online consciousness, transforming irrevocably the situation into which they break. Given the simplicity of image-macros and short edited videos, the specifically online phenomenon of memes has shown itself as a media manifestation that can accommodate the frenetic pace of online news content. The ideas of specific social and political groups can disseminate at such speeds that they can reframe news content at a speed that matches traditional media sources. As Dominic Pettman argues in his initiating contribution to this volume, the function of memes as shared modes of framing and reframing events takes us to the very fundaments of politics and technology. For Pettman, the political and technological find their origin in the ancient Greek notion of a steersman, and it is the capacity for both to provide a means for steering ideas, actions, and passions. Social media, as a "global meme machine", has seen an intensification of the speed of such framing and steering, to the extent

---

3   Matt Goerzen, "Notes Towards the Memes of Production," *Texte zur Kunst* 106 (2017): 82–108. Available at: https://www.textezurkunst.de/106/uber-die-meme-der-produktion/.

that rupture in political ideas and enthusiasms seems almost inevitable. This is a rupture which restructures thought rather than perpetuates continuations of political and social trends; memes must be taken as more revolutionary than evolutionary, whether they are put to use for the Right or the Left. Memes then, from the generally progressive perspective that we have taken in this volume, are a battleground on which the politics of the future must be fought.

Bibliography

Goerzen, Matt. "Notes Towards the Memes of Production." *Texte zur Kunst* 106 (2017): 82–108. https://www. textezurkunst.de/106/uber-die-meme-der-produktion/.

Lefebvre, Henri. *Critique of Everyday Life: The One Volume Edition.* Translated by John Moore and Gregory Elliott. London: Verso, 2014.

Contributors

Giacomo Bianchino is a writer, activist and compulsive producer of unfortunate memes. He runs a handful of popular pages online despite friends and critics agreeing that his sense of "humor" is indulgent and alienating. He has presented at conferences across Australia and writes on philosophy, media, and history. In 2017 he co-founded the Western Sydney Community alliance, a group that provides for the basic needs of Sydney's poor and homeless. He is now based in New York, where he is completing a PhD in comparative literature at the City University of New York.

Alfie Bown is the author of several books including *The Playstation Dreamworld* (Polity, 2017) and *In the Event of Laughter: Psychoanalysis, Literature and Comedy* (Bloomsbury, 2018). He also writes journalism for *The Guardian*, the *Paris Review*, and other places.

Dan Bristow: Recovering academic. Bookseller. Author of *Joyce and Lacan: Reading, Writing, and Psychoanalysis* (Routledge, 2016) and *2001: A Space Odyssey and Lacanian Psychoanalytic Theory* (Palgrave, 2017). Co-creator with Alfie Bown of *Everyday Analysis,* now based at *New Socialist* magazine.

DOI: 10.21983/P3.0255.1.22   415

Roy Christopher marshals the middle between Mathers and McLuhan. He has written about culture and music for three decades for everything from regional newspapers and home-grown zines and blogs to books, academic journals, and national glossy magazines. His dissertation was titled *Allusions of Grandeur: Figurative Language Use in Rap Lyrics,* and he most recently contributed to both the *St. James Encyclopedia of Hip-Hop Culture* (St. James, 2018) and *The Routledge Companion to Remix Studies* (Routledge, 2015). He was assistant editor to Paul D. Miller, a.k.a. DJ Spooky, on his *Sound Unbound: Sampling Digital Music and Culture* (MIT Press, 2008) and self-published an interview collection called *Follow for Now: Interviews with Friends and Heroes* (2007). He holds a PhD in Communication Studies from the University of Texas at Austin and is currently a Visiting Assistant Professor in the Department of Communication at the University of Illinois at Chicago. As a child, he solved the Rubik's Cube competitively. He writes regularly at http://roychristopher.com.

C_YS is an artist and writer based in and out of London.

Seong-Young Her is a graduate student from New Zealand with a background in public health and bioethics. He heads The Philosopher's Meme, an organisation of artists and philosophers who study memes. He is interested in the application of evolutionary ideas in abiological contexts, such as natural selection in the epidemiology of cybercultural artefacts.

Thomas Hobson is a PhD candidate at the University of Bath, UK. He also works as a consultant and advisor on issues related to security and ethics in governance of science research and emerging technology. His research takes place at the intersection between security, technology, politics, and society. He is particularly interested in how technologies and societies are co-produced — and more specifically, in how these sociotechnical interactions condition security practices and modes of technological warfare. Tom has a background in campaigning on a range of issues. He likes to write about technology and its relationship to society. He has, at least once, done a meme.

Roisin Kiberd writes about the Internet, culture, and Internet culture, and has been published in *The Guardian, Motherboard,* the *Dublin Review,* and the *Stinging Fly.* You can complain to her at @roisinkiberd.

Bogna M. Konior is the Media and Technology editor at the *Hong Kong Review of Books* and the editor of *Oraxiom: A Journal of Non-Philosophy.* She holds a Research Masters in Media Studies, a PhD in Cultural Analysis, and was recently a visiting researcher in Media and Culture at the ICON Center at the University of Utrecht. Her recent work is published in *Transformations: Journal of Media and Culture* and *Identities: Journal for Gender, Politics and Culture.* Her collaborative work exploring theory in the Anthropocene has been exhibited internationally, including at Tuning Speculations in Toronto and First Draft in Sydney. She teaches film and media studies at Lingnan University. Her research interests include media, extinction, ecology, and techno-feminism.

Kaajal Modi is a designer by day and artist/activist by night. In the former capacity they have worked on political design for the EU Remain Campaign, Jeremy Corbyn, and the Labour Party, and in the latter they work with organisations across London in order to deconstruct established hierarchies of knowledge through collaboration, participation and co-creation, utilizing a broad practice-based approach that includes textiles, digital, and print media, as well as live art and installation.

Jay Owens is a researcher and writer from London. She is interested in digital media and dust: both complex, ambivalent ecosystems where grand technological projects come to clash with messier realities. Her work on dust, developed through the "Disturbances" newsletter, has been produced for BBC Radio

4's "Four Thought" and featured in WIRED. She is also Research Director at audience intelligence platform Pulsar, helping media and technology companies understand the present state of things.

Ian Parker is a psychoanalyst in Manchester, UK.

Dominic Pettman is Professor of Culture and Media at the New School for Social Research and Eugene Lang College, and the author of numerous books on technology, humans, and other animals; including *Creaturely Love* (Minnesota, 2017) and *Sonic Intimacy* (Stanford, 2017).

Patricia Reed is an artist, writer, and designer based in Berlin. Her work concerns the entanglements between epistemology, diagrammatics, and modeling with politics adapted to planetary scales of cohabitation. She is also part of the Laboria Cuboniks technofeminist working group.

Angus Reoch is a writer from Sydney whose interests include radical political theory, imperialism, geography, and austerity. His work has been featured in the *Overland Literary Journal* and the *Hong Kong Review of Books*.

Francis Russell is the course coordinator of the humanities honors program at Curtin University in Perth, Western Australia. He has a PhD in Literary and Cultural Studies from Curtin University, and researches the political and philosophical implications of mental illness, alongside conducting broader research into neoliberal culture.

Gabriele de Seta is a media anthropologist. He holds a PhD in Sociology from the Hong Kong Polytechnic University and has recently completed a Postdoctoral Fellowship at the Institute of Ethnology, Academia Sinica in Taipei, Taiwan. His research work, grounded on ethnographic engagement across multiple sites, focuses on digital media practices and vernacular creativity in contemporary China. He is also interested in experimental music scenes, Internet art, and collaborative intersections between anthropology and art practice. More information is available on his website http://paranom.asia.

McKenzie Wark is professor of Media and Culture at Eugene Lang College and of Liberal Studies at The New School for Social Research. Wark is the author of *A Hacker Manifesto* (Harvard, 2004), *Gamer Theory* (Harvard, 2007), and *Molecular Red* (Verso, 2015), among other things.

Scott Wark is a PhD Candidate at the University of Warwick's Centre for Interdisciplinary Methodologies. His PhD research, "Meme Theory," investigates circulating online cultural production. He's also working on a project that theorizes the chemical element lithium as a mediator of the body.

Tom Whyman is a Teaching Fellow in Continental Philosophy at the University of Warwick. His PhD is from the University of Essex, and he has published a number of peer-reviewed articles, mostly on Theodor Adorno. His writing has also appeared in outlets such as *The Guardian, The Baffler,* and the *New York Times.*

Eric Wilson is senior lecturer of public law at Monash University, Melbourne, Australia. He received a Doctorate in History from Cambridge University in 1991 and a Doctorate of Juridical Science from the University of Melbourne in 2005. His publications include *The Savage Republic: De Indis of Hugo Grotius, Republicanism, and Dutch Hegemony in the Early Modern World System (c.1600–1619)* (Martinus Nijhoff, 2008). He is currently editing a series of volumes on critical criminology devoted to the relationships between covert government agency, organized crime, and extra-judicial forms of governance; the first volume in the series, *Government of the Shadows: Parapolitics and*

Criminal Sovereignty, was published by Pluto Press in 2009. The second volume, *The Dual State: Parapolitics, Carl Schmitt, and the National Security Complex,* was released by Ashgate Publishing in November 2012. Another volume on parapolitics, *The Spectacle of the False Flag: From JFK to Watergate* was published by punctum books in 2015. His most recent monograph is *The Republic of Cthulhu: Lovecraft, the Weird Tale, and Conspiracy Theory* (punctum books, 2016). His research interests are radical criminology, critical jurisprudence, and the application of the work of René Girard to Law and Literature.